CW01271978

Group 2

The genesis of world rallying
1946–1972

John Davenport ■ Reinhard Klein

McKLEIN
PUBLISHING

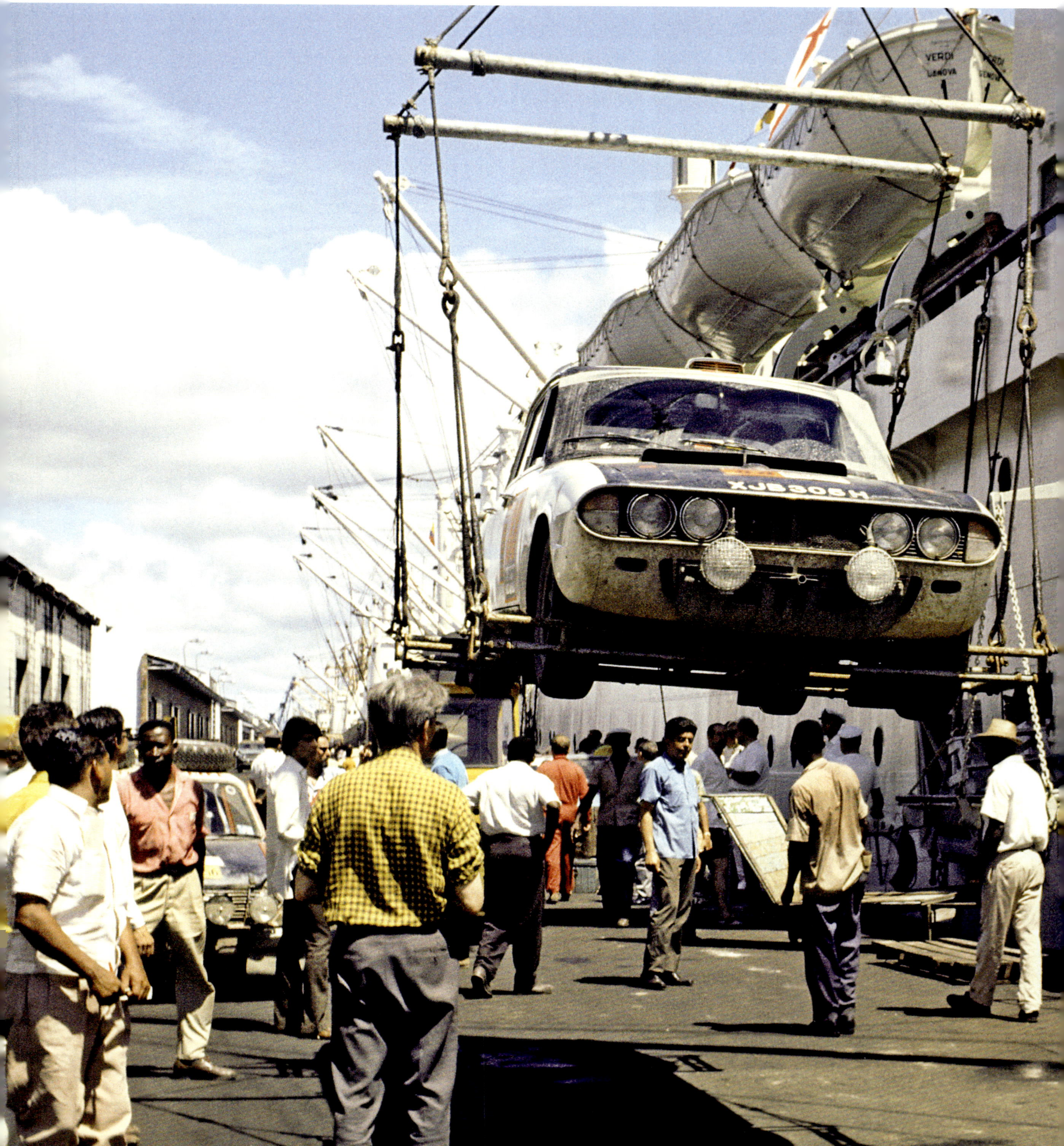
XJB305H
VERDI
GENOVA

Contents

	Foreword by Rauno Aaltonen	4
	Author's introductory note	5
	Terminology	6
Chapter 01	Rallying finds its feet 1946–1952	8
Chapter 02	Expansion in all areas 1953–1956	14
Chapter 03	The Scandinavians are coming! 1957–1959	24
Chapter 04	Into the Swinging Sixties 1960–1962	36
Chapter 05	Wonderful times 1963–1965	52
Chapter 06	A time of experiment 1966–1969	88
Chapter 07	A prototype of the World Championship? 1970-1972	132
Chapter 08	The works teams, their managers and their cars	174
Chapter 09	Appendix	198
	The fairer sex	199
	Getting technical	206
	Tour de Corse	208
	East African Safari Rally	214
	Long Distance Information	218
	Odds and Ends	222
	Epilogue	226
Chapter 10	Statistics 1953–1972	228

Imprint

Editor: Reinhard Klein
Authors: John Davenport, Reinhard Klein
Design and layout: Ellen Böhle-Hanigk
Coordination: Sarah Vessely
Editorial staff: Alexander Galitzki, Daniel Klein, Sebastian Klein, Colin McMaster, Sarah Vessely

Photography from the McKlein archive with the work of:
Hans Beijnoff, Hugh Bishop, John Davenport, Foste & Skeffington, Hans Georg Isenberg, Reinhard Klein, Peter Kumpa, Jeff Lehalle, Lars O. Magnil, Rolf F. Nieborg, Gunnar Palm, Kalle Riggare, Alois Rottensteiner, Colin Taylor Productions, Gerhard D. Wagner, Mike Wood

Other images:
LAT (p.9, 18, 19, 20, 25, 26, 41, 42, 48, 89, 193, 225), Mercedes (p.22, 37, 38, 41, 49, 50, 51), Audi AG (p.18, 19, 183), Porsche-Werkfoto (p.17, 120, 209), Corsa Research (p.26, 27), Saab (p.17, 199), Graham Gauld (p.75), John Ross (p.23), Squderia Naftalin (p.110), Citroën (p.34), Ford (p.185)

Statistics: Fred Gallagher & John Davenport

Special thanks to: Rauno Aaltonen, Fred Gallagher, Ursula Kleinmanns, Luis Podenco

Reproductions: McKlein Publishing/Verlag Reinhard Klein GbR
Printing: Himmer AG, Augsburg, Germany
Distribution: RallyWebShop (www.rallywebshop.com)

Copyright and publisher:
McKlein Publishing/Verlag Reinhard Klein GbR
Hauptstr. 172
51143 Köln
Germany
Tel.: +49-(0)2203-359239
Fax: +49-(0)2203-359238
publishing@mcklein.de
www.mckleinstore.com
www.mcklein.de

1st edition – 2014
ISBN: 978-3-927458-73-4

All right reserved. No part of this book may be reproduced, stored or transmitted by any means, mechanical, electronic, or otherwise without written permission of the publisher.

Foreword by Rauno Aaltonen

I was only eight years old when the first rally in this book was held and, when my interest in powered sport began in the 1950s, I participated in speedboat racing and on motorbikes. But finally, I saw the light and started rallying. Of course it was in a Saab and I was delighted to find that a lot of the things that I had learnt in boats and bikes could be translated into techniques that helped me to drive a rally car faster than some of the other guys.

So this book covers quite a lot of my rallying career as I won my first Finnish rally championship in 1961. The same year I co-drove – and did some of the driving, mainly on gravel stages! – with Eugen Böhringer in a works Mercedes. Then my father lent me his 220SE with which I won the 1000 Lakes Rally. The following year was my introduction to BMC and a long relationship with the Mini Cooper with which I won the European Championship in 1965.

Throughout my career, I have driven a lot of very different rallies in a lot of different cars including front-wheel drive Lancias, rear-wheel drive Datsuns, Opels and BMWs, in all some eleven works teams. I even took a Mini Cooper S on the East African Safari Rally in 1967 though it did not get very far. In fact the Safari is almost an obsession with me as I have finished second four times and retired from the lead on several other occasions.

If there are successes that I prize above others they both fall into the period of this book. They are the 1964 Liège–Sofia–Liège where, with Tony Ambrose, we won Europe's toughest-ever rally in a Healey 3000 and the 1967 Monte Carlo Rally that I won with Henry Liddon in a Cooper S. Both were sweet victories since in 1963 we had broken the steering of our Healey on the last night of the Liège and crashed while leading, while in 1966, all the Minis including mine had been thrown out of the Monte for 'illegal' lights.

This period of rallying is thus very special for me and I am delighted to have been asked to write the foreword of this book. The rallies of that era were real adventures, maybe a little unsophisticated compared with modern events that bristle with electronic wizardry, but very demanding on the whole team. Quite simply communications and logistics were a big challenge and the rallies had anything up to ten times the competitive mileage than in the rallies today. They were not kid's play! The cars were unsophisticated too but that meant the crews were often in a position to be able to repair them themselves. Doing a rally in those days was a challenge and I am so pleased to have been a part of that scene. I am sure that you will enjoy reading about it.

Rauno Aaltonen, Turku, 2013

Author's introductory note

I started rallying in 1959 not knowing the first thing about it except how to read a map – and that not very well. My first rally saw us have two accidents, rip off a front door so that I had to navigate with a torch from the back seat, and we finished next to last. But sometime during that long night in the Derbyshire Dales, I was bitten by the rallying bug. It is no coincidence that some years later, the first continental team I joined was called Ecurie les Mordus, in English 'The bitten ones'. Within three years, I was a rallying journalist and navigator, another year and I was doing European rallies, two more years and I was a works co-driver. Fast forward forty years of co-driving, organising events, journalism and team management and I found myself back writing books about rallies, a work that is still continuing.

All of my early rally career happened during the period covered by this book, which is why I have a particular fondness for it and the adventures that I – and others – enjoyed during those years. Doing my research, I have discovered that there are three classes of experiences in one's past: those that happened that you remember, those that happened that you don't remember, and those that you remember that didn't happen. I sincerely hope that there is none of the latter category in the pages ahead, but, if one should have crept in, then I claim the 'Liberty Valance' defence: 'When the legend becomes fact, print the legend'.

I would like to think that you will enjoy this book at least as much as I have enjoyed writing it. If there is a dedication to be made, it is to all those wonderful characters that made post-war rallying such incredible fun: competitors, organisers, officials, trade suppliers, journalists, mechanics and spectators. All of them were totally committed to enjoying the rallies and prepared to get involved. I remember with particular affection two gendarmes who rescued Geoff Mabbs and me from the Monte Carlo blizzard of 1965. Before coming out to officiate on the rally, they had had the foresight to arm themselves with two bottles of eau de vie …

John Davenport, 2013

On early rallies, co-driving skills extended beyond reading maps …

Terminology

Given man's competitive nature, it was inevitable that soon after he had invented the motor car, he invented motor sport. At first there were all kinds of events held on the public roads that were called runs, trials, races, trophies, and even rallies. To be frank, in the beginning, there was not a lot to choose between them. Even events designated as races like the ill-fated Paris–Madrid of 1903 started cars at intervals of one minute and used time cards, features that were later to become key elements of rallying.

The first time that the word 'rally' came into general use was for the 1911 event run by the Sport Automobile et Vélocipédique de Monaco (SAVM) and now known worldwide as the Monte Carlo Rally (Rallye Automobile Monte-Carlo). The original idea of young Anthony Noghès, son of the President of the SAVM, was to have an event that started and finished in Monte Carlo and went round all the capitals of Europe. What he wound up with was an event that started in all the capitals and finished in Monaco where, in wintertime, the empty hotels would be very keen to welcome guests. Since this meant that they were 'coming together from dispersal' [Chambers English Dictionary], he called it a 'rally'. The French word 'rallye' means much the same and the modern French dictionary, Hachette, gives it as a 'réunion' that, in English means 'a meeting'.

During the 1920s and 1930s, races migrated to permanent circuits leaving the normal roads for a mixture of trials, rallies and trophies that were to evolve into a recognisable class of motor sporting events that we would today recognise as rallies. While the racing fraternity had their cathedrals of worship like Monza, Nürburgring, La Sarthe (Le Mans) and Brooklands, the rallies took to the mountains and hills of Europe where gradients and changing weather conditions would test the crews and their cars. Consequently, as well as the aforementioned Monte Carlo Rally, there were other high profile rallies like the Österreichische Alpenfahrt (Austria), the Coppa delle Alpi (Italy), the Rallye International des Alpes (France), the Marathon de la Route (Belgium) and the RAC Rally (Great Britain).

However, it was not until the end of the Second World War that rallying began to expand, evolve and develop and it is that period that we shall look at in this book. And our title also needs a quick word of explanation.

In the immediate post-war period, rally organisers tended to draw up their own criteria for the cars that could enter their events. Any scrutineering undertaken at the rally was done on the basis of the modifications permitted in the event regulations and comparison with a car taken from a dealer showroom. It was not until 1957 that the FIA published its new Appendix J that classified cars and set out standard cylinder capacity classes. It also required that the national club of the country where a car was manufactured draw up a 'recognition form' – later to be known as the Homologation Form. The cars were split into Touring and Grand Touring cars, the former being four-seaters (unless the engine's capacity was below 1,000 cc when it was enough to have two) and the latter being two-seaters. Each of these two categories was split into three sub-groups: 'normal series production', 'improved series production' and 'special'.

As rallying evolved after 1957, the most successful and popular cars tended to come from the 'improved' groups and, as the sport moved towards special stages, the trend was for the Touring cars to become favourites. Volvos, Saabs, Mini Coopers, Fords, Mercedes, Citroëns, Renaults, Lancias, Fiats, Alfa Romeos, Peugeots, Sunbeams and Panhards all topped the results regularly during the period covered by this book. Even Porsche had their 911 T and 912 recognised as Touring cars for a while in the mid-1960s. Of course, there were still GT cars that won events – Mercedes 300SL, Austin Healey 3000, Porsche 356, Alfa Romeo GTZ, Alpine A110 – but the dominant strain was from the 'improved series production touring cars'.

Under the 1957 rules, these were known as 'second group' and when the Great Revision of Appendix J came for 1966, they were identified as Group 2 cars. Hence the title of this book that nevertheless tries to tell the story of them all.

Peking to Paris 1907, Prince Scipione Borghese/Ettore (Hector) Guizzardi, Itala 40-hp.

For the early Monte Carlo Rallies, speed and even regularity were not of great importance. In 1911, for instance, there were awards for "distance travelled", "comfort" and "number of passengers on board". This Gobron 40HP seen before the start in the Place de la Concorde, Paris, was evidently trying for the latter award.

Chapter 01
Rallying finds its feet
1946/1947/1948/1949
1950/1951/1952

Chapter 01
Rallying finds its feet

1946

As soon as possible after peace broke out in Europe, there was an immediate rush to start building cars again and to repair the roads. Motor sport enthusiasts generally were quick to get going and already in the latter half of 1947 there were four Grands Prix held in Switzerland, Belgium, Italy and France. However, rallying got in first with the Rallye International des Alpes when, on July 12th, 1946 just fourteen months after peace had been signed, thirty-two competitors were flagged off from Marseille on a four-day loop through the Alpes Maritimes. The same year, there was also a Circuit of Ireland though this event was called a 'trial' and did not adopt the patronym of 'rally' until 1956.

1947

In 1947, the Italians ran the first of a series of rallies called Stella Alpina based in Trento and Piero Taruffi in a Lancia Aprilia won the first of these events. The Stella Alpina ran for eight more years until it disappeared in the somewhat negative publicity for road events that was temporarily generated in Italy following the Marquis de Portago's fatal accident on the 1957 Mille Miglia.

Then to celebrate the eighth centenary of the Reconquista of Lisbon by Alfonso the First in 1147, the Automobile Club of Portugal (ACP) decided to hold an international rally called simply 'Rallye de Lisboa'. This had several starting places of which the furthest apart were Lisbon itself and Brussels with their routes converging on the resort of San Sebastian in north-eastern Spain. The competitors had all kinds of problems about fuel supply in the shortages prevailing so soon after the war. The sixteen Dutch and six British entrants found that there was no petrol available for 'competition purposes' while crossing France. For that very reason, there were no French entrants. After a long and difficult journey on main roads, the competitors arrived in Estoril where, after a night's sleep, they took part in a driving test outside the casino, a feature that was retained in later Portuguese rallies. The winner was Geoffrey 'Goff' Imhof driving an Allard J1 with Jorge Montereal second in a Bentley and Maurice Gatsonides third in a Gatso, a car of his own construction.

1948

There were no major newcomers to the rally scene in 1948 but in 1949, two of the most important pre-war events were revived. The first of these, and one of the most venerable – it had first been held in 1911 – was the Monte Carlo Rally. The event of 1949 was different from the pre-war version in that the main start was in Monaco and its ninety-three starters went on a three-day loop up to Amsterdam and back, picking up starters from peripheral cities such as Lisbon, Glasgow, Oslo, Stockholm, Prague and Florence along the way. They all passed through Paris and thence to Lyons from where there was a more difficult route back to Monaco. Of the total of two hundred and thirty starters, one hundred and sixty-seven arrived in Monaco. Jean Trevoux was victorious in a Hotchkiss 686 3.5-litre, an almost exactly similar machine to that in which he had finished equal first on the last pre-war rally in 1939.

This rare RHD example of a Peugeot 402 Special Sport was entered by Miss Dorothy Patten (on L) for the 1939 RAC Rally for her and her partner, Count Dorndorf.

Monte Carlo Rally 1949. Cars parked in the Jardin Exotique after arrival.

Monte Carlo Rally 1950. This Hotchkiss 686-2 driven by Marcel Becquart and Henri Secret narrowly defeated the Humber Super Snipe of Maurice Gatsonides.

The second of the established pre-war events to start up again was the Österreichische Alpenfahrt, the first of which had been held in 1910. In a war-torn Austria, motorcycles were more numerous than cars and, for a few years at least, the resurrected Alpenfahrt was an event for motorcycles with a few cars tacked on behind. Nevertheless in 1949, forty-eight cars started the event from Zell am See in the American zone and amongst them were two VW-engined specials: Wolfgang Denzel's own WD sports car and the Type 64 originally designed by Ferdinand Porsche for the cancelled Berlin–Rome event of 1940. Of the seventeen finishers, five were awarded Alpine Cups for class wins with Denzel winning the sports car category and Karel Vrdlovec in a Tatra T600 Tatraplan winning the touring car category.

1949

For some reason, the Dutch were very active in rallying in the immediate post-war period and it was inevitable that they would want an international event of their own. In April 1949, the first Tulip Rally was held and it was a very ambitious event. It had starts in The Hague, Rome, Monte Carlo, London, Brussels, Berne and Glasgow. All the starters from these cities then converged on Breda in Holland and thence via a driving test at the Zandvoort racing circuit to the finish at Noordwijk aan Zee, a seaside resort in the middle of fields of tulips. Of the one hundred and fifty-three starters tackling the event, more than half were Dutch but it was the British contingent of fourteen entries that came away with the top prizes. Ken Wharton won outright in his Ford Anglia Ten while Ian Appleyard was second overall in his Jaguar SS100.

In 1950, the Marathon de la Route was re-launched in the format that it had been run by the Royal Motor Union of Liège between 1931 and 1939, namely Liège–Rome–Liège. First held in 1927 as a non-stop run from Liège to Biarritz and back and then as Liège–Madrid–Liège for three years, the Marathon de la Route was firmly established as one of the toughest events around. Its unique system of timing that concealed high average speeds by 'adjusting' the opening and closing times of controls for individual crews made it a by-word for both speed and endurance. The 1950 event was reasonably mild by Liège standards. It went down through Luxembourg and France to Nice and thence to Genoa and Rome before turning back and passing through the Dolomites. It then crossed northern Italy to enjoy a last night in the Alpes Maritimes and then through the Vosges back to Belgium. The event was won by Claude Dubois in a 1,490 cc Peugeot Special featuring a low-blow supercharger and a Cotal automatic gearbox. His co-driver was Charles de Cortanze, the father of André de Cortanze, the engineer behind much Peugeot success in the 1980s and 1990s.

1950

That same year, 1950, the KAK (Royal Automobile Club of Sweden) launched its first 'Svenska Rallyt Till Midnattssolen', internationally known as the Rally to the Midnight Sun, with starts in Stockholm, Gothenburg and Falsterbo and the finish inside the Arctic Circle at Kiruna. Held over four days in June with thus very little night-time motoring thanks to the long days, the hundred and twenty-six starters had a pleasant run with various tests of braking, acceleration and manoeuvrability. There was a great deal of variety in the entry with eight-litre Bentleys, Cadillacs and Austin Atlantics mixing it with the recently launched Saab 92, Porsche 356s, Volvos and VWs.

1951

Then in 1951, both the Tour de France Automobile and the RAC Rally had their post-war re-launches while newcomers to the international rally scene were the Rally of the 1000 Lakes in Finland and the Viking Rally in Norway. Even the Italians got off the mark by running the first Sestriere Rally in February. This was almost an all-Italian event with a few French competitors and was won by two Grand Prix drivers and Ferrari team-mates, Luigi Villoresi and Alberto Ascari, in a Lancia Aurelia B10 saloon.

The RAC Rally was the first of the re-launched events to be held since its date was in June and, like so many rallies of the time, it imitated the Monte Carlo Rally by having multiple starting points. These were in Brighton, Cheltenham, Skegness and Harrogate and the two hundred and twenty-nine starters converged on Silverstone for a 30-minute high-speed driving test before tackling a route through Scotland, Wales and the West Country and then finishing at the southern seaside resort of Bournemouth. There was no overall winner but Ian Appleyard's Jaguar XK120 was the least penalised and won the Open Car category.

The Viking Rally was also pretty much a parochial affair and was shorter than many of the others rallies of the time since it only lasted one day. The format was a few driving tests on a not-too-demanding route and it was won by Per Bergan driving a 1.9-litre Citroën 11CV, perhaps one of the first major victories for a front wheel-drive car in rallying.

The Tour de France was held at the same time as the 1000 Lakes but the two events were catering for very different competitors and cars. The Tour de France started from Nice on September 1st and finished back there a week later after two hill climbs and four tests totalling just seventeen kilometres of pure competition. Ferraris dominated with Pierre Boncompagni and Alfred Barraquet winning outright in a Ferrari 212 Export ahead of two similar Ferraris with an ubiquitous Porsche 356 and a Jaguar XK120 behind them.

In its own way, the 1000 Lakes emulated both the more senior events as, although it had just one starting place in Jyväskylä – the event was sub-titled Jyväskylän Suurajot or the Grand Prix of Jyväskylä – it went beyond the Arctic Circle to Rovaniemi and then returned down the Baltic Coast and back to Jyväskylä. This was a trip almost entirely on gravel roads and covered in less than thirty-six hours so that, though it may only have had two tests amounting to some 1.65 kilometres, the whole event presented a tough task for cars of that era. It is a credit to the Finns that of the twenty-six starters, only three fell by the wayside.

As far as these major rallies of 1951 were concerned, the winner was always found by means of tests, though there were exceptions to that rule. The Liège was one right at the top of the 'tough' list. Up there too was the Rallye des Alpes where the road sections plus their infamous sélectifs and a small number of hill climbs to sort out any ex aequo produced the final result. The Tulip Rally too had got tougher with a much smaller proportion of the entry remaining unpenalised on the road sections. At least a couple of the rallies – Monte Carlo and Lisbon – confined their entries to saloon cars. As the rallies gradually moved away from short manoeuvrability or speed tests to more difficult road sections and eventually special stages, open cars would become less popular and were replaced by GT cars. There were also exceptions to that rule since some drivers continued to prefer open cars for driving in foggy conditions where they thought it could give them an advantage of wider vision.

Monte Carlo Rally 1951. Even a towel rail in this Hillman Minx!

1952

The 1952 season kicked off with a very snowy Monte Carlo Rally that saw Sydney Allard win outright in a car bearing his own name, a 4,375 cc P-type Allard saloon built on a M2X chassis, with Stirling Moss second in a 2.2-litre Sunbeam Talbot saloon entered by Rootes. Only fifteen competitors were unpenalised on the road sections and the rally was decided on a seventy-five kilometre regularity test held in the mountains behind Monaco. Rather sadly, Allard was not able to fully capitalise on his victory as, just one week after his unique win, King George VI died and that massively important piece of news completely took over the British media. It was not a time for advertising or selling fast cars.

Bad weather also visited the Sestriere Rally with fog and snow so that only twenty of its entrants were unpenalised on the road sections. It was a Lancia Aurelia B20-2000 coupé that won driven by Luigi 'Gino' Valenzano but ominously two Porsche 356s finished in second and third places showing that the German manufacturer was soon to be a major threat in rallying. Snow affected the first day of the second RAC Rally and led to the cancellation of the first test at Silverstone, but other tests at Castle Combe, Epynt, Hardknott Pass, Rest-and-be-Thankful hill climb and Oliver's Mount thankfully provided a result since one hundred and thirty-one of the two hundred and fifty starters were unpenalised on the road sections. There was no overall winner but the best performance was realised by Geoffrey Imhof in an Allard J2 sports car.

Timed tests and hill climbs allied to night sections in the French mountains gave a clear result on the Tulip Rally that in 1952 was won by Ken Wharton at the wheel of a Ford Consul with Ian Appleyard close behind in a Jaguar Mk VII. The class-improvement penalty system favoured saloon cars and the best sports car, the Jaguar XK120 of the Swiss driver Rolf Habisreutinger, was classified eleventh overall. To indicate how desperate rally organisers were to make their tests more difficult, one only needs to consider the test held at Schiphol Airport during the Tulip. Here, an official replaced the co-driver and had in his hand a piece of rope looped round the clutch pedal. Once the car was started and had got into top gear, the official would pull on the rope and no more gear changes were allowed while the car was driven through the manoeuvrability test.

The Lisbon Rally held in May was much as before with the cars converging on Estoril and the event was decided on a driving test outside the casino followed by a regularity test on the Estoril circuit. The outright winner was Joaquim Nogueira in a Porsche 356 ahead of the Conde de Monte Real in an Allard. And on the Rally to the Midnight Sun in Sweden, it was Porsches that dominated with Olle 'Grus-Pelle' Persson winning in a 356 ahead of similarly mounted Arthur 'Ärtan' Wessblads. The best foreign entrant was a certain Huschke von Hanstein driving – what else? – a Porsche 356 into fourth place. With Scandinavian police frowning on anything resembling fast driving on public roads, the Swedes and Finns were rapidly discovering that specialsträcka and erikoiskoe on closed private roads were the way to decide their results. They did not

Happy before the start but less happy once the 1951 Monte Carlo Rally got under way, Maurice Gatsonides and André van Luyck suffered from having their fuel tank filled with paraffin instead of petrol at the Digne control. Attempting to pull back the lost road time, "Gatso" made an uncharacteristic error and slid off the road.

eliminate manoeuvrability tests completely but they showed the way forward for rallying in Europe when hard driving on open pubic roads became less acceptable.

And two good examples of the latter were the Rallye des Alpes and the Liège–Rome–Liège. Held in the middle of July, the Alpine attracted eighty-eight crews and offered them a route from Marseille through France, Italy, Austria and Switzerland finishing back in France at Cannes by which time it had crossed no less than forty of the highest passes in the Alps and Dolomites. Ten crews finished with no road penalties and among them was Ian Appleyard in his Jaguar XK120. Appleyard was promptly awarded a Coupe d'Or since this was the third year in succession that he had performed that feat. Also winning an ordinary Coupe were the three Sunbeam Talbot drivers, Stirling Moss, Mike Hawthorn and George Murray-Frame, and they duly won the team prize. But the class-improvement factor meant that the overall winner was Alex von Falkenhausen in a pre-war BMW 328 ahead of Maurice Gatsonides in a Jaguar XK120 with Ernest de Regibus third in a 748 cc Renault 4CV.

Then in mid-August came the Liège, reported at the time as being 'the toughest rally ever run'. At 5,240 kilometres in four days, it was certainly no pushover for the one hundred and five starters and indeed only twenty-four of them came to the finish. No need for driving tests here since even the winners, Helmut Polensky and Walter Schlüter in a Porsche 356 Coupé, lost fifteen minutes over the demanding route and were seven minutes ahead of second placed crew, the Frenchmen Jean Laroche and Rémy Radix in a specially bodied Jaguar XK120. The Liège was always pretty casual about the cars that were entered and any number of 'one-off' specials or modified production cars could always be seen on its entry lists. Maurice Garot, the Clerk of the Course, always maintained that a route and schedule devised by him would penalise any car, no matter how much it had been modified. In later years, he was to go so far as to say that he would be delighted to have just one car finishing within the time limit.

The final major event of 1952 was the Viking Rally where the organisers contrived for no one to finish unpenalised. This was thanks to their incorporation into the event of a difficult navigation and regularity section that was kept secret until the last moment. The winner for the second year running was Per Bergan in his Citroën 11CV.

With a successful rally season coming to an end and major rallies attracting large entries, the CSI (Commission Sportive Internationale) of the FIA (Fédération Internationale de l'Automobile) announced that, for 1953, they would be running a European Touring Championship that would comprise the nine major international rallies of the day.

This recognition of rallying as a major international sport was very gratifying and, though few drivers and teams would necessarily try to attend all the events, one thing was for certain. This focus of interest would encourage more car manufacturers to participate directly as well as supporting – as already happened to a limited extent – private owners entering in their own cars. On top of that, there was also going to be an increase in the number of tyre and oil companies, spark plug manufacturers and electrical suppliers anxious to be associated with rally success.

Rallye des Alpes 1952,
Stirling Moss/John Cutts,
Sunbeam Talbot 90.

Chapter 02
Expansion in all areas
1953/1954/1955/1956

Rallye des Alpes 1954, Stirling Moss/John Cutts, Sunbeam Alpine. This year they won a Coupe d'Or for winning three consecutive Coupe des Alpes.

Rallye des Alpes 1956, Hans & Philip Kat, Triumph TR3. Five TR3s won Coupes des Alpes of which this was one.

Sestriere Rally 1956, Walter Schock/Rolf Moll, Mercedes 300SL. Note the chains on the tyres.

Chapter 02
Expansion in all areas

1953

As the 1953 season commenced, rallying had certainly found its feet and was even more popular than before the war. Indeed it was destined to become increasingly popular as the years passed and more major events were created. However, there is a saying that 'The past is a foreign country; they do things differently there', so it is important to remember several things about the rallying of the 1950s when one is reading this book some sixty years later.

The first is that the roads – even the major ones – were far different from what we find in Europe today. Apart from the German autobahns, there were no motorways, many of the minor roads did not have a tarmac surface, and there had been no policy of 'improving' them so that all the bends were still there from the days of the horse and cart. And the cars of that era with all their 1950s accessories such as tyres, lights and brakes were far less able to move quickly over those roads than a modern car would have been. Thus for them, a 50 kph (30 mph) average speed over public roads was actually very demanding.

The rallies themselves were still evolving from what might best be described as 'long touring events with occasional bursts of speed'. It is interesting that the FIA championship was called the 'European Touring Championship' since that title evokes the sentiment of long, leisurely drives with time for lunch. There were exceptions of course, of which the Liège–Rome–Liège was the most outstanding, and even the less demanding events had a strong element of endurance for the crew with early starts and few night halts. The rally organisers, even now they were part of the European Touring Championship, had no common template on which to base their events so that everything from control procedures to penalties, and from route definition to competitive tests were different on every event. And in this pre-digital age, timing clocks were certainly more unreliable than the cars.

The top rally crews were not professional in the sense that they were very rarely in full time employment by the car companies that 'supported' them. This would change, of course, but even in 1953 the crews that wanted to win took a highly professional approach to the sport and were quite prepared to recce rally routes and tests where this information was available beforehand.

All in all, there was immense variety in these rallies. The Monte Carlo might require the use of chains on your tyres and shovels to dig away the snow, or it could be a very pleasant drive to the Riviera. The Rallye des Alpes could sometimes have good weather but it was a complex event that required careful preparation to know when to try hard and when to stop and take fuel for the car and a drink for the crew. The Liège was just tough and non-stop in true Royal Motor Union fashion, so you were certainly going to be tired with the implication that both crew members had to be able to drive well, and, as with the Rallye des Alpes, you had to work out on what parts of the route you had to drive hard to stay in time. The RAC Rally was more of a British navigation rally and it is little wonder that many of the foreign entries struggled with the night sections on narrow lanes using Ordnance Survey maps. On the Scandinavian events, the tendency was towards moving the manoeuvrability tests from car parks to gravel roads and gradually extending their length so they became speed tests or special stages.

But that is already leaping into the future. The 1953 season kicked off with the Monte Carlo Rally and, in the absence of much snow and ice, this was not one of the classic rally's greatest moments. There was a large entry of over four hundred cars but more than half of them came to Monaco penalty-free. This put the organisers in a bit of a dilemma since only a hundred cars could take part in the regularity section in the mountains behind the Principality. Thus a hastily devised acceleration and braking test was created to give them a way of choosing who should undertake the mountain circuit. And there was further disappointment when the organiser's clocks on the regularity test showed some variances with those of the competitors. Maurice Gatsonides considered his victory over Ian Appleyard and Stirling Moss to be the result of good fortune.

The next event was the Sestriere Rally in Italy and this too was bit of a damp squib in competitive terms. The weather provided snow, ice and fog but the rally was severely let down by poor paperwork – translations from Italian – and thus non-Italians like Gatsonides and Helmut Polensky suffered as a result. Strangely, the winners were Gert Seibert and Alfred Bolz from Saarland who had bought their winning Citroën 11CV second-hand just a week before the rally. Behind them, Italians in Italian cars figured strongly.

It was only to be expected that there would be a home victory on the RAC Rally of Great Britain with its heavy emphasis on navigation and so it proved to be with Ian and Pat Appleyard winning in their works-supported Jaguar XK120. Very few foreign crews crossed the channel and of those the best-placed finisher was Marcel Becquart in his Jowett Javelin in sixty-seventh place. The Jowett with its 1.5-litre flat four engine and four-speed gearbox was a very popular rally car at this time and the Tulip Rally was won by Count Hugo van Zuylen van Nijevelt driving a Javelin. Initially the winner was given as Bill Banks in a Bristol 401 but he and eight others drivers were excluded for infringements of the technical regulations discovered at final scrutineering. This procedure was always quite rigorous at the Tulip Rally and hence Appleyard was delighted when his Jaguar Mk VII – in fifth place – passed with flying colours thus dashing the rumours that it possessed a C-type engine.

Probably the least said about the Rallye Travemünde the better, as it was what English navigators used to call a 'scatter event'. There was no set order in which one had to visit controls and victory went to the crew that, with an adjustment for the cylinder capacity of the car, visited the most controls. Cleverly choosing to drive in a Fiat 1100, Helmut Polensky and Walter Schlüter came out as winners ahead of the adept Alsatian, Seibert, in his now well-used Citroën 11CV. The next event was the Swedish Rally to the Midnight Sun where unsurprisingly almost all the entrants were Scandinavian. They were treated to five gravel special stages during the long route and on these, Porsche 356s reigned supreme with one taking the outright win with Sture Nottorp. With two more Porsches in fourth and fifth places the German manufacturer was thus assured of the team prize.

With only fifty percent of its entry finishing, the Rallye des Alpes might have been considered quite tough had it not been for the fact that almost half of the finishers were unpenalised on the road sections. They were thus eligible for a Coupe, the event's most prestigious award for an unpenalised performance on the road sections, and no less than twenty-five were awarded. The overall winner – decided by a class handicap system on the various tests and hill climbs – was the Porsche pair of Polensky and Schlüter. Having won the Liège in 1952, Polensky took up the offer of a Lancia Aurelia for the 1953 event. A Lancia was a good choice since an Aurelia won the event driven, almost singlehandedly, by Johnny Claes when his co-driver, Jean Trasenster fell ill shortly after the

Monte Carlo Rally 1953, Ian & Mrs Pat Appleyard, Jaguar MK VII.

start. Polensky was leading at Cortina d'Ampezzo but he retired when his Lancia suffered mechanical failure shortly afterwards.

With just two events left in the inaugural ETC, it was a close thing between Polensky and Appleyard but when they both went to the Viking Rally in Norway, it was Polensky who finished second with his Fiat 1100 and Appleyard who uncharacteristically left the road. On the final round, the Lisbon Rally, despite heavy rain and washed out roads, fourteen cars were unpenalised on the road and the Estoril driving test once again decided the result. The winner was local man, Joaquim Nogueira driving a Porsche with Appleyard second in his XK120 and Polensky third, once again in a Porsche, this one borrowed from the Belgian, Max Thirion. This result was sufficient to clinch the championship for Polensky.

Before leaving 1953, it should be noted that this year saw the debut of two events that were to become big rallies in the sport's future. The first was the East African Safari, or 'Coronation Safari', as it was then known. Held in Kenya, Uganda and Tanganyika (today's Tanzania) far from the birthplace of rallying, it was a legend waiting to grow and by the end of the 1950s had found a place in the heart of the sport if not yet within one of its championships. The other event was the Acropolis Rally in Greece. It too had a low-key start but was destined to grow into one of the hardest rallies in Europe once burgeoning restrictions had forced rallies like the Liège and the Rallye des Alpes into retirement.

Champions 1953

Lisbon Rally 1953, Helmut Polensky (on the right) Walter Schlüter, Porsche 356 1500S.

Ladies champion, Greta Molander seen here with Rolf Mellde and their Saab 92.

1954

The following year, 1954, saw two changes in the ETC line-up of events with the German event now called the Wiesbaden Rally and with the Geneva Rally coming in to replace Lisbon. It was a puzzling year since the European weather decided to play some distinctly twenty-first century tricks and provide summer weather in winter and vice versa. The Monte Carlo was thus one of the easiest events of the year and was again decided on the regularity run round the mountains behind Monaco. Here crews could choose what speed to average – between set limits – and Louis Chiron in a Lancia Aurelia made the best choice. Close to him was Ulsterman, Ronnie Adams, just 0.2 of a point behind in his Jaguar Mk VII but, with the rally finishing with a race around the GP circuit, it was inevitable that the Lancia would come out on top.

There was a lot more snow on the Sestriere Rally, so much indeed that chains were compulsory for the final test in Sestriere itself, and it was a Lancia 1-2 with Italian drivers very much to the fore. In much the same way, the RAC Rally was, with its peculiar ways and emphasis on navigation, was favourable to British competitors, though it now carried the subtitle of 'The Rally of the Tests'. The handicap system favoured sports cars and saw Triumph TR2s in first and second places. One of the very few foreign entries was Walter Schlüter, now driving a DKW. He had had a torrid time on the Monte Carlo Rally where he had finished in 222nd place and 37th in class. On

Monte Carlo Rally 1953, J. Risk/A. Gordon, Ford Zephyr. The windscreen broke when snow chains flew off from a car that they were following.

Monte Carlo Rally 1954, Louis Chiron/Ciro Basadonna, Lancia Aurelia. This was the winning combination.

the RAC, however, he did extremely well, considering that the DKW was not a sports car, to finish thirteenth overall and win his class easily. One suspects that he had a British navigator with him though the entry list is silent on that identity.

The RAC Rally had enjoyed some thick fog on the night sections and for the Tulip Rally there was more of the same with rain and mist in other places. It was thus a tough event and was won by the Belgians, Pierre Stasse and Olivier Gendebien who were sharing an Alfa Romeo 1900 TI and who only got the better of Werner Engel and Gilbert Ambrecht's Porsche 1500S on the final race at Zandvoort. Schlüter did not win his class as he was upstaged by Gustav Menz in another works supported DKW but nevertheless finished second in class and fifteenth overall to add to his points total. He increased that even further when he and Menz shared a DKW on the Wiesbaden Rally – this year open only to standard Touring cars – and won it outright.

On the Midnight Sun Rally, sports and GT cars were welcomed and Swedish drivers in Porsches took the first two places overall. There was no restriction on sports and GT cars either for the Rallye des Alpes who also opened its doors to 'improved Touring cars', the category for which this book is named though they did not get assigned the name Group 2 until the revision of the rules for the 1957 season. Despite some atrocious weather, including snow in July, which forced the cancellation of several of the higher passes, there were still eleven crews who finished unpenalised on the road section and thus qualified for Coupes. Among them was Stirling Moss who thus became the second recipient of a Coupe d'Or for finishing without penalties for the third year in a row. There was no official overall winner announced but, if there had been, it would have been Wolfgang Denzel from Austria driving a sports car of his own construction with a 1,300 cc VW engine.

Like the Rallye des Alpes, the Liège–Rome–Liège accepted almost any car but, as it turned out, the stormy conditions that prevailed throughout tended to favour closed cars. The rally turned into a battle royal between Helmut Polensky in a Porsche and Olivier Gendebien in a Lancia with the German driver coming home just over three minutes ahead of the Belgian. By comparison the rest of the field were nowhere. One performance that did stand out was that of Jean Rédelé who brought a modified Renault 4CV home in sixth place on an event for where there was no artificial bonus for cars with small engines.

Walter Schlüter did not compete on the Liège–Rome–Liège but he had his eyes set on the last two rounds of the European championship where he felt that his DKW would score points. He was right about that and on the Viking Rally where only standard Touring cars were admitted he won his class while on the Geneva Rally he truly excelled by finishing second overall and, naturally, winning his class. This was more than enough to make him European Touring Champion for 1954. For the ladies, Sheila van Damm followed him to Norway and Switzerland and was rewarded by two more Ladies Cup awards that, when added to the others she had won on the Tulip and the Rallye des Alpes, confirmed her as the European Ladies Champion.

After two seasons, various patterns could be discerned within the ETC. Firstly, German cars and drivers were being very successful and were strong supporters of the concept of a championship. The British, Dutch, Belgian and French competitors were keener on doing the tough rallies while the Scandinavians were developing their rallies and rally driving to prepare them for a takeover of the sport that, even in the twenty-first century, is not completely ended.

Champions **1954**

Geneva Rally 1954, Walter Schlüter poses with his DKW F91 3=6 Sonderklasse.

Sheila van Damm talks with a team-mate before the start of the Monte Carlo Rally in Stockholm.

1955

And so to 1955 and the day a motor racing accident touched rallying. Pierre Levegh's accident at Le Mans and the deaths of himself and eighty-three spectators sent its ripples out into the world. The restrictions placed on motor sport events by the French and Swiss authorities led to the cancellation of the Rallye des Alpes and the Geneva. Other changes were that the German event was now called the Internationale ADAC-Rallye Nürburgring and Yugoslavia obtained a spot for its 'Rallye Adriatique'.

The Monte Carlo Rally introduced secret controls to check adherence to the set average speeds on the common route into Monaco and this new tactic caught out many of the established crews. Thus the mountain circuit and the lap on the GP course had little effect on the final result that saw two relative unknowns from Norway win outright after being the only crew to arrive at Monaco with zero marks from the secret checks. This was Per Malling and Gunnar Fadum in their Sunbeam 90 and indeed it was Sunbeams that won both the Ladies prize and the Manufacturers award.

A Lancia Aurelia again won the Sestriere Rally though this one was a bit special in that it was a GT version with a lightweight body by Zagato and thus qualified in the Modified and GT category. Just as the Italians had their 'own' rally, the same was true of the British RAC Rally where the highest foreign entrant on this occasion was the German Prinz von Preussen whose Porsche 356 was classified eighty-first of the finishers. The overall winner this year was a modified Standard Ten saloon driven by Jimmy Ray and increasingly it was these modified cars that became more popular for rally drivers despite often having a higher handicap on tests. But everyone's ideas were about to be shaken up even more when the Mercedes 300SL made its debut appearance on the Tulip Rally in the hands

Monte Carlo Rally 1954, members of the DKW team (from L to R) Heinz Meier, Gustav Menz, Günther Ahrens and Walter Schlüter before the start.

of Willem Tak. Tinkering with their handicap system worked well and thus all the class winners were in the first twenty cars in overall classification. The winner might well have been Dutchman, Jan Martens, in a Fiat 1100 had he not broken down on the ten-lap race at Zandvoort that finished the event so it was Tak who showed the performance potential of the Mercedes by coming home 8.6 seconds ahead of Bill Banks's Bristol.

The Nürburgring Rally only attracted a small entry and, despite featuring over 200km of driving on the circuit of its title, it had a sufficiently tough handicap for Modified and GT cars to allow the two standard production works DKWs of Gustav Menz and Heinz Meier to win ahead of Paul Ernst Strähle's Porsche 1300 and Werner Engel's Mercedes 220A. Up in Sweden, a bad winter had left the gravel roads in a treacherous condition and this, coupled with a major increase in the length of special stages on closed roads, caused more than the usual crop of retirements on the Midnight Sun Rally. Swedish Porsches once again ruled the roost taking first and second places but a remarkable result was obtained by Heinz Meier who, in the land of the Saab, came fifth overall in his three-cylinder two-stroke DKW and won his class.

With the Rallye des Alpes and the Geneva both missing, the Adriatic Rally was the next event to be held and the new event turned out to be field day for German cars and drivers. A fairly standard European event of the time, it had a hill climb, an acceleration/braking test, a regularity stage on the Dubrovnik Circuit, and a five-lap race on the Opatija Circuit. The road section was sufficiently interesting to make sure that everyone was penalised but the final results were pretty tight with only seconds separating the top cars. The overall winner was Werner Engel in a Mercedes 300SL just ahead of Gustav Meier in a BMW 502 with the 1954 champion, Walter Schlüter, third in a DKW.

Next was the Liège–Rome–Liège and this was affected by the post-Le Mans restrictions imposed in France. Almost the whole of the rally had to be neutralised on its return through France but the Liège system of individual exclusion times was still in force and managed to reduce the field by fifteen cars during that last night of rain and fog. Amazingly, three crews managed to finish without losing any time on the road sections and, of these, Olivier Gendebien/Pierre Stasse had the best times from the five specially timed ascents of Italian passes. Behind them were René Cotton – later to be team manager at Citroën – driving a Salmson S4E and then Johnny Claes/Lucien Bianchi sharing a Lancia Aurelia. Claes was suffering from influenza and Bianchi did the lion's share of the driving, a reversal of the situation in 1953 where Claes had won despite his co-driver falling ill. One minute of penalty behind the leading trio was Werner Engel in a Mercedes 300SL thus racking up enough points to be declared European Champion.

The last rally of the 1955 season was the Viking won on this occasion by Lars Egeberg Jr and Amand Böhle in a Peugeot 203. The rapidly accumulating experience of the German rally drivers was emphasised once again by the second place going to Walter Schlüter in his DKW.

Monte Carlo Rally 1955, Per Malling/Gunnar Fadum, Sunbeam 90. The winning car stops for a quick under-bonnet check on the final mountain test.

Monte Carlo Rally 1955, Greta Molander/Monica Kjerstadius, DKW.

Champions **1955**

Werner Engel, Mercedes 300SL

Ladies Champion, Sheila van Damm (on L), poses with co-drivers Anne Hall and Françoise Clarke (on R) on their return to England with the 1955 Monte Carlo Coupe des Dames.

1956

After a few setbacks to its major events in 1955, the ETC bounced back in 1956 with all its old favourites plus a newcomer, the Acropolis Rally, and a return for the Lisbon Rally making a total of thirteen events. The championship catered for standard Touring and GT cars and thus these were the only ones that scored even if the events themselves chose to admit modified cars and sports cars. The limiting factor was that only a driver's best five scores could count.

Again it was the acceleration/braking test that decided which crews would go out on the final mountain circuit of the Monte Carlo Rally but this time there was a fair amount of ice and snow awaiting the lucky ninety cars selected. The best performance came from Ronnie Adams in a Jaguar Mk VII ably assisted by Derek Johnson and Frank Biggar. The GT and Modified Touring cars were disadvantaged by their handicap and thus Walter Schock and Rolf Moll took second overall in a standard Mercedes 220A. On the Sestriere Rally, Schock drove a 300 SL and made no mistake by winning outright. The best Lancia finished fifth and both second and third places went to German drivers in German cars.

Sixteen tests and three night navigation sections were the core of the RAC Rally this year and the final outcome was a win for Lyndon Sims in his Aston Martin DB2 navigated by Tony Ambrose and Roger Jones. They narrowly defeated another GT car in the shape of a Jaguar XK140 FHC driven by the Appleyards. On the Acropolis Rally, there was simply no one to take on the Mercedes 300SL of Walter Schock and, with fastest time on all the tests, he won relatively easily from a local driver in a standard DKW. It was hardly a power victory on the Tulip Rally where the British father and son team of Raymond and Edward Brookes took the win in a privately owned Austin A30. They did so from under the noses of the works Standard Triumph team whose Standard 8s – one of which was driven by Paddy Hopkirk – took the next three places in the general classification as well as winning the team prize. The Geneva Rally visited Monza and introduced the novel idea of a competitor being able to discard his worst test performance. The result was a win for a local man driving a modified DKW while Schock and Moll could only make tenth place.

For the first time in some years, a Porsche did not win the Midnight Sun Rally since the GT cars were handicapped out of it, but it was still a triumph for German cars as Volkswagens filled the first two places. Hot on their heels came two works Saab 93s, driven by Carl-Magnus Skogh and Erik Carlsson, two of the new breed of special stage experts. The Midnight Sun, like other Scandinavian events, was becoming more specialised and difficult for outsiders. For example, Schock brought a 220 A to Sweden and could only make sixth in class and 55th in overall classification. And it was a Saab driven by a Swede – Berndt Jonsson – who won the Wiesbaden Rally, an event almost entirely based on laps of the Nürburgring with little importance given to the road sections. The handicap system was, as in Sweden, in favour of small-engined cars so that Schock could only finish ninth overall though he did win his class.

The Rallye des Alpes returned to the ETC and for the first time took the event into Yugoslavia and had a night halt in Zagreb. However, authority got in the way again with the Italian police objecting to the use of some of the more testing passes and even forced the organisers to reduce average speeds on their 'Dolomite Circuit' based in Cortina d'Ampezzo. Thus there were more Coupes awarded than intended with seventeen crews unpenalised on the road sections. All the top places went to the modified Touring and GT cars with victory overall in the hands of Frenchmen Michel

Liège-Rome-Liège 1956, Willy Mairesse (on R of car)/Willy Genin, Mercedes 300SL. The winners of a very tough rally pause at a control in the Dolomites.

Rallye des Alpes 1956, Paddy Hopkirk/Willy Cave, Triumph TR3. They tackle a Stelvio hairpin on the way to winning a Coupe des Alpes.

Collange and Robert Huguet with their modified Alfa Romeo Giulietta. For the first time a manufacturer's prize was awarded and this went to the team of Triumph TR3s.

The Liège was also Yugoslavia-bound and chose Zagreb as the point where the route turned back to Belgium. As well as going to Yugoslavia for the first time and, despite keeping Rome in its title, it ceased to visit that Italian city as it was getting more difficult to get permission for open road events in Italy. From now on, its eyes were turned towards the possibilities offered by the less-used Balkan roads. It was this new territory that caused most retirements and penalties but in fact the winners, Willy Mairesee and Willy Genin, kept their Mercedes 300SL penalty free until the last night in France where a very tight schedule in pouring rain cost them nine minutes. However, they were comfortably clear of Claude Storez in a Porsche and Olivier Gendebien in a Ferrari.

The Viking Rally certainly identified where the threat to German supremacy was to be found for the coming years as Saab 93s took first, second and fourth places overall in the hands of Swedish works drivers headed by Skogh and Carlsson and even the third place went to a Swede, Bengt Johansson in a Peugeot 403.

Walter Schock was not on the Rallye des Alpes or the Liège but he did visit Yugoslavia for the Adriatic Rally where his Mercedes 300SL took fourth place behind two DKWs. He should have been first overall since his was the only car to have no penalties on the single special stage, but a minor mechanical problem caused him to check in late at the Zadar control. The overall winner was Paul Ernst Strähle in a Porsche 1300S. The rally was notable in that it gave the nascent Škoda team from Czechoslovakia it first international class win with their 1.2-litre 1201. Schock also went to the last event of the year, the Lisbon Rally now renamed the Rali Ibérico and featuring a route with more sections in Spain. The final regularity test was on a road circuit near Estoril where Schock's 300 SL was penalised so as to drop him to twenty-fourth place. He felt this was a mistake by the timekeepers and protested to the FIA but in any case, even without a result from the Ibérico, he had sufficient points to win the European title. By coincidence, it was a Mercedes 300SL that won the rally driven by a Portuguese with a slightly confusing surname, Fernando Stock.

The final positions in the ETC were Walter Schock first, five points clear of his fellow German Strähle, with Storez third a further fifteen points behind. Next was the Saab factory driver, Carl-Magnus Skogh, just one point behind the Frenchman and one point ahead of the British driver, William Bleakley. It is interesting to note that Bleakley scored points as both a driver in his own right with a Jaguar Mk1 and as co-driver to Johnny Wallwork on the Tulip Rally in a Standard 8. The Ladies champion for 1956 was Greta Molander. And one cannot leave 1956 without noting the appearance in late November of a new star on the international calendar known as the Tour de Corse. This was not to be given European Rally Championship status until 1970 but long before that, it became, in the eyes of European rally crews at least, the gold standard for tarmac rallies.

Champions **1956**

Nancy Mitchell was European Ladies Champion in 1956 when she drove an MGA with Doreen Reece. Here she is pictured (on the L) at the Liège-Rome-Liège of 1954 when she drove with Joyce Leavens in her own Ford Zephyr Six.

Walter Schock, Mercedes 300SL

Chapter **03**

The Scandinavians are coming!
1957/1958/1959

Chapter 03
The Scandinavians are coming!

1957

There were some changes implemented for 1957, starting with the technical regulations governing motor sport. The Commission Sportive Internationale (CSI) published their revised Appendix J to the FIA's Sporting Code during 1956. Much of what was done was commonsense and recognised that the habit of improving and tuning of cars was becoming more popular. It also accepted that such work might go much further and result in highly modified cars, something that was already accepted by events such as the Liège–Rome–Liège. This change meant that cars from all six groups were eligible to enter events of the European Championship though the quantity of points to be won in a class would depend on the number of starters in that class.

It is also important to remember that the rallies of this period were not, with the sole exception of the Liège–Rome–Liège, run on scratch times. There was little standardisation between events but it is generally true to say that difficult road sections, special stages and sélectifs were given set times for each class. Go faster than that time and you picked up no penalty; go slower and you were penalised whatever the difference was between your time and the set time for your class. More confusingly still, some events worked on a class improvement basis for their tests whether these were on roads or circuits. And the formulae that were introduced to set these times and speeds rather resembled something pertaining to Heisenberg's Uncertainty Principle.

The name European Rally Championship was adopted for the first time and, with thirteen events chosen for the championship, it looked as if it might be a vintage year for rallying. However, a little dispute over the Suez Canal in late 1956 and the imposition of fuel rationing throughout most of Europe in 1957 played havoc with a couple of the major rallies. The Monte Carlo and RAC rallies were cancelled as a direct result of the rationing. Later in the year, the Rallye des Alpes was a casualty of doubt concerning its Italian sections after the accident involving the Marquis de Portago on the Mille Miglia while the Rali Ibérico was simply not run. The final blow came when, on what would have been the final event, the Viking Rally, King Haakon VII of Norway died while the rally was taking place and it was immediately stopped.

Thus the European Rally Championship was decided on just eight events with a driver's best four scores counting. One man had set his heart on the title and by driving his Saab on some events and co-driving in a Borgward on others, Ruprecht Hopfen was able to keep the European title in Germany. He did not compete in the opening round, the Sestriere, where Italians in Group 2 Touring cars took the top places but was out in his Saab 93 on the Acropolis Rally. This was an event that was beginning to develop a tougher edge and, though it was won by a Ferrari 250 driven by the husband and wife team of Jean-Pierre and Lucille Estager, special stages were used for the first time and it was much less of a 'touring' event than previously. Hopfen finished eleventh overall and second in class thus commencing his scoring in the European Rally Championship.

The Tulip Rally saw Hopfen's score of a single point rapidly eclipsed by two drivers when Hans Kreisel won outright in a Group 2 Renault Dauphine and Martin Carstedt from Sweden – co-driven by his wife Gulli – took fourth overall and won his class with a Ford Fairlane.

Liège–Rome–Liège 1957, René Cotton/Jacques Leclère, Alfa Romeo Giulietta.

Willem Tak was unable to prevail with his Mercedes 300SL and had to be content with second on an event that was nowhere near as competitive as it had once been. The Deutschland Rally went further afield than its sister events had done in previous years with a route requiring a high standard of navigation through Austria and into Yugoslavia. There were still speed tests at the Nürburgring and Hockenheimring and a handicap that favoured standard cars over modified ones. The event was won outright by Leopold von Zedlitz and Rolf Hahn in a Group 1 BMW 502 but more interestingly, there was also a class for diesel-engined cars and this was won by Rudi Golderer and Alfred Kling in a Mercedes 180D who also managed to finish third overall. Hopfen was there with his Saab in which he won his class and finished fifteenth overall.

There were no surprises on the Midnight Sun Rally where Swedish drivers once again dominated the results sheets. The best that Saab could do was to win their class with Carl-Magnus Skogh and top honours went to a private Group 2 Volvo PV444 LS, this model now fitted with a new 1.6-litre engine and twin carburettors, driven by Thure and Lennart Jansson. They finished just 0.9 of a point ahead of Heimer Adiels and Anders Berg in a DKW with Mr & Mrs Carstedt an amazing third overall in their Group 1 Ford Fairlane. To give some idea of the gap now separating the Scandinavian drivers from the other Europeans, Tommy Gold and Willy Cave in a works supported Standard 8 finished 95th overall and 20th in their class just two places ahead of their team-mate, Paddy Hopkirk.

Like some of the other rallies, the Geneva turned out to be tougher than usual with a difficult road section and a few well-chosen hill climbs and circuit tests though the one at Solitude had to be cancelled thanks to terrible weather. There were two crews tied for first place, the Leto di Priolo brothers, Massimo and Salvatore in a Group 1 Alfa Romeo 1900 Berlina and Stefan Brügger/W. Tiefenhaler in a highly tuned DKW. Hopfen shared a Borgward Isabella with Horst Boes and they finished fifth overall and won their class. A month later, Hopfen took his Saab 93 down to Yugoslavia and, co-driven by von Lösch, won the Adriatic Rally outright. He was one of only three drivers to finish without penalty on the road sections and was quicker than the second placed DKW on the two hill climbs and the circuit test. The eight points gained here catapulted him into the lead of the European Rally Championship.

The Liège was by any standard the 'Rally of the Year' with top marks for endurance, speed and distance covered plus both the quantity and quality of its entry. In such a straightforward event with no form of handicap, it was not surprising to find that GT cars were at the forefront of the results with Claude Storez and Robert Buchet winning with their Porsche Carrera. They very nearly finished with zero penalties and only missed out by just twenty seconds. Second overall was a Mercedes 300SL crewed by Mr & Mrs Jo Schlesser – recently returned from Madagascar – while Bernard Consten came third in a Triumph TR3. Interestingly, Storez chose to drive in an open Speedster because he felt sure that one could see better in foggy conditions by sitting on a cushion and peering over the windscreen. He also wore a driving helmet with a substantial visor!

And finally, there was the Viking Rally that got cancelled at half distance and thus its result was not allowed to count towards the European Rally Championship. Hopfen did manage to finish the Liège with his Saab albeit in 48th place but, with no results counting from the Viking, the man from Frankfurt was safely European Champion. So too was Nancy Mitchell who was sixteenth overall on the Liège in an MGA and won the Ladies Prize which, with her previous results, was enough to confirm her as European Ladies Champion for 1957.

Champions 1957

▲ Lyon-Charbonnières Rally 1957, Nancy Mitchell, MGA

▶ European Champion in 1957 was Ruprecht Hopfen (on the R) seen here with his co-driver, Wolf-Albrecht Mantzel, and his 748 cc Saab 93 at the 1957 Liège-Rome-Liège.

The joy of the open road: This was Claude Storez and Robert Buchet driving their Porsche Carrera Speedster 1500 GS in beautiful weather on the 1957 Liège-Rome-Liège. They went on to win the rally by a clear margin from the Mercedes-Benz 300SL of Jo Schlesser and his wife, Annie.

1958

If 1957 had been something of a disappointment, then 1958 was just so much better in every way and with nearly all eleven European qualifying events running, made for a much more interesting and competitive year. Even the Monte Carlo produced a much-appreciated event and, though winter weather affected the routes that crossed the Vosges and created a lot of road penalties, the mountain circuit was sufficiently competitive to allow crews penalised in that way to fight back. Even the eventual winners, Guy Monraisse and Jacques Féret lost time into Chambéry that under normal circumstances would have ruled them out of any consideration for victory. Even more amazing was the ascent of Maurice Gatsonides and Marcel Becquart to sixth overall from 58th at the start of the mountain circuit.

The Sestriere Rally also had its share of winter snow and most people were penalised on a route that went all the way down to San Marino and back. In fact, one driver did come back to Sestriere without penalty and that was Ludovico Scarfiotti in a Fiat 'Otto Vu' sports car powered by a two-litre V8 engine. Sadly he made such a mess of the final manoeuvrability test in Sestriere that he did not even win his class and overall victory went to Lanzo Cussini in a Fiat-Abarth 750 cc fitted with a body by Zagato.

Probably the less said about the RAC Rally the better. It was like a meal prepared from the best raw materials by a bad chef who made the result seem like a dog's breakfast. The tests seemed to count for nothing and even following all the route instructions and visiting all the controls did not seem to be a recipe for success. However there was some justice in that the winners, Peter Harper and 'Doc' Deane in a Sunbeam Rapier, were one of the seven crews who did go round the entire route. The event claimed to have three overseas entries of which one was Paddy Hopkirk. As usual, Standard Pennants did well and Pat Moss showed what the Ladies were capable of by finishing fourth in a Morris Minor.

The Acropolis Rally was now relying on special stages and two hill climbs to supplement the final race on the Tatoi military aerodrome outside Athens but still the race played an over-important part in creating a result since its times were allied to a performance index. Nevertheless, it gave a pretty mixed classification with five very different cars – Lancia Aurelia, Chevrolet, Volvo, Jaguar and an Auto Union (the DKW name had temporarily disappeared) – occupying the top five places. The winner was Luigi Villoresi in the Lancia while the new Scandinavian on the block, Gunnar Andersson, was third in a Volvo PV444. Volvo drivers also did well on the Tulip Rally where a PV444 won the event outright driven by the German pair of Günther Kolwes and Ruth Lautmann. Veteran organiser, Piet Nortier, had toughened up the rally which now featured ten special stages – each with set times for each class – and no less than eleven tests. And unfavourable weather in the Vosges added to the difficulties.

The Deutschland Rally added three French circuits – Reims, Montlhéry and Le Mans – to its itinerary while keeping its allegiance to the Nürburgring. It also added special stages and hill climbs that were built into a more demanding route so that only five crews remained unpenalised other than on the tests. With a French emphasis, it was not surprising to find that Bernard Consten and Jean Hebert turned out to be the winners in their Alfa Romeo Giulietta Zagato but hot on their heels were Max Riess and Hans Wencher from Germany in a standard Alfa Romeo Giulietta TI who thus repeated their second place on the Tulip Rally. Third was Andersson in his Volvo ahead of Hans-Joachim Walter and Paul Ernst Strähle in a Porsche 1500.

Liège-Rome-Liège 1958, Paul Ernst Strähle/Robert Buchet, Porsche 356 1500. The descent of the Passo del Vivione.

Monte Carlo Rally 1958, Guy Monraisse (on L)/Jacques Féret, Renault Dauphine 845. They look pleased because they had won the rally outright!

The Midnight Sun Rally came with special stages having yet more difficult set times and only two cars were able to achieve their class targets. The eight tests included in the rally worked on a class improvement basis so by being fast on the stages and regularly winning his class on the tests, Gunnar Andersson notched up his first major outright win that catapulted him into the lead of the European Championship. On the Rallye des Alpes that followed, there had been some tinkering with the format of the event with four so-called regularity tests added to the usual mix of road sections, hill climbs and circuit tests. Unfortunately, two of these proved to have been set at too high an average speed for anyone to achieve and, had they been allowed to stay in the results, then the organisers would have had no Coupes to award. The two 'tests' were retained as tie-deciders and seven Coupes were awarded. Amazingly, Andersson led the event on the last night until he crashed when the Volvo ran out of brakes. It was left to Alfa Romeos to take the prizes with Consten – on this occasion sharing his Zagato with Roger de Lageneste – winning ahead of two more standard Giuliettas of which the third placed one was driven by Riess and Wencher.

With three events left to run, it was still Andersson out in front with his Volvo and when he promptly won the Adriatic Rally in Yugoslavia ahead of Wolfgang Levy, who was driving an old model DKW, he put himself practically beyond reach. However, on the Liège–Rome–Liège it was Consten's turn and in a dramatic event, he emerged as the winner with his 1,300 cc Alfa Romeo ahead of Paul Ernst Strähle's Porsche 1500. Consten had overtaken Strähle on the last night when the Porsche had a small excursion on the descent of the Col de Soubeyrand. The three Austin Healey 100-6s entered all finished and won the Manufacturers Team Prize but significantly, it was Pat Moss and Ann Wisdom who led them home and finished fourth overall. The story of the rally was that of Maurice Gatsonides who finished fifth in his Triumph TR3 despite breaking all his additional lights after coming back into Italy and having to drive right through the last night on headlamps alone. Gunnar Andersson and Max Riess both started the Liège, but the Volvo crashed while Riess, driving a factory Porsche, cracked the sump on the last night and also retired.

As it turned out, the Viking Rally did not affect any of the main championship results since Andersson was penalised in a police speed check and Riess was not able to win his class. Norwegian Volvos dominated with four of them in the top five and most interest was focussed on the Ladies since Pat Moss could be overtaken for the title by Greta Molander in her Saab if the factory Morris Minor failed to score points. The British girl was second in the separate female classification with Molander third and thus the title was hers. And with no sign of the Ibérico Rally being run, that was it for 1958 with the main European title going to a Scandinavian for the first time.

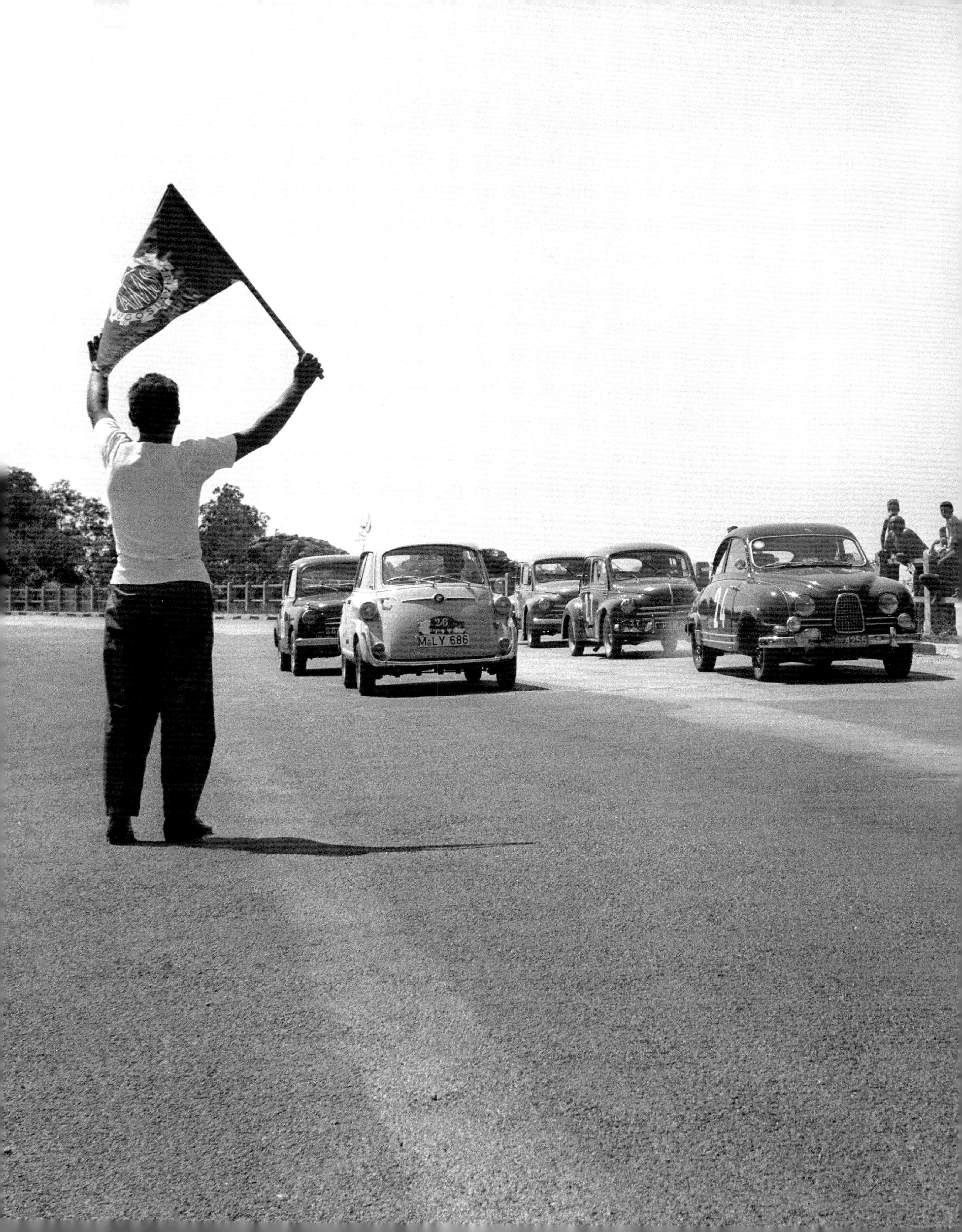
AMS
26
M-LY 686

Adriatic Rally 1958, Kurt Otto/Hermann Henf, Wartburg 311.

Adriatic Rally 1958, Alex von Falkenhausen/Mrs Kitty von Falkenhausen, BMW Isetta 600.

Champions 1958

Pat Moss/Ann Wisdom, Austin Healey 100-6. They pose with their Coupe des Dames from the 1958 Rallye des Alpes.

Gunnar Andersson, Volvo PV444

◀ Adriatic Rally 1958. The smaller capacity cars on the starting grid for their race on the Opatija street circuit.

1959

The season of 1959 was one that began well and ended badly. It was also a period during which it became evident that rally organisers had to devise new solutions to the problem of finding a winner. European roads were getting more crowded and high average speeds were only possible in remote areas at night and even then just one ordinary traveller could cause havoc. Closed roads for special stages along the lines pioneered in Scandinavia were the way to go but not all could seek this remedy immediately.

The Monte Carlo decided to increase the number of secret checks and average speed changes on its Mountain Section thus forcing the event to be decided on very precise timing. The road sections down to Monaco were timed at ten marks per minute lost whereas the Mountain Circuit could cost the same penalty for just ten seconds early or late. The consequence was that arriving in Monaco the first time with zero penalties was no guarantee of a good result at the finish. Still, the winner was Paul Coltelloni, a good driver in a Citroën ID19 who was modest enough to credit his win to the efforts of Pierre Alexandre and Claude Derosiers who did all the navigation and calculations. The rally was very much a French affair with Gallic cars and drivers filling the first four places, but 1956 winner, Ronnie Adams, accompanied this time by Ernie McMillen in a Sunbeam Rapier did pick up fifth place and second in class behind Coltelloni. Pat Moss drove an Austin A40 to finish tenth and win the Ladies prize.

If it had been French cars and drivers that led the way on the Monte Carlo, it was Italian cars and drivers who dominated the Sestriere Rally which, rather in contrast to the Monte, turned out to be a tough event. It was won by Giancarlo Castellina and Piero Frescobaldi in a Fiat Abarth 750 GT but more surprising was that Ada Pace, the lady racing driver known as 'Sayonara' after the name she put on the rear of her race cars to bid farewell to gentlemen drivers after she had passed them, was second overall after a spirited drive in an Alfa Romeo Giulietta Zagato accompanied by Carlo Toselli. Other ladies present were Pat Moss who won the Coupe des Dames in a Riley 1.5 ahead of Annie Soisbault in a Triumph TR3.

The Tulip Rally too was harder and, after encountering heavy rain and mist in the Ardèche, only five crews emerged unpenalised at time controls. Most of the success was British with the outright win going to Don and Erle Morley in a Jaguar 3.4 ahead of Keith Ballisat in a Triumph TR3A and Peter Riley in a Ford Zephyr. Erik Carlsson accompanied by multi-lingual Karl-Erik Swenson finished fifth but did not win his class as his highly modified Saab 93B was in the same class as the Porsches. But Saab did win the Ladies Prize with Greta Molander. The Acropolis Rally hit the same high note and had toughened yet again to the point where the hill climbs and speed tests were not needed to declare a result. The outright winners, Wolfgang Levy and Hans Wencher, were least penalised on the road in their Auto Union 1000, an uprated model of the old DKW 3=6 now with a one-litre three-cylinder two-stroke engine and a four-speed gearbox. Hans-Joachim Walter and Max Nathan were second in a Porsche Carrera while Annie Soisbault took the Ladies prize with her Triumph TR3.

The scene now shifted to Sweden where on a Midnight Sun Rally that was bristling with new special stages, Erik Carlsson took the outright win for Saab with a Group 5 version of the 93 ahead of team-mate Carl-Magnus Skogh in a Group 2 car. Volvos and VWs also had to take a back seat to the amazing Ferrari 250 of John Kvarnström who finished third and showed that, in the right hands on the right event, big GT cars like this were not yet totally superseded. Volvo had their latest lady driver, Ewy Rosqvist, in one of their new PV544s and she came away with the Ladies Prize albeit in sixtieth place overall.

For some reason the Rallye des Alpes abandoned a general classification and made two lists, one for Touring cars and one for GT cars. In addition they decided to make the road section times set in the classes all but impossible for the bigger GT cars. Thus the smallest capacity GT car won its category and the only Coupe in the GT category while no less than eight Coupes were awarded in the Touring category. The best of these was the Renault Dauphine crewed by Paul Condriller and Georges Robin whose 850 cc just stayed ahead of the 1,000 cc Auto Union of Hermann Kühne and Hans Wencher. Interestingly, Wencher was effectively the team

Swedish Rally to the Midnight Sun 1959, Wolfgang Levy/Oscar Matti, Auto Union 1000 Spezial Hardtop.

Sestriere Rally 1959, Gianfranco Castellina/Piero Frescobaldi, Fiat Abarth Zagato 750.

Swedish Rally to the Midnight Sun 1959, Erik Carlsson/Mario Pavoni, Saab 93B.

Swedish Rally to the Midnight Sun 1959, Bengt Söderström/Roger de Faire, VW Beetle.

manager of the Auto Union/DKW team at this time and took in turns to co-drive with his drivers in order to encourage them to greater efforts.

A class winner on the Rallye des Alpes, Paul Coltelloni went one better on the Adriatic Rally by repeating his outright win on the Monte Carlo. This time it was not super-accurate time-keeping that won the day but fast driving on gravel roads not to mention a couple of hill climbs and tests on circuits. The Citroën driver was the only one to finish with no penalties on the road sections and stages while Erik Carlsson, who finished second, had a total of twelve points. To be fair, the Citroën was tuned and prepared to run in the GT category while the Saab and the third placed Auto Union of Kühne were running in Group 2. A new entry into the championship was the 1000 Lakes Rally in Finland and, for only the second time in its history, a Swedish driver, Gunnar Callbo in a Volvo PV544, won the rally though it has to be admitted that he did have a Finnish co-driver, Väinö Nurmimaa. Erik Carlsson who had won this rally in 1957 was only able to finish fourth in his Group 5 Saab 93 and scored no points by winning his class since there were insufficient entries. At this time, Saab were choosing to enter rallies with a car prepared to either Group 2 or Group 5, using the lightweight car wherever this gave no handicap in terms of points scoring.

Like the Rallye des Alpes, the Liège decided to have separate results for Touring and GT. This was something of a shame since both categories were competitive with one another and the change proved nothing. In Touring, it was the Renault Dauphines that made the running and won with Jacques Féret and Guy Monraisse finishing with just over a minute fewer penalties than the sister car of Willy Mairesse and Maurice Desse. In fact Mairesse nearly retired when his Dauphine lost two of its five gears on a liaison section. However, in trying to keep up the schedule on the next difficult section, he went slightly off the road, banged the underside of the car on a rock and suddenly they were all working again. The winning car in GT was the Porsche of Robert Buchet and Paul Ernst Strähle. They also had gearbox problems that were only solved when Buchet found time on an easier section to change the complete gearbox, fortunately a reasonably fast procedure on a Porsche.

The Viking Rally was, as might have been expected, a Scandinavian affair. It was won over seven gravel special stages by Hans Ingier, brother to Arne who had won the previous year, and who was also driving a Volvo PV544. Second was Erik Carlsson and both he and Coltelloni won their classes while Pat Moss in an Austin A40 narrowly failed to beat Ewy Rosqvist for the Ladies prize. The Deutschland Rally gave Carlsson's championship chances a major boost when he won it outright. In fact, he and Pat Moss – now driving one of the new Austin Healey 3000s – actually tied for first place on penalties and Carlsson won as he was driving the car with the smaller engine. Wolfgang Levy in an Auto Union and Paul Coltelloni in a Citroën both won their classes.

Next event was the RAC Rally and this had moved to what was now to become its traditional date in November. Unsurprisingly, winter conditions played a part in the result though not perhaps in the way that the organisers might have hoped. Most of the rally was straightforward stuff with navigation sections and tests, but as the rally made its way south from the Western Highlands of Scotland, the route lay over the highest road in the Cairngorm Mountains. From Tomintoul to Braemar is a mere thirty-two miles (fifty-one kilometres). Sadly this was completely blocked by snow and even with shovels and chains, no one could get through. Some crews quickly realised that the only way to reach the control in Braemar was to go a longer way round. The shortest alternative route through Dufftown would add forty-five miles (seventy-two kilometres) to the section and, if you had spent too long shovelling in the snow before choosing it, you would certainly be out of time at Braemar. Thus the majority of the hundred and thirty starters cut out Braemar altogether and went to the next control in Blairgowrie. But sixteen crews went via Dufftown driving like devils on the public roads and got to Braemar within their maximum lateness. The least penalised of these were Gerry Burgess and Sam Croft-Pearson in a works Ford Zephyr. Wolfgang Levy, co-driven by Stuart Turner, was one of the sixteen, but his Auto Union (the 1000 SP sports version known to the Germans as 'Schmalspur Thunderbird') was seventeen minutes later into Braemar than Burgess's Zephyr.

Levy was not happy about finishing eighth and lodged a protest at being required to average some 45 mph (72 kph) on the open road. The protest was rejected by the RAC and he promptly appealed through the German Automobile Club to the FIA though eventually in January of the following year this was withdrawn. It had been a totally unsatisfactory situation. The organisers knew that the Tomintoul-Braemar road was impassable and could have saved everyone a lot of trouble by announcing that fact, specifying an alternative route and making an extra time allowance. The self-examination at the RAC generated as a result of this led to Jack Kemsley, himself a keen competitor and who had been involved in the 1959 event, being confirmed as the man in sole charge for the 1960 RAC Rally. This was a move that was to set the British event on its road to fame and fortune.

Sadly the last rally of the year, the Rally of Portugal was even more disrupted by protests and bad feeling. Somewhere in the regulations, it was written – probably only in Portuguese – that the large side numbers on the cars had to be black on a white background. Since the FIA regulations allowed other combinations, Erik Carlsson's Saab had white numbers on the blue background of the car. When the rally was over, Carlsson found that he had been given a penalty of fifty marks for having the wrong colour numbers. He was just writing out the protest when the results were changed again and he dropped right out of the leaders – the organisers had docked him another fifty marks for the co-driver's door!

Before the RAC Rally, it had looked as if Carlsson was going to be European Champion as his nearest rival on points was Hans Wencher who did not plan to do the last two rounds. The gap between them was a single point with Carlsson on thirty-six and Wencher on thirty-five. Behind them lay Coltelloni with thirty-two points and Levy four further points behind Coltelloni. The effect of the RAC on the results was not known until Levy withdrew his protest in the early part of 1960. At that point, Levy gained five points from his class result while none of the others scored anything thanks to either retiring or non-starting. So going to Portugal, Carlsson still led Wencher by one point with Levy now third two points behind Wencher and Coltelloni one point further back still.

As we have just seen, the Portuguese Rally at first sight appeared to give nothing to any of the main contenders for the championship but when Levy, Coltelloni and Carlsson all made formal appeals against their penalties to the FIA through their national automobile clubs, the CSI was compelled to convene and hear them, which they did in March 1960. They concluded that the organisers and their stewards were wrong to penalise cars for the colour of their number backgrounds and reinstated those competitors in the results. The man who came off best was Coltelloni who, now with third overall and a class win to his credit, took eight more points bringing him to a total of forty. Carlsson found himself not highly placed in the overall classification due to other problems and only picked up three points within his class taking him to a total of thirty-nine. Levy had five points from his class and thus a total for the year of thirty-eight while of course, Wencher had not competed in Portugal and stayed on thirty-five.

So in the end it was a close result and a championship for the cheval noir (black horse), Paul Coltelloni. It was also the closest that Erik Carlsson came to winning the title for sadly, like his brother-in-law, Stirling Moss, despite winning many things in the coming decade, he was also to be a 'champion without a title'.

Champions **1959**

Ewy Rosqvist, Volvo PV544

Paul Coltelloni (at the wheel of his Citroën ID19) after winning the 1959 Monte Carlo Rally. He is flanked by his co-drivers, Pierre Alexandre (on L) and Claude Derosiers.

Safari Rally 1959, Ronnie Adams/John Boyes, Humber Super Snipe.

Safari Rally 1959, Denis Scott/Peter Davies, Ford Zephyr Mk II.

Some of the Mercedes team before the start of the 1959 Safari. From L to R, the cars are those driven by Jim Heather-Hayes/Keith Savage (220S), Jim & Lucille Cardwell (190), Nick Thomas/David Lead (219), Donald & Neil Vincent (190D) and Bill Fritschy/Jack Ellis (219).

Safari Sputnik!

By 1959, the Safari Rally was already six years old and had been a full international event for two years. Its reputation as one of the great motor rallies of the world was growing but there was, as yet, no place for it in an FIA championship. Unlike many of the European rallies, it catered for what were known as 'showroom' cars and categorised them on showroom price. However, once the so-called 'overseas' crews started to arrive with factory supported cars, all this changed and its reputation shot up faster than a Sputnik. A victory on the Safari could sell a lot of cars – and not just in East Africa.

However, the visitors seemed fated not to succeed. Many were the reasons advanced for this – lack of experience in the conditions, inability to speak Swahili, etc. – but it was probably just that they drove too fast. They expected to be able to drive at special stage speeds and that the speed of their reactions would avoid disaster. The locals drove expecting the unexpected and survived to win. Until 1972, that is, when everything changed.

In 1959, Peter Hughes and Tommy Fjastad drove together in this Ford Anglia 105E with its 1,172 cc side-valve engine and three-speed gearbox and finished fourteenth.

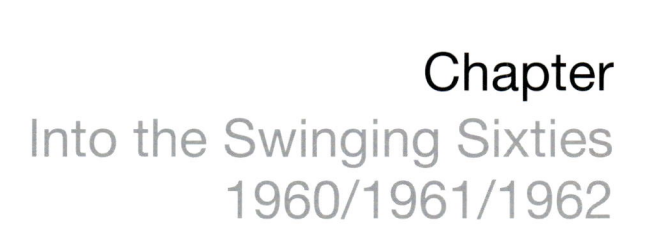

Chapter **04**
Into the Swinging Sixties
1960/1961/1962

Chapter 04
Into the Swinging Sixties

1960

Two things characterised the opening years of the 1960s. The first was the fact that manufacturer support and manufacturer teams became the norm rather than the exception. A lot of what had gone on behind a façade of private entries became more open and overt. In its turn, this led to rally organisers realising that they had to sharpen up their act and produce events that had clear and indisputable results that could be used to promote car sales. And that meant less reliance on cylinder capacity handicaps or class improvement bonuses and more emphasis on scratch speed from point A to point B.

Naturally, all this did not happen overnight and some big rallies were still using handicaps and formulae well into the middle of the decade. But the message gradually got across and the sport of rallying grew in strength and status as a result. Another thing that rally organisers had to take into account was that the European authorities were getting itchy feet about fast cars on their roads. Before the 1960 season got under way, the French announced that as of March 1st, no average speed higher than 50 kph (31 mph) could be required unless the road was closed to other traffic. It was things like this that helped to ease the sport towards special stages. Several events in France were cancelled while their organisers thought about solving the problem, but of course it did not affect the Monte Carlo Rally, run as it is in January and thus benefiting from bad weather making even low averages difficult to achieve.

Regrettably, the Automobile Club de Monaco had learnt little from the 1959 event and the adverse comments that it had generated. This was a shame as the weather was much more co-operative and produced a lot of snow and ice only some of which thawed before the start. The problem once again was that the road penalties down to Monaco, where just ten crews were unpenalised, meant little when compared with the points amassed at six times the rate on the 580 kilometres (360 miles) of regularity on the Mountain Circuit. The situation was made worse by the electronic results system that gave some unwarranted results. This and decisions by the scrutineers led to a record number of protests and subsequent appeals.

The most significant of these was that of Ido Marang and Jacques Badoche in a works Citroën DS19 who were penalised 500 marks for a missing scrutineering seal. They and their team hotly denied that they had removed it but nevertheless they were put into tenth place instead of third place. It is not certain that there was any inter-team politics here, but their third place would have spoiled what turned out to be a 1-2-3 for Mercedes with their new injection 220SE. There is no doubt that the winners, Walter Schock and Rolf Moll, fully deserved their place since their performance over the Mountain Circuit was just so much better than even their team-mates, Eugen Böhringer/Peter Socher and Roland Ott/Eberhard Mahle. The meticulous reconnaissance of the Mountain Circuit by the Mercedes crews had paid off since, beforehand, they were classified 22nd, 33rd and 48th respectively.

The next event was the Geneva Rally, returning to the European Rally Championship after missing two years and here a new breed of French rally drivers made their presence felt. The outright winners were Roger de Lageneste and Henri Greder driving a Group 2 Alfa Romeo Giulietta TI ahead of René Trautmann and Jean-Claude

▲ RAC Rally 1962, Rosemary Smith/Rosemary Seers, Sunbeam Alpine.

◀ Monte Carlo Rally 1960, Walter Schock/Rolf Moll, Mercedes 220SE. They won the event outright ahead of two other Mercedes 220SEs.

Ogier in a Citroën ID19. The rally was very largely decided on the narrow, twisty roads of the French Haute-Savoie where the two French crews plus the Swiss crew of Jean-Pierre Schild and Jean Briffaud (Alfa Romeo Giulietta TZ) were the only ones to stay without road penalties. One interesting result here was that the Morley twins, Don and Erle, won their class in a Group 2 850 cc Austin Mini and in doing so finished ahead of Erik Carlsson in his Group 2 Saab. Schock and Moll were fifth overall and second in their class to another Mercedes driven by Eberhard Mahle and Herbert Ott who had been in the third 220SE on the Monte Carlo Rally.

The car that won the Tulip Rally could so easily have been penalised for damage since René Trautmann fell asleep at the wheel just a few miles from the finish and the Citroën he shared with Guy Verrier arrived with its bonnet strapped to the roof and a door on the rear seat. The rally had gone right down to Monaco for a night halt before making its way back to Noordwijk aan Zee. Curiously despite all the hill climbs and tests on the Nürburgring, the section that sorted out the entry was one instigated by the French gendarmes who had insisted that the rally tackle the snowy ascent of Col de Turini, twelve kilometres in as many minutes depending on class. Only eleven crews made the summit on time and behind Trautmann at the finish were Carl Orrenius and Rolf Dahlgren in a Saab 96 with Schock third in his Mercedes.

Twelve special stages incorporating gravel sections and an unrelenting road section on the Acropolis Rally found just four crews unpenalised so that the Tatoi race circuit test was the decider. To give an idea of the complexities that some organisers came up with to get a result on such tests, in Greece, the task for each crew was to beat the best time of the class just below them and be within three percent of the best time of the class above. The one man who did that was Walter Schock and he thus won the rally ahead of Carlsson's Saab, Levy's Auto Union and Peter Harper's Sunbeam Rapier all of whom were unpenalised on the road sections and stages.

There was Scandinavian domination on the Midnight Sun with the honours going to Carl-Magnus and Rolf Skogh in a works Saab 96 who came home ahead of Harry Bengtsson and Åke Righard in one of the new more powerful Porsche Super 90s. Gunnar Andersson took third with a works Volvo PV544 and a rising star – he came up so fast that he was nicknamed 'Sputnik' – in the person of Harry Källström who won his class in a VW Beetle. By chance, the Rallye des Alpes this year was also decided on gravel roads though in this case, it was just one road and that not so far from the finish in Cannes. Many weary crews failed to spot this sting-in-the-tail and thus only six crews were unpenalised and won Coupes. Throughout the rally, three cars were in contention for the win with Henri Oreiller's Alfa Romeo Giulietta SZ leading right until that crucial last section where he spun and lost the lead. Also in trouble there was his main rival, Pat Moss in a Healey 3000, and thus it was the Alfa Romeo SZ of Roger de Lageneste and Henri Greder that won outright. Schock did not take part in either the Midnight Sun or the Rallye des Alpes but Eugen Böhringer was fourth on the Rallye des Alpes only being denied a class win by Jean Behra in a Jaguar 3.8.

Saab continued their winning ways in the 1000 Lakes where they captured the three top places with Carl-Otto Bremer leading home Erik Carlsson and Carl-Magnus Skogh. Both Schock and Böhringer were there for Mercedes but they retired. Thus Stuttgart honour was upheld by Rauno Aaltonen driving his father's Mercedes 220SE who finished seventh overall and won his class. It was on this rally that the young Aaltonen discussed with Böhringer the arrangement whereby they were to team up on certain gravel rallies during the following season. Mercedes did not enter the Liège and this turned out to be one of the toughest yet with over half the entry failing to re-emerge from the Yugoslav sections. Indeed as the rally entered

The victorious Mercedes team from the 1960 Monte Carlo Rally pictured with their prizes. On the far left is Eugen Böhringer while in the centre, holding the big cup, is team manager, Karl Kling.

Swedish Rally to the Midnight Sun 1960, Tom Trana/Gunnar Palm, Volvo PV544. This car was fitted with the new 1.8-litre B18 engine that was not yet in production.

Swedish Rally to the Midnight Sun 1960, Harry Bengtsson/Åke Righard, Porsche 356 Super 90.

Italy for the second time, there were two Healeys in the lead – Pat Moss and Ann Wisdom in a Healey 3000 followed by John Sprinzel in a 975 cc Austin Healey Sprite. Moss kept her lead through the last night in the French mountains but the little Healey dropped back to third behind the more powerful Porsche Super 90 of the Sanders, Guy (father) and Willy (son). The fact that two ladies had just won the most revered rally in Europe did much to lift the public interest in rallying and certainly did a lot of good for the reputation of British cars.

Next was a new rally and, since Yugoslavia was not regarded as being fully under the sway of Moscow, this was the first time that a championship rally had been held entirely behind the Iron Curtain. The 'Rajd Polski' was run in the Tatra Mountains and based in Zakopane. It was a tough event resembling a combination of the Scandinavian stage rallies and the older European events that had their home in the Alps. The winner proved to be the well organised Walter Schock and Rolf Moll who managed to hold off the two-stroke challenge from Bremer's Saab 96 and a brace of factory Wartburgs from East Germany. This situation was reversed for the Viking Rally in Norway where Carl-Magnus Skogh walked away with the win for Saab while Schock had to be content with 22nd overall and second in class. He was probably hoping for better on a Deutschland Rally that went further south into France but its competitiveness suffered from the 50kph average imposed by the authorities. The first three places were decided on a single tough section – the infamous 'circuit' of St Jean en Royans – that was held in torrential rain and where only three crews achieved their set time. Thus it was that Gunnar Andersson won with his Volvo PV544 ahead of René Trautmann's Citroën ID19 and Rolf Kreder's Mercedes 190. Kreder was in the invidious situation of keeping Schock's works Mercedes in fourth place but happily the 220SE driver won the over two-litre class thus helping his championship position.

The final round of the year was the RAC Rally that was now firmly established in November and with the introduction of many more special stages on private roads. Walter Schock started but then rather dented his sportsmanship credentials by pulling out once he discovered that René Trautmann, his closest rival for the championship, had gone off the road and retired. In every other respect, the rally was a great success and resulted in a win for Erik Carlsson and Stuart Turner in a Saab 96 who managed to finish free of penalties on both the road sections and special stages despite the handicap of Carlsson driving with two broken ribs. Close behind them was the amazing John Sprinzel in a Sebring Sprite with another Healey, this one a 3000, driven by the Morley twins into third place. The Ladies prize was hotly contested since, should either Pat Moss or Ewy Rosqvist win, then the European championship title would be theirs. Eventually, it was Anne Hall and Val Domleo who came out ahead of both contenders by finishing ninth overall in a Ford Anglia 105E but Pat Moss was next best driving her Healey 3000 with Ann Wisdom and that was sufficient to give the British girls the European title.

Thus the European Rally Champion for 1960 was Walter Schock who proved beyond doubt the qualities of the new 220SE and the efficacy of the Mercedes team approach that covered everything from recceing – where that was possible – to car preparation and servicing. The other teams of BMC, Saab, Volvo and Citroën were no less professional in their approach but at this stage their preparations were not as comprehensive as that of the team from Stuttgart under the direction of Karl Kling. But all had victories that they could celebrate and advertise.

RAC Rally 1960, Erik Carlsson, Saab 96.

RAC Rally 1960, Erik Carlsson/Stuart Turner, Saab 96. This was Carlsson's first of three consecutive victories on the RAC Rally.

Champions **1960**

Pat Moss and Ann Wisdom with their Austin A40 prior to the 1959 Monte Carlo Rally.

Victory on the Monte Carlo Rally of 1960 got Walter Schock and Rolf Moll off to a good start in their successful title chase.

1961

In contrast to the 1959 season, 1961 started badly but ended well. There were to be eleven championship rallies with a 'revived' Mile Miglia coming in to represent Italy while the Geneva was cancelled and the Viking was not part of the championship anymore.

The Monte Carlo was a disappointment despite its introduction of special stages on the common run to Monaco. This was mainly because the organisers had devised a handicap formula to be applied to the special stage times that was frankly ridiculous. Based on a power-to-weight ratio, it favoured standard, heavy saloons with small four-stroke engines. It thus came as no surprise that Panhard PL17s should occupy the top three positions in the results. This was despite Erik Carlsson choosing to drive a slightly heavier Saab 96 estate car – that incidentally benefited from a four-speed gearbox – but the two-stroke handicap that had caused Auto Union to withdraw their entries before the start was just too much for him and he finished fourth. The crew of the second placed Panhard were German, Walter Löffler and Hans-Joachim Walter, and Walter's second place was to help him considerably in his privately funded chase of the European title.

Incidentally, Paul Coltelloni worked out later what the result of the rally would have been if the stages had been marked on scratch rather than handicap. Calculated in that way, René Trautmann would have won for Citroën with Carlsson second in his Saab estate car, Gunnar Andersson third for Volvo, Pauli Toivonen fourth and Jean Rolland fifth both for Citroën. Mercedes would then have filled the next three places with their 220SEs driven by Onni Vilkas, Roland Ott and Eugen Böhringer. With the handicap, Böhringer was classified thirtieth overall instead of eighth.

For the Tulip Rally, relying on French roads meant that the event was rapidly becoming a 'Rally of the Tests' like the RAC Rally of the 1950s. Also its 'class improvement' marking system showed its weakness when the Triumph team were able to ensure that Geoff Mabbs could win the rally outright in his Herald Coupé. The way they did it was by deliberately retiring the similar car of Tiny Lewis and thus making Mabbs's difference to the remaining cars in his class that much greater. Fortunately after these two bizarre events, things reverted to normal on the Acropolis Rally. This was fast becoming a highly respected event and rising to be on a par with other longer established events. Loose surface special stages, some in pouring rain, were the order of the day and thus hill climbs and the Tatoi racetrack faded into the background. The Greeks had also come up with the novel idea of grouping stages together so that the second or third one commenced when the previous one ended – no neutralisation, just stamp the card and go. It was a Scandinavian triumph with Erik Carlsson – back in a Saab 96 saloon now with the four-speed gearbox homologated – winning outright ahead of fellow Swede, Gunnar Andersson, in a Volvo PV544. Third overall was Peter Riley in a Healey 3000 ahead of Eugen Böhringer in a Mercedes 220SE.

The Mille Miglia was a real oddity and this event that was mainly on racing circuits was shunned by most of the top drivers except for two clever ones. These were Gunnar Andersson who bought himself a Ferrari GT in which he won outright and Hans-Joachim Walter who shared a Porsche Abarth with Paul Ernst Strähle and took fifth place and second in class. On the Midnight Sun, it was victory once more for the Skogh brothers in a standard Saab 96 ahead of Bertil Söderström in a Group 2 VW. The set times on the Swedish stages still varied according to the class. Hans-Joachim Walter again hitched a ride and won his class together with Harry Bengtsson in a 1,600 cc Porsche.

The Rallye des Alpes came up with a much tougher event by virtue of including many more special stages – they called them sélectifs – held on French roads that were not 100% closed but

Monte Carlo Rally 1961, Maurice Martin/Roger Bateau, Panhard PL17. Thanks to a good handicap favouring heavy cars with small engines, this Panhard won outright ahead of two others. Very few photographers had thought to take pictures of them in action ... this is from a liaison section with one of the crew sleeping!

▲ Winners of the Rally to the Midnight Sun for the second year in succession, the Skogh brothers – Carl-Magnus and Rolf – are closely followed by two other Saab 96s crewed by Erik Berger/Lars Anderson and Olle Bromark/Kjell Lyxell. These three finished 1-2-3 in class.

◀ RAC Rally 1961, Erik Carlsson/John Brown, Saab 96, wait behind Pat Moss/Ann Wisdom, Austin Healey 3000. The Saab won again and the Healey was second overall.

were nevertheless run at 60 kph (37 mph). After one third of the rally, only three crews were still in the running for a Coupe. One of them was Hans-Joachim Walter, this time in his own Porsche 356, but he retired on the way to Italy with a broken valve spring. The other two unpenalised cars were both Healey 3000s. However, when Peter Riley crashed his on the descent of the Stelvio when the brakes went, it left the other Healey 3000 crewed by the Morley twins to come home in first place and win the one and only Coupe. With just one minute lost, Jean Rolland was second in his Alfa Romeo Zagato and one minute behind him was Paddy Hopkirk in a Sunbeam Rapier.

Böhringer drove a Mercedes 300SE on the Rallye des Alpes and was doing well up until the last night when he set fastest time on the Col d'Izoard. He then tried to repeat that on the Col d'Allos and went off the road for a few minutes. He finished but scored no championship points. His fortunes were better on the Polish Rally where he teamed up with Rauno Aaltonen in a 220SE and, sharing the wheel, they won the event outright with its mixture of tarmac and gravel roads. Mercedes were naturally pleased and even more so when Aaltonen won the 1000 Lakes Rally outright in Dad's 220SE. This year, the Finns were on top of the Swedish challenge and Pauli Toivonen in a Citroën DS19 was second with Esko Keinänen third in a Škoda TS.

As usual, the Liège proved to be the toughest of them all and it now had a new title – Liège–Sofia–Liège – indicating that it would be turning for home at the capital of Bulgaria. In fact the run down to Sofia was, for a Liège, relatively gentle but the long run back to the Italian border over new Bulgarian roads plus all the Yugoslav favourites completely decimated the entry. It was dry, dusty and harsh going and of the ninety starters just eight were classified as finishers. Crossing into Italy from Yugoslavia, René Trautmann was leading in his Citroën but his suspension failed and it was a team-mate, Lucien Bianchi, who inherited the lead and kept it to the end. At that point Bianchi had been forty minutes ahead of the Böhringer/Aaltonen 220SE and the Hans Walter/Hans Wencher Porsche 356 was almost nine minutes further back. During the last night, both Walter and the Citroën DS19 of Bob Neyret/Jacques Terramorsi managed to overhaul the Mercedes on the classic Italian passes of the Croce Domini, Vivione, Gavia and Stelvio.

The Deutschland Rally clashed with the Tour de France Automobile and that plus poor organisation the previous year kept many competitors away. But the serious contenders for the championship were there and fought it out between them. Victory went to Hans Walter in his Porsche with Böhringer/Aaltonen second for Mercedes and Gunnar Andersson third for Volvo. By contrast, the RAC Rally, now to be the decider for the championship, was very well attended. And it was to be the first RAC Rally to use Forestry Commission roads as closed special stages though these were not yet run on a scratch basis but with set times for each class.

Erik Carlsson repeated his dominance of the event and won for Saab but more surprising was that Pat Moss was second in a Healey 3000. It would be hard to find two cars with greater dissimilarities than a saloon car with front wheel drive and a two-stroke 850 cc engine, and a GT car with rear wheel drive and three-litre four-stroke engine, but over 165 miles (265 km) of forestry roads they were a mere forty seconds apart at the finish. Some benefit was given to Touring cars in that on the four-lap Oulton Park test the GT cars were given a target time one minute less than the Touring cars.

Anyone watching the cars before the start would have been amazed to see Hans-Joachim Walter going round and very carefully putting a dent in each of his Porsche's panels with a hammer. The regulations said that body damage would be penalised at the finish but that you could declare pre-rally dents, which meant that damage there would not then count. He nearly lost his class win by doing one lap too many at Oulton Park but thankfully hung on to claim victory in his class and the points. This meant that, when Gunnar Andersson finished sixth overall but only third in his class thus not adding to his annual points total (only the best six scores could count), Walter was champion, nine points ahead of Andersson. And, despite her performances on the Monte, the Tulip and now the RAC, Pat Moss, had to defer to Ewy Rosqvist who won the Ladies championship for the second time in her Volvo.

Rallye des Alpes 1961, Don & Erle Morley, Austin Healey 3000. The rallying twins won outright and claimed the only Coupe des Alpes awarded that year.

RAC Rally 1961. For his second RAC victory, an Englishman again accompanied Carlsson, this time it was John Brown. However, for this driving test at the finish in Brighton, it was a case of 'driver only'.

Champions **1961**

Ewy Rosqvist won her 1961 European Ladies title at the wheel of a Volvo PV544.

A clever choice of cars for the various European rallies saw Hans-Joachim Walter drive a Panhard, an Abarth and various Porsches to gain the European title. On the 1961 Midnight Sun Rally in Sweden, he shared a Porsche 356 with Harry Bengtsson.

1962

The end of the 1961 season had seen excellent competition and it was only to be hoped that 1962 would keep up that trend. This proved to be the case with a titanic struggle for the European Championship between Eugen Böhringer in the Mercedes against Erik Carlsson in his Saab. First blood went to the Swede with an outright victory on the Monte Carlo Rally with the Mercedes second. On the five special stages down to Monaco, there was a handicap system depending on cylinder capacity but it was not as ridiculous as the previous year and when Carlsson arrived in Monaco his lead over Böhringer was just 43.5 seconds some of which – or maybe all if the Saab ran into trouble – could be taken back on four laps of the Monaco GP circuit where no handicap applied. In the actual event, Carlsson kept clear and was only fifteen seconds slower than his rival.

The battle was even closer for the Ladies Prize between Pat Moss in a 997 cc Mini Cooper and Anne Hall in a Ford Anglia 105E as, before the race, only eight seconds separated them but the Cooper proved faster round the circuit. This was the first appearance of the Mini Cooper with two cars entered by the works team. The second car was for Rauno Aaltonen who had an accident on the descent from the Col de Turini where the car rolled and caught fire. He was trapped in the wreck and was only freed by the swift action of his co-driver, Tulip Rally winner, Geoff Mabbs. The Sunbeam Rapier team were there in force with Peter Procter, Graham Hill, Tiny Lewis and Peter Harper all finishing in the top twenty, but it was Paddy Hopkirk who netted them third place overall behind Böhringer.

▲ Monte Carlo Rally 1962, Paddy Hopkirk/Jack Scott, Sunbeam Rapier.

▼ Monte Carlo Rally 1962, Peter Proctor (wearing sunglasses behind the cup)/Graham Robson, Sunbeam Rapier. They finished fourth overall and helped to win the team prize for Rootes.

Monte Carlo Rally 1962, Erik Carlsson/ Gunnar Häggbom, Saab 96. After defeat by the Panhards the previous year, this was to be the first of Carlsson's two great victories on the Monte.

The Tulip Rally was a bit of a disappointment in some ways with just 4.5% of its route down to Monaco and back to Holland used for competition. But BMC, now under the direction of Stuart Turner, were not upset when Pat Moss and Ann Riley – Miss Wisdom had married Peter Riley – won the event outright in a 997 cc Mini Cooper from Gunnar Andersson driving a Volvo 122S that was slightly heavier but more powerful than the PV544 he had used previously. Carlsson was fourth but was denied his class win by Pierre Gelé in a DKW Junior powered by a 796 cc three-cylinder two-stroke engine while Böhringer, who finished seventh, did win his class with a Mercedes 220SEb, one of the famous fintails.

With twelve special stages, gravel roads and a couple of hill climbs, the Acropolis was more in keeping with what rally drivers expected as a test of their skills and it produced a magnificent fight between the two leading championship contenders. The victory went to Böhringer but only by the very narrowest of margins from Andersson. René Trautmann pursued them the whole way in his works Citroën DS19 and finished barely a minute behind the Volvo.

The next happening was a midsummer date clash between the Rallye des Alpes and the Midnight Sun that should surely have been avoided with better co-ordination between the CSI and the various rally organisers. In the Alps, the Morley twins won for BMC but their Healey 3000 was harried all the way by Hans-Joachim Walter's Porsche Carrera which, in its turn, stayed ahead of Pat Moss's Healey 3000. All three won Coupes as did the fourth and fifth placed finishers, Mike Sutcliffe (Triumph TR4) and René Trautmann (Citroën DS19). Meanwhile in Sweden, both Carlsson and Böhringer had entered, Böhringer in a Group 1 Mercedes 220SEb and Carlsson in a Group 2 Saab 96. Both won their classes and finished in the top five but it was a new name on the winner's trophy, Bengt Söderström. Driving a Group 1 Mini Cooper from BMC Sweden, the burly Swede, who had been driving a Saab a year earlier on the 1000 Lakes, now showed his mastery of a much smaller car and earned himself an invitation to drive a Mini on the RAC Rally later in the year.

High-speed roads were on the menu for the Polish Rally and in trying to keep up with the bigger-engined cars, Carlsson posted his first retirement of the year. Unfazed, Böhringer won outright and his nearest challenger was Pat Moss accompanied by Pauline Mayman in a Healey 3000 since Ann Riley was having a baby. Indeed, had the Healey not run out of petrol at one point, the ladies might have won but finally had to be content with second place ahead of another Mercedes fintail driven by Hermann Kühne.

Eugen Böhringer did not venture to the 1000 Lakes Rally and, with Rauno Aaltonen having a drive in a works Mini, the way was left open for Carlsson to close the gap to his German rival. By finishing third and winning his class, the Swede put himself equal on points with Böhringer. Winning the rally was Pauli Toivonen in a Citroën DS19 with Esko Keinänen second in a Škoda, and there was a new face too among the ladies with Sylvia Österberg from Sweden in a Volvo very nearly beating Ewy Rosqvist's all-conquering Mercedes. Also worth noting was a young driver, Simo Lampinen, who finished fourth in his own Saab. His first major rally had been the 1000 Lakes the previous year when he entered with the Jaguar 3.4 that his father had bought for him to drive to essential therapy sessions following his recovery from poliomyelitis.

As everyone had come to expect, the Liège was the best rally of the year, its unique blend of impossibility and improbability with speed and endurance proving so attractive that it got one of its biggest entries to date. At Sofia, two Healey 3000s – those of David Seigle-Morris and Paddy Hopkirk – were tied for the lead with Böhringer. As an indication of the destructive nature of the Yugoslav roads,

Rallye des Alpes 1962, David Seigle-Morris/Tony Ambrose, Austin Healey 3000.

Swedish Rally to the Midnight Sun 1962, Bengt Söderström (seated)/Bo Olsson, Mini Cooper 998. They won the rally outright.

Acropolis Rally 1962, Eugen Böhringer/Peter Lang, Mercedes 220SE (fintail). They won the rally outright.

Mercedes had opted to replace Böhringer's usual co-driver, Peter Lang, by someone with more mechanical expertise, Hermann Eger. Among the seventy cars that dropped out on the return run through Yugoslavia was Carlsson whose suspension cried 'enough' while Hopkirk retired and Seigle-Morris gradually dropped back to finish eighth.

At the finish, Böhringer had a lead of almost half an hour over Paul Coltelloni and Ido Marang in a works Citroën DS19. They were perhaps a bit surprised to find themselves so well placed since their team manager, René Cotton had such little faith in them that for this rally he had persuaded them to pay their own way. With Guy Verrier fourth and Claudine Bouchet seventh, Citroën also picked up the Manufacturers Cup plus the Nations Trophy for France. One hopes that the crews were not buying their own drinks at the prize giving!

The next rally was the Baden-Baden, Germany's contribution to the European Rally Championship. It was not a happy event with all kinds of wrangles about cars, eligibility and a generally negative approach from the organisers towards the competitors. It also suffered from a class improvement system that should have worked for the Mercedes team but eventually proved to be their undoing. Basically it was the four hill climbs in France that decided the result as all the top crews completed the road sections with zero penalties. Aware that class improvement could be manipulated as by the Triumph team on the previous year's Tulip Rally, the organisers discarded the second fastest time in the class if it was too far away from the fastest man. On the last hill climb, there must have been a bug in the Mercedes computer for, instead of enhancing Böhringer's improvement, the other two works Mercedes in his class went too slow and he did not get any improvement at all. The result was that Pat Moss emerged, after much calculation, as the winner in her Mini Cooper just ahead of Böhringer. Trautmann finished third for Citroën and a delighted Hans-Joachim Walter was fourth and GT winner in his Porsche Carrera after a magnificent performance where he set fastest time on all of the hill climbs.

Acropolis Rally 1962, Eugen Böhringer/Peter Lang, Mercedes 220SE.

Liège-Sofia-Liège 1962. The four Rover P5 3.0 accompanied by a service Land Rover are pictured at the Solihull factory before leaving for the start. Two finished, Ken James/Mike Hughes sixth overall and Bill Bengry/David Skeffington eighteenth overall.

Carlsson was also there. He finally finished sixth and won his class but it left his situation in the championship a bit desperate as he needed to win both the final two rallies if he were to defeat Böhringer. At first, things looked good for him as Mercedes would not be contesting the Geneva Rally as the team were off to Argentina for the Gran Premio Internacional Standard Argentina. But there were too few entries on the Geneva Rally for full points to be awarded and thus, even finishing second and winning his class, Carlsson could not keep his hopes alive. Thus Böhringer won the championship on a rally in which he did not compete and before his rival even crossed the start line!

The winner in Geneva was Hans-Joachim Walter accompanied on this occasion by Werner Lier from that same city. As with so many major rallies, the route lay not in Switzerland, where the authorities were definitely unfriendly towards motor sport, but in France where, despite the imposed 50 kph average speed, there were roads that could prove sufficiently challenging to make a good rally. The organisers had also enlivened things by running some 'chronometric' sections that had set times for the various classes – sélectifs by another name – in addition to major hill climbs like Chamrousse and Mont Ventoux. Walter set fastest time on every single one while second fastest was Jean-Jacques Thuner in a works Triumph TR4 except for the last one where he stopped with a broken throttle. Thanks to the rain and some fog, only four cars were without penalty on the normal road sections.

The RAC Rally was the final event of the year and, though it was now well into its tough special stage format, it attracted more entries than the previous year. There were twenty-nine stages all of which had set times but now there was no handicap and it was a straight fight. Thus it was all the more surprising that Erik Carlsson with his 850 cc Saab 96 set seventeen fastest times and came home a comfortable winner from Paddy Hopkirk and Pat Moss in Austin Healey 3000s. This was in some ways an even more remarkable achievement than Carlsson's two previous wins in his hat trick of RAC victories. Paddy Hopkirk had made a name for himself driving Triumph TR3s and for almost four years had been driving Sunbeam Rapiers for Rootes but after finishing third on this year's Monte Carlo, he had been snapped up by BMC and was now proving his worth. Other notable names now driving for BMC and cropping up in the top ten finishers were Rauno Aaltonen and Timo Mäkinen both driving Mini Coopers and who, with Hopkirk, were about to create a major stir in the rally world. The Midnight Sun Rally winner, Bengt Söderström, was also driving a Mini Cooper but after setting some fast times retired with a broken gearbox shortly after leaving Scotland.

The RAC Rally had now really come of age and being won three times by a Scandinavian ace had done nothing to harm its prestige with European drivers. New champion Böhringer had even hurried back from Argentina to take part – with number 1 on his 220SEb – and chosen a British driver, Brian Culcheth, to go with him. Sadly, their rally was over quite quickly when a Yorkshire tree proved to be stronger than a Stuttgart radiator. Ewy Rosqvist did not start for Mercedes as she was still in Argentina reaping the rewards of her victory on the Gran Premio.

Champions **1962**

Eugen Böhringer (on L)/Peter Lang and their Mercedes 220SE.

Pat Moss was 1962 Ladies Champion driving Mini Cooper 998s and Austin Healey 3000s.

Chapter **05**
Wonderful times
1963/1964/1965

Chapter 05
Wonderful times

1963

European rallying was about to enter a period that contained some of the best moments of the century. But what was the first thing that happened? The Commission Sportive Internationale (CSI) decided that they were going to do without a European Rally Championship for 1963 and that it would recommence in 1964 when they had had time to think things over. Well, championship or not, the vigorous youngster that was rallying was going to continue to grow and the event organisers, all of whose clubs were part of the FIA, were going to continue organising events. All it meant was that those events that had been included in the championship previously for reasons other than the quality of their organisation and the challenge of their route lost the interest of the works teams and other top competitors.

The Monte Carlo was blessed with snow and ice. Indeed there was so much in places that none of the starters from Athens or Lisbon got through to Chambéry to start the common route south to Monaco. Of the 296 cars starting, 216 reached Chambéry, only 96 reached Monaco and of those just twenty-seven were unpenalised. The handicap formula was still in place for the special stages of which there were six and here there was a genuine surprise in store. One car was fastest over all six stages and it was an American V8, a Ford Falcon Futura. Admittedly it was driven by a Swede, Bo Ljungfeldt, but the fact that he could go some fourteen minutes faster over 145 kilometres of stages than Eugen Böhringer in his works Mercedes 220SEb stunned the rally world. Fortunately for all concerned – with the natural exceptions of Ljungfeldt and Ford USA – the Falcon had lost a whopping amount of road marks when its clutch had to be replaced in the Cevennes on the run-in to Chambéry. Thus Ljungfeldt was finally classified 43rd overall but without that problem, he would have won outright despite the handicap.

The winner was – again – the incredible Erik Carlsson now with a new co-driver, Gunnar Palm. In fact the man that had been with Carlsson on the 1961 victory, Gunnar Häggbom, was sitting alongside Ljungfeldt. Despite the best efforts of the Swedish/American effort, this snowy rally was a triumph for front-wheel drive cars and Citroëns and Mini Coopers filled out the next six places behind the Saab. And in there were names like Pauli Toivonen, Rauno Aaltonen and Paddy Hopkirk that would soon be even better known to rally fans. If there was any sadness, it was that the handicap, now much fairer towards larger engined cars, was still capable of keeping the GT cars out of the Monte Carlo's top places. Timo Mäkinen driving a works Healey 3000 with the British Mini racer, Christabel Carlisle, could only finish thirteenth just two places behind Böhringer while the next best GT car was the Porsche of Hans-Joachim Walter who finished 38th overall.

Monte Carlo Rally 1963, Rauno Aaltonen/Tony Ambrose, Mini Cooper 998. They finished third overall and won their class.

Monte Carlo Rally 1963. The small but successful Saab team pose in their Trollhättan workshop. Gunnar Palm is on the far left, then Bo Hellberg (team manager), Per-Olof Rudh (mechanic), Erik Carlsson (at the door of the winning car, 283) and Sven Olsson (mechanic).

The next big European event was the Tulip Rally and this was a better event than in the past few years. The endurance and cost aspects had been improved by cutting out the night halt in the south of France and the fourteen special tests were well chosen even if the route itself was not able to be made very demanding. And to add interest, Piet Nortier had decided to have separate Touring and GT categories plus a category for Amateur drivers. The fly in the ointment was, as usual, the class improvement system whereby a dominant performance in a weak class produces a winner. It happened here with Henri Greder taking one of the ex-Monte Falcon Futuras – now left in the control of Ford France – and simply running away from the chasing Jaguar 3.8 saloons and Ford Zodiacs in his class. Paddy Hopkirk and his new co-driver, Henry Liddon, had a much harder time of it with their works Mini Cooper since they had to deal with the very fast DKW F12 of Pierre Gelé who kept hard on their heels. Still Hopkirk was second to Greder in the Touring Category while the BMC entry of a Healey 3000 for the Morley twins, Don and Erle, was enough to finish second in the GT category and keep a trio of works Triumph TR4s driven by Vic Elford, Roy Fidler and Jean-Jacques Thuner behind it in its class. The overall GT winner was L.H. Bakker from Holland driving a Porsche Super 90 while Pat Moss with a new co-driver – Jenny Nadin – in a new team – Ford – won the Ladies prize with a Cortina GT. The Amateur category was won by Geoff Allen in what was actually a works Vauxhall VX 4/90 and second was Andrew Cowan, making one of his first forays abroad in his own Sunbeam Rapier after winning the 1962 Scottish Rally.

Monte Carlo Rally 1963, Erik Carlsson/Gunnar Palm, Saab 96.

Monte Carlo Rally 1963, Bo Ljungfeldt/Gunnar Häggbom, Ford Falcon Sprint 4.2. The big surprise of the rally was the Swedish crew in the American car. Without time lost on the concentration run with transmission trouble, they would certainly have won.

Monte Carlo Rally 1963. Everyone wants to interview the winners and Bo Ljungfeldt (partly hidden behind Carlsson) is keen to listen.

The GT category had looked as if it was going to be won by another Dutch driver in a Porsche, Ben Pon, the sports-racing driver turning out to do the rally in his Abarth Carrera. Unfortunately, his support crew was seen to follow him through one of the tests and he was excluded. There was also an unfortunate incident on the Trois Epis hill climb where the Healey 3000 of Derrick Astle went off, hit some tree branches that dislodged the Healey's hardtop that then broke the driver's neck. This was a most unusual incident and was one of the very rare fatalities that rallying suffered in these years.

Mercedes had opted not to do the Tulip. They were perhaps aware after the Monte Carlo that a Ford Falcon with a 4.3-litre V8 engine could be quite quick uphill. But they were back with a vengeance on the Acropolis Rally where they found plenty of opposition from the Saab, Volvo, Ford and Citroën teams though BMC had elected for once to give it a miss. Saab lost Erik Carlsson early on when he had a brush with a stone bridge on one of the fast stages in the north. The normal Greek sunshine and dust were missing on this occasion and were replaced by rain and mud with the occasional early morning fog added for good measure. With Carlsson's exit – and Saab lost Olle Bromark on the same stage – Böhringer's nearest challengers were the works 122S Volvos of Gunnar Andersson and Carl-Magnus Skogh but his 300 SE proved too fast for them.

The Ford Cortina GTs showed well in these conditions and Henry Taylor finished fourth while Pat Moss – briefly reunited with Ann Riley – was sixth and won the Ladies Prize. Mercedes had strength in depth with two 220SEbs driven by Dieter Glemser/Klaus Kaiser and Ewy Rosqvist/Heike Krause who finished fifth and twelfth respectively. The Citroën DS19s proved reliable but not fast enough and Pauli Toivonen, René Trautmann and Guy Verrier finished in line astern behind Pat Moss.

The Midnight Sun of 1963 will be best remembered for its last special stage. This was held in the bowels of the earth using the tunnels of an iron ore mine near the finish at Kiruna. The cars had to first descend to the bottom using the same route as the stage but in reverse and were then released up the adits into the open air. Fastest man here was Berndt Jansson in a Porsche Carrera with a time of 2 min 46 sec and indeed he had been fast throughout the nineteen special stages and thus won the rally by a narrow margin from Erik Carlsson's Group 2 Saab 96. Not far behind was the Monte Carlo sensation, Bo Ljungfeldt, but this time he was driving a Cortina GT for Ford Sweden. As well as the 350-metre vertical ascent out of a mineshaft, the Kiruna finish-ramp also provided a welcome 'refresher' for this mid-summer rally in the form of a snowstorm.

One performance that almost went unnoticed in Sweden was that of Tom Trana. The young Volvo driver had been going well in a works 122S on the Acropolis Rally until he had an accident. Here too he left the road a couple of times early on but recovered and finally finished fourth in class with his PV544 and ahead of Sylvia Österberg, also in a PV544, who won the Ladies Prize. It is also worth noting that Pat Moss was entered in Group 3 with one of the new Lotus Cortinas – it had to go into Group 3 as not enough had been made for Group 2 homologation – and thus shared a class with all the Porsches. She finished third in class but on this occasion was only fourth in the Ladies classification.

For the Rallye des Alpes, there was no clash of dates with the Midnight Sun this year and it showed in the quantity and quality of the entry it received. The rally measured up to the challenge and only a quarter of the starters arrived at the finish of which just six were awarded Coupes. One of those, René Trautmann, also won a Coupe d'Argent after having already won Coupes in 1960 and 1962

Acropolis Rally 1963, Vjatsheslav Mosolov/Aleksei Matissen, GAZ-M21 Volga. The Russian factory entered Volgas in rallies like 1000 Lakes and Acropolis during the mid-1960s but they were heavy and had a low-tech 2.4-litre engine giving 80 bhp.

Swedish Rally to the Midnight Sun 1963. Rally cars queue to venture down the iron ore mine in Kiruna, the ascent from which was the last special stage of the rally.

Swedish Rally to the Midnight Sun 1963, Berndt Jansson/Erik Pettersson, Porsche 356 Carrera. They pose with their trophies after winning.

Acropolis Rally 1963, Eugen Böhringer/Rolf Knoll, Mercedes 300SE. The car may have been bigger, the man the same size, but the result was the same with Böhringer winning his second Acropolis Rally.

but generally Citroën were outclassed on this event and Trautmann finished fifth. Early retirements came from the GT category where BMC lost two Healey 3000s and Triumph a TR4 through accidents – Hopkirk set fastest time on the first hill climb but went off just after the flying finish – but there was trouble of a different kind for others. Eugen Böhringer was sidelined with engine failure while his Mercedes team-mates joined him soon after with electrical problems in the case of Ewy Rosqvist and an accident with a non-competing car for Dieter Glemser. Triumph also lost its two other TR4s, a bent wishbone for Vic Elford and a faulty clutch for Jean-Jacques Thuner.

Through all this, Don and Erle Morley carried on unflustered, concentrating on trying to win a Coupe and thus a Coupe d'Or, awarded for finishing without penalties for three years in a row, despite the fluctuations in the weather that went from too hot to rain and then back again. Sadly, on the last day, their works Healey 3000 broke its differential on the start line of the Col d'Allos. This meant that Jean Rolland/Gabriel Augias could carry on to win the GT category in their lovely Alfa Romeo GTZ. It also meant that the Reliant team could chalk up a class win with one of their Sabre Sixes driven by Bobby Parkes with a certain Roger Clark finishing behind him in another Sabre Six.

The main battle amongst the Touring category runners was between the Mini Coopers and the Ford Cortinas. At the end of the day, the Minis had the best of it with Rauno Aaltonen winning the Touring category and the rally outright with Henry Taylor and David Seigle-Morris in Ford Cortina GTs finishing second and third in the category. BMC also won the Ladies prize with a Mini Cooper driven by Pauline Mayman, now promoted to a Number One driver after the departure of Pat Moss to Ford. Pat did not start the Rallye des Alpes thanks to a bout of pleurisy. Henri Greder was out in the Falcon Futura again and was pushing Aaltonen and Taylor hard but a minor indiscretion on the Col d'Allos saw him lose time though he did have the consolation of winning his class.

The date of the 1000 Lakes fell just nine days before the start of the Liège and thus that event was deprived of a few of the big names. But there was no need to fear as there were plenty of new names rising to the top and this event highlighted them. The outright winner was Simo Lampinen, the young man who had impressed by following Carlsson home in 1962. Now, at the wheel of a Finnish Saab 96, he kept Tom Trana, Volvo's new golden boy, in second place with his PV544. Lampinen also beat the man who taught him left-foot braking, Rauno Aaltonen, who was driving another Finnish Saab 96 and came third. While it was evident that a two-stroke Saab with fifteen-inch wheels might yet have an advantage over a Mini Cooper with not much more horsepower and ten-inch wheels, it is worth recording that Timo Mäkinen managed ninth overall with an imported Mini.

With few changes to its format or route, the Liège looked as if it was going to be straightforward but that was discounting the effect of the weather. Rain, mud and terrible thunderstorms were the order of the day. They hit just as the rally entered Yugoslavia by means of the Moistrocca Pass, the first difficult section, and continued on the route down to Belgrade. The rain and accompanying fog caused chaos with many fancied crews having accidents and either being delayed – Paddy Hopkirk in a Healey 3000 – or retiring – Pat Moss in a Cortina GT. Somehow, eleven drivers were still unpenalised at the one hour halt in Sofia and these included Eugen Böhringer in the new Mercedes 230SL sports car, Rauno Aaltonen in a Healey 3000, Erik Carlsson in a Saab 96 and Anne Hall in a Ford Cortina GT.

Going back from Sofia, initially dust was the problem and, when it got dark, the rally lost car number 2, the Healey 3000 of Timo

RAC Rally 1963. Before the start, competitors look at the route – until then, secret – through Scotland.

RAC Rally 1963, Harry Källström/Gunnar Häggbom, Volkswagen 1500S. By finishing second, Källström shot to fame – and was promptly nicknamed 'Sputnik'.

◀ Liège-Sofia-Liège 1963, Eugen Böhringer/Klaus Kaiser, Mercedes 230SL.

◀ Liège-Sofia-Liège 1963, Paddy Hopkirk/Henry Liddon, Austin Healey 3000. This was the only works Healey to survive Le Marathon de la Route in 1963. It finished sixth overall.

Mäkinen when it hit an unlit truck coming the other way. But then the rain started again and Lucien Bianchi lost ten minutes drying out his electrics of his Citroën while Carlsson fumed behind a truck on a narrow road and lost about the same. Going back into Italy, Aaltonen led Böhringer by just two minutes with Carlsson eight minutes further back. It could not have been closer but the fight at the front came to an end when the Healey developed a steering problem on the Passo del Vivione and tried to launch itself into space with a bit of help from the adjoining rock face. From then on, over the last two passes, Böhringer kept his cool and won with the 230 SL. That was something that had not been expected before the start since it is rare for a new car to do well first time out. Carlsson was a very well deserved second with Bianchi's Citroën third. In fact Citroën came out of the rally quite well since they collected the team prize and Claudine Bouchet the Ladies Prize.

The Liège is always a difficult act to follow but this time the RAC Rally very nearly eclipsed it. The rally in the British forests had reduced its night stops to a single night in Blackpool and upped the quantity and length of its special stages. There was no doubt that this was a tough event calling for speed, strength and endurance. And the Scandinavians dominated it to such an extent that one magazine likened it to a repeat of the 8th Century Viking invasions of Britain. And there were plenty of new faces to welcome since the winner was Tom Trana from Sweden who simply revelled in the wet conditions and kept his Volvo PV544 in the lead throughout. His closest pursuer was Harry Källström driving a VW 1500 S. He was one of a team of four similar VWs from Scania-Vabis in Sweden with the others driven by Berndt Jansson, Rune Larsson and Bertil Söderström. They nearly won the team prize as all four finished in the top twenty but that award went to Ford GB with Henry Taylor, Pat Moss and Peter Riley bringing their Cortina GTs home in sixth, seventh and fifteenth places overall and with Pat Moss collecting yet another Ladies award. Showing that there was still life in the Healey 3000, Timo Mäkinen and Don Morley finished fifth and ninth respectively but, as a portent of the future, Hopkirk's Mini Cooper beat both of them.

And what of the winner for the last three years? Erik Carlsson tried hard right to the very last stage in his Saab and in fact finished equal on points with Harry Källström. However, he was unfortunate enough to have encountered a navigational problem on the very first stage of the rally and it was the times from there that were used as a tie-decider so he had to be content with third overall.

Although this was a year without an official European Rally Championship, there was an unofficial one that was administered by the Sports Department of the Automobile Club von Deutschland (AvD). This was based on the results of seven rallies – Monte Carlo, Tulip, Acropolis, Alpes, Wiesbaden, Sardinia and Geneva – and was split into two parts, a Trophy for Touring car drivers and a Cup for GT drivers. Gunnar Andersson won the Trophy in Volvo 122S and PV544 and was proclaimed overall champion while Hans-Joachim Walter took the GT Cup in his Porsche Carrera.

Champions **1963**

Tom Trana and Gunnar Andersson (on R) the unofficial European champion in the year when there was no championship.

Valerie Domleo and Pauline Mayman (on R), another unofficial champion.

Acropolis Rally 1963, Gunnar Andersson/Walter Karlsson, Volvo Amazon 122 S.

RAC Rally 1963, Tom Trana/Sven Lindstrøm, Volvo PV544. They won the rally outright and here they tackle one of the last stages on a military area near Lulworth.

1964

For 1964, the good news was that the FIA's Rally Championship was back but the bad news was that the CSI had missed the opportunity to turn it into a championship worthy of the name. It was still focussed firmly on Europe despite there now being candidates for inclusion in an FIA Championship such as the Safari in East Africa and the Shell 4000 in Canada. Its points scoring system was as impenetrable as an Italian tax return and some, like the Liège's Maurice Garot, saw fit to withdraw from the championship in disgust. All this having been said, it was a really good year for rallying and when the dust had settled, there was a worthy champion in the person of Tom Trana whose Volvo PV544 had come from behind and won three major events in the second half of the year.

The Monte Carlo Rally once again provided a bit of a shock. Pat Moss had left Ford to join Erik Carlsson at Saab – they were married the previous March – and the pair of them were determined to make the best of the handicap factor to defeat the army of Ford Falcon Futura Sprints entered by Ford USA. These beasts were now sporting 4.7-litre V8 engines and acres of lightweight fibreglass panels and, of course, Bo Ljungfeldt was behind the wheel of one of them. This time, there were no clutch problems on the run-in to Chambéry and in conditions that were just a fraction less snowy than the previous year, the Ljungfeldt Falcon once again set fastest time on all the special stages.

But there was a new toy in the equation as BMC had come with their new 1,071 cc Mini Cooper S that had more power and bigger brakes than the old Cooper. They entered examples of these for Paddy Hopkirk, Timo Mäkinen and Rauno Aaltonen and the result was everything for which they could have wished. Hopkirk won outright with Mäkinen fourth and Aaltonen seventh to win the Manufacturers award. The handicap coefficient favoured smaller-engined cars but it was the fact that Hopkirk was able to set such remarkable times in the Cooper S that after the five special stages – he was equal fastest with Ljungfeldt on Saint-Apollinaire – he was just eighty-one seconds on scratch behind Ljungfeldt. Once the handicap had been applied, the order on arrival in Monaco was in fact Hopkirk first with the two Saabs of Erik Carlsson and Pat Moss next and then Mäkinen's Cooper S. The final test of four laps round the Monaco GP circuit however enabled Ljungfeldt to pull up into second place. See table for details:

There was a bit of a surprise in the GT category whose handicap was even heavier than for the Group 1 and 2 cars. The Porsche Carrera of Günter Klass was beaten by the Morley twins in a works MGB with Jean-Jacques Thuner third in a works Triumph TR4. With 120 cars eligible to take part in the circuit test, several sessions had to be organised and these led to the occasional problem. First Mäkinen and Carl-Magnus Skogh (Volvo 122S) were shown the chequered flag one lap too early and their penalties had to be calculated from those laps they had completed at full speed. Then in the penultimate heat, Peter Harper's Falcon crashed and the heat was stopped. The organisers insisted on having a re-run, which meant that Piero Frescobaldi ran out of fuel in his Lancia. He had checked into *parc fermé* with enough to do his four laps but he had been asked to do seven. Naturally he protested and that slowed up the results. All this indicated to everyone that such a circuit test was anomalous in a major rally.

A new event in the championship was the Rallye dei Fiori based in Sanremo. It had first been held in 1961 and had thus only just started to mature. Its special stages were in fact regularity tests and that caught out Pauli Toivonen in a VW 1500 and Franco Patria and René Trautmann in Lancia Flavias all of whom checked in ahead of schedule and were heavily penalised. Normally on a special stage, if you drove it in less than the set time, you were given the set time.

Monte Carlo Rally 1964. Bo Ljungfeldt in action with his Ford Falcon in the circuit test where he easily set fastest time.

Monte Carlo Rally 1964, Bo Ljungfeldt (in car wearing trademark cap)/Fergus Sager, Ford Falcon Futura Sprint 4.7.

Driver	Co-eff	SS1	SS2	SS3	SS4	SS5	Circuit Time in seconds	Total Penalty
Hopkirk	0.3345	16 min 13 sec	34 min 11 sec	15 min 23 sec	17 min 41 sec	23 min 46 sec	384.1	2536.2730
Ljungfeldt	0.3489	15 min 54 sec	33 min 53 sec	15 min 23 sec	17 min 13 sec	23 min 29 sec	350.5	2566.7128
Carlsson	0.3298	17 min 00 sec	35 min 20 sec	15 min 45 sec	18 min 33 sec	23 min 42 sec	390.5	2573.7760
Mäkinen	0.3345	16 min 40 sec	34 min 59 sec	15 min 42 sec	17 min 54 sec	25 min 10 sec	377.8	2593.8625
Pat Moss	0.3298	17 min 07 sec	36 min 05 sec	15 min 48 sec	18 min 16 sec	23 min 51 sec	398.2	2596.9766

Monte Carlo Rally 1964. The winning driver, a very happy Paddy Hopkirk, takes lunch in the Monaco sun with his wife, Jenny.

With regularity, it was double the penalty per second for being early. Anyway, two visitors who got on top of the timing were Erik Carlsson and Pat Moss whose Saab 96s finished first and second with Piero Frescobaldi third in his Lancia Flavia.

For the Tulip Rally, BMC upped the ante by arriving with their latest Cooper S, the 1,275 cc model. The rally was slightly shorter than the previous year but still the easy road sections linking the stages far exceeded them in mileage. This did not stop there being some very exciting tussles and, though Timo Mäkinen may have won the Touring category in the sole works 1275 Cooper S, behind him a very determined Henri Greder in an ex-Monte Falcon had a real fight on his hands with Carl-Magnus Skogh's Volvo 122S. And behind them there was a battle royal between the Saab 96s of Mr & Mrs Carlsson and Kurt Pfnier's DKW F11 that was finally resolved in favour of the German driver with Pat Moss then taking sixth place behind her husband and the Ladies prize.

In the GT category, the long-time leader was Ben Pon returning to try and win the Tulip Rally at the wheel of a Porsche, this time a 904 GTS. He kept ahead of the Morley twins in their works Healey 3000 until on the last day he suffered a broken suspension – and this time there was no service car handy. The demise of the Pon Porsche was not the end of the struggle, however, as Berndt Jansson was chasing the Morleys hard with a Porsche Abarth Carrera that arrived at the finish with a driver's door that was now much nearer the driver than at the start of the rally. All in all, the Tulip had improved and by comparing the times in a class with those above and below instead of just within the class, the handicap was much fairer. The rally had its usual variations in weather with rain at Zolder and sunshine at Solitude but nothing in the extreme.

As one had come to expect, the Acropolis was a tougher proposition altogether so that it came close to rivalling the Liège. The reason for this was that the organisers, ELPA, had decided to tighten up the road sections between the stages and chose rougher roads to make those links. Time for service was short and this showed in that only nineteen of the seventy-two crews that started were classified as finishers. And there were some big names amongst the retirees with Eugen Böhringer heading the list when his Mercedes 300SE succumbed to petrol pump failure. Also out were the two 1275 Cooper Ss of Hopkirk and Aaltonen that had led the event until Aaltonen broke his steering and Hopkirk fell prey to an electrical short-circuit.

As a further indication of the severity of the road sections, at the finish there were only two crews without road penalty, Jean-Claude Ogier in a works Citroën DS19 and Pat Moss in a Saab 96. However, their times on the stages were sufficiently eclipsed by Tom Trana in a Volvo PV544 that his loss of a minute on the road was not sufficient to stop him winning the rally ahead of the two front-wheel drive cars. The Rover company who had made a good showing on the 1963 Safari, Liège and RAC rallies with their big 'Auntie' three-litre saloons came to Greece with five cars and, though they lost Anne Hall and Logan Morrison, the rest – Ken James, Toney Cox and Richard Martin-Hurst with his co-driver, Roger Clark – got theirs to the finish. The Mercedes team were thrown into confusion before the start when Dieter Glemser fell ill but an engineer by the name

Tulip Rally 1964, Don & Erle Morley, Austin Healey 3000 Mk III. The rallying twins drove the new Mk III and are seen here about to set fastest time at the Nürburgring test. They went on to win the GT category of the rally.

▲ Tulip Rally 1964, Timo Mäkinen/Tony Ambrose, Mini Cooper S 1275. They won the touring category.

◀ Acropolis Rally 1964, Erich Waxenberger (nearest camera)/Klaus Kaiser (behind), Mercedes 220SE. Waxenberger, a Mercedes test engineer, stepped in to drive when Dieter Glemser was taken ill with appendicitis.

Acropolis Rally 1964. Waxenberger's Mercedes 220SE might be in the lead on the final race at Tatoi Airfield but it was Tom Trana's Volvo PV544 that won the rally.

of Erich Waxenberger stepped in and drove the 220SE brilliantly to finish fourth overall just one place ahead of the similar car of Ewy Rosqvist. Erik Carlsson had a problem in the Peloponnese when he slid off the road in heavy rain and, when the tow rope pulling him back on again broke, it cost him almost an hour to build a track back to the road and continue to finish thirteenth.

The Austrian Alpine, probably the oldest rally in the world, since it was first run in 1910 one year before the first Monte Carlo Rally, was for the first time part of the European Championship. It attracted works cars from Steyr-Puch, BMW and Citroën but it was a lone Healey 3000 – the new Mk3 – driven by Paddy Hopkirk that emerged as the winner. The route was based on Velden and there were six special stages with a complex handicap system whose calculations meant that the winner actually had more points than the rest of the finishers. Second place went to the amazing Steyr-Puch 650 TR of Johannes Ortner that not only managed to stay with the Healey but also outdistanced both the Italian champion, Arnaldo Cavallari, in his Alfa Romeo Guilia TI, and Wilfried Gass in a Porsche 356. There were two odd features of this event that are worth noting. The first was that the regulations permitted a car to be driven without a co-driver provided that he was replaced by a 60-kilogram weight. The second was a kind of 'reliability test' whereby at each morning's start, the cars had to be pushed to a line and the driver was then given 30 seconds to start it up and drive to another line 30 metres away. The reluctant starting of the big Healey cost Hopkirk ten penalty marks for each of the three days.

Tom Trana's winning ways continued in Sweden where he won the Midnight Sun in his now familiar Group 2 PV544. This had the usual format of gravel stages with set times representing high average speeds and with comparatively gentle road sections between them. But this was to be the last Midnight Sun since the KAK (Swedish Automobile Club) let it be known that from 1965, their principal event was going to become a winter rally known as the Swedish Rally. The problem really was that modern rally cars performing on gravel roads owned by local municipalities did quite a bit of damage and this would be dramatically reduced in the winter when the normal road surface was covered by a few inches of ice and snow.

The most interesting aspect of the results from Sweden is the car/driver combinations that did well behind the flying Mr Trana. For instance, in the smallest capacity Group 1 class, Ove Andersson finished ahead of Erik Carlsson and was the highest placed Saab ahead of the Group 2 Saabs of Rauno Aaltonen, Simo Lampinen and Olle Bromark. Second overall was Harry Källström in a Cooper S narrowly ahead of Bengt Söderström, now signed by Ford, in a Cortina GT. The remarkable Bo Ljungfeldt was seventh in one of the ex-Monte Falcons still bearing its USA number plates. Also worthy of note were the first green shoots of the Opel rally connection that were to become so important in later years. Opel Kadetts under the direction of Ragnar Ekelund from GM Sweden won their Group 1 and Group 2 classes with Ove Eriksson and Håkan Lindberg respectively.

The Rallye des Alpes had heavy rain on the first and last days of its five-day jaunt from Marseille to Monaco via Cannes and Chamonix. Accidents and mechanical faults were the main cause behind the reduction of its seventy-six starters to just twenty-five finishers of whom seven went home the proud owners of Coupes. Particularly unfortunate was the early exit after two accidents – the second proved definitive – of René Trautmann in his Lancia Flavia Zagato since he had been on course for a Coupe d'Or. An early bath too for Eugen Böhringer whose Mercedes 230SL collided with a non-competing car, as did the Triumph Spitfire of Jean-Jacques Thuner. Pat Moss's problem was a blown head gasket on her Saab while Timo Mäkinen's Cooper S broke its engine mountings. Even Paddy Hopkirk lost his chance of a Coupe when he had to have a rear hub changed.

If things had carried on like that, there might have been no one left by the finish. However, the second part of the rally from Cannes to Chamonix proved more gentle though not before Hans-Joachim Walter's ex-Le Mans Porsche 904 retired with a broken rear axle. Another 904 driven by Günter Klass had been threatening the GT supremacy of Jean Rolland's Alfa Romeo GTZ but a minor accident removed most of the Porsche's front bodywork and lights. In the Touring category, it was Ford that led the way with David Seigle-Morris and Vic Elford in Cortina GTs ahead of the truly amazing Erik Carlsson. Henri Greder had entered in one of the 1963 Falcons but the small, uneven roads broke his rear springs and, with no threat from the BMC brigade, it was Citroën who followed the leaders. Aaltonen's Cooper S was entered as a GT car but was hard pushed to deal with the Porsche 904 of Jacques Rey who he failed to

Swedish Rally to the Midnight Sun 1964, Bengt Söderström/Bo Olsson, Ford Cortina GT Mk I.

Austrian Alpine Rally 1964, Paddy Hopkirk/Henry Liddon, Austin Healey 3000 Mk III. They won the rally outright.

Swedish Rally to the Midnight Sun 1964, Tom Trana/Gunnar Thermaenius, Volvo PV544. They won the rally outright.

beat on scratch but took third place on index of performance. And Aaltonen did pick up a Coupe and thus put himself in line for a Coupe d'Or the following year. The man who had lost his golden chance the previous year, Don Morley, took his Healey 3000 to second place in the GT category plus a Coupe and thus collected a Coupe d'Argent.

Another bright spot for BMC was that Pauline Mayman won the Ladies prize in a Cooper S while for Rover there was the sight of one of its 2000s crewed by Peter and Ann Riley finishing fifth overall on the car's rally debut. Two more of the Rover 2000s retired with broken oil connections to the engine, these driven by Anne Hall and Roger Clark. The cruellest blow fell on one of the Fords and was saved right to the end. In fact it came on the last test at the Col de Braus, literally within sight of Monaco. The Cortina GT leading the Touring category, that of David Seigle-Morris, broke its head gasket and handed the win to his team-mate, Vic Elford. But it was still an outright victory for Ford to add to the Cortina's win on the East African Safari that year and they were delighted with it despite missing out on a 1-2 finish.

The Polish Rally saw an outright win for the smallest-engined car currently competing, the 650 cc Steyr-Puch – an Austrian manufactured Fiat 500 – when Sobieslaw Zasada took advantage of a favourable handicap plus his local knowledge – he lived in Zakopane – and came home ahead of Erik Carlsson. Pat Moss was third in her Saab 96 but Gunnar Andersson's Volvo crashed and retired. The full story is that Andersson had taken a Polish co-driver to bring his local knowledge to bear on some of the tricky navigation. At one point, the co-driver asked if he could drive and, when he had the wheel, promptly went off the road. Andersson was badly hurt in the accident and for some time, it was not certain that he would regain the use of his arms. After a long period of convalescence, he was able to do so but since he was team manager as well as driver, this did not have a positive effect on the Volvo competition programme.

After Poland, Saab went one better on the 1000 Lakes where Simo Lampinen won for the second year in a row with Tom Trana chasing him all the way to the finish. The gap between them at the finish was two and quarter minutes while the man in third place, Rauno Aaltonen, also in a Saab, closed to within twenty seconds of Trana. There were indications here too of how the future might be with Timo Mäkinen coming fourth in a 1275 Cooper S and Bengt Söderström taking fifth in a Cortina GT.

There is no doubt in anyone's mind that the 1964 Liège–Sofia–Liège was the best that had ever been run, even surpassing the almost legendary 1961 event when only eight cars finished. This year there were twenty-one finishers but the principal reason for that was that Maurice Garot, that hardest of hard-man organisers, weakened during the rally and at Sofia extended the lateness period at subsequent controls by two hours. The cause was the earlier section from Novi on the Adriatic coast to Zagreb where a detour thanks to a blocked road added almost sixty kilometres to the route with no extra time. For Rauno Aaltonen in his Healey 3000 this was usually a 'co-driver section' and thus Tony Ambrose was driving when they set out. Ambrose then had the deviation handed in through the window, realised the problem, decided that it had just become a 'driver's section' and woke up the Finn.

Before that section, Aaltonen had been leading from Böhringer – back with a 230SL – with Henry Taylor's Ford Cortina and the two Saabs of Pat Moss and Erik Carlsson not far behind. Only four cars made it to Zagreb on schedule and they were the Mercedes 220SE that Ewy Rosqvist was sharing with Hans Schiek, Lucien Bianchi's

Ford GB's newly opened competitions department at Boreham during 1964. To the right, the author, John Davenport (with beard!) is talking with rally manager, Alan Platt. In the foreground on the right is one of the Ford mechanics, Derek Smith.

Citroën, Vic Elford's Cortina and Erik Carlsson's Saab. Aaltonen lost time to Zagreb but still led now from Carlsson, Taylor and Bianchi with Böhringer fifth.

Coming away from the turning point at Sofia to Montenegro, the trio of Aaltonen, Carlsson and Böhringer began to pull away from the rest. It was helped by Paddy Hopkirk losing all the gears in his Healey 3000, Henry Taylor smashing a wall with his Cortina GT and Vic Elford matching it by putting his through a parapet onto a railway line. Unlike some previous marathons, this one was blessed with hot and dry conditions and, on their third day without sleeping in a bed, many of the crews might well have been hoping for a shower of rain to wash away some of the dust. The last night in the Dolomites did not change anything and Aaltonen was able to arrive at the foot of the Stelvio ready for the run back to Liège confident that he had beaten the Vivione gremlins. Indeed, this time it was the Passo di Gavia that caught out Rolf Kreder and Alfred Kling in their Mercedes 220SEb and though the accident was more severe than Aaltonen's in 1963, they were both unhurt.

In finishing second overall on scratch so soon after winning a Coupe on the Rallye des Alpes, both in a car with just an 850 cc engine, Erik Carlsson had achieved something far more difficult than all his wins on the Monte Carlo, the Swedish, and the RAC rallies. At the finish he was just two minutes ahead of Böhringer in his 230 SL that was probably giving at least double the horsepower of the Saab while of course weighing more. But it says a great deal for Carlsson's ability to make up time downhill. While the story of this amazing event has necessarily to focus on its leaders, one story is quite remarkable and that is the Cooper S that finished the Liège. After many others had tried and failed, John Wadsworth and Mike Wood brought their Mini through to finish 20th, last but one – but first among Minis.

And it was Carlsson again who got a podium finish on the Geneva Rally coming home third overall in an event teeming with hill climbs and mountains. He was behind the winner of the Touring category, Henri Greder with a 1964 Falcon and the GT winner, Terry Hunter in a Triumph Spitfire co-driven by Patrick Lier, son of Hans-Joachim Walter's co-driver, Werner Lier. The Walter/Lier combination had forsaken Porsche and drove a factory BMW 1800 TI into fourth place just ahead of Jean-Jacques Thuner in another Spitfire. Pat Moss was seventh overall just behind Tom Trana's Volvo and just ahead of a certain Gérard Larrousse in a Renault R8. The rally was notable also for the rally debut of three Sunbeam Tigers in a Rootes team run by the ex-BMC team manager, Marcus Chambers. After some alternator belt problems, all three finished outside the top ten but dominated their class that was won by the Tiger driven by Tiny Lewis.

Liège-Sofia-Liège 1964. At the proper start in the town of Spa, thirty-four kilometres from Liège, the cars were lined up in threes and released one after another. Here the Belgian Mercedes of Cosins/Roland is next to the Humber Sceptre of Adrian Boyd/Beatty Crawford with the Cortina GT of Henry Taylor/Brian Melia just moving away.

▲ Liège-Sofia-Liège 1964. The three works Austin Healey 3000s and their crews before the start: from L to R, Timo Mäkinen, Don Barrow, Rauno Aaltonen, Henry Liddon, Tony Ambrose and Paddy Hopkirk. Aaltonen and Ambrose were the only ones to finish and that was in first place.

◀ Liège-Sofia-Liège 1964, Erik Carlsson/Gunnar Palm, Saab 96. With only a 850 cc engine, the Swedish pair were second overall for the second year running in this most difficult rally.

And so it came to the final event of the year, the RAC Rally. This one started in central London just off the Kings Road at the Duke of York's Barracks and went first to the West Country before heading up through Wales and the Lake District to Scotland and the only night halt at Perth. That was three days and two nights of driving and what with black ice in Wales and fog before the Lake District and then more ice and even snow in Scotland, it made for a very tough event.

From the start, the leader was Timo Mäkinen in a Healey 3000 hotly pursued by Trana's Volvo PV544 and a trio of Cooper Ss driven by Hopkirk, Källström and Aaltonen. Erik Carlsson was a bit further back, a victim of the organiser's new tactic of not issuing Tulip-type road books for the stages but relying entirely on arrows, some of which had been obscured. Saab lost Simo Lampinen with a massive roll on an icy piece of Epynt tarmac and many other cars including the Healey 3000 of the Morley twins spent time off the road in Wales. There was dense fog for the test at Oulton Park that got worse and affected those cars with high starting numbers. Fortunately the rally had seeded its entry so that all the serious competitors were close together at the front, but it was hard luck on some of the more enterprising private owners.

Before the Lake District, Aaltonen held a narrow lead of several seconds over Trana with Källström half a minute further back but by Carlisle, Trana had surged into the lead by almost a minute. Once into Scotland, Aaltonen had a double puncture and fell back so that when the cars arrived into a freezing Perth, he lay fifth ahead of Pat Moss in her Saab and Mäkinen in his Healey. The Ford Cortinas had not been having a happy time with both Vic Elford and Henry Taylor visiting the scenery while Carl-Magnus Skogh retired his Volvo PV544 after a fairly major accident in the slippery conditions. After Perth, BMC lost both Aaltonen and Hopkirk with a gearbox failure and an accident respectively and Saab lost Åke Andersson also with a crash. One man revelling in the conditions in a car that should not have suited them was Mäkinen who pulled up to lie third with the big Healey.

As the rally returned to England and went into Kielder Forest, a fantastic battle commenced between Trana and Källström with the Mini driver gaining almost a full minute on the Redesdale stage and taking the lead. It was not to last long, however, since the Cooper's gearbox broke just a few stages later to leave Trana unchallenged for the lead. Rather sadly, the last part of the rally was something of a disappointment, as some stages planned in East Anglia had to be cancelled. The results service too was below standard, partly due to adverse weather conditions, and the results peppered with corrections took some time to appear. Mäkinen had retained his second place and it was a brace of Cortina GTs, Elford and Söderström, who had fought their way back into the top five to finish either side of Pat Moss. Erik Carlsson did finish and won his class but it was not enough to stop Tom Trana taking the European title for 1964.

If this had been a good year for rallies, then 1965 was to eclipse it in many ways. The only sadness was that the Royal Motor Union of Liège had decided to take their 'Marathon de la Route' off the open roads and confine it to three and half days of driving round the Nürburgring. It was sad but inevitable. There had been too many accidents with non-competing vehicles in both Bulgaria and Yugoslavia and the authorities there, though welcoming foreign visitors, were getting a bit chary about some of the average speeds that were being required on the rallies.

RAC Rally 1964, Rosemary Smith/Margaret McKenzie, Hillman Imp.

RAC Rally 1964, Roy Fidler/Don Grimshaw, Triumph 2000. They finished sixth overall, one place ahead of Erik Carlsson's Saab, in this Group 3 Triumph.

Champions 1964

Tom Trana (on R) and Gunnar Thermaenius pose with their trophies after winning the 1964 Acropolis Rally.

Pat Moss-Carlsson (on L) and Liz Nyström.

1965

The new season started with one of the great rallies of all time – the 1965 Monte Carlo Rally. And the reason was simply the weather since, on the night the rally was to pass, the region between Geneva and Gap was hit by the most massive blizzard that turned the event into an epic. It was an epic with two stars: Timo Mäkinen and his Cooper S and Eugen Böhringer and his Porsche 904; front engine, front wheel drive against rear engine, rear wheel drive. Porsche had decided to enter two 904s for Eugen Böhringer and Pauli Toivonen and, with some reluctance, team manager Huschke von Hanstein, had released a new 911 to be driven by Herbert Linge and Peter Falk from the engineering department. Had the Monte Carlo been dry or with just a modicum of snow and ice, then the 904s were expected to overcome their handicap and 'do a Ford Falcon' on the BMC Mini Coopers. As it was, the British team hedged it bets with Mäkinen entered in the GT category with a lightened car and the others in Group 2.

As the rally started from its eight cities, the weather gave no warning as to what was in store. The Athens starters saw a little ice in Yugoslavia but there was no question of snow blocking the road. Among them was Rauno Aaltonen but he was not to reach the converging point in Chambéry thanks to a broken distributor. Perhaps that was his good luck for, as the routes drew together in the Jura mountains to the northwest of Geneva, it started to snow. And now the lottery started since the Warsaw, Stockholm, Minsk and London starters were the first arrivals and got through to Chambéry with the minimum of trouble. The Frankfurt, Paris, Lisbon and Monte Carlo starters had considerably more snow and more of a struggle and a large number of them never made it in time to start the main route down to Monaco with its special stages. The two 904s had differing fortunes since Böhringer got through with a minimal loss of time while Toivonen was beached on a snow drift and was out of time at Chambéry. So it was a case of early number = good, late number = bad. Just thirty-five crews eventually reached Monaco of which ten were from Stockholm, six from Minsk, eight from London, four from Frankfurt, three from Paris, two from Lisbon, two from Monte Carlo and none from Athens.

Conditions on the first three stages also became worse for those with late numbers. Fastest time over the three cols of the Chartreuse was set by Carlsson (car no. 40), next fastest was Mäkinen (car no. 52) a minute and half slower while Böhringer (car no. 150) was thirteen minutes slower than the Saab. For all the crews, it was a nightmare of fighting their way through the soft, falling snow that froze on lights and windscreens and stopped windscreen wipers in their tracks. If one should wonder how the Mäkinen Mini with its ten inch wheels could compete with cars like the Saab and Porsche on much larger diameter fifteen inch wheels, then you should know that Mäkinen had brought some Finnish ice-racing tyres called Rengas-Ala that were fitted with steel blades and used them for the Chartreuse. Carlsson's other stage times were still good but he lost over an hour on the road when his Saab's engine iced up with the build-up of soft snow under the bonnet.

Once beyond Gap, the blizzard had blown itself out but by the time the rally reached Monaco, Mäkinen had set three fastest times and established a lead over the Citroëns of Lucien Bianchi and Bob Neyret who had both started from Minsk. His Cooper S was also the only car without road penalties and was thus comfortably ahead of Böhringer who had lost four minutes on the road and had been docked a further 20 seconds at scrutineering for an exhaust that was too noisy. Behind Böhringer there were several other performances of note with Peter Harper a very creditable fifth in a Sunbeam Tiger, Pat Moss there as usual in sixth and Roger Clark an

Monte Carlo Rally 1965, Eugen Böhringer/Rolf Wütherich, Porsche 904 GTS. This was a truly great drive in blizzard conditions with a low-slung GT car to finish second to Mäkinen's winning Mini Cooper S.

amazing seventh in a Group 1 Rover 2000. Rounding out the top ten at this stage were Linge in the Porsche 911, Guy Verrier in a Citroën DS19 and Simo Lampinen at the wheel of a Triumph Spitfire.

Now came the mountain circuit. This was not the regularity affair of the old Monte Carlos but a double loop round six special stages including the Col de Turini with little time to hang around being serviced. BMC lost Hopkirk when a welded-up wishbone broke while both the Triumph Spitfires of Lampinen and Jean-Jacques Thuner retired with mechanical problems. Citroën lost Bianchi when he ran out of petrol that then meant he did not have enough service time to change to new tyres and, driving on the old ones, went off the road into a tree. The Mäkinen versus Böhringer battle raged through the night and at one point it looked as if the Porsche might come out on top when the Mini stopped with a broken spring in its distributor. But, having had the same problem on his reconnaissance, Mäkinen was carrying a spare and continued. With this plus the time taken to fit new studded tyres before each stage, he lost four minutes on the road by the time the cars were back in Monaco putting him on equal time loss to Böhringer. However, five fastest times were enough to ensure that he was comfortably ahead of the Porsche to win both the rally and the GT category.

Pat Moss was third ahead of Peter Harper's Sunbeam Tiger while the Porsche 911 was fifth overall on its international debut. Before they left Stuttgart, Von Hanstein had exhorted them 'Please do not scratch this car as it must be immaculate in Monaco' and sure enough Linge and Falk brought it through in perfect condition. Bob Neyret had been outclassed on speed during the last night – only two drivers, Böhringer and Carlsson were without road penalty on the last night – and he had lost a further nineteen minutes but still finished seventh ahead of the works Cortina GTs of Bengt Söderström and Henry Taylor. Rounding out the top ten was the works-supported BMW 1800 TI of Hans-Joachim Walter who had made a smart move by starting in Stockholm and thus drawing number 58.

This Monte Carlo Rally had been one of the most exciting and thrilling in the event's history and, for once, there was not a single protest. But what of the European Rally Championship? There were again thirteen rounds with a new event in Spain and now three events venturing behind the 'Iron Curtain', an event called the Vltava Rally in Czechoslovakia, the Polish Rally and the Munich–Vienna–Budapest that gave a chance to try Hungarian roads. The problem was that factory teams were not prepared to send cars to all of the thirteen events but chose to do the ones that their marketing departments could use for meaningful advertising. Events like the Monte Carlo, Tulip, Acropolis, Alpes and RAC were all reasonably well-known and meaningful to the car-buying public. The newcomers tended to get ignored unless, as happened, towards the end of the year there was a chance of scrambling round to score some championship points and net the title.

On the new Spanish round for example, there was a field of entirely Spanish and Portuguese entrants with a GT car taking the honours since a Porsche 904 GTS crewed by Joan Fernández and Arturo Saenz won from Estanislao Reverter and José Marquez in an Abarth 1000 Bialbero.

The Rallye dei Fiori was mainly an Italian affair with only minimal entries from outside. Volvo came with two cars for Tom Trana and Sylvia Österberg but Trana retired with a broken drive shaft while

◀ Monte Carlo Rally 1965, Peter Harper/Ian Hall, Sunbeam Tiger 4.2. Again, this was an excellent performance in a GT car to finish fourth overall in such poor weather conditions.

▶ Monte Carlo Rally 1965. Timo Mäkinen was someone who liked to check everything himself!

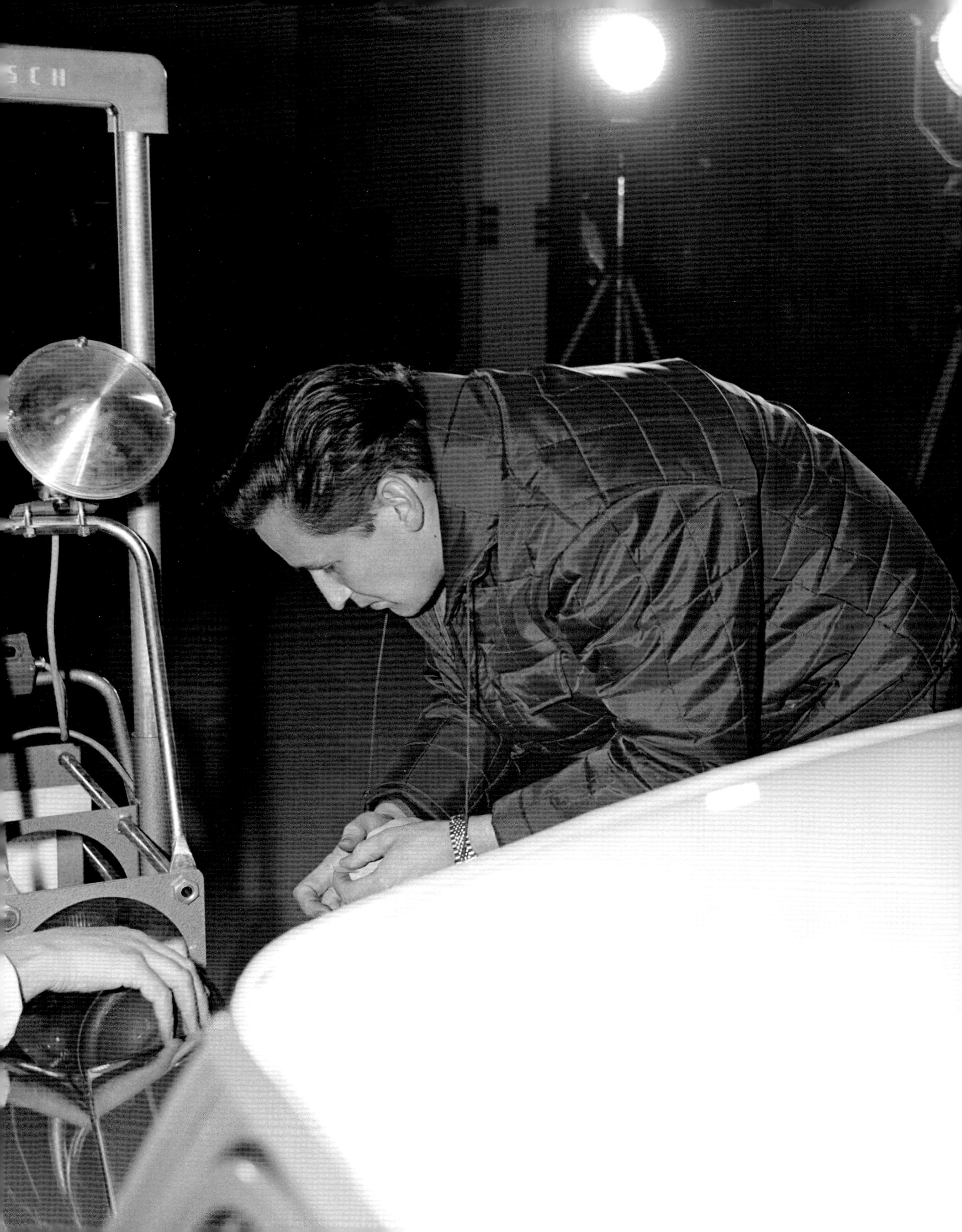
SCH

Swedish Rally 1965. This was the year that Sweden's championship event went from being a summer rally to a winter one. The winner was still Trana's Volvo, but on the ice and snow, the big Opel Rekord Coupés started to make their presence felt.

Österberg finished sixth and won the Ladies prize co-driven by Siv Sabel. There were three Renault R8 Gordinis of which by far the quickest was that driven by Berndt Jansson. Indeed he would have won the rally outright had not his co-driver Gunnar Liljedahl, repeating the mistake of Pauli Toivonen the previous year, allowed him to cross the finish line of the first stage ten seconds 'early' thus provoking a 75 mark penalty. Nevertheless, he finished third behind the Lancias of Leo Cella and Gigi Taramazzo. Cella's victory was significant since this was the first appearance of a Fulvia in a major international though this was the 'sit-up-and-beg' saloon version, the 2C, and not the Coupé that was to become famous in the succeeding years. Taramazzo was driving a Flavia Coupé powered by a flat-four engine as was Giorgio Pianta in fourth place while René Trautmann brought a second Fulvia 2C home in twelfth place. The other R8 Gordinis were driven by Jean-Pierre Nicolas who was seventh and the interesting combination of Jean-François Piot and Henri Pescarolo who came home forty-third overall.

The Midnight Sun was no more and the KAK's annual event had metamorphosed into a full winter rally. Held in March, it ensured plenty of snow by going more than halfway up Sweden to Lycksele in Swedish Lapland though this was nowhere near as far as it had gone the previous summer to Kiruna that was well inside the Arctic Circle. The early leader was Timo Mäkinen whose Cooper S beat Tom Trana by twenty-four seconds on the first stage but it was not long before the Mini gearbox broke and he was out. After that it was Trana the whole way pursued by the new Opel Rekord Coupés of Ove Eriksson and Bertil Söderström. Indeed so fleet were these three that, even if the rally penalties had been calculated on scratch times, they would have kept their places in the classification.

Elsewhere it was a field day for Saabs since they completely dominated their Group 2 class with Åke Andersson and Ove Andersson taking the first two places while in Group 3, Hans Lund came home ahead of Pat Moss and Erik Carlsson. BMC did not win their class as Berndt Jansson's Renault R8 Gordini was too quick for Lennart Eliasson's BMC Sweden Cooper S but Hans Lannsjö driving a 997 cc Cooper did manage to beat the Opel Kadetts in the smaller Group 2 class. And newcomers to the international scene were the DAF team with their Daffodil 33s powered by a 746 cc flat twin engine and using a belt drive CV transmission. Rob Slotemaker and Claude Laurent finished fifth and sixth in their class.

During 1965, Rosemary Smith got used to picking up awards – and not always for the Coupe des Dames.

The Tulip Rally of 1965 should have been a really great event since the weather in the Jura Mountains was almost as bad as it had been for the Monte Carlo Rally but its class performance system produced a somewhat skewed result. That is not to detract from the achievements of Rosemary Smith in a Group 3 Hillman Imp and Hans Lund in a Group 2 Saab 96 who won the GT and Touring categories respectively since everyone knew the rules before the start. But as with the Monte Carlo, your start number was important. When the snowy conditions started, hills climbs were cancelled and the rally arrived at Champagnole from where there was to be a southern loop towards the Haute-Savoie. When about half the competitors had set out on this loop and had passed through Saint-Claude, a traffic accident between two cars that were nothing to do with the rally shut the road. Consequently, the second half of the entry had to either turn back to Champagnole and wait for the others, or try to go round by another route and amass sufficient penalties to get them excluded. With the Group 3 cars running first on the road, there was bound to be a benefit to the Imps since behind them were all the Touring cars. The Cortina GTs had a particularly bad time and Bo Ljungfeldt and Bengt Söderström both retired though Gilbert Staepelaere got through but with road penalties.

Swedish Rally 1965, Berndt Jansson/Erik Pettersson, Renault R8 Gordini.

Also two of the most competitive GT cars retired when both the Sunbeam Tigers of Peter Harper and Peter Riley went out. Harper hit a van while Riley was unable to get his Tiger back up the snowy Col de la Faucille to Champagnole. Even the Morley twins only just made it by pushing their Healey 3000 up the snow-covered hill. Rob Slotemaker went one further by taking the carpets out his works Triumph 2000 and using those to get traction, but it was to no avail as he retired later with a blown head gasket. Timo Mäkinen used studded tyres thoughtfully provided by BMC but when the final reckoning came, back in Noordwijk, the Imps of Rosemary Smith/Val Domleo and Tiny Lewis/David Pollard were ahead of everyone. In the much-depleted Touring category, victory went to Hans Lund in his private Saab 96 ahead of Olle Dahl's similar car with both of them ahead of Mäkinen. The best that Staepelaere could manage for Ford was sixth and a class win while the Morleys were fifth in GT only just ahead of Claude Laurent in a DAF 33.

There was no snow on the Acropolis Rally and in complete contrast, this was a rally clearly won on the stages. Its popularity can be measured by the fact that there were no less than ten works teams at the start. As usual, the route went north from Athens towards Thessalonica and then came south again to cross by ferry to the Peloponnese for a last night of action. The early leader was Eugen Böhringer in a works Mercedes 300SE closely pursued by his team-mate, Dieter Glemser this time in a 230SL. But both were eventually overtaken by Timo Mäkinen in a Cooper S who had an advantage in terms of the set times on the stages. Behind them, Carl-Magnus Skogh and Tom Trana in Volvo 122Ss and Giorgio Pianta and René Trautmann in Lancia Flavias were in their own private battle.

Before reaching Thessalonica, Böhringer retired with a mechanical problem, as did Tom Trana while Hans-Joachim Walter broke a radius arm on his works BMW 1800 TI and was also forced to stop. Now it was Glemser who set all the fastest times but he had to keep a constant watch for the Volvos, Lancias and the two Saabs of Erik Carlsson and Åke Andersson who were, like Mäkinen, benefiting from having smaller engines and thus longer set times. Perhaps it was this that caused him to take a wrong road in the middle of the southern loop and he lost nineteen minutes on the road. The leading Cooper S was being serviced using a method that was devised during the 1964 Liège to work on the Wadsworth Mini and involved tipping the car on its side. This was actually its nemesis as, with just one stage and the two final tests remaining, the Mini caught fire from leaking petrol while on its side and the damage was such that it stopped shortly afterwards.

From all this destruction, the victor emerged as Carl-Magnus Skogh in a Volvo accompanied by Lennart Berggren. Erik Carlsson by virtue of an intelligent drive and a reliable car was second in a Saab 96 with Trautmann, showing that the Lancias had strength as well as speed, was fourth. And the incredible little Steyr-Puch of Zasada snatched seventh place from Pianta's Lancia. None of the three Rover 2000s entered came to the finish since Roger Clark and Logan Morrison both had accidents while Andrew Cowan broke the de Dion tube of his rear axle. The slow-but-sure Wartburg team were deprived of the Manufacturers prize when one of their 311s retired with a broken engine just 100 km from the finish.

As the halfway point of the year approached, no one could imagine that Rauno Aaltonen was a contender for the championship since he had virtually no points on the board and had not won a major rally since the Liège 1964. This was about to change and he gave notice of his intention by winning the Geneva Rally from two of the men who were to be his main rivals, Trautmann in a Lancia Flavia and Zasada in a Steyr-Puch. This was a tougher event than previous Geneva rallies and required a much more 'press on' approach to the road sections, many of which had been set on small roads and with more time controls. The winners of the GT category were the regal pairing of Jean Rolland/Gabriel Augias in their Alfa Romeo GTZ prepared by Virgilio Conrero and behind them was the local hero, Jean-Jacques Thuner in a works Triumph Spitfire and then the Morley twins in a works Healey 3000.

At the beginning of July in the UK, a new international rally hit the scene. This was the Gulf London organised by David Seigle-Morris and using many of the same forest stages as the RAC Rally. It attracted a good entry with works cars there from Volvo, Saab, Triumph, BMC and Ford. It was won by Roger Clark in his works-supported Cortina GT fresh from its win on the Scottish Rally. But it had a wider significance in that Tom Trana's Volvo 122S hit a non-competing car on the first night and this resulted in the death of his co-driver, Gunnar Thermaenius.

Acropolis Rally 1965, Sobieslaw Zasada/Longin Bielak, Steyr-Puch 650 TR.

Geneva Rally 1965, Rauno Aaltonen/Tony Ambrose, Mini Cooper S 1275. The victorious Mini rounds an uphill hairpin. The points scored here got Aaltonen started on his late chase for the European title.

Two weeks later and Aaltonen had won the Rally Vltava in Czechoslovakia ahead of the Lancia Flavias of Trautmann and Giorgio Pianta. This new event to the European Rally Championship insisted that there should be no servicing and this certainly took its toll on the entry since only twelve cars finished from one hundred and thirty starters. Both Czechoslovakian car manufacturers were represented with Škoda and Tatra running teams and, though Škoda had cars in fourth and fifth places at the finish, it was Tatra that took the team prize. With two wins under his belt, Aaltonen was now looking in much better shape and he could approach the next big rally, the Rallye des Alpes, with some confidence since he had won Coupes there for the past two years in Mini Coopers and was now in the hunt for a Coupe d'Or.

However, in the Alps luck ran out simultaneously for BMC, Ford and Rootes on a rally that had been made slightly tougher by the simple expedient of pruning the odd minute off the high average sélectif sections. But the first major loss was the Alfa Romeo GTZ of Jean Rolland who, like Aaltonen, was chasing a Coupe d'Or. During the first night in torrential rain, the Alfa's windscreen wipers packed up and first lost him a chance of a Coupe and then visibility was so bad that he had to retire. Aaltonen's nemesis came in the middle of the second leg when a helpful Gendarme directed them away from a blocked road in a village just a few kilometres before a time control. Sadly the subsequent junctions appeared to tie in with the road book and it was not until he and Tony Ambrose had travelled some ten kilometres down the wrong road that they realised the mistake. They were four minutes late at the next control and this was sufficient to drop them to fourteenth overall at the finish and lost them their Coupe d'Or.

Two of the other works Cooper Ss did win Coupes with Timo Mäkinen second in the Touring category and Paddy Hopkirk fourth, the latter picking up a Coupe d'Argent as well. Between them was the Lotus Cortina of Henry Taylor who had been slowed in the opening leg by a lack of second gear. But the major sadness for Ford was that Vic Elford had been leading the category right up to the end of the third leg when his Cortina's contact points in the distributor broke. Team-mate David Seigle-Morris towed him to the top of the Col St Martin so that he could freewheel down to the control but he was six minutes late there and then it took another forty minutes to get a Ford service car to him. With forty-six minutes of road penalties, he was eventually classified twenty-first. When he had run into trouble, he had been more than two and a half minutes ahead of René Trautmann in a Lancia Flavia Zagato and it was the Lancia that now inherited the win.

In the GT category, Robert Buchet led at the end of the first leg in his Porsche 904, the similar car of Pauli Toivonen having been delayed by a spin on the first hill climb. But Toivonen recovered to set a string of fastest times and had it not been for time lost on sélectifs he would have won outright instead of finishing seventh. Buchet retired during the second night and it was the Alfa GTZ of Bernard Consten who emerged as the GT winner by virtue of losing just two minutes on sélectifs as against three for the Morleys in their Healey 3000. There was also a Prototype category where Porsche had entered Böhringer in a 904/6 and naturally he led until on the third leg, the 904/6 started losing gears and he had to retire. The winners – indeed the only finishers – in the prototype category were thus the Triumph Spitfires of Lampinen and Thuner.

Rallye des Alpes 1965, Simo Lampinen/Jyrki Ahava, Triumph Spitfire. Entered as a prototype against Böhringer in a 6-cyl Porsche 904, the Triumph survived to win the category.

Of the other teams, the Rover 2000s went well and Roger Clark missed winning a Coupe by just one minute, but there was disappointment for Rootes when Peter Harper's Tiger was disqualified at post-event scrutineering. He had clearly won the GT category and lost merely a minute on the road but when his engine was stripped, it was discovered that the exhaust valves were smaller in diameter than the ones detailed on the homologation form. It was a clerical error, of course, but the scrutineers were adamant that it would have 'improved the efficiency' of the V8 engine and Harper was out.

There were no Coupes for the GT or Prototype finishers but there were eight in the Touring category of which two were won by Renault R8 Gordinis driven by Jean-François Piot and Jean Vinatier, one by Jean-Claude Ogier in a Citroën DS19 and one by a new face from England, a certain Tony Fall driving his own Cooper S. His employer was none other than the 1952 Coupe d'Or winner, Ian Appleyard, so it was an appropriate way to start a rally career.

Better fortune followed Aaltonen to Poland where he won a tough rally that was once again based on Zakopane. Road sections were run at average speeds of up to 82 kph (51 mph) and Aaltonen was the only car to remain without penalty on these. His opposition came from the 'Super Mouse' otherwise known as the Steyr-Puch of Zasada who lost just one minute on the road but was well behind the Cooper S on the hill climbs. Saab, Volvo and Lancia were all there with third place going to Erik Carlsson with Pat Moss fifth in the other works Saab. Trautmann took fourth for Lancia and kept his lead in the European Rally Championship while sixth was Skogh in a Volvo 122S.

It was Cooper Ss also winning on the 1000 Lakes, but this time Mäkinen ahead of Aaltonen supported by a very determined Paddy Hopkirk taking on the Finns – with a Finnish co-driver – to finish sixth and give BMC the team prize. Mäkinen's win was quite definitive since he was almost two and half minutes quicker than his team-mate over the twenty-seven stages totalling some 200 km (125 miles). The winner for the previous two years, Lampinen, took fourth for Saab behind Pauli Toivonen in a very well sorted VW 1500S. And there was a new talent making itself known in the person of Jorma Lusenius whose private Cooper S was holding third place until just before the end of the rally when he dropped back to fifth with a mechanical problem. His reward was to be given a drive in a works car on the RAC Rally. Trautmann started with the Flavia Zagato but dropped out after twenty stages at the same point where the rally lost the Saabs of Mr & Mrs Carlsson.

The situation in the championship now was that Trautmann still led with 61 points but Aaltonen was only two behind him and Mäkinen was on 54 points. Thus the Three Cities Rally – the Munich–Vienna–Budapest – assumed great significance. Only Aaltonen and Trautmann among the leading contenders made the trip and tackled the relatively easy rally with its six special stages totalling some 57 km (35 miles), two in each of the three countries visited. On the tarmac stages, Trautmann had the advantage and led most of the way but on the gravel stages the Mini Cooper S was normally fastest. There was a complicated method of scoring but eventually it did not matter too much as Trautmann's Flavia Zagato holed a piston just before the finish in Budapest and thus was not classified. A similar fate awaited Arnaldo Cavallari and Sandro Munari – another name to note – whose Jolly Club Alfa Romeo Guilia TI went out with electrical trouble.

Thus Aaltonen won again from a Ford Cortina GT driven by the Austrian Herbert Tunner who finished just ahead of Arnulf Pilhatsch in a private BMW 1800 TI. In fact, this BMW finished ahead of

Zasada in his Steyr-Puch and also ahead of two works BMW 1800 TIs driven by Alfred Kling and Peter Ruby, the latter co-driven by Helmut Bein who would later become BMW team manager. One rallymanship ploy by BMC to get round the 'no service' regulation on this event was to enter three Cooper Ss for Tony Fall, Paul Easter and Geoff Halliwell since a competitor was allowed to 'give assistance' to another. It worked all right with the one exception that Halliwell crashed his car on one of the tests before even leaving Germany.

Approaching the final round, the RAC Rally, the situation was that Aaltonen now had seventy-five points to Trautmann's sixty-one so that the French Lancia driver needed to win the rally outright to lift his total to seventy-seven and for the Finn to either not score at all or just take a single point. It was always going to be unlikely that Aaltonen would not score at all, but the RAC Rally was visited with weather conditions that echoed those of the Monte and Tulip rallies at the beginning of the year so that anything was possible. BMC decided that they would put Mäkinen in a Healey 3000 – in fact it is said that he himself chose to drive that car – so that he would not jeopardise Aaltonen's chance by finishing ahead of him in the class as well as in the general classification. To make doubly sure, the Cooper Ss of Hopkirk and Jorma Lusenius were entered as Group 3 cars. As it turned out, putting Mäkinen in the Healey was the catalyst that turned the rally into an unforgettable event with two Finns battling to show who was best and which car was most suitable to win this kind of rally.

1000 Lakes Rally 1965, Rauno Aaltonen/Anssi Järvi, Mini Cooper S 1275.

Rallye des Alpes 1965, René Trautmann/Mlle Claudine Bouchet, Lancia Flavia Zagato. Running in Group 2, this coupé won the Touring category outright and also won one of the eight Coupe des Alpes awarded.

Roger Clark/Jim Porter, Rover 2000

Simo Lampinen/John Davenport, Triumph 2000

Timo Mäkinen/Paul Easter, Austin Healey 3000 Mk III

Paddy Hopkirk/Henry Liddon, Mini Cooper S 1275

Andrew Cowan/Brian Coyle, Hillman Imp

British best

There could be little doubt that in the 1950s and 1960s, the British adored their rallying. And with works teams from Ford GB, BMC, Rover, Triumph, Rootes all sending cars off to compete on European rallies, they had plenty of success to show for it. Though there were not always British drivers behind the wheel, the Scandinavian drivers frequently took British co-drivers who had been brought up on national rallies that placed great emphasis on map reading.

But it was the variety of the cars that impressed most. The Mini Cooper proved conclusively that front wheel drive could win in adverse conditions on a Monte Carlo or RAC Rally as well as on tarmac events. More conventional cars with front-engine and rear-wheel drive like the Austin Healey 3000, the Sunbeam Tiger, the Rover 2000, the Triumph 2000 and the Ford Cortina GT and Lotus were better all-rounders capable of handling rough roads while the little Hillman Imp with its rear engine layout proved, on occasion, to be a giant killer.

RAC Rally 1965, David Seigle-Morris/Tony Nash, Ford Lotus Cortina

The rally started from London airport and went to the West Country stages before running up through Wales, across to Yorkshire and then into Scotland for a night halt at Perth. This meant two full nights of rallying without a break. The Volvo team elected not to start as Tom Trana was facing charges of dangerous driving following the fatal accident on the Gulf London Rally while Trautmann too stayed at home and thus gifted the European Rally Championship to Aaltonen before the start. Nevertheless, there was to be plenty of action and it should be remembered that even in the face of ice and snow, studded tyres were not allowed on the RAC Rally. It was bitterly cold at the start but the first stages were free of ice yet still managed to claim Bo Ljungfeldt's works Lotus Cortina and Ove Andersson's works Saab while Peter Harper broke the radiator in his Sunbeam Tiger. At Bristol, Mäkinen led with the Norwegian Ford driver, Trond Schea, second in a Lotus Cortina followed by Hopkirk, Fall, Carlsson and Aaltonen.

The Welsh stages were universally icy and one bend on Myherin claimed Schea and thus left the field clear for an all-BMC fight. After a test of several laps at Oulton Park, the crews headed off across the Pennines to Yorkshire where falling snow greeted them. It was on an uphill section towards the end of a short stage in Pickering Forest that the first car on the road, Mäkinen's Healey, came across an official's car blocking the road and slithered to a halt with no traction and a flat battery. The other leading contenders queued up behind him and, until spectators had helped them push and shove their way to the top, they were at the mercy of the clock. On a 3.6 mile (5.8 km) stage with a set time of 4 min 23 sec, Mäkinen took 24 min 23 sec and other rally leaders were equally delayed like Aaltonen with 17 min 05 sec, Hopkirk on 18 min 48 sec and Pat Moss-Carlsson 19 min 19 sec. The incredibly determined Carlsson forged around some of the others to record 11 min 02 sec but the fastest cars were those with much later numbers and the fastest time was recorded by Sten Lundin in a VW 1600 on 7 min 17 sec with Jerry Larsson next on 7 min 28 sec in his privately owned Saab. Lampinen, who had been fighting with Mäkinen and Aaltonen, got through in 18 min 51 sec but his works Triumph 2000 blew its head gasket just before Peebles and had to retire. The times from both Cropton (where there was a timing error) and Pickering stages were later removed from the results so that the true position at Peebles was that Mäkinen led from Aaltonen and the about-to-retire Lampinen.

Mäkinen now reeled off a string of fastest times in Kielder to extend his lead and throughout the Scottish stages was never out of the top three stage times. When the rally re-started from Perth on the Wednesday morning, the weather had turned to rain and it seemed as if ice and snow would play no further part in the rally as it headed back south through Ayrshire, the Lake District and into Wales. Unfortunately for Mäkinen, this was not to be the case and, in Coed-y-Brenin Forest on some old ice now freshly lubricated with rain, the Healey once more ran out of grip on an uphill section. While it was there and sorting out how to go up with no spectators handy to help him, along came Aaltonen's Mini. He later recalled that 'I saw Timo on the hill and realised what had happened, so I drove off the road and went up through the bracken where there was more grip.' That was sufficient to win him the rally and put the finishing touch to a year when he had become European Champion and won five rallies outright.

His final gap to Mäkinen at the finish was just over three minutes. The Healey had set twenty-eight fastest times over the fifty-one stages that had been run and certainly, without its delay in North Wales, would finally have won the RAC Rally after three previous second places in the space of just four years. Behind it came the two Saabs of Larsson and Carlsson, the privateer preceding the works car again thanks to the Yorkshire delays, and then a full fifteen minutes further back, the works Triumph 2000 of Roy Fidler. Jorma Lusenius and Lars Ytterbring both finished with their Cooper Ss and beat the Swedish Volkswagens. Although he did not finish, one of the VW drivers, a certain Björn Waldegård, impressed with some fast times. It was an unlucky rally too for Ford who lost the Lotus Cortinas of Vic Elford and Bengt Söderström and thus their best finisher was Brian Melia – normally Henry Taylor's co-driver – who drove his own Cortina GT into eleventh place. From a starting list of 162 cars, just 61 were classified at the finish back in London at the end of what had been a truly tough rally.

This RAC Rally had been a fittingly difficult and glorious end to a season that had been enlivened by excellent driving, good events and some interesting weather. It now remained to see whether the new Appendix J regulations that had been published in the middle of the year would raise 1966 and the following seasons above the high standard already set.

RAC Rally 1965, Rauno Aaltonen/Tony Ambrose, Mini Cooper S 1275. Part of the success of the Minis was due to using 10-inch diameter racing tyres for tarmac stages as seen here on Aaltonen's winning car performing at Oulton Park.

RAC Rally 1965. Rauno Aaltonen (on L) and Tony Ambrose pose with the spoils of victory on the bonnet of their Mini Cooper S. This win also confirmed Aaltonen as European Rally Champion for that year.

RAC Rally 1965, Björn Waldegård/Lars Nyström, VW 1600 Fastback. Waldegård was not yet in a Porsche 911 but, round Oulton Park race circuit, he got valuable experience of swing-axle rear suspensions for the years to come.

Champions **1965**

Rauno Aaltonen collects his RAC Trophy.

Pat Moss-Carlsson examines damage on her Saab inflicted during the Safari.

Chapter **06**

A time of experiment
1966/1967/1968/1969

Chapter 06
A time of experiment

1966

The new Appendix J, created by the Commission Sportive Internationale (CSI) during 1965, was to be in force from the beginning of 1966. This was clear from the 1966 Monte Carlo Rally regulations that had been published a couple of months before the end of 1965. But the problem for team managers and private entrants alike was that the new regulations were rather vague on several points. The complication arose from the fact that the Automobile Club de Monaco (ACM) had decided to favour Group 1 cars to the detriment of the new Groups 2 and 3. Their famous formula had been adjusted so that only a Group 1 car stood any chance of victory. Thus anyone who wanted to win the Monte Carlo Rally would have to homologate one of his cars into Group 1 with its 5,000 cars per annum requirement. The combination of new homologations with trying to understand the new elements of Appendix J and reconciling them with the regulations as published by the ACM meant that the new season started in a fair degree of confusion. Indeed the British team managers submitted a set of forty-two questions to both the CSI and to the ACM to try and make sure that they were preparing their cars within the rules.

This lack of certainty was sufficient to persuade both Saab and Volvo that they were wasting their time even entering the Monte Carlo. But BMC, Rootes, Rover and Ford GB persisted for all of them had cars that they thought could win or at least do well – the 1275 Cooper S, the Hillman Imp, the Rover 2000 and the Lotus Cortina. With additional homologation meetings laid on in December 1965, they all eventually came to the start line in January to take on the Renaults, Citroëns and Lancias. For Porsche and anybody else with a GT car in Group 3, taking part was to do so without any hope of winning as their handicap was even heavier than for Group 2.

It is worth explaining that in addition to introducing new rules and encouraging organisers to favour more standard cars, the CSI had also juggled around with the format of the European Rally Championship. This had become three separate championships for drivers in Group 1, Group 2 and Group 3 with each of the fourteen rallies allotted scoring chances for just two of those championships. For instance, the Monte Carlo was for Groups 1 and 3, the Acropolis for Groups 2 and 3 and the 1000 Lakes for Groups 1 and 2. Cars of other groups could enter those rallies but would not score championship points. For example, Dieter Lambart won Group 1 with an Opel Kadett on the Rallye dei Fiori but, since the event counted for Groups 2 and 3, he scored no points. The result was that interest in the series was divided and some works teams did not go to rallies in which they might otherwise have competed. For a start, the Monte Carlo Rally had fewer entries than on any Monte since 1949.

Monte Carlo Rally 1966, Timo Mäkinen/Paul Easter, Mini Cooper S 1275.

A time of experiment 1966

By most standards, the 1966 Monte Carlo Rally was quite a good one but the underlying theme was much darker and when three works Cooper Ss finished in the first three places with Timo Mäkinen leading home Rauno Aaltonen and Paddy Hopkirk, it was not such a big surprise that the scrutineers wanted to virtually tear them apart to find some fault. Eventually, the only thing on which they could fail the BMC Minis was their lighting system. In the new Group 1, only two supplementary lights were permitted over and above whatever came on the car as standard. To maximise the effect of the new iodine vapour bulbs, for which no double-filament version yet existed, the Minis were fitted with iodine bulbs in their two headlamps and in their two supplementary fog lights. To dip their headlights, all that happened was that the headlights were switched off and the fog lights left on. This, the ACM scrutineers declared, did not conform either to the requirements of French law or to the modifications carried out under the rules of Appendix J.

The fact that British cars travelling for a short period in France did not have to comply with French requirements plus a less-than certain interpretation of Appendix J did not deter the ACM and they threw out not just the three Minis but also Roger Clark's Lotus Cortina and Rosemary Smith's Hillman Imp. The most reluctant winner in Monte Carlo history, Pauli Toivonen, was then obliged to accept his prize after his Citroën DS21 was elevated from fifth position. It also made the two Lancia Flavias of René Trautmann and Ove Andersson second and third with Bob Neyret's Citroën DS21 fourth while Leo Cella in a Group 1 Fulvia Coupé rose to fifth overall. The whole fuss – and it should be noted that the ACM received more than thirty protests on technical matters, other than this one, all of which had to be dealt with before results could be issued – rather detracted from the actual achievements of the Citroën and Lancia teams who had done well in any case. Also forgotten in the controversy was the fact that Günter Klass had won Group 3 and finished sixteenth overall ahead of two other Porsche 911s driven by Jo Schlesser and Hans-Joachim Walter. The Group 2 winner was Joachim Springer in a Ford Taunus 20 MTS who was classified twenty-seventh overall.

It is fair to say that this was a bad start to the year and the fault lay more with poorly worded and tardily issued regulations than with the competitors, though a slightly less partisan approach from the men at the ACM would have helped.

The next event was the Swedish Rally, the second winter version and an absolute cracker of a rally. The conditions were 100% snow and ice with temperatures dropping to -40 °C thus allowing the organisers to make use of roads ploughed out on frozen rivers and lakes as well as the usual forest roads. The severe cold took its toll on transmissions but, in addition, the powdered snow blowing in the wind made it difficult to see exactly where the road was and Carl-Magnus Skogh in a Volvo was an early victim of poor visibility. Simo Lampinen's Saab lost seven minutes after hitting a rock and bending the suspension while even Tom Trana found the early conditions hard going in his Volvo, but both of these were set to recover to finish in the top three.

At halfway, Berndt Jansson led in a Renault R8 Gordini but was subsequently to retire with a broken water pump while Åke Andersson (Saab) swept into a lead that he then held to the finish. His team-mate Erik Carlsson retired with a blown engine but Pat Moss finished in her Saab to take the Ladies prize. The Lotus Cortinas were doing well initially but Roger Clark dropped out with fuel problems thanks to the cold while Bengt Söderström broke his axle so it was left to Vic Elford to win his class and finish second in Group 1.

Monte Carlo Rally 1966. From L to R, Gunnar Palm, John Davenport, Henry Liddon (looking away), Rauno Aaltonen, Bo Ljungfeldt, Lennart Berggren and Erik Carlsson with his father-in-law, Alfred Moss.

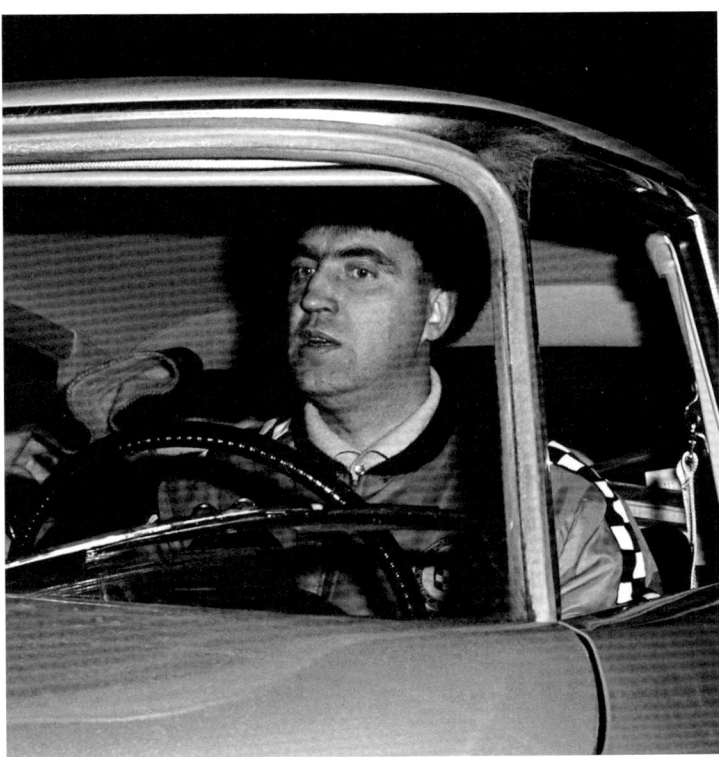

Monte Carlo Rally 1966. When the ACM officials came to tell how and why they had excluded the three Mini Coopers, the two Lotus Cortinas and the Hillman Imp, everyone wanted to hear what was said. It was a scandal erupting. The controversial dipping system that used the foglights of the Mini Cooper was the excuse to deprive Mäkinen of a second victory in Monaco (above L), and Pauli Toivonen inheritated the 1st place (above R).

HOW THEY REALLY FINISHED

1	LIS	T. Makinen/P. Easter	SF	Mini-Cooper S	2		5307.00			7345.00	12,652.00	1 2	1
2	ATH	R. Aaltonen/T. Ambrose	SF	Mini-Cooper S	242		5429.00		20	7349.00	12,778.00	1 2	2
3	WAR	P. Hopkirk/H. Liddon	GB	Mini-Cooper S	230		5492.00		20	7444.00	12,936.00	1 2	3
4	LON	R. Clark/B. Melia	GB	Lotus Ford Cortina	75		5480.00			7477.00	12,957.00	1 2	4
8	OSL	B. Soderstrom/G. Palm	S	Lotus Ford Cortina	205	100	5878.00			7458.00	13,436.00	1 1	5
25	LON	Miss R. Smith/Miss V. Domleo	EIR	Hillman Imp	107	440	7413.00	15	220	8935.00	16,348.00	1 1	2

Rauno Aaltonen/Tony Ambrose, Mini Cooper S 1275

Roger Clark

Bengt Söderström/Gunnar Palm, Ford Lotus Cortina

Timo Mäkinen/Paul Easter, Mini Cooper S 1275

Paddy Hopkirk/Henry Liddon, Mini Cooper S 1275

Monte Carlo 1966

It will forever be a blot on the reputation of the Monte Carlo Rally that a national passion for blue cars was allowed to rule in the scrutineering bay and thus turn the results of an excellent rally upside down. Even the drivers who profited from the exclusion of the British cars – in particular Pauli Toivonen, René Trautmann and Ove Andersson – were upset by what went on and showed their displeasure as much as they were able.

The way the whole thing was handled pointed directly to the fact that the French – not Monegasque – scrutineers were determined to find something with which to disqualify the winning trio of Mini Coopers. After the finish of the rally, they literally took the leading car apart hoping to find some mechanical discrepancy that would enable the Minis to be disqualified without resorting to the matter of the lights. They had already examined the lighting systems on these cars before they went out on the final night in the mountains so, if they were indisputedly illegal on that count, why let them continue in the rally?

Rosemary Smith and Val Domleo won the Coupe des Dames only for their Hillman Imp to be subsequently disqualified.

Perhaps it was too cold to start taking cars apart and protesting, but Sweden passed off without any of the distractions of the Monte Carlo. The same was not true on the Rallye dei Fiori that followed. After an excellent rally with difficult special stages and not an early penalty in sight, the winner appeared to be Elford in a works Group 2 Lotus Cortina but, when the scrutineers examined his car, they found several discrepancies. On the homologation form, it said that a connecting rod should weigh 960 kilograms. That is almost the weight of the complete car and what the form should have said was 0.960 kg. Similarly, none of the gearbox ratios tied up with the number of teeth in the gearbox. As a hapless Henry Taylor, the new team manager for Ford, explained 'There have been some typing errors'. Sadly this was considered irrelevant and the car was thrown out. Tony Fall in a works Group 1 Cooper S was not even allowed to re-start after the concentration run when it was discovered that there was no air filter element in its air cleaner while even Trautmann's works Lancia Flavia was thrown out for having the wrong exhaust manifold.

The man who inherited the win was Cella, repeating his win of 1965 but this time in a Lancia Fulvia Coupé with Ove Andersson bringing a similar car home in third behind the Porsche 911 of Klass. The Fulvia Coupé had gone well in Monte Carlo where Cella had not been as fast as his team-mates in the old two-litre Flavias but had taken fifth place behind them and the Citroëns. With the Lancias and Porsches all in Group 3, the Group 2 winner in the Rallye dei Fiori was Sobieslaw Zasada with his incredible Steyr-Puch after Paddy Hopkirk's Group 2 Cooper S had been delayed with the fan going into the radiator. Both the Renault R8 Gordinis of Jean-François Piot and Jean Vinatier suffered from problems caused by the rough stages and retired but four Group 2 Italian R8s made it through to the finish. The winner of Group 1 was Dieter Lambart in his Opel Kadett and he was also ninth overall.

The Tulip Rally was very much a Ford versus BMC affair with Mäkinen's Cooper S slugging it out with Bengt Söderström's Lotus Cortina in Group 1 and Aaltonen's Cooper S staying ahead of Elford's Lotus Cortina in Group 2. The Fords were under a bit of a handicap on this all-tarmac rally since their tyre supplier, Goodyear, did not have any racing tyres suitable for rallying and their team manager thought that they would be quicker on the wide Ultragrip gravel tyre. With the Minis shod with Dunlop racers, this did not prove to be the case.

For the first time, the Tulip had abandoned its class-improvement handicap system and each of the three groups was decided on scratch. In Group 1, Mäkinen took the win by a narrow margin from Söderström with the Opels of Dries Jetten (Rekord) and Lambart (Kadett Coupé) winning their respective classes. In Group 2, the fast-starting Alfa Romeo GTA of Rob Slotemaker gave Aaltonen and Elford something to worry about until it broke a drive shaft on the Col de la Charbonnière, while the sister car of Arnaldo Cavallari was content to come home third in the category. In the overall classification, it was the Group 2 cars that came out on top but third overall was the winner of Group 3, a very determined Peter Harper in a works Sunbeam Tiger. He had a long battle with the Porsche 911s of Wilfried Gass and Gijs van Lennep but kept them comfortably at bay. Happily, post-rally scrutineering was brief and raised no problems.

Three weeks later in Austria, it was a win for another Mini with Hopkirk's Group 2 Cooper S taking the overall honours ahead of the Group 3 cars. But it was not like that from the start since Klass in the works Porsche 911 dominated on the first day of the two-day event. But then he broke a drive shaft while the other competitive Porsche of Gass went off the road. The main opposition in Group 2 came from a works BMW 1800 TI/SA driven by local hotshot, Arnulf

Swedish Rally 1966, Åke Andersson/Sven-Olaf Svedberg, Saab 96. They won the rally outright.

Swedish Rally 1966, Björn Waldegård/Lars Helmer, VW 1600 S fastback.

Tulip Rally 1965, Peter Harper/Robin Turvey, Sunbeam Tiger 4.7. They won the GT category.

Tulip Rally 1966, Timo Mäkinen/Paul Easter, Mini Cooper S 1275.

Pilhatsch, but he eventually retired with a combination of brake and fuel supply problems.

This rally was run on traditional lines and used Austrian gravel roads plus a few more in Yugoslavia of which some were quite rough. The emphasis was on not losing time on the road sections and only three cars managed to finish with no such penalty and they were Hopkirk, Günther Wallrabenstein whose Porsche won the Group 3 category, and Alfred Burkhart whose Ford Taunus 20 MTS was second in Group 2. Also as usual, there was a handicap system within the categories based on cylinder capacity.

Down in Greece at the Acropolis Rally, Ford and BMC were again the main protagonists but, as in the Monte Carlo and the Rallye dei Fiori, there was an element of controversy in the result. The long-time leader was Mäkinen but his Cooper S broke its suspension on the last night and he lost half an hour on repairs. Aaltonen was not even that lucky, dropping out with a broken timing chain on his Mini a short while later. This left Hopkirk fractionally ahead of the three Lotus Cortinas but unfortunately he had a leaking sump. At a very confused service point in the early hours of the morning, he had the Mini worked on within a control area, something that the marshal noted down but told Hopkirk that he would not be penalised. Until that is, someone within the Ford team pointed out the indiscretion to the organisers after the finish. Hopkirk was duly docked marks for arriving early into a control and for working on his car within its zone. This dropped him to third place behind the Lotus Cortinas of Söderström and Clark. Elford was disqualified for taking a 'short cut' on almost the last special stage when he cut across an uphill hairpin as his car had lost its clutch.

There was tragedy too on this Acropolis Rally since a Volvo service crew were killed when a bulldozer came off a transporter and landed on their car. The remaining members of the Volvo team, Tom Trana and Gunnar Andersson, promptly retired, Carl-Magnus Skogh having already gone out with brake system problems. Joginder Singh upheld Volvo honour by winning his class in his private 122S. For Lancia there was the honour of winning Group 3 with one of their Fulvia Coupés and this car, driven by Ove Andersson, was also classified fourth overall behind the three Group 2 cars.

The Geneva Rally was not of particular interest to the main works teams as it only scored points for Groups 1 and 3. Citroën went with DS21s for Guy Verrier and Lucien Bianchi who finished fourth and fifth overall but both were beaten by team-mate, Jean-Claude Ogier, trying out a Panhard 24CT. The overall winner also came from Group 1 thanks to the handicap and that was the Belgian driver, Gilbert Staepelaere in a Lotus Cortina. Second in Group 1 and also second overall was Tony Fall in a works Cooper S but the Group 2 Cooper S entered for Hopkirk was forced to retire at about half-distance when its gearbox broke. Jean-Jacques Thuner won the Group 3 category in a works Triumph Spitfire ahead of Klass's Porsche 911.

Next it was behind the Iron Curtain for the Czechoslovakian contribution, the Vltava Rally. The Ford effort suffered when Elford went off on a gravel stage but Söderström was able to stick close to the flying Cooper Ss of Mäkinen and Aaltonen. In the 'Battle of the Minis', Aaltonen was getting the better of things but, on the penultimate special stage, he ran out of fuel and dropped back behind Mäkinen. However he was able to regain the lead at the last test. This was a re-run of a stadium race in Prague where bonus points were awarded for bettering the time done at the same test held at the beginning of the rally. Aaltonen was able to take back time from Mäkinen who was thirty-six seconds slower than on his first attempt when a valve rocker broke during his last lap. In fact, Mäkinen's time dropped him back just four points (equal to one second) behind Söderström who had lost a minute on the road during the night. Fourth overall was Zasada in a works Group 1 Cooper S with Pat Moss fifth and picking up the Ladies Prize in her Saab 96.

Austrian Alpine Rally 1966, Paddy Hopkirk/Ron Crellin, Mini Cooper S 1275. After the retirement of Klass's Porsche 911, Hopkirk not only won the Touring Category but also won the rally outright.

Acropolis Rally 1966, Vic Elford/John Davenport, Ford Lotus Cortina. Smiles before the start from L to R: Brian Melia, Vic Elford, Gunnar Palm & Bengt Söderström (both sitting on car) and John Davenport.

Three Cities Rally 1966, Timo Mäkinen/Paul Easter, Mini Cooper S 1275.

Starting in Cortina d'Ampezzo, the Deutschland Rally made the most of the Dolomites before heading to Austria and then into Germany. As it was a Group 2 and 3 event, Ford sent Elford while BMC had Hopkirk and Fall, both in ex-Acropolis Cooper Ss. None of these three were lucky with both Minis retiring while Elford was amongst the leaders until a half-shaft broke on the start line of the Rossfeld hill climb. The eventual winner was Klass in his works Porsche 911 ahead of Cavallari in an Alfa Romeo GTA. Springer took third overall and won his class with a works BMW 1800 TI while Zasada, now back behind the wheel of his formidable little Steyr-Puch, was fifth in Group 2 and won his class.

BMC sent three cars to the Polish Rally and Ford sent one. It was the Cooper Ss that came home first and second but in an unexpected order. Fall had been given one of the new 970cc Cooper Ss and it had naturally been supposed that he would dutifully follow behind the 1,275cc versions of Mäkinen and Aaltonen. However, during the last day, Aaltonen retired with broken transmission while Mäkinen picked up a lateness penalty at the re-start plus a dodgy stage time to put him second overall behind the smaller-engined car. It was a good event for small engines as Zasada was third overall in the Steyr-Puch ahead of Clark's Lotus Cortina that had lost time on one of the difficult sections when he had to wait at a closed level crossing. It was a good result for BMC since Krzysztof Kormonicki also won the Group 1 category with a 1275 Cooper S.

The scene now shifted to Finland for the 1000 Lakes Rally that had been allotted Groups 1 and 2 by the men in the CSI. Of course none of the Scandinavians were much interested in driving a Group 1 car on the event. They wanted to win outright so the organisers combined Groups 1 & 2 and anything from Groups 3 to 5 were lumped into a single class irrespective of capacity. Mäkinen won the rally relatively easily from Trana (Volvo 122S) with Aaltonen third. The best Saab was Simo Lampinen in fifth and one had to scan down to thirty-ninth place to find the winner in Groups 3/5, Antti Aarnio-Wihuri in a tuned-up VW. During the opening stages, the rally leader had been Söderström in a Lotus Cortina but on the night stages he fell back slightly, only to retire with a broken gearbox just before the rest halt the next day.

The allocation of Groups was more sensible for the Rallye des Alpes that was given Groups 2 & 3 but again, just showing that the rally organisers and the CSI were not singing from the same hymn sheet, the Rallye des Alpes also allowed cars of Groups 4 and 5 to enter. The early leader on this five-day epic round the mountains was Mäkinen but his Cooper S was soon to overheat and blow its head gasket while Hopkirk quickly followed him into retirement with a broken differential. Fall retired soon after with broken suspension joint thus leaving the BMC challenge in the hands of Aaltonen with yet another Group 2 Cooper S. His principal opposition came from Jean Rolland in an Alfa Romeo GTA and Elford, the leader of Ford's foursome of Lotus Cortinas. At the end of the first leg, it was Elford leading Rolland with Aaltonen in close attendance. The rate of attrition was extremely high with good weather, clean roads and excellent grip punishing the car's transmissions. Renault lost four of its five Group 5 R8 Gordinis in the first leg but the surviving car of Piot won the Group and finished fifth overall. The three Group 3 Hillman Imps entered for Peter Harper, Rosemary Smith and Andrew Cowan also retired as did the two Saab Sonetts entered for Mr and Mrs Carlsson, he with an accident and she with engine failure. Similar fates were also in store for the three works Lancia Fulvias that started the rally.

There were tears too in the Ford camp when Elford's engine broke a tappet on Mont Ventoux and he retired, thus leaving the field clear for Rolland to come home the overall winner, victor in Group 2 and winner of a Coupe d'Argent for three non-consecutive Coupes. Clark took second place with his Lotus Cortina while Aaltonen was third overall despite losing two minutes – and his Coupe – on the last section into Cannes when he suffered a temporary total electrical failure. There were seven Coupes awarded this year and one of them went to Jean-Pierre Nicolas in a Group 2 R8 Gordini who finished fourth overall.

The Three Cities Rally – Munich, Vienna, Budapest – was a scoring event for Groups 1 and 2 and that was where the main competition lay. BMC sent two 1,275cc Cooper Ss for Mäkinen and Fall but, as expected, it was the big Finn that made the running against the Group 2 Lancia Fulvia Coupé of Cella and, rather surprisingly, the Group 1 Opel Rekord of Lillebror Nasenius. Both Zasada in his

Vltava Rally 1966. Group 2 versus Group 1 – the Ford Lotus Cortina of Bengt Söderström/Gunnar Palm is flagged off at the start of the stadium test in Prague. Alongside him is the Group 1 Mini Cooper S 1275 of Sobieslaw Zasada/Zenon Leszczuk.

Acropolis Rally 1966, Bengt Söderström/Gunnar Palm, Ford Lotus Cortina.

German Rally 1966, Arnaldo Cavallari/Dante Salvay, Alfa Romeo GTA.

familiar Steyr-Puch and Staepelaere in his Geneva-winning Group 1 Lotus Cortina fell victim to a damp corner on the first special stage in Germany but, while Zasada retired on the spot with a broken transmission, Staepelaere was able to continue. On the gravel stages in Austria, Pat Moss damaged a door on her Saab and had to swap it for one from a service car. In Hungary, the roads were rougher and the average speeds higher but Mäkinen kept his advantage to the end ahead of Cella and Nasenius. The Group 3 honours went to Gass who was fourth in his Porsche 911.

By the time of the RAC Rally, the last round of the European Rally Championship, one might have expected to know who stood a chance of becoming a champion. Indeed in Group 3, the picture was clear as Klass was well clear of his nearest rival but, with outstanding appeals on the Monte Carlo and Acropolis from BMC and an unresolved 'enquiry' from Ford about the Rallye dei Fiori result, the rest was far from certain. Finally the CSI issued a formal decision that was published on the eve of the RAC Rally in which they rejected the BMC appeals and left all three results standing. This meant that Mäkinen trailed Zasada in Group 2 and, since the RAC Rally counted for Groups 2 and 3, he could, in theory, win the Group 2 championship.

As it turned out, Zasada did not consider the Steyr-Puch suitable for an RAC Rally without pace notes and could not find another Group 2 car for the task. Mäkinen, after blazing away into a lead of some seven minutes at halfway was first slowed by gear-change problems and finally retired when his Cooper S's clutch blew up coming south through Kielder Forest. The leader of the pack behind Mäkinen was Söderström in his Lotus Cortina and when the Mini retired, the burly Swede carried on to win by a comfortable margin of some thirteen minutes over his compatriot, Harry Källström, in another works Cooper S with team-mates Aaltonen and Fall in close attendance behind him.

Kielder Forest was where the rally lost Erik Carlsson's Saab with a blown engine, Pauli Toivonen's R8 Gordini with no oil in the engine and Vic Elford's Lotus Cortina with no oil pressure. The Swedish Opel Rekords had also had a torrid time losing Nasenius in Wales with a broken differential and Ove Eriksson in Scotland with a broken gearbox. Even the remaining BMC Minis were in problems with disappearing fan belts while Tom Trana damaged his suspension and lost time. Lancia lost Cella with a cracked sump while Ove Andersson somehow managed to finish seventh after a catalogue of problems including a broken oil cooler, the temporary loss of second gear in his Fulvia's four speed gearbox, fuel starvation, a broken alternator and a broken seat mounting.

Thus the end of year position was that Nasenius had won Group 1 by two points from Staepelaere, Zasada had triumphed with his Steyr-Puch in Group 2 ahead of Trana, Mäkinen, Aaltonen and Söderström while Klass had simply walked it with his Porsche in Group 3. The sad thing is that practically no one cared and certainly Opel, Steyr-Puch and Porsche did not rush to take full-page advertisements to advertise their success. To the manufacturers, the championship had been devalued by splitting it and success on individual events that were important in their own right were of more use to their marketing departments. It appeared that, at least so far, the CSI's experiment had not proved a great success.

RAC Rally 1966. Bengt Söderström (on R)/ Gunnar Palm with their Ford Lotus Cortina and the winner's trophy.

Champions **1966**

Three Cities Rally 1966, Lillebror Nasenius/Fergus Sager, Opel Rekord 1700.

Lillebror Nasenius (on R) was Group 1 champion.

Sylvia Österberg was Ladies champion.

Sobieslaw Zasada was Group 2 champion driving both Steyr-Puch and Mini Cooper S.

Rolf Wütherich and Günther Klass (on R) pose at Monte Carlo Rally 1966.

Günther Klass was Group 3 champion for Porsche.

1967

There had been a rumour that for 1967 there would be a championship title for car manufacturers but nothing came of this and the same three championships for drivers in the three Groups remained. The only change for 1967 was that the number of events counting for the championship rose to sixteen and there was no 'allocation' of Groups to events. Much more significant was the action taken by Porsche. Fired with enthusiasm for rallying after Klass's modest success in 1966 and seeing that there could be something in it for them in saloon car racing as well, they took a magnifying glass to Appendix J and a tape measure to the rear seats of their 912/911 cars. They discovered that the internal dimensions were sufficient, with of course the right production numbers certified, to allow a 912 with its four-cylinder 1,582 cc engine to qualify in Group 1, and that their 911 and 911S with six-cylinder, 1,991 cc engines could be homologated in Group 2 and Group 3 respectively. With Zasada driving a 912 and Elford, now a refugee from Ford after trying a 911 on the 1966 Tour de Corse, at the wheel of a 911S, they could do a lot more rallying and probably be successful. And so it was to prove.

Their first big hit was so nearly the Monte Carlo Rally of 1967 where it looked as though Elford would quite easily triumph over the front-wheel drive cars from BMC and Lancia. The Italians now had their Fulvia Coupé with a 1.3-litre engine as opposed to the 1.2-litre version that they had used previously. However, the ACM had come up with a new rule. They had junked the old idea of handicap formulae and decided that all timings would be on scratch, but each car would only be allowed eight tyres for each of the two main parts of the event. These had to be chosen before the start, marked and then all eight carried with the car at all times. The Minis and Porsches carried two on the roof and two inside while the Lancias had one in the co-driver foot well, one behind the driver and two in the boot.

Crazy though it sounds, it all worked quite well. And the ACM was flexible enough to allow a tyre to be substituted if there was evidence that the original was not available as when Simo Lampinen had a puncture on his works Mini and the tyre came off the wheel in the stage. When the cars arrived back in Monaco, Elford led by more than half a minute followed by the Cooper Ss of Mäkinen, Hopkirk and Aaltonen with the Lancia Fulvia Coupés of Ove Andersson, Cella and new boy, Sandro Munari close behind. There had not been much snow, just some old ice on the stages and this knowledge affected everyone's choice of tyres for the last night in the mountains behind Monaco. Then, naturally, it started to snow and the combination of front-wheel drive and left-foot braking enabled Aaltonen and Andersson to push to the front while Elford's Porsche lost time and dropped back to third and was nearly caught by Cella and Munari.

The gap between the two leading cars was down to just eleven seconds at the finish after Andersson had set three fastest times and taken forty-four seconds from Aaltonen in just the last two stages of the rally. Indeed he might have won had he not hit a rock, punctured and lost thirteen seconds to Aaltonen on the second of three runs over the Turini. Fallen rocks caused the retirement of Mäkinen's Cooper S with a broken sump and Källström's R8 Gordini with irretrievably bent steering. After Lucien Bianchi hit another piece of fallen scenery, he dropped back and Lillebror Nasenius in an Opel Rekord finished in sixteenth place eventually winning Group 1. Klass driving a Porsche with Robert Buchet got lost and exceeded his maximum lateness, thus effectively retiring.

Monte Carlo Rally 1967, Rauno Aaltonen/Henry Liddon, Mini Cooper S 1275. Aaltonen always liked to be fully knowledgeable about his rally car.

Monte Carlo Rally 1967, Vic Elford/David Stone, Porsche 911S. This was the year that the cars had to carry eight tyres with them throughout both competitive halves of the rally.

Monte Carlo Rally 1967, Rauno Aaltonen/Henry Liddon, Mini Cooper S 1275. C'est Shell que j'aime: Liddon supervises a re-fuel to the winning car, while on the right, Simo Lampinen prepares to look under his Mini's bonnet.

The Swedish Rally was a bit of a parochial event and this was partially due to the fact that the Scandinavians seemed to have an excessive familiarity with the 'secret' route and their door pockets on previous events had been stuffed with pacenote books. This may have reduced overseas participation and success but could not detract from a forceful victory by Bengt Söderström driving one of the new Mk2 Lotus Cortinas. Ford were not doing many rallies this year, preferring to spend their money on a big effort for the East African Safari but they prepared two Mk2s for Söderström and Ove Andersson to drive under the Ford Sweden banner. Andersson was suffering from influenza during the rally and retired to seek a doctor but the eventual winner, Söderström, was showing the same form that had won him the RAC Rally – consistency and determination.

The early leader was Björn Waldegård in a Scania-Vabis Group 2 Porsche 911 but he fell prey to a common 911 fault when it broke its drive shaft coupling. This was the first big event for the new Saab 96 V4 and it distinguished itself well by finishing second overall with Simo Lampinen in Group 2 and seventh overall and third in Group 1 with Olle Bromark. Aaltonen brought a Cooper S home in third place after Mäkinen had retired and this was the first time that the BMC team had registered a finish here with a works Mini since the Swedish went to being a winter rally in 1965. Group 1 was won by Nasenius in his now familiar Swedish Opel Rekord with Pauli Toivonen second in Group 1 with a Lancia Fulvia Coupé.

The Rallye dei Fiori saw the inevitable clash between BMC and Lancia but to their considerable surprise, Jean-François Piot walked off with first place in a works Renault R8 Gordini. Piot had been seventh overall in the Monte so it should have come as no surprise that in his 'mini-Porsche' with its rear mounted 1.3-litre engine he should have been able to match Paddy Hopkirk in a 1,275 cc Cooper S. The gravel roads were in a poor state and recent snow had made them narrower and quite rutted. Piot led initially but then Hopkirk came back and won four stages to give himself a lead. However, on the very last part of the last stage, a fault with the gearbox made it almost impossible to drive the Mini forward. It got out of the stage eventually from where 95% of the route to the finish was downhill so, with a little 'help' from a service car placed very close behind, they made it into the centre of Sanremo and managed to retain second place.

The Lancia team had mixed fortunes as Munari was quick but broke his Fulvia's sump while Cella, not realising that a stage had been cancelled, wasted time looking for the marshal thus losing four minutes on the road. It was left to Ove Andersson to take third place ahead of Fall's works Cooper S that had broken its rear suspension and finished with large amounts of negative camber on both rear wheels. And, as there were no works Porsches entered, Elford was out in a Lancia Fulvia seeing how the other half lives. He finished fifth.

Elford was back in a Porsche 911 for the Lyon-Charbonnières and he was not alone. There was a veritable clutch of 911Ss entered some of whom eventually managed to claim the first four places on this all-tarmac rally with Elford finishing more than sixteen minutes ahead of Jean-Pierre Hanrioud. The leader for most of the rally however was Jean Rolland in his Group 2 Alfa Romeo GTA. He had taken an initial advantage on the Solitude Circuit test where the handicap favoured Group 2 against Group 3. He had maintained a narrow lead through ten of the twelve stages, all of which were on scratch, until his rear axle failed on the ascent of the Col de Pennes. Group 1 went to Citroën with Bob Neyret bringing his DS21 home fifth behind the Porsche phalanx while a private R8 Gordini that finished seventh and was driven by Fernand Schligler won Group 2.

Swedish Rally 1967, Ove Andersson/Agne Nordlund, Ford Lotus Cortina. Now alternating between Lancias and Fords, Andersson retired on this occasion with influenza.

▲ Rally dei Fiori 1967. Paddy Hopkirk/Ron Crellin (no 67) needed help from Tony Fall/Mike Wood (no 82) to leave the *parc fermé* after claiming second and fourth overall respectively.

◀ Swedish Rally 1967. Bengt Söderström/Gunnar Palm were happy winners in their Ford Lotus Cortina.

▼ Rally Rally dei Fiori 1967. One of the works Renault R8 Gordinis passes through the banks of unexpected spring snow. In a similar car, Jean-François Piot/Claude Roure won the rally outright.

It was a similar story on the Tulip in that Elford romped home in first place by setting fastest times on fourteen of the fifteen tests and stages with a Group 3 Porsche 911S. On the very fast hill climb of La Roche–Samrée he was quickest despite having a deflating tyre and nearly understeering into the timing marshal at the finish. On the next test, the narrower Route de Mont, Mäkinen beat him with the Cooper S by just three seconds. Mäkinen was in his own private fight with Aaltonen for supremacy in Group 2 and needed that time to put pressure on his Finnish rival who promptly spun on the penultimate test at a military proving ground. The two Minis finished second and third overall not far ahead of a Group 2 Porsche 911 driven by Björn Waldegård while a second 911 from Sweden driven by Åke Andersson was going well before it split its gearbox casing and retired.

A night navigation section with lots of time controls in the Haute-Savoie saw Simo Lampinen's works DAF 44 emerge as the class winner amongst the tiddlers while a broken driveshaft on her Saab 96 V4 cost Pat Moss any chance of a high placing but she did win the Ladies Prize for the umpteenth time. After a couple of years competing with his own car, Dieter Lambart was finally given a works Opel from Sweden, a Group 2 Rekord, with which he finished a creditable eleventh overall and just two places behind Rob Slotemaker's factory-built BMW 2000 TI on an event that did not suit the big Opel.

There were Wartburg 353s competing on the Tulip Rally where, within their class, they were easily beaten by an English private owner, Mike Marsden, in a 970 cc Cooper S. But on home territory in East Germany with nothing much in the way of opposition, they were able to claim a 1-2-3 finish on the sixth round of the European Rally Championship.

Sobieslaw Zasada had been driving the early rallies in his own Porsche 911S and had been third on the Lyon-Charbonnières but then crashed on the Tulip. Thus Porsche lent him a 911S for the Austrian Alpine and, after Walter Roser had fallen back after an electrical fault on his extremely rapid R8 Gordini, Zasada won outright. He was not the quickest of the finishers over the special stages since that accolade went to the man who finished second, Lasse Jönsson in a semi-works Saab 96 V4. Unfortunately for the Swedish crew, they had a wheel come off during a tight road section – of which there were many – and lost three minutes fitting it back on again. Richard Bochnicek was third in a Citroën DS21 just two seconds ahead of Dieter Lambart in his Opel Rekord.

The result on the Acropolis Rally smacked a little of sweet revenge since Paddy Hopkirk finally won that tough event for BMC in a Cooper S. Thanks to the political upheaval of the Colonels' military coup, the entry was down on previous years. Indeed the Swedish consul in Athens had advised the Saab and Volvo teams not to come to Greece, but Ford, BMC and Lancia were there to slug it out in what was, as usual, an enjoyable and highly competitive rally. From the start, the pattern that emerged was that the Minis were fastest on the tests, many of which were driveable in the time allowed, followed by the Lancias and then the Lotus Cortina of Bengt Söderström. But it was also necessary to keep up the gruelling pace on the tough road sections. When the rally passed from the Peloponnese to the mainland, the classification saw Hopkirk and Mäkinen leading ahead of Aaltonen and then Ove Andersson's Lancia. But then Mäkinen broke his gearbox and Aaltonen hit a private car in the middle of a test where the road should have been closed, and both retired. Pauli Toivonen split his Lancia Fulvia's petrol tank and retired while Cella, also in a Fulvia, suffered a navigational error and the time lost ruled him out of a top ten placing.

Tulip Rally 1967. In the *parc fermé* at Noordwijk-aan-Zee, the GT cars are lined up behind the Jaguar E-type of J. Gordon/P. Whiting. The Tulip Rally was very popular with private owners largely thanks to the fact that it did not use damaging roads.

▲ Lyon-Charbonnières Rally 1967. Starting in Stuttgart and finishing at the Casino of Charbonnières outside Lyon, this rally for many years had the unique distinction of making its cash prizes in gold coins.

Vic Elford/David Stone, Porsche 911S – winners of the 1967 Lyon-Charbonnières Rally.

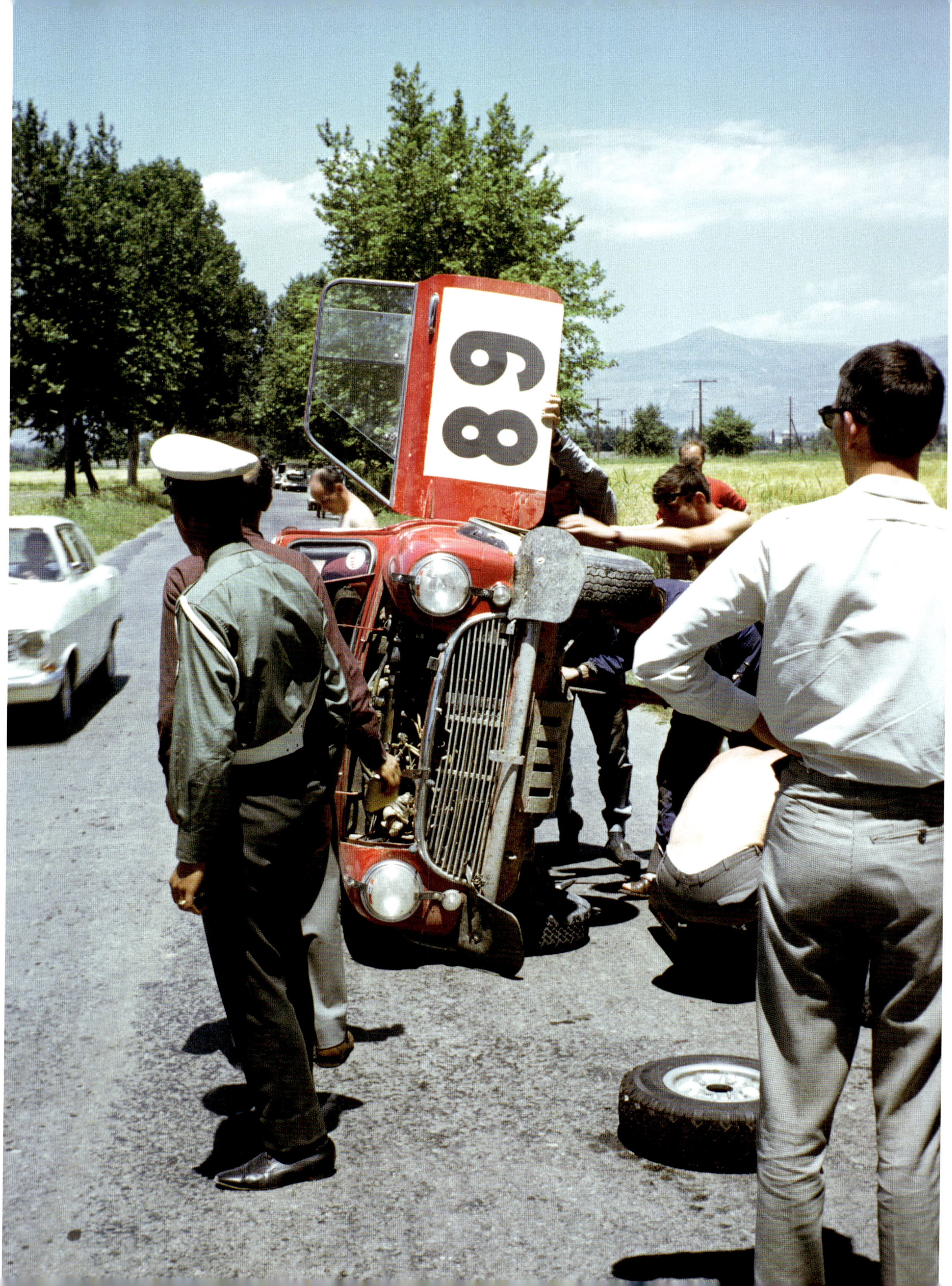

Thus in its closing stages, the rally was between Hopkirk and Andersson with Söderström in a lonely pursuit. Behind the Cortina was the BMW 2000 TI of Pilhatsch that had suffered a major setback when it had had a puncture, fell off the jack and, in trying to lift it, Pilhatsch had badly burned his hands on the exhaust. The result was never in much doubt with Hopkirk winning by seventy seconds from Andersson though it was clear that the Lancia Fulvia was steadily improving and would soon have the measure of its rivals. There were two other works teams in Greece though, like BMC and Lancia, they did not reach the finish intact. Datsun had three 1600 SSS for Finnish drivers and they got two to the finish with both in the top ten while DAF had to be content with fifteenth place and a class win for Claude Laurent in his works DAF 44. Dieter Lambart drove a sensible rally in his Opel Rekord with some quick stage times, but a puncture right near the end dropped him to eleventh place.

The Geneva Rally was on wet tarmac roads and, for a while, Munari's Lancia actually led from Elford's Porsche 911S but Elford restored his domination with some incredible times on classic tests like St-Jean-en-Royans and won from the upstart Italian combination. BMC were there with Fall who collared the Group 2 honours while Zasada made his first appearance with a Group 1 Porsche 912 and won Group 1. This new Group 1 car was also in evidence on the next round in Czechoslovakia, the Vltava Rally, where the main competition came from two works Saab 96 V4s driven by Mr and Mrs Carlsson and a flock of locally driven Škodas. With a slightly favourable handicap for Group 1 cars, Zasada was able to split the two Saabs finishing behind Carlsson's winning car but ahead of Pat Moss-Carlsson. Back in a Group 1 Kadett, Lambart finished seventh overall and moved into the lead of the Group 1 section of the European Rally Championship.

The Austrian-organised Danube Rally was a bit of a strange affair thanks to a misunderstanding between its organisers and the Hungarian border officials that resulted in several crews not being allowed to enter Hungary. One of these was the hot favourite, Aaltonen, in a works Cooper S. It looked as if the might of France – a full team of Renault R8 Gordinis from both their home country and Sweden plus supported cars from Hungary and Romania – would easily carry the day. But it was not to be Renault's day as they lost nearly all their cars and the one that was still in contention, that of Jean Vinatier, had the misfortune to get stuck behind several other cars in dust on the first long stage in Romania thus losing several minutes. Out of all this, the Austin 1800 driven by Fall emerged as a very surprise winner. Zasada, who had nearly called it a day in Romania, finally found the ignition problem on his Porsche 912 and continued to once again win Group 1. This time, Lambart was out in a Group 1 Commodore and won his class while Wallrabenstein won Group 3 and finished third overall in his Porsche 911S.

▲ Geneva Rally 1967, Julien Vernaeve (in Dunlop jacket)/Henry Liddon, Mini Cooper S 1275.

▶ Acropolis Rally 1967. Bengt Söderström and Gunnar Palm lean on the bonnet of their Ford Lotus Cortina Mk2 before the start.

◀ Acropolis Rally 1967, Paddy Hopkirk/Ron Crellin, Mini Cooper S 1275. Using a technique pioneered by John Wadsworth and Mike Wood during the Liège-Sofia-Liège of 1964, BMC mechanics change a drive shaft coupling on the winning car.

At the end of the Danube Rally there was sadness when the news broke that Günter Klass had been killed in an accident in practice for the Mugello race. After making a contract with Ferrari in April, he had started to race the two-litre Dino 206 Spyder and was driving one at Mugello when he left the road and hit a telegraph pole.

Another result, almost as incredible as that of the Danube though of a different nature, came on the Polish Rally where Lancia were out in strength but knew that, in order to beat the Group 1 Porsche 912 of Zasada and the Opels, their three Group 2 Fulvias had to overcome a fairly hefty handicap. With the rally steadily increasing in difficulty and with a massive amount of fog and rain on the second night, Ove Andersson managed to forge a substantial lead of some eight minutes. But then a combination of fog and a misplaced road sign saw his Fulvia leave the road. For nearly all the entry, what with trying to keep on the road and struggling to keep up the tight schedule, most of them dropped out. At the finish, there were just three cars left running – and they were all in Group 1. By winning outright, Zasada moved into the championship lead with the man in second place, Lillebror Nasenius, also displacing fellow Opel driver, Lambart, in the title chase.

The 1000 Lakes Rally of 1967 will always be remembered for Timo Mäkinen's iconic drive on the swoops and jumps of the classic Ouninpohja stage. After a few kilometres, the bonnet of his Cooper S flew up and he had to drive the rest of the stage peering through the tiny strip of the windscreen that was not obscured. In fact, he had a hard fight all through this damp and misty rally with a rejuvenated Simo Lampinen in a Saab 96 V4 who pressed him the whole way. Indeed Mäkinen could scarcely afford to lose ten seconds to Lampinen on Ouninpohja since the gap between them at the finish was a mere eight seconds. The Porsche 911s of Waldegård and Åke Andersson took to the woods quite early in the rally with Andersson retiring on the spot and Waldegård delayed but continuing to finish twelfth. The man flying along behind the two leading protagonists was Hannu Mikkola who managed to coax his large Volvo 142S into third place ahead of both works Lotus Cortina Mk2s of Söderström and Ove Andersson. The 1000 Lakes stirred a small amount of controversy before the start by rejecting cars at scrutineering that had iodine lamps in any lamp other than in fog lamps since that is what Finnish traffic law stated at that time. However, Renault made a protest and they were allowed to use them on the R8 Gordinis.

Danube Rally 1967, Tony Fall/Mike Wood (both at the front of car 5), BMC Austin 1800. A clean car must have helped as they won the rally outright.

Danube Rally 1967. Servicing both before and during rallies of the 1960s was very much a non-regulated affair. Here Renault, BMC, Porsche and Dunlop share the same area outside Rally HQ.

If the Rallye des Alpes of 1967 proved anything, it was that this was very much a Paddy Hopkirk year. Having won the Acropolis, the Irishman went out and won the second most arduous event on the calendar against a formidable array of talent in Porsche 911s, Alfa Romeo GTAs and Renault R8 Gordinis not to mention his three BMC team-mates. The Porsche and Renault teams both fell prey to mechanical woes with the Porsches going out with transmission failures while many of the Group 6 engines in the works R8s proved too strong for their mountings and broke free. With Rolland breaking his GTA's axle and Mäkinen and Aaltonen also falling out with transmission problems, Hopkirk's adversaries were much reduced. After an impeccable drive, he headed home the GTAs of Bernard Consten and Jean-Claude Gamet with the Swedish prepared R8 Gordini of Harry Källström finishing fourth and, like the other three, winning a Coupe des Alpes.

On the Spanish Rally, Lancia went with a Group 6 Fulvia for Ove Andersson and a Group 2 Fulvia for Munari. Their sights were set on winning a major rally after second places in Monte Carlo, Geneva and Acropolis and they succeeded with Andersson first and Munari second overall. They were helped in this task by wet weather, especially at the circuit race on the Circuito de Guadalope at Alcañiz and the downhill special stages that followed. Bernard Tramont in a local Alpine Renault A110 and Arnaldo Cavallari in an Alfa Romeo GTA were the closest contenders for the Lancias but Cavallari, who used to be co-driven by Munari, suffered a piston failure and he was lucky to limp round the final test on the Jarama Circuit to finish eighth. There were insufficient Group 1 cars entered for either Nasenius or Lambart to score more points for the championship and indeed Zasada, who had entered, withdrew before the start when he realised that this would be the case.

The last-but-one rally in the championship was the Three Cities and both Piot and Söderström turned up in R8 Gordini and Lotus Cortina respectively. This time, it was the Ford that failed with Söderström suffering the cruel fate of breaking his clutch on the last test around the streets of Budapest when he was leading. By virtue of his win, Piot moved to within four points of the burly Swede and might well have hoped to grab the title on the last event of the year, the RAC Rally, had that event not been cancelled due to a widespread outbreak of foot-and-mouth disease (aphtae epizooticae) in mainland Britain.

As with the previous year, having three European Champions tended to dilute any publicity generated in the mind of the public. For the record, Zasada won Group 1 with his Porsche 912 (its last year in Group 1 before it became a Group 3 car) with a nine-point advantage over Nasenius in his Opel Rekord. In Group 2, it was victory for Bengt Söderström and Gunnar Palm in a Lotus Cortina MK1 ahead of Piot's Renault R8. Group 3 was almost naturally a Porsche benefit with Vic Elford and David Stone way out in front thanks to their three outright victories. Jean-Pierre Hanrioud, also driving a 911S, was second, twenty-six points behind the title winner.

So 1967 ended in a minor key with some of the rally cars that were already in the UK performing on a single stage outside London for the benefit of television. What then was in store for the coming year? It was known that the FIA had decided to scrap the idea of running a European Rally Championship in three categories for drivers and were to replace it with fifteen events split into two championships. One of these would be for drivers – seven events – and the other would be for manufacturers – eight events. As an experiment, it was another dismal failure. What should a team do when they would like to win the manufacturer championship but discover that the driver championship contains the Monte Carlo, the Acropolis and the 1000 Lakes Rally? What happened, of course, was that most of the teams ignored the European Rally Championship and entered the rallies that best suited their marketing aims.

1000 Lakes Rally 1967, Timo Mäkinen/Pekka Keskitalo, Mini Cooper S 1275. Despite having to peer round the edge of his flapping bonnet, Mäkinen lost just ten seconds in sixteen minutes to his nearest pursuer and won the rally.

Champions 1967

Sobieslaw Zasada winning the Polish Rally in a 4-cylinder Group 1 Porsche 912.

Sobieslaw Zasada was Group 1 champion.

Bengt Söderström did not finish the Safari Rally in this Ford Cortina GT Mk2.

Bengt Söderström was Group 2 champion.

Lucette Pointet, seen here co-driving for Jean-Claude Ogier (Citroën DS prototype) on the Rallye des Alpes was ladies champion.

Vic Elford was Group 3 champion.

1968

A small shock was to find the opening manufacturer round, the Swedish Rally, coming first on the menu before the Monte Carlo Rally. The reason was that the Swedish organisers did not want to compete for media coverage with the Winter Olympics that were to be held in Grenoble on Sweden's traditional February date. With the majority of rally crews practising for the Monte, all but a few entries on this winter rally were Swedish. Porsche now had their 911T homologated in Group 2 and Waldegård proved simply invincible in his example. The main opposition came from Saab but when Lampinen retired with a major oil leak in his Saab 96 V4, it was left to Trana and Håkan Lindberg to chase the rapidly disappearing Porsche. Also disappearing – though in a different sense – were Åke Andersson who bent his Porsche's steering, Mikkola who left the road in his Volvo 142S, and Clark who was suffering from influenza and thus retired at the halfway halt in his works Lotus Cortina Mk2.

It was a Porsche too that won Monte Carlo with Elford making no mistake about it this time – and with no restrictions on tyre quantities and no handicaps – to rocket home in a works 911T ahead of team-mate, Pauli Toivonen. Behind them came a traffic jam of three works Minis driven by Aaltonen, Fall and Hopkirk who found that in the relatively snow-free conditions, they were no match for Stuttgart's finest. Many of the stages, including the Turini, were driven on racing tyres. In a particularly unfortunate incident where spectators had shovelled snow into the middle of the road on the Turini, Gérard Larrousse, whose Alpine Renault A110 had been leading at the end of the first arrival in Monaco, went off the road and had to retire. Mikkola did his career no harm by finishing ninth overall in a Datsun Fairlady ahead of Waldegård's Porsche and Söderström's Lancia Fulvia. This latter combination was a function of Ford being happy to release one of their works drivers as the Monte Carlo did not count for the manufacturer championship. The laisser faire attitude created by the CSI's latest rallying experiment saw Ove Andersson, a new signing for Ford, also allowed to drive on the Monte for his previous employer whom he rewarded with a sixth place in – to give it its full title – a Lancia Fulvia Coupé 1.3 HF now competing in Group 2.

Andersson had been driving Lotus Cortinas for Ford for some time alongside his main Lancia duties and indeed had won the non-championship Gulf London Rally – a UK forest event even tougher than the RAC Rally – for them in July 1967 with a Lotus Cortina Mk2. Now he and Ford were to take a major step by debuting their new rally car, the Escort Twin Cam on the newly named Sanremo Rally. Initially homologated into Group 3 for lack of production numbers, at this stage of its development the Escort still had its rear dampers in the standard position inclined at 45 degrees to the axle. This was rapidly changed – and homologated – with vertical dampers in time for Roger Clark to give the car its first international victory on the Circuit of Ireland in April. Back amid the snows of Sanremo, Andersson did well to bring the new car home in third place behind the winning Porsche 911 of Pauli Toivonen and the Lancia of Pat Moss.

The next European rallies were the German twins, East and West. Both were qualifiers for the driver championship and thus neither attracted much of an entry from the main teams. Porsche did however send Pauli Toivonen and he delivered two perfect victories to establish him clearly in the lead of that championship. Between the two German rallies came the good old-fashioned Tulip Rally – a round of the manufacturers championship – where Ford's Escorts, driven by Clark and Andersson, recorded a resounding 1-2 victory just five seconds apart. For some reason, the organisers did not publish an overall classification so, though Julien Vernaeve got

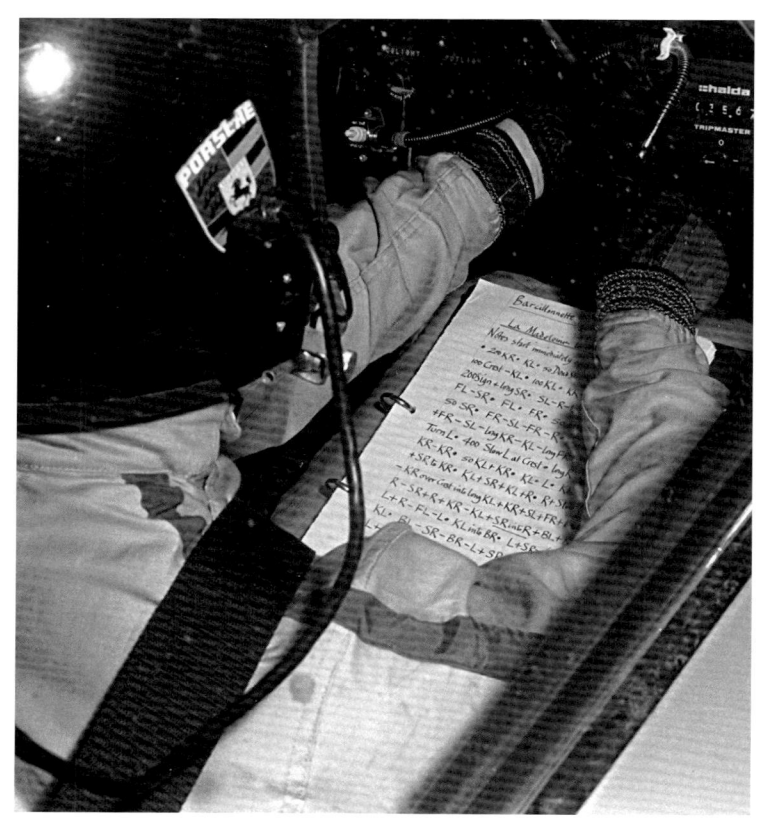

▲ Monte Carlo Rally 1968. The co-driver's workplace in the winning Porsche 911T of Vic Elford/David Stone. Pace notes, Halda tripmaster and helmet with intercom.

▼ Vic Elford proves that you do not have to take off your helmet to relax briefly while winning the Monte Carlo Rally.

Monte Carlo Rally 1968, Vic Elford/David Stone, Porsche 911T

Monte Carlo Rally 1968, Vic Elford/David Stone, Porsche 911T. The Monaco prize-giving system was that the Prince presented the winners with the permanent trophies belonging to the club and then the Palace security staff immediately repossessed them. Here Elford has a champagne moment beyond the presentation dais with a cup that will be his to keep.

Few people recall that some of Hannu Mikkola's early international exploits were with a Datsun Fairlady sports car. This is his team-mate, Jorma Lusenius's Datsun before the start of the Tulip Rally 1968.

the Group 2 win in a Cooper S, he was in fact third behind the two Group 3 Escorts. The most commendable performance must go to Jorma Lusenius who took fourth place – and third in Group 3 – with a Datsun Fairlady. Mäkinen was leading Group 2 when he had a rare off-road excursion on the Col du Brabant stage. It took him an hour to get back on the road but he was fast enough on the long road section not to be penalised at the subsequent time control. Thus though he was classified forty-first overall from his time on the stage, he was one of the few cars with no road penalty!

The Austrian Alpine was a round for manufacturers and thus Ford was there as well as Lancia and Saab but not Porsche or Alpine who had other things to do. The Austrian event was still rather set in a traditional mould with set times for stages and difficult navigation sections but, unlike the Tulip Rally, its timing was perfect. The rally evolved into a three-way battle between Söderström's Escort, a Lancia Fulvia driven by Mikkola, and the works Saab 96 V4 of Carl Orrenius. Söderström led initially but first Orrenius and then Mikkola overhauled him. On a soaking wet road section, Orrenius's co-driver, Arne Hertz, slid off the road and rolled the Saab out of contention. Now Mikkola led and as things dried out, Söderström came back at him and over the last four stages the lead changed three times with Söderström eventually winning by just fourteen seconds.

Saab had an unfortunate time of it in Austria with Trana losing sufficient time off the road early on and only be able to recover to ninth overall while Lars Jönsson, driving a Saab Sonett, threw away fourth place and the Group 3 win when he failed to conserve his comfortable lead on the second leg. He went off the road and the Sonett was then hit by Joachim Springer's BMW rendering both cars hors de combat. But the Austrian drivers fared well since Walter Roser brought his Renault R8 Gordini to third place while Arnulf Pilhatsch upheld the honours of BMW by finishing fourth in his 2002.

Next event was the Acropolis Rally, a driver event that saw all the works teams present except Alpine whose cars could not be got ready thanks to a strike in the Dieppe factory. This was to be the last major event for the BMC team whose efforts after the Acropolis were to be directed to their entry of Austin 1800s on the London to Sydney Marathon. Mäkinen was not fated to improve on his tenth place in 1966 as, in the middle of the Peloponnese, his Cooper S engine overheated and he retired. At one point, the three Escorts of Clark, Andersson and Söderström were lying 1-2-3 but then

Toivonen and Zasada got going in their Porsche 911s and the lead shifted around several times before the cars reached the halfway point. By then Andersson and Clark led the field but not by much. Then at the tyre change after Volos, Andersson did not have his rear wheel nuts properly tightened and he lost a wheel on the next difficult road section. The twenty-nine minute penalty was sufficient to drop him to ninth place at the finish behind a trio of Lancia Fulvias driven by Harry Källström, Amilcare Ballestrieri and Pat Moss.

Of the front runners, it was only Clark that had no major problems and those that he did have – an alternator failed coming into a service point rather than leaving it – always seemed to cost him very little. Whereas, Toivonen had a puncture and a broken wheel that surely cost him the win and certainly dropped him behind his team-mate Zasada who had puncture problems of his own. Söderström was penalised when his Escort would not re-start to go to the final race at Tatoi Airport and he was docked enough points for not doing the race to drop him down into fourth place. They may not have got a 1-2-3 but Ford did win the team prize from Lancia even with Andersson's road penalty. Both Datsun Fairladys broke down, Mikkola losing his brakes and Lusenius his engine, but there was a consolation for Mikkola who was signed by Ford – on the strength of his Austrian performance – to drive an Escort on the 1000 Lakes Rally.

The Geneva Rally was postponed so that the next event was the Vltava Rally in Czechoslovakia where the winner was Vinatier at the wheel of an Alpine A110 powered by a 1,300 cc Renault engine. The Alpine team had already made something of an impression outside their native country by taking third and fourth places overall on the West German Rally with Piot and Vinatier respectively. But this was the little Group 3 car's first major European win. Second overall was Lampinen in a Saab 96 V4 ahead of Staepelaere in a Ford Escort TC with another Saab driven by Lindberg fourth and Piot's Alpine fifth. The second Alpine had been unlucky enough to fracture a water hose just before the initial circuit race and took eight minutes penalty having it repaired. Running second for much of the rally was the Porsche 911T of Zasada but, as with several other crews, he missed a passage control and was excluded. Despite a clash with the Gulf London Rally in the UK that had attracted many of the top crews, Lancia sent Pat Moss and Källström to this manufacturer's round but both retired with, respectively, an engine that would not run properly and broken steering.

Acropolis Rally 1968. Rallying in the Europe of the 1960s involved travelling through remote and beautiful parts of the countries that were hosting rallies.

Austrian Alpine Rally 1968, Bengt Söderström/Gunnar Palm, Ford Escort Twin Cam. In its debut year, the Escort could do no wrong and won rallies with ease.

Acropolis Rally 1968. Two of the BMC works crews take sun with their beer: from L to R, Henry Liddon, Brian Culcheth, Rauno Aaltonen and Mike Wood.

A time of experiment 1968

It was a bit of a walkover for Pauli Toivonen on the Danube Rally where his Porsche 911T set fastest time on all eleven special stages. There was no major opposition from the factory teams on this event and his hardest challenger was Pilhatsch in a works supported BMW 2002 until the rear axle broke on the last leg. Another car to drop out was the Ford Taunus 20 MTS of Staepelaere who had been holding station behind the BMW until the Ford went off the road into a tree when co-driver, Andre Aerts, was driving. Zasada was a non-starter since he preferred to spend the time preparing for his home event, the Polish Rally.

There were no big manufacturer teams in Poland either so Zasada might well have hoped for an easy win and indeed he did lead for most of the rally, winning all the special stages. But then on the last night and in torrential rain, he made a small error on a very fast stage and slid off the road into a tree. This enabled Renault to claim their second European win of the season when Krzysztof Kormonicki headed the field in his R8 Gordini. In many ways, there were too many rallies shoved together in this period with events like the Gulf London Rally and the 84 hours of Nürburgring draining off interest. This event at the Nürburgring was the new 'Marathon de la Route' after the Royal Automobile Club of Liège had decided in 1965 to cease running its road rally that used to go all the way from Liège to Sofia in Bulgaria and back.

But there was no such problem for the 1000 Lakes Rally as all the Finns headed for their summer speed-fest. It should have been a four-way fight between Porsche (Toivonen and Leo Kinnunen), Saab (Lampinen, Orrenius and Jari Vilkas), BMC (Mäkinen and Lars-Ingvar Ytterbring) and Ford (Söderström, Ove Andersson and Mikkola) but only the Ford team were not Finnish importer cars. Thus though the Porsches led from the start, they were soon to suffer a string of mechanical maladies and drop out. There was trouble too for the BMC surrogates as Mäkinen's car lost its alternator and then broke the gearbox while Ytterbring flew too high on a jump and landed off the road and out of the rally. The Saabs showed great reliability – indeed they won the team prize – but even Lampinen could not match the pace of Ford's new man, Mikkola. Despite heavy rain throughout the rally, Mikkola won from Lampinen by almost two and half minutes. His Ford team-mates suffered from various problems with Andersson dropping out when his differential broke and Söderström losing time with a bent front suspension. Perhaps the drive of the rally came from Atso Aho (later to co-drive Mikkola to 1000 Lakes success in a Toyota Corolla) who was entered in his private Cooper S and finished fourth behind Söderström. And the surprise of the rally was the speed of Pentti Airikkala driving an Isuzu Bellett who was holding second place until he rolled just two stages from the end.

The Rallye des Alpes was held in early September and the bad weather plus a tough route saw the entry reduced from 64 starters to just twelve finishers. The works Ford Escorts of Clark and Andersson were delayed by multiple punctures early on and eventually both of them retired as the result of accidents while Söderström had the engine fail in the third Escort. Alpine was there in force with 1,440 cc engines in its A110s. While their quickest driver, Gérard Larrousse, was out very early with a broken clutch, Jean-Pierre Nicolas got to the very last test, made fastest time and then his engine blew up. With Piot also retiring mid-rally with a fuel blockage, it was left to Vinatier to battle it out with a horde of Alfa Romeo GTAs. Sadly these did not include Jean Rolland who had died testing for Alfa at Montlhéry in a Type 33 the previous September. In the vanguard of the Alfa attack was the GTA driven by the Gamet brothers, Jean-Claude and Michel, while Bernard Consten and co-driver Jean Todt were also chasing the Alpines. However, it was Jean-Louis Barailler who stayed the pace and finished second behind Vinatier. Third was

Danube Rally 1968, Pauli Toivonen/Martti Tiukkanen, Porsche 911T.

1000 Lakes Rally 1968, Hannu Mikkola/Anssi Järvi, Ford Escort Twin Cam. In his first drive for Ford, Mikkola showed that he was quite capable of winning rallies outright. Even the un-seasonal rain and mud did not slow him.

Danube Rally 1968, Gilbert Staepelaere/Andre Aerts, Ford Taunus 20 MTS. The big Ford from Köln was not an ideal European rally car. First Staepelaere had a small accident and then his co-driver had a worse one involving a Romanian tree that resulted in their retirement.

the Lancia of Trautmann after being delayed by four minutes at a closed level crossing. Those three were awarded Coupes despite losing time on the road as Coupes were now being awarded to the winner and to anyone who stayed within 2% of him on combined test and sélectif times.

With the Rallye des Alpes allowing cars of Groups 4, 5 & 6 to compete and to be counted in the final classification, the CSI did not permit it to be a points scoring event, so the Spanish Rally was drafted in as a last minute replacement in the manufacturer championship. Once again the combination of Toivonen and a Porsche 911T proved invincible winning ahead of Piot's Alpine and Staepelaere's Escort.

Another late runner was the postponed Geneva Rally that also took place in October. Not quite as demanding in terms of average speeds as the Rallye des Alpes, the Geneva was still a tough event thanks to a long route and little rest. There was a rally-long battle between Toivonen's Porsche and Vinatier's Alpine that was finally resolved in favour of the Porsche when the Alpine broke its transmission coming away from the last test. Behind these two, the Alfa Romeo GTAs of Lucien Bianchi and Guy Verrier had disputed third place with Staepelaere's Escort and, with Vinatier's exit, it was Bianchi that inherited second overall with Staepelaere fourth behind Verrier.

The next and final championship event was the RAC Rally. This too suffered a little from its proximity to the start of the London to Sydney Marathon to which Ford (UK, Australia and Germany), BMC (now known as British Leyland), Porsche, Citroën, Rootes, Volvo (Australia), Simca, DAF and Moskvitch were all committed. Not that this reduced the RAC's entry by very much as Saab turned out in force with four cars, Lancia with five, Porsche with three while Mäkinen had managed to get a works Ford Escort TC entered by the private team of Clarke and Simpson (a.k.a. David Sutton). What was peculiar was that the RAC had decided to run a separate rally for Groups 4, 5 & 6 that they called the 'European Club Rally' since it was to comprise mainly British club drivers in the anything-goes cars that they drove on UK national rallies. However it was here that Lancia entered three of its works cars – Fulvia Coupés with 1.6-litre engines and five-speed gearboxes that would not be homologated into Group 3 until July 1969 – with Munari, Mikkola and, another refugee from the cessation of mainstream BMC activities, Aaltonen.

Early disappearances were the works Saab 96 V4s of Trana and Lindberg, both with differential failure while Pat Moss rolled her Group 3 Lancia in North Wales and Mikkola's 1.6-litre Lancia wound up in a ditch in Scotland. At halfway, Mäkinen led by a hair's-breath from Lampinen's Saab and this was despite the Escort suffering a host of minor troubles like breaking a drive shaft and a steering arm in the West Country and cutting a brake pipe in Wales. As the rally headed south, Elford started to set good times with his Porsche 911T but then, in Kielder Forest, the suspension cried enough. Mäkinen was in trouble with a leaking head gasket and this eventually brought the Escort's run to an end. Källström was sidelined when he broke the sump while Munari in the remaining 1.6-litre Fulvia went off the road in Craik Forest in heavy morning mist.

As the rally entered Yorkshire, it was clear that only mechanical problems would change a situation where Lampinen led Orrenius by some fifteen minutes with the next best competitor, the private Escort of British Rally Champion, Jimmy Bullough, some forty minutes behind the two Saabs. From this point on, it was a case of proceeding with care for the two leaders with Lampinen even freewheeling round corners on the last tests at Mallory Park and Silverstone to ensure his transmission lasted to the end. The Club Rally had been led from the start by Aaltonen who was frequently setting faster times than either Mäkinen or Lampinen in the main rally, but his rally ended off the road in Kielder with the car too badly damaged to continue.

Thus at the end of the year as the London to Sydney departed for 'Down-Under', the situation was that Ford had won the championship for manufacturers and Pauli Toivonen was the worthy winner of the championship for drivers. Ford's supremacy was largely thanks to the quantum leap in performance that the Escort Twin Cam had given them over the Lotus Cortina and was also helped by good private owner results on rallies that the works team did not contest. As for Toivonen, he scored more than double the points of his nearest rival, Zasada, and also won two manufacturer events, the Sanremo and the Spanish.

RAC Rally 1968, Simo Lampinen/John Davenport, Saab 96 V4. With many teams concentrating on the London-Sydney that was starting just three days after the RAC Rally finished, the entry list lacked many familiar names. But there were works cars from Porsche, Lancia and Saab, plus Mäkinen in an Escort Twin Cam, so that the young Finn's victory was no walkover.

A typical scene on a 1960s international rally. During the 1968 Rallye des Alpes, Jean Vinatier waits in the Alpine Renault while co-driver, Jean-François Jacob confers with the time control officials.

Champions **1968**

Only one Driver champion in 1968 – Pauli Toivonen with co-driver, Martti Kolari, at the German Rally.

Sanremo Rally 1968. First international rally for the Escort Twin Cam that went on to win the first Constructors championship for Ford GB. From L to R: John Davenport, Ove Andersson, Bill Meade (on roof), Bill Barnett, David Rowe, Derek Smith and Dave Stevens.

1969

For 1969, the CSI kept the European Rally Championship formula much the same and chose fifteen events that were almost the same as those used in 1968 but with the Munich-Vienna-Budapest (Three Cities) Rally substituted for the East German Rally. The East Germans had forgotten to apply for inclusion and although their event ran as usual in April, it was not a round of the ERC. The events had been moved around a bit between the two championships for manufacturers and drivers so that the former comprised Monte Carlo, Acropolis, Geneva, 1000 Lakes, Danube, West German and Three Cities while the drivers took the other eight. As it turned out, the manufacturers list was jinxed. Monte Carlo ran but was not counted by the CSI since it ran a Group 6 event concurrently despite the fact that this was precisely what the RAC Rally had done just months earlier. Then, thanks to a fatality in a hill climb the Swiss authorities cancelled the Geneva shortly before it was due to run. Thus there were only five events in the manufacturer half of the championship.

The Monte Carlo was a better event in 1969 thanks to being able to use its traditional tests around the Chartreuse and Chamrousse now that the 1968 Winter Olympics had gone. And there was more snow than there had been the year before with at least fifty percent of the fifteen stages having some snow or ice. Despite having the advantages of front-wheel drive, Lancia had a generally poor event with Aaltonen and Fall going out with accidents on Pirelli racing tyres in the Ardèche and Pat Moss finishing sixth behind the Group 1 R8 Gordini of Jean-Luc Thérier. They had one consolation in that Källström won the Group 6 rally driving a 1.6-litre Fulvia Coupé. Ford did little better with their Escorts as Andersson was troubled with a leaking head gasket right from the start while Mikkola had wheel stud problems. Both retired and it was left to new Ford signing, Piot, to come home fourth and win Group 2. Alpine also lost early leader Jorma Lusenius with a broken valve spring and Jean-Claude Andruet with suspension damage after an accident and it was left to Vinatier to come through to take third place behind his ex-team-mate, Larrousse who was now driving for Porsche. Nicolas drove a 1.6-litre A110 in the Group 6 rally and was within seconds of Källström until on the last stage his engine threw a spark plug. He lost eleven minutes fixing the problem but finished second nevertheless.

Indeed it was a Porsche benefit for their new fuel-injected 911Ss and they could so easily have been 1-2-3 had not Elford, granted the lead on the last night when Waldegård had brake problems in service that cost him four minutes road penalty, uncharacteristically slid off the road on a liaison section and retired. As it was, Waldegård was simply in a class of his own and Larrousse was happy to be second just twenty-three seconds clear of Vinatier. The two works BMW 2002 TIs entered for Timo Mäkinen and Åke Andersson had both retired with rear brake troubles quite early on but the Dutch BMW entry for Rob Slotemaker finished in seventh place.

It was a Porsche too that won in Sweden though this time Waldegård was driving the lighter and shorter 911T. Plenty of snow and freedom to practice the roads – there were 44 special stages totalling over 1,000 kilometres – made for an excellent rally. Lancia arrived with two 1.3-litre Fulvia Coupés for Munari and Källström while Ford had two Escorts for Ove Andersson and Söderström but the main opposition to Porsche came from the Saab factory who fielded five cars for Lampinen, Trana, Orrenius, Lindberg and a new talent, Stig Blomqvist. Waldegård was a lone entry from Scania-Vabis, the Porsche importer, but his old team-mate, Åke Andersson, was in a BMW 2002 TI again with a second Munich car driven by Anders Gullberg. There was also a host of Swedish Opel Team Rallye Kadetts.

Monte Carlo Rally 1969. Porsche drivers Vic Elford (on L) and Björn Waldegård chat with team boss Rico Steinemann (on R) at the harbour.

Swedish Rally 1969, Björn Waldegård/Lars Helmer, Porsche 911L.

Sandro Munari/Sergio Barbasio,
Lancia Fulvia Coupé 1.6 HF. DNF

Harry Källström/Gunnar Häggbom,
Lancia Fulvia Coupé 1.6 HF. 1st overall.

Jean-Pierre Jabouille/Peter Marchesi,
Matra 530 V4. DNF

Henri Pescarolo/Johnny Rives,
Matra 530 V4. DNF

Henri Pescarolo/Johnny Rives,
Matra 530 V4. DNF

Rally in the Rally

The FIA did not like prototypes in rallies and when the ACM decided to run a rally for them within their main event called the Rallye Méditerranée, the FIA threw the Monte out of the 1969 Championship. The RAC Rally had done exactly the same thing for their 1968 event and nobody had said a thing.

There were just fourteen starters in the Rallye Méditerranée. Lancia had taken the opportunity to try their yet-to-be-homologated 1,600 cc Fulvia Coupés. It proved to be worthwhile with both Harry Källström and Sandro Munari figuring in the fastest times, until Munari suffered from being first car on the road and was excluded when he drove through a passage control before the marshal had arrived. However, Källström had an untroubled run to first place.

Alpine too were keen to try out one of their A110s with a 1,600cc engine that would not be homologated until twelve months later. Jean-Pierre Nicolas drove well to finish second and chased Källström hard. Matra Sports entered four standard 530As to be driven by a selection of French racing drivers but none finished.

Jean-Pierre Nicolas helps with the quick-lift jack on the Alpine Renault A110 he shared with Claude Roure. They finished 2nd overall.

There was never much doubt about the leader since Waldegård set twenty-nine fastest times but he did have two worries. The first was a failing gearbox and, just where he needed to have it changed, his service car had rolled and a taxi had to be sent back to fetch the spare gearbox. The other was fresh snow that got in around his carburettors and slowed his pace for a while. Behind him, Ove Andersson retired when his gearbox broke and thus the men fighting for second place were Lampinen and two Opel drivers, Anders Kulläng and Ove Eriksson. At one point, Kulläng got ahead of Lampinen but then broke his differential and he dropped back to fourth. Munari retired when he rolled and broke his windscreen while Källström finished amid a bevy of Saabs in sixth place.

There was snow too on the gravel stages of the Sanremo Rally and Lancia pulled an amazing tyre change between two stages in a single tight road section to grab an advantage they were never to concede. Despite losing their fastest man, Munari, they still contrived to have a 1-2-3 result with Källström heading home Rauno Aaltonen and Sergio Barbasio. The two works Escorts of Hannu Mikkola and Roger Clark both had problems with Mikkola crashing in thick fog and Clark delayed with a misbehaving clutch. For Porsche, Zasada slid off the road and broke his suspension and it was left to the Italian 911 of Luigi Taramazzo to uphold Stuttgart's honour by taking fourth place just ahead of the Yugoslavian 911 of Jovica Palikovic.

Just three weeks after Sanremo came the non-championship Sestriere Rally. It had been won outright by Pat Moss for Lancia in 1968 and this rally was about to be united with the Sanremo Rally in order to produce the Rallye d'Italia for the new 1970 FIA rally championship due to be announced in the summer. There were massive amounts of snow on some parts of the route and, out of the confusion of blocked stages, came a solid victory for Munari ahead of Andersson's Escort and Källström's Lancia.

The problems that assailed the Tulip Rally were financial rather than meteorological though the fog in the Vosges and Haute-Savoie did make it rather more difficult than it might have been. Fortunately new sponsors were found at the last minute – the city of Rotterdam and Esso – which caused the rally to move its start from Noordwijk to Rotterdam. Staepelaere led in his Escort from the beginning and his closest rival, after the retirement of Källström's Lancia and Zasada's Porsche 911S, was Slotemaker in a BMW 2002 TI. Sadly, the BMW took a wrong turning in fog during the night and lost three minutes and this enabled Staepelaere to take a relatively untroubled win. There was sadness too at the finish since for the first time the traditional silver Tulips were not given as class and overall awards and, like any other rally, there were just cups and other such trophies.

In Austria, Mikkola notched up his first major win outside Scandinavia for Ford by winning outright in an Escort. In many ways, this was a repeat result of the previous year with an Escort beating a Lancia but this time it was Mikkola in the Ford and Källström in the second-placed Lancia. Among the sixty-five starters, there were a few strange additions to the European scene with Hopkirk in a works Triumph 2.5 PI and double Safari winner, Joginder Singh trying his hand in a Porsche 911S. Neither of these two finished but more serious competition was expected from Zasada in a Porsche 911S and Staepelaere in a Taunus 20 MRS. Many of the crews found the navigation difficult and all but a few lost time on the road sections. On the fourteen special stages, when he was not fastest, Mikkola was in the top three and this kept him ahead of Källström and the pursing trio of works Saab 96 V4s driven by Orrenius, Lampinen and Lars Jönsson who finished behind the two leaders in that order.

Hannu Mikkola was gaining experience fast and won the Austrian Alpine in 1969 for Ford.

Sanremo Rally 1969, Harry Källström/Gunnar Häggbom, Lancia Fulvia Coupé 1.3 HF. Lancia finished 1-2-3 with Källström at the head of the trio.

Tulip Rally 1969, Gilbert Staepelaere/André Aerts, Ford Escort Twin Cam. They won the event outright.

Austrian Alpine Rally 1969, Gilbert Staepelaere/André Aerts, Ford Taunus 20 MRS.

Austrian Alpine Rally 1969, Hannu Mikkola/Mike Wood, Ford Escort Twin Cam.

▲ Acropolis Rally 1969. But for an untypical excursion, Roger Clark and Jim Porter might well have won in Greece.

◀ Acropolis Rally 1969, Ove Andersson/Gunnar Palm, Ford Escort Twin Cam. While leading the rally, a puncture forced Andersson to drive hard on a road section and, when something failed in the front suspension, this was the result.

At last the manufacturer championship reached its second round, the Acropolis Rally, though in fact by then it was actually the first since the Monte Carlo results had been ignored. Here too the roles were reversed since the previous year's winner, Clark, spent twelve minutes off the road on the first night and was only able to recover to second place behind the man he beat in 1968, Toivonen. The other members of the Ford and Porsche teams did not fare well at all. Mikkola's Escort lost a wheel complete with half-shaft and bearing after only a couple of stages while Andersson who was setting all the fastest times had a front strut mounting break and parked his Escort thirty metres down in a chasm. Inheriting the lead from Andersson was the Porsche of Larrousse but, in the far north, he first encountered suspension problems and then, like the Porsche of Waldegård, sustained engine failure. Behind Toivonen and Clark, the best of the nineteen finishers was the works DAF 55 of Claude Laurent.

Now it was back to driver championship events and the first of these was the Vltava Rally in Czechoslovakia followed two weeks later by the Polish Rally. On these events, the three main contenders for the title were out to improve their positions. For Zasada, the Czech event ended in disaster when he split his Porsche's fuel tank and it was left to Staepelaere's Escort and Källström's Lancia to battle it out for points. Although the 1.6-litre Fulvia Coupé was homologated from July 1st, Källström was still driving a 1.3 in both of these rallies. Thus he did extraordinarily well to be leading at halfway only to then lose two minutes on a road section with a broken damper. After reeling off fastest time on six of the eight remaining stages, he and Staepelaere finished the rally exactly equal on points. But then stage 11 had to be cancelled thanks to dodgy timing. This was one stage where Staepelaere had not been quicker and thus the rally was his by fifteen seconds. Lampinen in a Saab 96 V4 suffered from engine problems that saw him finish fourth behind a local R8 Gordini while Lindberg's Saab lost a wheel and crashed.

In Poland on home ground, Zasada was determined that nothing should go wrong for him and, on the fast tarmac stages that he knew so well, that is how it turned out. He led from the first test – a circuit race outside the start town of Kraków – and was never under any real pressure finishing three and half minutes ahead of the others. On tarmac, Staepelaere just about had the best of Källström, as had been the case in Czechoslovakia, but at the finish this time there were only ten seconds between them with Staepelaere again having the upper hand. Källström still led the title race but with a reduced margin of only five points from Staepelaere though both were well clear of their nearest rival, Lampinen, who lay some twenty-seven points behind Källström.

The Danube Rally was a manufacturer round but you could have been forgiven for not realising it with none of the major works teams present. It was something of an Austrian fiesta after the only semi-factory car on the event, the Ford Taunus 20 MRS of Staepelaere pulled out while leading when one of his service cars, crewed by his wife, was involved in a road accident. The Porsche of Walter Pöltinger won the rally from the BMW 2002 of Alexander Kaja and the Renault R8 Gordini of Walter Wieltschnig.

The 1000 Lakes did not have to rely on manufacturer status to get entries and almost exactly one hundred cars left the start in Jyväskylä for the annual Finn-fest of rallying. The hot, dry weather that persisted throughout the event meant that the jumps and landings of this unique rally were taken at high speeds and the punishment thus handed out to the cars reduced the field to just thirty-six finishers. First among these was the works Escort of Mikkola, winning for the second year in a row after an untroubled and dominant run. However, his rally was nearly over before it had started when the drive to the Twin Cam's distributor disintegrated as the car was driven to Jyväskylä and an all-night rebuild was

Danube Rally 1969, Walter Pöltinger/Hans Hartinger, Porsche 911T. Rally organisers simply love roads with lots of hairpins as it keeps down the average speed that they have to set and that keeps the national authorities happy. The Romanian variety of hairpin has a mixture of surfaces with gravel repairs intruding on the tarmac. Pöltinger won the rally outright.

necessary before the start. His biggest threat came from the local Porsche 911s of Hans Laine and Leo Kinnunen with Laine holding a small lead at one point, but both suffered from suspension problems and retired shortly after halfway. Behind Mikkola, the Finnish Saabs of Lampinen and Mäkinen toiled in vain though Lampinen did make four fastest times over the last few stages to finish second some five minutes behind Mikkola. In the very dry conditions, the dust kicked up on this event was sufficient that the organisers allowed two-minute gaps between the competing cars.

Though not a championship event thanks to its love affair with prototypes, the Rallye des Alpes did attract a large and varied entry. Porsche sent a single 911T for Larrousse who, while driving a steady rally with the evident aim of finishing, somehow managed to pop it off the road. Ford came with three 1,852-cc-engined Escorts for Andersson, Mikkola and Piot plus a 2.3-litre V6 Escort for Clark but eventually all four ran into varieties of transmission trouble and retired. For Piot, who went the furthest of the Fords, his retirement was also the cruellest as his axle case broke just six hours from the finish when he was lying second. The rally was thus a straight fight between the 1,440 cc Alpines and their 1,598 cc Lancia rivals. At the finish, the first three places went to the Alpines of Vinatier, Andruet and Lusenius though, but for a couple of Lancia problems, that might have looked very different. Trautmann's Fulvia had an oil filter unscrew and at one service point Källström's car was fitted with standard brake pads so that both lost time on the road and yet they finished within five minutes of the second and third placed Alpines.

One week after this came the next manufacturer event. This went under the name of the Deutschland Rally though it was in fact the Baltic Rally that started in Copenhagen and had a route that lay through Sweden, Denmark and Germany. From the start, the fight for victory raged between Helmut Bein's BMW 2002 TI and a private Porsche but when the Porsche went off the road and Bein had a lengthy chat with the Danish police – after which he blew up his engine on the motorway trying to get back on time – the way was left clear for Willy Jensen to win in his BMW 2002 TI ahead of a private 1,300 cc Ford Escort driven by Jochi Kleint. This turned out to be a very important result for Ford since Kleint scored ten points and thus ensured that they would win the title at the end of the year.

It was an Alpine victory on the Three Cities Rally in October and here the Alpines were restricted to using their 1.3-litre engines in Group 3 as there was no prototype class. Three such cars were entered for Vinatier, Jean-Luc Thérier and Walter Roser, the Austrian who had faithfully campaigned an R8 Gordini in previous years. There was also Pöltinger's Danube-winning Porsche, a host of BMWs, the works Wartburg team and an unusual entry from Ford of a Zodiac Mk4 for Clark. The winner should have been Vinatier had it not been for a misunderstanding on delay time allowed between the two gravel stages in Austria where the Frenchman got penalised two extra minutes thus gifting the win to Roser. The leader going into Hungary had been Thérier but he left the road on the first of three stages and was not able to continue. Roser and Vinatier thus headed the field home with Vinatier initially proclaimed the winner. When the organisers dredged up the two-minute penalty and the situation in the classification reversed, the Alpine team – including Roser – showed their displeasure by walking out of the prize giving. The ungainly Zodiac made it to the finish, winning its class and finishing sixteenth overall.

The championship for manufacturers was now over with just five events of which only the best three scores could count. On that basis, Ford won by two points from Porsche with BMW third just one point behind the Stuttgart marque.

The focus of attention now swung to Spain and the next driver round where Källström and Staepelaere were due to go head-to-head again. Since the homologation of their 1.6-litre Fulvia Coupé in July, Lancia's fortunes had been on the up. They had won the 84 hours at the Nürburgring with Källström partnered by Fall and Sergio Barbasio while, just a week earlier, Fall had won the TAP Rally in Portugal for them. Except that he did not as he had been disqualified after the finish for carrying an additional passenger – his wife had joined him and Henry Liddon in the car for the last few yards up to the finish ramp.

Lucky: Jochi Kleint won the Championship for Ford by finishing second on the German Rally in a private Escort 1300.

Unlucky: Jean Vinatier was robbed of victory by a quirk of the timing on the Austrian stages of the Three Cities Rally.

Three Cities Rally 1969, Walter Roser (behind the wheel)/Leopold Mayer, Alpine Renault A110 1300.

Rallye des Alpes 1969, Jean Vinatier/Jean-François Jacob, Alpine Renault A110 1440.

Three Cities Rally 1969, Walter Roser/Leopold Mayer, Alpine Renault A110 1300. During 1969, the Alpine A110 began to prove that it was not just a performer on tarmac but could handle rough gravel roads as well.

The Spanish Rally was important since Källström had a slender five point lead in the championship with two events left. It was a weak position since he had only one victory to Staepelaere's two and had scored in five events already while Staepelaere had only scored in four. Thus Lancia did not need to have the drama of all its service vans, tyres and spares stuck in customs at Barcelona. The rally car and a chase car at least were released and reached Madrid on time but only on gravel tyres – and the first test was on Jarama race circuit. Finally, ten racing tyres in the company of Henry Liddon made their way in first class seats on Iberian Airways to allow Källström to tackle the Jarama test. But there was also a worry for both title chasers that there might not be enough starters in the rally to give full points. The organisers did their best so that there was the bizarre sight of practice cars and even local taxis doing the first test to bring the number of starters up to the forty-two required.

On only the second special stage, Källström punctured one of his racing tyres and, in stopping to change it, lost four minutes to Staepelaere. Now he needed fast times on the gravel stages to get back in front and, by halfway, his deficit to Staepelaere was down to 1 min 40 sec. Lancia lost Alcide Paganelli on his second major accident of the rally which meant that, with Raffaele Pinto still running and their full complement of service cars now present, they were able to give Källström the best tyres for each stage. He rewarded them by taking 45 seconds off the Escort on just one stage and at the finish, despite Staepelaere doing fastest time on the final Jarama test, Källström had won by 1 min 20 sec and kept himself in the lead of the championship with 54 points to Staepelaere's 51 points.

The final round was the RAC Rally where, rather sadly, the final confrontation between the two contenders did not come off when the Belgian decided not to start. It was a classic RAC with snow and ice making things difficult right through Yorkshire, into Scotland and then down to Wales. The man who revelled in these conditions was Waldegård with a Swedish Porsche 911 who led the rally from the start though the ultimate winner, Källström, was never more than a few minutes behind. On the tricky north Wales stages, the gap between them began to close and, when he went to respond, Waldegård slid off the road and spent 24 minutes getting back on to eventually finish twelfth.

This was a superb opportunity for front wheel drive cars to show their pace and it was a quartet of Saab 96 V4s that chased Källström home with Fall in another works Lancia getting in amongst them to finish third behind Orrenius. Indeed, Lancia's only sorrow was to lose Munari with a broken drive shaft in the Scottish borders. Staepelaere was probably wise to stay at home if he knew the conditions would be like this for, of the works Ford Escorts, Mikkola crashed in Yorkshire while Andersson and Clark found rear-wheel drive a handful in the snow. However once they got to snow-free stages in south Wales and the West Country, they set all the fastest times and rose to finish fourth and sixth respectively. Aaltonen had made another change of works team and drove a Datsun 1600 SSS into eighth place and, together with Roy Fidler and Jack Simonian driving similar cars, Datsun won the Manufacturer Team Prize.

Thus the 1969 season ended with a worthy champion driver, the quiet Swede, Harry Källström. The CSI had already made it known what lay ahead for 1970. They had been lambasted by the car manufacturers during the past year and had decided that the star feature of the 'FIA Rally Show' for the future was going to be a Championship for Constructors. Was the time of experiment now over?

Three Cities Rally 1969, Roger Clark/Jim Porter, Ford Zodiac Mk IV. Ford got British Vita Racing to prepare this 3-litre V6 saloon as an experiment to see if it was suitable for the 1970 World Cup Rally. Clark won his class but did not vote for its use on London-Mexico!

RAC Rally 1969. Winning the British round of the European Rally Championship was the icing on the cake for Lancia since Harry Källström (on L) and Gunnar Häggbom had become European Champions at the start of the rally. It was all to the evident delight of team manager, Cesare Fiorio (on R).

RAC Rally 1969. The car is the Saab 96 V4 of Stig Blomqvist. On this occasion, he was navigated by Scotsman, Ian Muir. After an excursion in Kielder Forest that damaged the car, they were forced to retire before entering Scotland. Here the Saab mechanics work to try and fix it under the watchful eye of Erik Carlsson.

RAC Rally 1969, Björn Waldegård/Lars Helmer, Porsche 911L. After leading for seventy-five per cent of the rally in this Swedish-prepared Porsche, Waldegård spent almost half an hour off the road in Wales and finally finished twelfth overall but still managed to win his class.

Champions **1969**

Harry Källström was the Driver champion.

Ford GB was the Constructor champion.

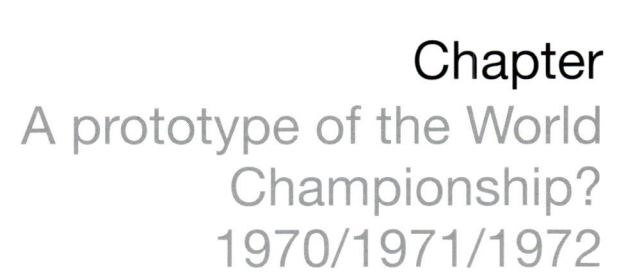

Chapter 07
A prototype of the World Championship?
1970/1971/1972

Chapter 07
A prototype of the World Championship?

1970

The plan of the Commission Sportive Internationale (CSI) for 1970 was to have a championship for manufacturers based on just eight events ranging from the Monte Carlo Rally through to the RAC Rally with many familiar events but also including the East African Safari. Only homologated cars from Groups 1 to 4 were allowed to compete, the route had to be of at least 3,000 km (1,860 miles), and there had to be a minimum of fifty starters for the points to count. Its full name was the International Rally Championship for Makes that we will shorten to IRCM. The European Rally Championship (ERC) was now solely for drivers and comprised no fewer than twenty-two rallies, again with some familiar names like the Tulip, Poland, 1000 Lakes, Danube and Spain plus others new to championship status. These latter included the Tour de Corse and the Tour de France Automobile. Biggest surprise of all was that all these events could include cars from Groups 1 to 6 though to allow cars of Groups 5 and 6 was not mandatory.

The car manufacturers may have been happy with all this, but it did seem to many people that the general public had a greater interest in a winning driver rather than the car he was driving. A contemporary comment was that the 'Man in the Street' would be more likely to recognise the name of World Champion, Jackie Stewart, than the name of the car he had been driving, a Tyrrell. Also the ERC's scoring was complicated with a driver only able to retain his six best scores and, of those, a maximum of three could come from the newly introduced events that had not previously been a part of the ERC. In addition, a driver could only count two scores obtained on rallies held in the same country. This was not an easy task for rally fans or journalists to follow!

As it turned out, the IRCM for 1970 comprised only seven rallies as the Rallye des Alpes ran into major problems in getting road usage permissions and was not held. Porsche got off to a flying start with that man, Björn Waldegård, repeating his Monte victory and following it up a few weeks later by completing a hat-trick on the Swedish Rally. For 1970, the familiar 911 was re-homologated in four versions, all with 2.2-litre engines but the most important of which for rallying was the lightweight 911S in Group 3. Three were entered from Stuttgart for Björn Waldegård, Gérard Larrousse and Åke Andersson. Also with a new homologation was Alpine who had 1.6-litre versions of their familiar A110 entered for Jean-Claude Andruet and Jean Vinatier and with 1.3-litre versions for Jean-Luc Thérier and Jean-Pierre Nicolas. Ford had four Escort TCs for Hannu Mikkola, Roger Clark, Timo Mäkinen – on his first rally as a Ford works driver – and Jean-François Piot while Lancia trumped all that by entering six 1.6-litre Fulvia Coupés for Sandro Munari, Harry Källström, Simo Lampinen, Tony Fall, Sergio Barbasio and Amilcare Ballestrieri.

The weather did not look to favour front-wheel drive as there was not a great deal of snow around and thus on the opening stages the three Porsches, with the occasional interruption from an Alpine, set all the fastest times. However, on the three cols of the Chartreuse with a modicum of snow on each, it was Lampinen who set the pace with only Ballestrieri, Nicolas and Mäkinen within a minute of his record time. Nevertheless, back in Monaco with the Mountain Circuit to come, Waldegård led comfortably from Nicolas with Larrousse, Åke Andersson and Lampinen behind him. Alpine had already lost Andruet who missed a passage control, Vinatier who had crashed and Thérier with a broken gearbox while Munari, Fall and Källström had retired their Lancias with engine problems. Mäkinen, suffering mainly from starting as last car thanks to a late entry and having to pass many slower cars on the stages, had dropped back with problems concerning the centre-lock wheels on his Escort while Mikkola was an early retirement.

The final night saw the stages mainly clear of ice but with perhaps a couple of kilometres of ice and snow at the summits. Choice of tyres was all-important and, by taking the risk of using racers on the first time over the Col de Turini, Waldegård was able to extend his lead. Larrousse fought back and set fastest time on the next five stages but Waldegård was usually right behind him and his victory was thus assured by almost exactly two minutes. One of the principal retirements of the night was that of Piot whose Escort broke its rear axle on the last stage and thus denied Ford three cars at the finish. Porsche, who did achieve that, had forgotten to enter a team and thus missed out on the manufacturer team prize.

Monte Carlo Rally 1970, Björn Waldegård/Lars Helmer, Porsche 911S. For Waldegård this was his second victory and a hat-trick for Porsche.

Monte Carlo Rally 1970, Roger Clark/Jim Porter, Ford Escort Twin Cam. The Escort was not as fast as had ben hoped, but three of them did finish in the top ten.

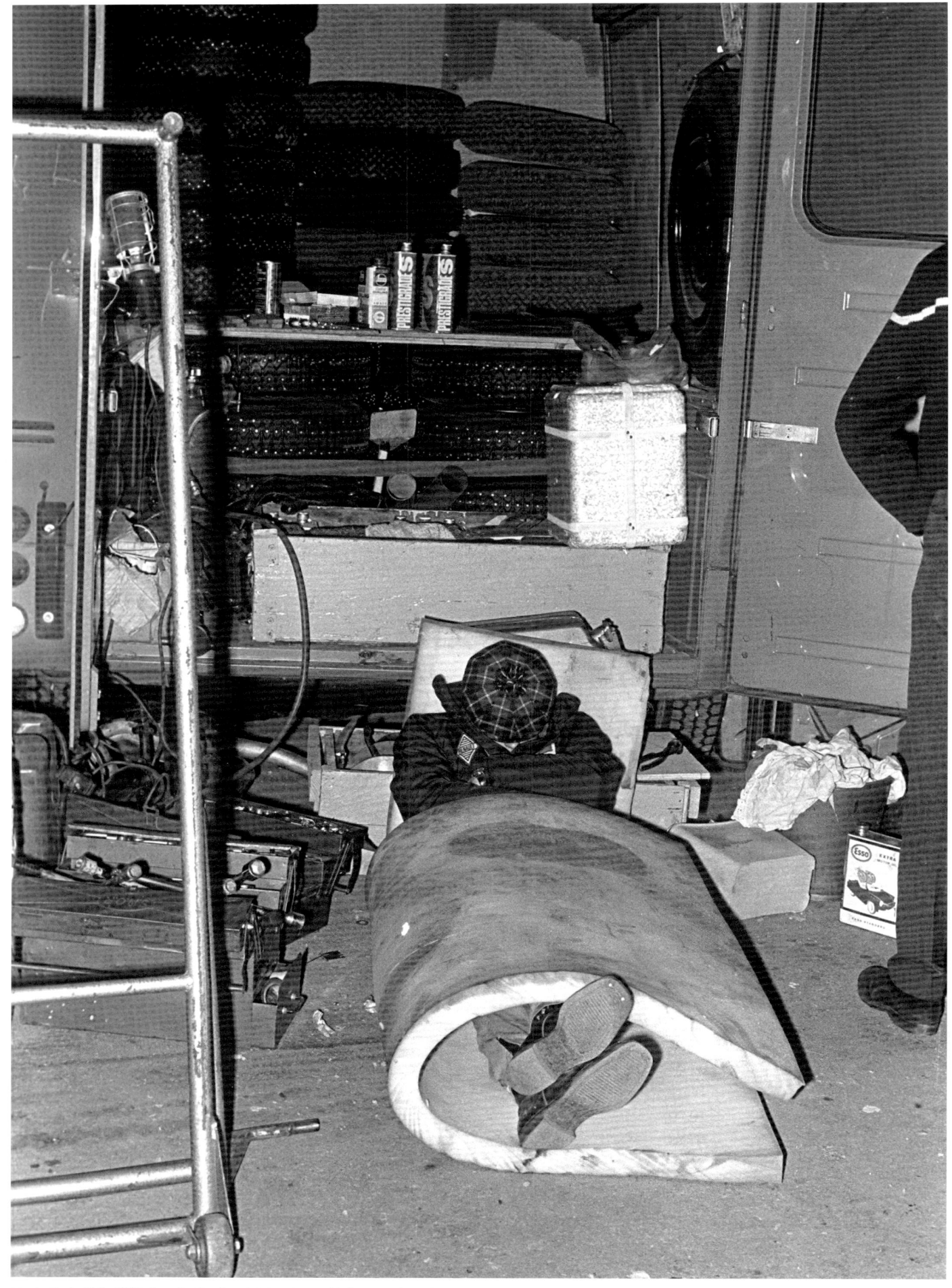

Monte Carlo Rally 1970. Despite the Scottish headgear, this is a member of the French Alpine team taking a break while waiting for the rally cars to pass his service point for the second time.

One way to appreciate the view! Practice days were lengthy affairs in those days and there was time for sightseeing. This is Simo Lampinen during 1970 Monte recce on the St Jean-en-Royans to Cime du Mas stage.

There was plenty of snow on the Swedish Rally, the second round of the IRCM and there was a familiar sound to the designation of the winner: Waldegård in a Porsche 911S. Quite simply, he led from start to finish and, once Håkan Lindberg fell away with transmission failure in a fuel-injected Saab 96 V4 and Källström's Lancia had its differential fail, Waldegård could live with a dodgy gear-change and a slide into a log pile. The rest simply could not keep up and Lancia lost Munari and Lampinen off the road in snow banks while both works Escorts of Mäkinen and Mikkola retired with broken sumps. Alpine lost both 1.6-litre A110s, Vinatier with an accident and Jorma Lusenius with a broken clutch, but their third-placed man from the Monte, Nicolas, again in a 1.3-litre car, kept seventh place until his engine broke just before the finish.

Thus it was the remaining Saabs and a clutch of locally prepared Opel Rallye Kadetts that kept up the chase with second place finally going to one of the Saab 'Junior' team, Stig Blomqvist, after Tom Trana had gone out with a dropped valve and Carl Orrenius with a seized piston. The Swedish Opel contingent that had been so prominent in chasing championships outside Sweden in the late 1960s showed that they had lost none of their verve. Anders Kulläng was the leader of this gang until he had a puncture and lost five minutes changing the wheel so that he was the third Kadett at the finish in seventh place, three down on his 1969 result. Only thirty-one cars finished from 121 starters and the only manufacturer team to finish intact and thus win the prize were three Triumph 2.5 PIs prepared and driven by Swedes.

Swedish Rally 1970. This is one of the three Swedish-prepared Group Triumph 2.5 PIs that finished 1-2-3 in class and won the manufacturer team prize.

At the same time as the Swedish, the draw took place for starting numbers on the next major marathon rally, the 1970 World Cup (London to Mexico). The British Leyland Motor Corporation (BLMC) competition department at Abingdon was making an entry here with Triumph 2.5 PIs and had already run single cars on the 1969 Austrian Alpine, Scottish and RAC rallies so they were naturally pleased with the Swedish result. The Daily Mirror, a major UK newspaper, was sponsoring the World Cup Rally and thus they were probably not too pleased when the car that drew the coveted number one was a Triumph 2.5 PI supported by Abingdon and co-driven by a reporter from their rival, the Daily Express. In addition to BLMC, major works teams due to start the World Cup on April, 19th included Ford and Citroën.

In Italy, politics are never far beneath the surface of anything. The Sestriere Rally, last held as a championship rally in 1959, was very much in the fiefdom of Fiat and when that company was starting to have an increased visibility in international rallying – all unofficial of course even though the Fiats entered on the Monte Carlo all bore Turin number plates – it felt it would be nice to have a major rally based in Turin. Hence the Sanremo got a large injection of lire to join with the revived Sestriere to produce the Rallye d'Italia. It was to be memorable for more than just the new format that saw the start remaining in Sanremo, the halfway halt in Turin and the finish in Sestriere. It will always be known as the rally with the 'Sabotage Scandal'.

Quite simply, three of the five works Lancias entered were out before the start of the second special stage with identical problems caused by various bits of rag, rubber and other foreign bodies in their fuel tanks, fuel filters and carburettors. These were the cars of Lampinen, Barbasio and Ballestrieri so that only Källström and Munari were left to fly the Lancia flag. With fresh snow and slush on the stages, it was a major advantage to be starting further down the field and so it proved for Thérier in one of the factory Alpines. After just one stage and one tight road section, he was leading Lindberg's Saab by two minutes and had extended that to nearly six minutes by the halfway point, though now it was Källström who had risen to lie

Swedish Rally 1970, Björn Waldegård/Lars Helmer, Porsche 911S. The scrutineer checks the hardware while a helper puts on the organiser's advertising.

Swedish Rally 1970. For the third year in a row, Waldegård and Helmer hold aloft the spoils of victory at the finish in Karlstad.

Sanremo-Sestriere Rally 1970, Jean-Luc Thérier/Marcel Callewaert, Alpine Renault A110. At the finish in Sestriere, Cesare Fiorio of Lancia (in white coat) talks to the winner, Thérier.

second. Munari was out with an oil filter that had unscrewed and, with dozens of crews excluded due to being out of time when a car crashed on Monte Ceppo and blocked the road, there were only twenty-two cars still running in Turin.

The second half was plagued with punctures – all from bright shiny nails – and a confrontation with some of the crews that had been put out at Monte Ceppo who blocked another road with a felled tree and caused two stages to be cancelled. With all this going on, there were also individual disasters such as Nicolas – once again in 1.3-litre A110 – who had his differential break and Lindberg who broke an engine mount on his Saab. In the ski resort of Sestriere, there was plenty to talk about but only fifteen finishers.

Now came the big newcomer to the championship, the East African Safari Rally. First run in 1953, this had now grown to a major international event with lots of manufacturer interest particularly from the Japanese who were conscious of the sales potential for their cars in Africa as a whole. The previous year, it had been won by a Ford Taunus 20 MRS driven by Robin Hillyar but in 1970, its date was a mere three weeks before the start of the World Cup so that European interest was muted. Ford Germany returned this time with three fuel-injected Capri 2300s to be driven by Hillyar, Rauno Aaltonen and Dieter Glemser, all under the direction of Jochen Neerpasch. Matched against them were three Lancia Fulvias driven by Munari, Lampinen and Källström and a lone Porsche 911S loaned to Sobieslaw Zasada by the Porsche factory. Peugeot, winners in the past, had locally entered 504s for past winner, Nick Nowicki, and Mike Armstrong. For a while it looked as if Peugeot would have to miss the services of Bert Shankland since he was an adopted Tanzanian. The start and finish were in Kampala – the capital city of Uganda – and the Tanzanian government would not let him take part as they were in a dispute with Uganda. There was an eleventh-hour change of mind but it meant that Shankland had to start as almost the last car on an event where to get a good starting number is seen as highly desirable. Added to this, their car was a Group 1 504 injection but, probably so annoyed at the hand fate had dealt him, Shankland drove the rally of his life and finished third overall.

In the event, all three Capris and all three Fulvias retired though Aaltonen did lead from Munari in the early sections before succumbing with a broken oil cooler. Poor Munari was very badly served as he had fought his way to second place down on the coast at Mombasa where he was informed that he was going to be excluded for checking in too early on too many occasions in the first part of the rally. An appeal was promptly lodged and he continued. On the way back to Kampala, he caught and passed the then leader, Zasada, but in rain, slid wide on tarmac and collected a bridge parapet that put the Fulvia out and himself, after hours sheltering from the rain, in hospital with pneumonia.

And Zasada did not last long since his car was fitted with a small sump-guard and magnesium alloy sump so that during the Ugandan loop, he retired with oil pouring out through a crack. So who was left to take the honours on this important rally? The answer was a horde of Datsun 1600 SSSs of which the best were driven by Edgar Herrmann, the ex-patriate German hotelier from Malindi, and Joginder Singh, a double winner of the Safari in VW and Volvo. Of the ninety-two starters, only nineteen cars finished and six of these were 1600 SSSs. Indeed if further proof of the little car's ability was needed, after Aaltonen's retirement, the leader for quite some time was Jack Simonian in another 1600 SSS. Incidentally, both Herrmann and Zasada got back to Europe in time to start the World Cup Rally, Herrmann in a Mercedes 280SE and Zasada in one of the seven works Ford Escorts fitted with 1.8-litre pushrod engines.

The next IRCM event was the Austrian Alpine and this was held while the rally world watched Ford, Triumph and Citroën battling for victory on the World Cup as they made their way northwards through the Andes. Thus the Ford contingent in Austria comprised those people not involved in the World Cup and two Escorts were entered for Ove Andersson and Piot. Ranged against them were two Stuttgart Porsche 911Ss driven by Waldegård and Åke Andersson, two Saabs driven by Lindberg and Orrenius and two Lancia Fulvias driven by Lampinen and Källström. There was a team of Austrian Bosch Racing Porsche 914/6s entered of which one went out with an oil leak while Günther Janger in another one was unfortunate enough to hit a post-bus and also retire. But the award for earliest retirement had to go to Thérier in an Alpine A110 whose gearbox failed after three kilometres of the first stage. This rally was not at all kind to Alpine as Bernard Darniche was delayed when fellow A110 driver, Walter Roser, rolled and blocked the road on the third stage.

Safari Rally 1970. The prize giving in Kampala, capital of Uganda, was al-fresco. Here the winner, Edgar Herrmann, leads his team-mates with the second place man, Joginder Singh, close behind him while Jamal Din who finished fourth is to the right of Herrmann. Between them, they won the team prize for Datsun.

Safari Rally 1970. One of the three Ford Germany Capris photographed in a pre-rally shoot. This was the car of Dieter Glemser/Klaus Kaiser. Despite the team from Köln winning in 1969 with their 20MRS saloon, all three V6 Capris were destined to retire.

The two Swedish-driven Porsches were easily fastest but Waldegård had to continue alone after Andersson retired with a bent engine valve. His Ford namesake was also out quite early with his Escort's engine cooked after a thermostat seized shut while Lampinen had his Fulvia's chassis break up and retired. At halfway, Waldegård led by a good margin from Lindberg's Saab 96 V4 – despite its engine making noises associated with a faulty piston ring – ahead of Piot's Escort and Källström's Lancia. Shortly after the re-start, Källström broke an oil pipe and lost time getting it fixed so that the best he could do was to finish ninth while Orrenius broke a drive shaft too far away from service to be reached in time to continue. Thus the rally was Waldegård's and, with three outright victories from five events and only two rounds left, it seemed as if the IRCM title was as good as won before mid-summer. But in the end it proved not to be the walk-over that everyone had expected.

It was easy to detect that the manufacturers had not been captivated by a championship that they themselves had lobbied to create as, just a week before the Austrian Alpine, Citroën and Renault had taken their teams to the Rallye du Maroc. On this 'European' African rally, Citroën prevailed with their DS21s of which the leading pair was driven by Bob Neyret (Group 5 prototype) and Bernard Consten (Group 1). Renault – not Alpine – had turned up with prototype R12 Gordinis for Vinatier, Thérier and Nicolas all of whom spent time within the top three before retiring, mainly with suspension failures. But Renault's cause was well served by a team of Moroccan R16 TSs that contrived to finish in fourth, fifth, sixth and seventh places overall. At the same time as Morocco, Lancia had a Fulvia in the ERC Tulip Rally for Sergio Barbasio who looked to be a certain winner until he took a wrong turning before the last test at the circuit of Zolder. As a consequence, he was late and thus dropped back to third behind the private BMW 2002 TI of Cees van Grieken and the GM France Opel Kadett of Jean Ragnotti.

Meanwhile in Mexico, Ford could celebrate the achievement of winning the World Cup marathon with the pushrod 1,850 cc Escort of Hannu Mikkola and Gunnar Palm. Both they and BLMC had entered large teams and the first five places were split between the Escorts and the Triumph 2.5 PIs with Brian Culcheth/Johnstone Syer second and Paddy Hopkirk/Tony Nash/Neville Johnstone fourth, the latter sandwiched between the Escorts of Rauno Aaltonen/Henry Liddon and Timo Mäkinen/Gilbert Staepelaere. Only twenty-three cars finished the event from over one hundred starters and the best non-Ford or Triumph was the Citroën DS21 of Patrick Vanson. The total distance covered was about 16,000 miles (25,750 km) in Europe, South and Central America.

◀ Austrian Alpenfahrt 1970. Before the start, the eventual winner, Björn Waldegård looks quietly confident as he leans on his works Porsche 911S.

▶ World Cup Rally 1970. "All cars on deck, please !" The need to by-pass the Darién Gap meant that the London to Mexico rally cars had to be transported for a second time by sea, this time from Buenaventura in Colombia to Panama City.

46
FORTIS
SWISS WATCHES
46
98
XJB 302H
GB
26
TRIO PACKING LTD
CRANHAM TRANSPORT
26
Daily Mirror
World Cup Rally
GB

Next, and the penultimate, IRCM event was the Acropolis Rally held at the end of May in weather that was weirdly unlike a Greek summer with rain making an appearance and turning the tarmac roads that were used into skating rinks. In other respects too, it was not a classic Acropolis with much distance and little stage action. The hot favourites before the start were the two works Porsche 911Ss of Waldegård and Åke Andersson but both retired with broken engines, though Andersson had been lying second at the halfway point. The man who was leading most of the way, despite a spin on the very first stage, was Thérier whose nimble Alpine was able to make best use of its low weight and Michelin racing tyres on the slippery tarmac stages. Ford's representatives were identical to those in Austria and it was Ove Andersson's Escort that emerged as the strongest challenger to the Alpines. He was able to hold off Vinatier's A110 to hold second place for some time. However, the lack of gravel stages plus the onset of more rain towards the finish took away any advantage the Escort might otherwise have had and Vinatier made it an Alpine 1-2 by just two seconds. The Alpine of Nicolas could easily have displaced both Escorts and made it a 1-2-3 but he lost over half an hour of road penalty having his starter motor changed in the Peloponnese and had to be content with sixth overall. Just behind him came Håkan Lindberg now driving a Fiat 125S and who was part of what was becoming a more overtly Fiat works team with every passing event.

Between the Acropolis and the final round at the RAC Rally in November, the IRCM had a break of more than five months. This dissipated nearly all interest in the newly-formed championship. But at least there was action in the European Championship.

In June came the Geneva Rally, now one of the leading lights of the ERC and this event, ninety per cent of which was held in France, saw the third ERC win of the year for Jean-Claude Andruet's Alpine A110. You may remember the rule that said that a driver might only count two results obtained in the same country. Well, Andruet won the Lyon-Charbonnières and the Geneva that did not count as 'French' events since they started outside France and were organised by clubs based in Germany and Switzerland respectively plus the Rallye de Lorraine that was totally French. He added points from the Tour de Corse at the end of the year and, with his two results from behind the Iron Curtain, was able to win the ERC. Indeed, Alpine domination on the Geneva Rally was total with the little blue cars finishing 1-2-3 with Nicolas second and a private car driven by Jean-Luc Maurin third with Claude Haldi fourth in a Porsche 911S. Life might have been harder for the Alpines had Piot not been involved in a road accident with his Escort three hours before the start while the semi-works French Porsche 911Ss of Claude Ballot-Lena and Guy Chasseuil were withdrawn since there had been insufficient time to do a reconnaissance after their successful run to sixth place and GT victory at Le Mans in a Porsche 14/6.

Still within the ERC, the Polish Rally in July was once again treated to heavy rain and fog while flooding caused the last 300 kilometres of the event to be cancelled. Initially the winner was announced as Zasada in his Porsche but Andruet successfully protested that he had been penalised for delay in a section that was later removed from the results. Once this had been corrected, Andruet emerged as the victor ahead of Zasada and Staepelaere in his Escort. However, both Andruet and Staepelaere took home ten points as there were insufficient starters in Andruet's Group for him to score the usual maximum and he had to be content with 4 (first overall) + 6 (first in group) = 10 while Staepelaere took 1 (third overall) + 9 (first in group) = 10.

The Danube Rally later in July used a higher proportion of high-speed tarmac stages as the bad weather prevented them from using many of their normal gravel sections. Both Andruet and Staepelaere came straight from Poland to compete and, though they were initially holding the first two places, the Escort ruptured its radiator and then the Alpine its sump. Janger then took the lead in a Porsche Salzburg 911S and at the finish had a comfortable lead over Carl Christian Schindler in a 914/6 also entered by Porsche Salzburg. Tony Fall was driving a private Escort but had all kinds of problems including a shortage of tyres and a broken suspension so it was left to that most unusual of combinations, an Englishman driving an Alpine A110 – Nigel Hollier – to take third place overall.

August may have lost its IRCM round, the Rallye des Alpes, but it still had a star event in the 1000 Lakes Rally, cruelly condemned for three years to ERC status. Nevertheless there were only two mainstream manufacturer teams present, namely Ford and Lancia, but various Finnish importer teams such as Saab, Sunbeam, Volvo, Renault and Opel compensated for this. Among the six drivers entered in Rallye Kadetts was a certain Markku Alén making his second 1000 Lakes appearance. Mikkola had drawn start number 13 and for a while it looked as if this might not be a good omen as his Escort refused to run on more than three cylinders, but this situation did not last long and he was soon in a massive scrap for the lead with team-mate, Mäkinen. By halfway, he was ahead of Mäkinen by a small margin that became a bigger one when Mäkinen jumped his Escort, the throttle link came off and he lost two minutes fixing it. This also elevated Lampinen to second place behind Mikkola and it

Geneva Rally 1970, Achim Warmbold/Wulf Biebinger, Opel Kadett 1.9 Rallye.

Geneva Rally 1970, Jean-Claude Andruet/Michèle Veron, Alpine Renault A110 1600.

Danube Rally 1970. An Alpine mechanic tops up the A110 of Jean-Claude Andruet/Michèle Veron during a pause in the action. This was one of Andruet's least successful outings in the ECR of 1970 since he retired with a cracked engine sump.

looked as if Lancia might well take the second step on the podium until Lampinen slid off the road, bending wishbones and shattering wheels. The Lancia mechanics fixed things but he had to be content with third.

One of several additions to the ERC for 1970 was the TAP Rally in Portugal. It had attracted a good entry in 1969 and this was repeated again when several works teams sent entries and many works drivers turned up in loaned cars. These included Waldegård in a Porsche 911S, Ove Andersson in an Alpine A110 and Tony Fall in an Escort. But the heavy hitters in this contest were Lancia with cars for Lampinen and Munari and Ford with cars for Clark and Piot. In the end, it turned out to be Lampinen who led from start to finish and mastered the tricky strategy of time control procedure to ensure that he stayed first on the road in the very dusty conditions that prevailed throughout. Second was Munari with Waldegård third. Both works Fords retired, Clark with a broken valve in the engine and Piot with a broken axle but Fall ran second to Lampinen most of the way until his Escort broke both rear springs and stopped with the propeller-shaft touching the ground.

Lampinen went on to win the 1000 Minutes Rally in Austria despite having to drive three night stages without a functioning alternator. Janger was second in a Porsche 911S ahead of Källström in another works Lancia. But these late points gains made very little difference to the final outcome of the ERC since Andruet had won the Munich–Vienna–Budapest at the beginning of October with Staepelaere second which put them well clear of the rest and Andruet well ahead of Staepelaere. Even when Nicolas won in Spain later that month with Staepelaere finishing sixth and winning Group 2 and then Staepelaere winning the Tour de Belgique, it did not change things greatly. And thus when Andruet finished second on the Tour de Corse to his Alpine team-mate, Bernard Darniche, in early November, the European crown was placed firmly on his head.

All that then remained of 1970 was the final IRCM round, the RAC Rally, on its traditional date in late November. There were two manufacturers in with a chance of the title: Porsche and Alpine. Both sent three cars as did Ford and Lancia while Saab, Opel and Fiat were there as well with the addition of Datsun who came with a team headed by Aaltonen and using their new 240Z sports coupés. The rally started by going north from London to Yorkshire where some snowy stages and more again in Scotland saw a massive amount of retirements with the three works Fords of Mikkola, Clark and Mäkinen, the two quickest Porsches of Waldegård and Åke Andersson, three of the four works Saabs, the 240Zs of Fall and Herrmann, the Lancia of Munari and the Alpine of Ove Andersson all dropping out. In fact, Andersson stalled his Alpine with mud in the radiator and was then hit up the back by Fall's 240Z and the damage was sufficient to cause the Alpine to retire. At halfway in Blackpool, the leaders were Källström and Lampinen for Lancia with Thérier third for Alpine then Ove Eriksson in an Opel Rallye Kadett, Blomqvist in the sole remaining Saab 96 V4 and Nicolas sixth for Alpine.

With so many retirements, it might have been thought that the action was over but it was not so. Soon after entering Wales, Lampinen was in trouble with his gearbox and by Machynlleth was out of all gears but top. He coasted into the town and the service area where he found Källström's Fulvia suffering from big-end bearing failure. It was quickly decided to remove the bearings from Lampinen's car and transpose them into Källström's engine. Thus Källström, still the rally leader, left Machynlleth to drive through five special stages and a 100 mile (160 km) road section in which he had to make up the hour lost by the exchange of parts in service. He arrived at the subsequent time control with seconds to spare but hit a truck that was manoeuvring at the control. The Fulvia had to be taken through the control area on a trolley jack and repaired at the subsequent service from where it proceeded to go to the finish and win.

But there were equal dramas behind concerning the Alpine and Porsche teams. The French still had three A110s in the fight but on the last Welsh sections they lost Nicolas when his car caught fire. The situation was that Thérier was in third place and Andrew Cowan in a semi-works Alpine in sixth place ahead of Gérard Larrousse in the last of the works Porsches. Finishing like this would give Alpine the IRCM title. However, fate struck at Thérier on the very last stage of the rally close to London when he broke a driveshaft and retired. The fact that this stage was subsequently cancelled was a bitter blow for Alpine as this meant that Cowan's fifth place with Larrousse finishing sixth was not enough to displace Porsche from the title.

In late May of 1970, the CSI had published their initial thoughts on the format for both the IRCM and the ERC for 1971. It revealed just how far off the beaten track were the minds of the men making the decisions in the smoke-filled committee rooms of the FIA. It certainly showed that they had no interest in promoting championships that were viable from a competitor's point of view whether that was a professional team or an amateur. The proposal for the IRCM was for thirteen events of which eleven would be in Europe, one in East Africa and one in Canada. Three of the events were to be held in August on virtually the same dates and in other places in the calendar there was clearly insufficient time to recce between two events. The only thing that could be applauded here was the inclusion of the 1000 Lakes and the Tour de Corse in the list. And a point of wonderment was that failing events like the Tulip, Austrian Alpine and the Rallye des Alpes were included.

It would be nice to say that after careful consideration, changes were made that improved things but this was not true. The final IRCM list was down to nine events but the mistakes had multiplied. Canada had gone and so had the Tulip and Danube but they had also axed the 1000 Lakes and Tour de Corse. Morocco had come in and once again eight of these nine events were to be held before July 1st with only the RAC Rally coming in the second half of the year. The ERC stayed much the same with the event count down slightly to twenty-one events including the rejections from the IRCM, the 1000 Lakes and the Tour de Corse.

RAC Rally 1970. Lancia mechanics work feverishly on the Fulvia Coupé 1.6 of Harry Källström and Gunnar Häggbom to repair damage from a road accident that had literally just taken place in a time control area.

RAC Rally 1970, Harry Källström/Gunnar Häggbom, Lancia Fulvia Coupé 1.6. Källström was the winner for the second year in succession but this result was unable to lift Lancia higher than third in the manufacturer contest behind Porsche and Alpine.

RAC Rally 1970. The overall winners pose with their trusty Lancia Fulvia Coupé and a lot of extra weight on the bonnet.

Champions 1970

Jean-Claude Andruet was the Driver champion.

Porsche was the Constructors champion.

1971

So things kicked off for the 1971 season as usual with the Monte Carlo Rally and this edition provided quite a few surprises. For a start there was lots of snow and lots of works entries so that it promised to be an excellent event right from the beginning. It was also a tough one for only thirty of the 171 starters finished the Common Run that on this occasion was a very large loop from Monaco to Chambéry and back to Monaco. By the time the Mountain Circuit was complete, the list of runners was down to twenty-two and only six of those had no road penalty.

The first special stage was at the end of the Concentration Runs as the cars converged on Monaco. Here, fastest man was Ove Andersson in an Alpine A110 and he went into a lead that he was never to lose. It was expected that Alpine's greatest rivals would be Porsche and Lancia but the boys from Stuttgart had been persuaded to run three 914/6s instead of the 911s that had won them the three previous Monte Carlo rallies. These were just not as quick and even the talent of Waldegård could only come home with third place. And actually that was 'equal third' as he and Andruet were level with two stages to go and then matched each other second for second to finish up evens. As for Lancia, their 1970 form did not continue and though Munari was fifth in Monaco at the end of the Common Run, his engine dropped a valve on the first test of the Mountain Circuit. This left Lampinen to show his skill by two fastest times over the Col de Turini and work his way up to sixth at the finish.

From being the 'Chris Amon' of rallying with bad luck lasting almost two full seasons, Ove Andersson now led the Monte but it was not a comfortable lead since his team-mate, Thérier, was not far behind him. Indeed with one stage to go, Andersson's lead was thirty-two seconds and he knew that on the last stage when it had been run as the opening stage of the Mountain Loop, Thérier had beaten him by thirty-two seconds. Andersson later admitted that perhaps his drive over that last stage was not very pretty but it was effective since he beat Thérier by eight seconds and won the rally by forty. One notable result was the fifth place for Aaltonen in the Datsun 240Z. This was a car not much suited to the Alps and developed more with Safari in mind but somehow he wrangled the big sports car through the snows of the Alps to finish as the best front-engined, rear-wheel drive car.

If there had been good snow on the Monte Carlo Rally, then Sweden before the start was so short of frozen water that several stages had to be cancelled due to lack of snow. Then during the rally it snowed so hard that even the snow ploughs could not cope but generally, it was a warm Swedish Rally with no frighteningly low temperatures. Ford had sent Timo Mäkinen with the first of the Group 2 Escort RS1600s that had been homologated in October 1970 while Saab were also parading their 1.8-litre Saab 96 V4 with Stig Blomqvist and Opel had 2.0-litre Kadetts. There were singleton entries of a Porsche 911S for Björn Waldegård and a Lancia Fulvia HF 1600 for Harry Källström while Alpine had sent two A110s for Ove Andersson and Jean-Luc Thérier.

Monte Carlo Rally 1971, Björn Waldegård/Hans Thorselius, Porsche 914/6. The neutral-handling 914 was not as popular with Waldegård as that of his trusty 911 and he struggled to match the pace of the Alpine Renaults. Porsche's choice of car for this rally was a marketing one.

Monte Carlo Rally 1971. Three happy men pose beside the winning Alpine Renault A110. From L to R, David Stone the co-driver, Ove Andersson the driver and Jean Rédélé, founder and owner of the Alpine marque.

▲ Swedish Rally 1971, Lars Nyström/Gunnar Nyström, BMW 2002 TI. In a year when there was a lot of snow, it was a good thing to have a high starting number and let the early numbers clear it away. Nyström proved this conclusively by taking this dealer-supported car to second place overall.

◀ Swedish Rally 1971. After the rally there was an informal press conference with the three top crews. The compere was Erik Carlsson (extreme L) and then on the stage are (L to R) Gunnar Nyström, Lars Nyström, Sverker Benson (event PR manager), Stig Blomqvist, Arne Hertz, Harry Källström and (slightly in the gloom) Gunnar Häggbom.

The heavy snowfall during the first loop caused a high retirement rate as crews struggled to find tyres to cope with these conditions rather than the hard packed ice and snow that they had been expecting. Both Alpines went out, Andersson with a broken engine and Thérier into the scenery while Per Eklund's Saab broke a connecting rod. At halfway, Blomqvist had a magisterial lead of two minutes ahead of Ove Eriksson in a Kadett who was just in front of a battle between Lars Nyström's BMW 2002 TI and Kulläng also in a Kadett. At that point, Waldegård was sixth and Källström tenth but both of them speeded up in the second half where there was less fresh snow. They could not catch the leading Saab and BMW and it looked as if Waldegård would take third and Källström fifth behind Eriksson. That was before penalties from reported speeding offences dropped the Porsche and the Opel back to fourth and fifth overall and gifted Lancia some useful points from third place. It is worth noting that the BMW result was rather unexpected and had much to do with the fact that Nyström was running at number 50. Like that, he had many more cars running through the fresh snow ahead of him compared with, say, Åke Andersson in his Swedish Porsche 911S who was running at number 1. Running first, Andersson was hard pushed to finish sixth overall from a lowly twelfth place at halfway.

The Sanremo-Sestriere (Rallye d'Italia) followed Sweden by less than three weeks and was, in its turn, just over two weeks before round four of the IRCM, the East African Safari Rally. None of this left much time for recceing for a works team like Lancia and it meant that instead of entering a full team in, say, Sweden, some crews would be in Africa preparing for the Safari and then coming back to Sanremo. Recceing for Sanremo was not made any easier by the cold weather. Frozen snow had to be bulldozed out of the way to enable cars to pass over the highest of the minor cols that the rally uses in the mountains between Turin and the Mediterranean coast. All this had been done and the recce completed when, on the night before the start, it again snowed heavily. It meant that quite a lot of the early part of the rally was cancelled and long tedious road sections took the cars to a few short special stages.

The early leaders in this confusing situation were the Alpines of Ove Andersson and Thérier but, as the rally approached the brief halt in Sestriere, a couple of tight road sections on snow saw Lancia tyre technology leapfrog the Fulvia of Munari ahead of Andersson and bring Lampinen up to within ten seconds of the Alpine. For Thérier the news was much worse for he hit a barrier while trying to make up time into the halt after having a long service on an ailing engine. After the re-start, a really snowy section at Bibiana saw Munari go through clean as first car while behind him all kinds of mayhem broke loose with Andersson puncturing and others getting stuck or blocked around him. The result was that Munari now led by four minutes with Lampinen second and Sergio Barbasio in another works Lancia, third. Andersson was fifth behind Darniche in another Alpine.

The re-start order away from the Sanremo halt was in classification order. Andersson was 3 min 12 sec behind Munari on penalties that could be recouped as pure road time (timing on the road was to the second) or be considered as 6 min 24 sec of special stage time, or any combination of the two. Running first on the road over fresh snow on the first stage/difficult road section, Munari lost one minute of stage time and 90 seconds of road time to Andersson who thus at one stroke reduced the Lancia's lead to a minute and half. On the next stage, Lampinen beat both of them so all three were now covered by just 48 seconds. The rally now went back towards Turin and, after a brief halt, Munari retired when his alternator failed and he first lost all his lights and finally the ignition. This put Lampinen in the lead with a 44 second gap to Andersson. But with just two stages remaining, he too was out when a drive shaft broke and the combination of Andersson and Alpine had their second IRCM victory of the year with Amilcare Ballestrieri and Barbasio picking up the other podium spots for Lancia.

Next round was the Safari at the beginning of April and here a new factor took a hand in the form of the American catalogue company, Sears Roebuck. With a recently signed deal for road tyre supply from Michelin, they had been persuaded by a gentleman called Jack Brady to sponsor a number of works rally teams on tough events like Safari and Acropolis. The result was that there was a strong works representation on Safari of European works teams who might not otherwise have considered their budgets adequate to be in Africa. Sears had all of the works Porsches and Saabs plus a works Datsun 240Z and one works Ford Escort Twin Cam all of whom had to run on the Sears branded road tyres. Also in attendance were Lancia, DAF and the local Peugeot importers

With such a high proportion of non-African resident drivers on the start line, everyone felt sure that the moment had come when an overseas driver would finally win the Safari. It was not to be and in fact, the winner in 1971 was the same man as in 1970, Hans Herrmann, except that this time his Datsun was a 240Z. From the early positions, one would not have guessed this as at the end of the first leg in Dar-es-Salaam, Waldegård led with a Porsche by twenty minutes from Mikkola's Escort and Blomqvist's Saab almost another twenty minutes further back. Herrmann was fourth but picked up to second place over the fast, dry and rough roads of western Tanzania so that at Nairobi, he was just thirteen minutes behind the Porsche. The Fords had been in all kinds of problems the worst of which affected Clark who lost five hours having the engine and gearbox removed to replace the latter and weld up the engine supports. Mikkola deliberately lost time on preventative service and was now fourth behind Aaltonen's 240Z.

As the cars headed down into Uganda and the Congo border, Lampinen retired with a broken Fulvia gearbox and three of the four works DAF 55s stopped with transmission bushes burnt out. But the most bizarre thing was that Waldegård came up behind team-mate, Sobieslaw Zasada, in the dust, and requested via the Porsche plane that he be given the road. What happened next is open to debate. Perhaps Zasada had turned his radio off and genuinely did not know that the rally leader was behind him. Anyway, he did not pull over for some time and, when he did, it was to release Waldegård through the dust into a very solid bank. Exit one Porsche 911.

Through a damp Uganda, Aaltonen was in trouble with his rear suspension and Mikkola retired with a broken head gasket so that as the cars crossed back into Kenya for the final sections round Mount Kenya, Herrmann still led but only by eight minutes and when he stopped for service, Shekhar Mehta moved into the lead with his 240Z. Then the heavens opened on the infamous Meru to Embu road where Herrmann struggled through 47 minutes late while Mehta lost 52 – and thus the rally – after being towed out of a particularly slippery patch by a taxi. Thanks to Aaltonen's persistence, Datsun had first, second and seventh places and won the team prize from Peugeot by more than ten hours of penalty. The best-placed Peugeot 504 was that of Bert Shankland who finished third for the second time in a row just one minute ahead of Robin Hillyar, the 1969 winner, now driving a Ford Escort Twin Cam. Zasada was fifth and Vic Preston Junior sixth in another works Escort.

Safari Rally 1971. When the East African Safari Rally comes to town, it fills the high street. Sobieslaw Zasada's Porsche 911 (no 19), Shekhar Mehta's Datsun 240Z (no 31) and Björn Waldegård's Porsche 911 (no 33) head the line up with Robin Hillyar's Escort TC (no 3) behind Mehta.

Safari Rally 1971. Dutch economics to the fore. The DAF team used their recce cars as service cars for the four DAF 55s entered.

Safari Rally 1971, Edgar Hermann/Hans Schuller, Datsun 240Z.

Austrian Alpine 1971. Before the arrival of mobile phones, rally organisers frequently used short wave radios to keep in touch with the marshals and pass a competitor's times back to Rally HQ.

Two weeks after the Safari came the second African event of the IRCM. This was the Rallye du Maroc that received entries from Lancia and Fiat but these were never taken up. Instead, the battle was fought out between Citroën, Alpine and Peugeot with DAF also in attendance. Normally this rally is run on dry, rocky desert pistes but untypical heavy rain made everything damp and floods caused the cancellation of two of the twelve long special stages. The early leader was Nicolas in a private Alpine but he left the road and did sufficient damage to the suspension getting it back on again that it broke very soon afterwards. This left the way clear for Jean Deschazeaux, a Moroccan farmer and a previous winner – known as the Desert Fox – to power his way to victory in a works Citroën SM, the Maserati V6-engined star of Citroën's road-car range. He had a margin of some twenty-five minutes over Guy Chasseuil in a Peugeot 504 who in his turn was over an hour ahead of Bernard Consten in a Citroën DS21. Of the sixty-one starters, just nine were classified as finishers and among them was the DAF 55 of Claude Laurent who took eighth place, almost ten hours of penalty behind the winning Citroën.

Two weeks after the Rallye du Maroc, the IRCM scene shifted from the plains of North Africa to the Austrian Alps where Alpine faced up to two works BMWs, two Fiats and a Lancia. Ove Andersson and Thérier drove the Alpines and it was the latter that went into an early lead until he broke a front wheel hub. The same problem – caused apparently by Michelin's efforts to strengthen their tyres against gravel road punctures – also afflicted Andersson but he was saved from retirement by the team repairing Thérier's car and then sending Thérier as a chase car with a supply of spare hubs. After a mid-stage hub change, Andersson relinquished the lead to Fall, now in a works BMW 2002 TI, who was in a major fight with Paganelli in a Fiat 124 Spider 1600. This was finally resolved when Fall took a wrong turning and lost a few minutes and then Paganelli ran out of fuel and spent some time finding more. Thus it was a very surprised Ove Andersson who found that he had won his third IRCM event. Paganelli was second ahead of Klaus Russling and Georg Fischer, both in Porsche Salzburg VW 1300 Ss, with Fall fifth for BMW.

The Austrian Alpine was a much improved event over some of its past manifestations and showed what could be done in terms of results and good PR. Unlike some occasions in the past, the officials of the Austrian Automobile Club, ÖAMTC, were friendly and helpful while the concentrated route and good choice of stages that they had chosen were definitely competitor-friendly. They had drafted in some help from the Austrian army to provide radio teleprinters so that results arrived almost instantly in the rally HQ from the end of the stage while closed circuit TV cameras relayed some of the special stage action.

In the ten-day gap between the end of the Austrian Alpine and the start of the Acropolis, the Wiesbaden Rally was run as West Germany's contribution to the ERC. It was notable in that Walter Röhrl chalked up his first win here with a Ford Capri 2600 while in second place was Achim Warmbold in an Opel Rallye Kadett. Both these names would become well-known in rallying circles in the future.

▲ Austrian Alpine 1971. One of the Porsche Salzburg service vans that were looking after their entry of VW 1302Ss for Austrian drivers.

▲ Austrian Alpine 1971, Klaus Russling/Franz Mikes, VW 1302S. Although they were not quick enough to beat the Alpine and the Fiat, Porsche Salzburg's Käfers proved ultra-reliable.

◀ Austrian Alpine 1971, Ove Andersson/Arne Hertz, Alpine Renault A110 1600. A very successful pair during 1971 since Andersson won four IRCM rallies for Alpine, two of them with Hertz, while Hertz won two more IRCM rallies alongside Stig Blomqvist in a Saab 96 V4.

With such a short space between IRCM events and since several of the top crews who had been in Austria were also doing the Greek event, there was an unseemly rush down through Yugoslavia to get started on the recce. Källström had been Lancia's man in Austria where he had retired but Lancia had entered a single Fulvia on the Acropolis and this was for Lampinen. Alcide Paganelli had done so well in Austria that Fiat felt he could skip Greece and return to Italy to practice hard for the next Italian championship event, the Quattro Regioni. Thus the only proper works team in Greece was Alpine with Ove Andersson, Thérier and Nicolas while Fiat sent two of their B-team, Lindberg and Pino Ceccato, both in 124 Spiders. There was also a team of Citroën DS21s in the rally but they were not the French works team. They were the Z-Team from Vienna ('Z' coming from 'Zentralsparkasse') with Richard Bochnicek, Franz Wurz, Wolfgang Petzl and Alexander Kaja.

The rally started in sunshine and the three Alpines soon established themselves at the head of the field followed by Lampinen and then Lindberg. A shower of rain on a tarmac stage saw Nicolas off for a few minutes but he did not lose his place in the running order and thus Andersson had to follow in the dust of both Thérier and Nicolas through two stages, though life improved for him when Thérier ran out of petrol and lost eight minutes. Petzl retired with a broken drive shaft and all of the other three Citroëns were in trouble with their front suspensions breaking up and all were out of the rally within hours of reaching central Greece. The rain returned this time in full force for the night stages so that mud and oily tarmac turned the roads into nightmares. Nicolas had found his clutch starting to slip and, with Thérier losing his engine through a bent crankshaft pulley, Andersson now led. But he too found he had a non-operational clutch and, towards the end of the rally, the two leading Alpines were doing 'flying starts' on stages with the co-drivers jumping in at the last moment. Lampinen, in third place, was so far ahead of Ceccato that he was stopping for preventative surgery on his Lancia as the rally returned to Athens. From a modest entry of fifty-nine crews, only nine survived to the finish and, unlike Morocco, these did not include Claude Laurent's private DAF as it had retired with broken engine mounts.

Thus by the first of June, Alpine had already clinched the IRCM title by winning four of the six events so far held. And the amazing thing is that the same driver, Ove Andersson, had won all four events. Had there been a driver championship run concurrently with that of the manufacturers, then he would have been undisputedly the champion. It also seemed as though Alpine were reluctant to acknowledge his status as works driver for they kept up the pretence of his being a sort of semi-private entry who was just borrowing cars from them. In Sanremo, for instance, Andersson drove a white Alpine instead of the normal works colour of blue. Rather sadly, the message of driver popularity with the public – if not the manufacturers – was lost on the CSI who, even when they had created the World Rally Championship for 1973, forgot about drivers until 1979.

Rather as in 1970, the second half of the year was a bit of damp squib. The Rallye des Alpes was run and was a showcase for Alpine who finished first and second with Darniche and Vinatier ahead of Piot's Ford Escort RS1600. But, with so much doubt that it would actually take place, it only received thirty-five entries and thus it fell below the criterium of fifty starters required to have its results count for the IRCM. One nice touch was that because the rally had not been run in 1970, the Automobile Club de Marseille–Provence decided that Vinatier's Coupes won in 1968 and 1969 together with his 1971 Coupe would qualify him for a Coupe d'Or and he thus became only the third man – the other two were Ian Appleyard and Stirling Moss – to be awarded that coveted trophy for three consecutive Coupes. For Vinatier, there was also the bizarre situation of beating the official Ford France entry and then, just a few days later, being appointed the new Director of Ford France's competition activities.

There were five works Alpines at the start of the Rallye des Alpes matched against Trautmann's lone Lancia Fulvia and Piot's Escort. Laurent rolled his DAF 55 out of the event on the first stage while retirements for the Thérier and Andersson Alpines soon followed with both leaving the road after breakages of rear hubs. Evidently the

▲ Acropolis Rally 1971, Ove Andersson/Arne Hertz, Alpine Renault A110 1600.

◀ Acropolis Rally 1971. The end-of-rally race at Tatoi Airfield was good fun for all concerned and usually had little effect on the results. Here Simo Lampinen's Lancia Fulvia Coupé chases the Alpine Renault A110 1600 of Jean-Pierre Nicolas.

Sometimes the quickest way is not always the best. On the Acropolis Rally of 1971, the Turkish-entered BMW 2002 TI of Aytaç Kot and Necat Sengur came off the road – which can just be seen in the middle of the photo at the bottom left – and it was evidently suggested to them that to push it out forwards was the quickest way to release it. True, but then it became even more stuck in the river bed ! This car did not finish the rally.

going was hard on the Alpine transmissions as Nicolas retired before the end of the first leg when a drive coupling broke. At that point, Darniche led Vinatier by nine minutes with the gap from Vinatier back to Piot a further eleven minutes. Ragnotti lay fourth in an Opel Rallye Kadett but he had an accident towards the end of the second leg and did not continue. With Trautmann now in fourth delayed by punctures, the field was so spread out by the last leg that the cars might almost have been competing on a Safari.

In complete contrast, the same weekend in Belgium, the 12 Hours of Ypres that was not even an ERC event, attracted 113 entries and proved a lively competition with Noél 'Pedro' Vanasche winning in a BMW 2002 TI from Staepelaere in a works prepared Escort RS1600.

There was a large entry too on the 1000 Lakes Rally held in mid-August with 117 crews taking the start. These were predominantly Finnish with the next best-represented countries being the Soviet Union and East Germany with teams of Moskvitch 1500Ms, Wartburg 353s and Trabant P 601s. There were also a few Swedish crews headed by Blomqvist and Eklund in works Saab 96 V4s and it was these that turned the Finns hopes upside down as Blomqvist romped home to win, the first non-Finn to do so since Erik Carlsson in 1957, also in a Saab.

Quickest car in the early stages was the semi-works Escort RS1600 of Mikkola who had but a single service car from Ford (and a few Finnish friends) to look after him. Behind him, a mixed bag of Volvo 142s, Saab 96 V4s and Opel Rallye Kadetts were in the hunt and Markku Alén was driving the fastest of the Volvos. Thanks to the dusty conditions, cars were being run at two-minute intervals so that the relatively unknown Alén with start number 40 was running about an hour and a half behind Mikkola who had start number two. In those days before the mobile phone, the Escort driver was not always aware of what some of his rivals were doing. Thus when he had one stage where he knew that his time was poor, he went flat-out on the next one, jumped too high and flipped the Escort into a large rock. He broke some ribs and was taken to hospital but his co-driver, Gunnar Palm, emerged unscathed.

The situation now was that Seppo Utrainen in a Saab Finland 96 V4 was leading from Alén with Tapio Rainio in an Opel Kadett and Blomqvist in close attendance. Blomqvist now took charge and set a whole string of fastest times to take the lead. He was helped in this by Alén having his Volvo stick in fourth gear for one whole stage while Utrainen retired with a broken petrol pump and Eklund's works Saab was slowed by leaking piston rings that required him to fit new spark plugs for every stage.

The following weekend in the Dolomites, Munari won the San Martino di Castrozza Rally. This was an ERC round but its importance to Lancia was for their national championship where it was very important to prevent the upstart Fiat team from gaining an upper hand. Since Fiat had acquired Lancia in 1969, Lancia's motorsport director, Cesare Fiorio, knew it was important to be seen to win these rallies so that the mother company would not switch all sporting funding to its own nascent team. Thus, while Barbasio picked up the points with a steady run and eventually became Italian champion, Munari or Lampinen (who had won the Quattro Regioni the week after the Acropolis) would appear at these rallies and go for victory to deny any of the Fiat drivers the glory. In addition, Munari was chasing the Mitropa Cup, a German/Austrian/Italian championship that he won by virtue of adding victory on the Bavaria Rally in late September to wins on the Semperit and the San Martino.

The next big rally was also an ERC event, the TAP Rally that, with 133 starters easily eclipsed many of the IRCM rounds. Its popularity was based on two things. Firstly, it was a tough rally that presented a real challenge to come to the finish just as the old Liège–Sofia–Liège had done. Of the 133 that started, just thirteen were still running at the finish. Secondly, it was generous with the help it extended to its entrants with the TAP airline providing a lot of free air tickets. Lancia was back with Munari and Lampinen to see if they could repeat their success of the previous year but now they had works Alpines, Porsches, Saabs, Citroëns, DAFs, Fiats and Datsuns to contend with plus a host of private Escorts from the UK and private Opel Kadetts from Sweden and Germany.

Fastest man out of the starting blocks was Nicolas in the Alpine but Munari kept him in his sights and after the rally passed from tarmac to gravel stages, the Italian went into the lead. Blomqvist had a puncture with his Saab and somehow lost the wheel nuts so that by the time he had sorted things out, he was out of time. Similarly plagued by punctures was the Austrian Z-team with their Citroëns

▲ 1000 Lakes Rally 1971, Stasis Brundza/Gunnar Holm, Moskvitch 1500M-412.

◀ 1000 Lakes Rally 1971, Stig Blomqvist/Arne Hertz, Saab 96 V4.

▶ Rallye des Alpes 1971, Henri Greder/Marie-Madeleine Fouquet, Opel Commodore GS/E.

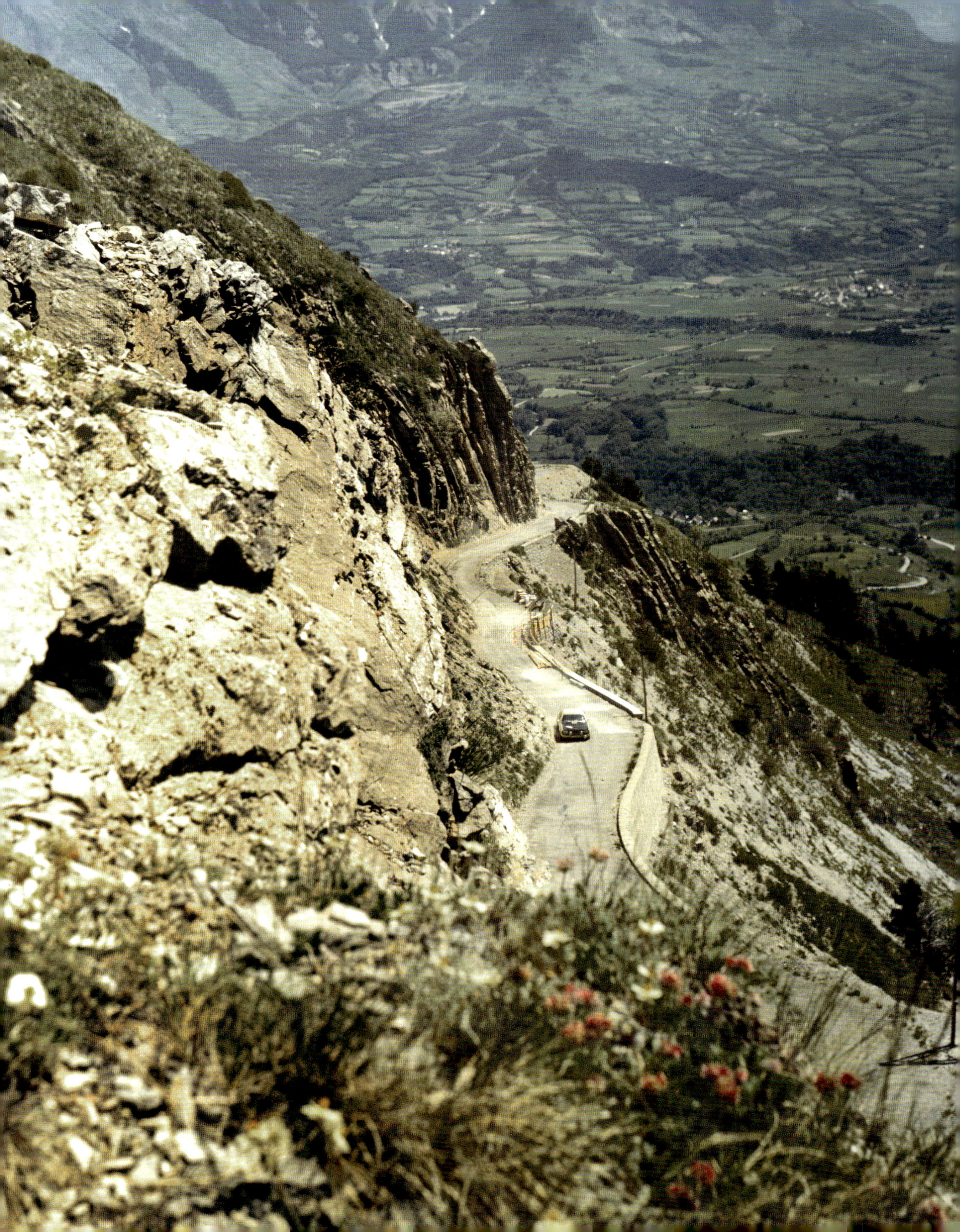

and both Petzl and Walter Lux retired. Soon after, Waldegård was out with broken transmission in his Porsche while Munari retired when the pounding on his sump guard finally broke the sump. For a short while the rally leader was Paganelli in a Fiat 124 Spider with his team-mate, Lindberg, third behind Nicolas but then all three Fiats broke their Panhard rods far from service and retired.

At this point, Nicolas was benefitting immensely from running first on the road with no dust in his face from preceding cars. Behind him was a South African Datsun 1600 SSS (but fitted with an 1.8-litre engine) of Ewold van Bergen. However, even Safari winning Datsuns have their weak points. Fall retired in his works 240Z when he lost a wheel and then Van Bergen retired with broken rear suspension. This left Nicolas and Lampinen far out in front as in third place was now the private Alpine A110 of Bob Neyret, almost fifty minutes behind the Lancia. Of the thirteen cars that made it to the finish, four were out of time and thus not classified and of the nine that remained, three were Opels with Reinhard Hainbach finishing fifth and Gomes Pereira eighth in Kadetts and Henri Greder taking seventh with an Ascona 1.9.

Only one man appeared to be taking the ERC seriously and that was Zasada who, for the majority of the year, drove a BMW 2002 TI borrowed from the factory and set about collecting points for all he was worth. He won the East German Rally and the Polish Rally but crashed in Czechoslovakia. He fought back by scoring good points on events like Semperit and 1000 Minutes in Austria and the Danube in Romania. By October, Munari decided that he had an outside chance of winning the European Rally Championship. Fortune did not favour him on the TAP Rally where Zasada did not start, but Munari did win the 1000 Minutes in Austria where Zasada was fourth while on the Spanish Rally, where Nicolas won in an 1.8-litre Alpine, Zasada was fourth and Munari sixth, both scoring nine points.

With the Tour de Corse not held in 1971 thanks to financial woes, the final round of the European Rally Championship was the Tour de Belgique. This Munari needed to win outright with Zasada scoring no points. In 1970, it had been a tough event with forest-like stages but for 1971, it copied the Tour de France format with a combination of circuit tests and hill climbs. It was a case of 'Gentlemen, choose your weapons' for the finale. Munari opted for an open Abarth 2000 Spider while Zasada chose a race-prepared BMW from Alpina with racing driver, Nick Koob, as his co-driver. On the event, it poured with rain and the Abarth virtually drowned out and retired. The winner was Jean-Marie Jacquemin in an Alpine A110 from Darniche in a similar car with Zasada third in the BMW. The Polish driver also won his class and thus sailed home to win the European championship by fourteen points from Munari.

The final fling of the year was again the last IRCM round, the RAC Rally. With the title already taken by Alpine, it was still an event with a large entry – probably the best of the year – and with no one looking to do anything but try to win outright. With seven works teams plus supported Opels from France, Finland and Sweden, a Swedish Porsche 911 for Waldegård and the Z-team Citroëns, it was going to be a free-for-all. Starting from Harrogate in Yorkshire, the 231 starters were launched immediately into some of the worst snowfalls that England had experienced and, back at the halfway halt in Harrogate after the first Scottish leg, only half the entry was still running. Nine of the scheduled forest special stages were blocked and had been cancelled. It was an event that would not easily be forgotten by anyone who took part.

Predictably, it was Scandinavian drivers who made the best of the conditions and at the halfway point, Blomqvist led for Saab ahead of Mäkinen's Ford Escort RS1600 and the Porsche of Waldegård. But other Scandinavians had a tougher time with Källström sliding off the road for half an hour with his Lancia and Aaltonen breaking a drive shaft on his 240Z, rolling it three stages later and then stopping with a puncture and getting irretrievably stuck. Mikkola bent the rear axle tube on his Escort and dropped out of the top ten before getting it fixed and finally surged back to come fourth ahead of team-mate Mäkinen. Lampinen had a few unexpected problems starting with a broken exhaust and then the much less welcome one in such freezing weather of having the windscreen of the Fulvia pop out in Kielder Forest.

The route through Wales was cold and icy but with far less snow. Blomqvist's Saab held on to its lead and, after Mäkinen suffered gear selector problems in the Escort, he was joined in the top three by his Saab team-mate, Carl Orrenius. Indeed at the finish, Saabs occupied first, third, seventh and tenth places and thus it came as no surprise that they won the manufacturer team prize with ease from Ford and Lancia. In the wintry conditions, non-Scandinavian names in the top twenty of the 104 finishers were to be commended. Amongst these were Munari in ninth place for Lancia, Warmbold in fourteenth place for BMW and East Africans, Herrmann and Mehta driving Datsun 240Zs into seventeenth and nineteenth places respectively.

1000 Minutes Rally 1971, Sandro Munari. A win in Austria lifted Munari's chances of becoming European Champion but a retirement on the final round in Belgium scuppered his chances.

TAP Rally 1971. The Portuguese were generous – and inventive – with their prizes as Jean-Pierre Nicolas discovered when he won for Alpine. The airline's sponsorship meant that team members and journalists benefitted from free travel to Portugal and there were still funds for impressive prizes.

TAP Rally 1971. The Portuguese made extensive use of local facilities to run a rally that covered more than seventy per cent of the entire country. The help in this case is a fire engine with a full complement of firemen who will provide emergency cover for a special stage.

RAC Rally 1971. The combination of lots of snow and the fact that studded tyres were not allowed led to a high retirement rate – 104 finishers from 231 starters. Three crews to fall prey to the conditions were Richard Hudson-Evans/Colin Taylor, Skoda S100L (no 95), Michael Bennett/Eddy Bamford, Ford Capri 3000GT (no 64) and David Childs/John Dymond, Ford Escort TC (no 153). Even the professionals found the going tough. Here Pentti Airikkala/John Taylor, Opel Rallye Kadett (no 48) are ahead of Harry Källström/Gunnar Häggbom, Lancia Fulvia Coupé 1.6 (no 1) between special stages.

TAP Rally 1971, Jean-Pierre Nicolas/Jean Todt, Alpine Renault A110 1800.

RAC Rally 1971, Stig Blomqvist/Arne Hertz, Saab 96 V4. Outright winner of a snowy event, Blomqvist was also capable of keeping up the pace when the conditions were more normal. Particularly when, in the latter part of the rally, he was being hotly pursued by the Porsches and Escorts.

Champions **1971**

Alpine Renault won the 1971 Makes Championship with a total of 36 points all of which were scored by Ove Andersson, seen here winning the Austrian Alpine Rally.

Sobieslaw Zasada won the European driver title.

1972

As far as the major championships were concerned, things stayed much the same for 1972 with ten events planned for the IRCM of which the new arrival was the Press-on-Regardless (PoR) in Michigan, USA. Eventually, only nine counted as the Rallye des Alpes, though nominated, had been held for the last time. This plus the fact that the Austrian Alpine had moved from May to September, the Sanremo had thrown off its partnership with Sestrière and moved into October, the PoR was held in November and the RAC Rally in December all meant that the championship looked much better balanced. For the ERC, twenty-seven events were on the originally published list with additions like the Olympia Rally in Germany and the Yugoslavia Rally while old favourites like the Tulip and Geneva rallies eventually failed to materialise so that by the end of the season, twenty-four events had been run for the championship.

The season opener was, as usual, the Monte Carlo Rally and this did not produce the follow-on victory for Alpine that most people had anticipated despite a works line-up that certainly impressed. The Dieppe firm had Thérier, Darniche, Nicolas, Andruet and Andersson but things did not turn out well for them. To start with on the first two ice-free stages, the semi-works Porsche 911Ss of Waldegård and Larrousse set fastest times and led by about a minute and a half from a chasing bunch of Munari (Lancia Fulvia), Mäkinen (Ford Escort RS1600) plus Thérier and Nicolas. Even Aaltonen's big Datsun 240Z was in there with a chance.

But on arrival in the Ardèche to the west of the Rhône valley, it began to snow. Pure racing tyres had always been used for the long stage over the Col de la Fayolle but now, with snow falling, all kinds of mistakes were made. For instance, only Andersson of the Alpines took studded tyres and the other Alpines together with the two Porsches found it hard to even arrive on time at the subsequent time control on their slicks or plain snow tyres. And the next stage over Burzet was literally a white hell where visibility was down to zero and snowdrifts were forming over the ploughed-out road. In the blink of an eye, the Porsche lead was gone and they also lost time on the long road section after Burzet which they had to drive on their studded tyres fitted for this stage that were now worn out. Munari and Waldegård fared best on Burzet but the only car not to have road penalties from the Ardèche was the Alpine of Darniche. Andersson lost a minute because he had to wait for the tyre change before Burzet when another Alpine was up on the speed jacks in the service point. Munari lost two minutes and thus, back in Monaco with their stage times all roughly compatible, Darniche led from Andersson with Munari third.

On the last night having already lost Thérier to an accident, Alpine also lost Nicolas and Andruet in crashes and then first Andersson and then Darniche retired with broken gearboxes. The only man to salvage any honour for the French firm was Bob Neyret in his private A110 who finished seventh. Ford lost Mäkinen to a broken clutch and a failed alternator on the last night while Piot came home fifth despite losing five minutes on the road sections in the Ardèche. Otherwise, it was a Lancia festival with Munari winning by ten minutes from Larrousse with Fulvias also fourth and sixth with Lampinen and Barbasio while the most remarkable result of all was third place for Aaltonen in the 240Z. Waldegård had retired as the result of an accident on the last stage of the Common Run.

A fortnight later in mid-February, studded tyres were needed again for the Swedish Rally. However, just one day before the rally started, the organisers announced that all cars taking part had to use studs in their tyres that complied with Swedish road regulations. This promptly excluded 84 of the 91 cars scrutineered all of whose tyres complied with international motor sport regulations. Naturally some compromise had to be made and all cars started, but the 'push-through' studs – as opposed to the 'shoot-in' normal variety –used by Pirelli for Lancia were ruled out and thus Lancia had to rely on a limited number of Finnish Hakkapeliitta tyres to furnish their cars. The weather stayed cold throughout with no fresh snowfall so fortunately everyone was moderately happy.

Monte Carlo Rally 1972. Sandro Munari (on R) and Mario Mannucci face the press at Monaco harbour when they arrive victorious from the final nights of the rally.

Monte Carlo Rally 1972, Sandro Munari/Mario Mannucci, Lancia Fulvia Coupé 1.6.

▶ Monte Carlo Rally 1972, Jean-Claude Andruet/Pierre Pagani, Alpine Renault A110 1600.

calberson
elf
CIBIE
6
1972 6 1972
RALLYE MONTE-CARLO
ALPINE
929 HB 76

Swedish Rally 1972. Björn Waldegård and Lars Helmer in their ex-Monte Carlo Porsche 911S are ahead of Stig Blomqvist and Arne Hertz on the trotting track test in Karlstad, but at the end of the rally it was the Saab that had won by a clear margin.

Instead of coming with A110s, as part of their new role as a Renault competition organisation, Alpine turned up with two untried Renault R12 Gordinis for Ove Andersson and Thérier. As an experiment, it was unsuccessful with Thérier retiring with a broken engine and Andersson finishing a lowly fifteenth overall. The real battle for victory was between the Group 2 Saabs of Blomqvist, Orrenius, Eklund and Åke Andersson, the Group 2 Opel Ascona 1.9s of Kulläng and Ove Eriksson, and the Group 3 cars represented by the lone Porsche 911S of Waldegård (the same car that he had used on Monte Carlo) and the Lancia Fulvia 1.6 of Källström.

Right from the start, Blomqvist set seven fastest times in the first ten stages. Hot on his heels was Kulläng's Opel with Källström third despite a clutch problem on one stage. Then just as Källström and Waldegård looked as if they might catch Kulläng, they both spent time off the road on a particularly sinuous stage ploughed out on the snow-covered surface of a frozen lake. The consequence was that Kulläng stayed second and Blomqvist eased even further ahead. And that was the way it remained most of the way to the finish. Behind them, Källström, Eriksson and Waldegård all had minor excursions but then towards the end of the rally, Kulläng's engine started to go sick after he had run for a while with fuel starvation and both Waldegård and Källström got ahead of him.

Interest now centred on the East African Safari and it was at once apparent why Ford had only two Escorts on the Monte Carlo and no presence in Sweden. After their experiences the previous year, they were determined to tame this difficult event using the Escort RS1600 with its sixteen valve, belt-driven camshaft engine that they had twice rejected, once for the London–Mexico World Cup Rally and then again for the 1971 Safari. Their knowledge of long rough-road events had been honed in South America and, with a service organisation that was co-ordinated from the air, they proved unbeatable – and got the first win for an overseas crew, the same Hannu Mikkola and Gunnar Palm who had triumphed in Mexico.

This year, the Safari Rally started in Dar-es-Salaam in Tanzania and despite a few weather worries before the start and some fearsome mud holes in the first section, it stayed dry throughout. This meant that rally cars were arriving at dry riverbeds and other obstacles far too fast. Peugeot lost three of its 504s on the first leg up to Kenya's capital Nairobi with radiators holed by fans and ensuing head gasket failures while Raffaele Pinto simply broke his Fiat 125S by failing to slow for one concrete drift. Ford was not without problems as Timo Mäkinen's car developed an enormous appetite for fan belts while it constantly had McPherson struts coming loose. Indeed, Joginder Singh crashed his Ford Escort when one of his strut tops actually came off. Mäkinen lost more time when a rear wheel came off while Mikkola had to stop and adjust his front track after hitting a drift too hard.

Thus on the first leg up to Nairobi, Edgar Herrmann led in a Datsun 240Z with a gap of twenty minutes to Mikkola with Vic Preston Junior (Ford Escort RS1600), Sobieslaw Zasada (Porsche 911S) and Shekhar Mehta (Datsun 240Z) spread over the next ten minutes. Herrmann had two punctures on the way to Kampala in Uganda and dropped back to fourth while team-mates Mehta and Aaltonen both lost time changing their 240Z's clutches. On the tough leg from Kampala to Nairobi that took in the famous escarpments of Tot and Tambach, both Mikkola and Preston managed to squeeze their Escorts past Zasada and thus ran in clear air with no dust. In just two sections, Mikkola extended his lead over the Porsche by fourteen minutes and continued to ease away despite being 58 minutes late in just one 137 km section as the others were slower still. However, going round Mount Kenya, Mikkola had to stop with a puncture and, since the cars had been closed up at the brief halt at Eldoret, Zasada swept past and managed to pull back to within fifteen minutes of the leader at Nairobi. It was in these escarpment sections that Datsun's debutant 1800 SSS driven by Ove Andersson was stopped for almost three hours sorting out a comprehensive wiring fire.

Safari Rally 1972, Hannu Mikkola/Gunnar Palm, Ford Escort RS1600. After first trying to win the Safari with the Escort TC and burning their fingers, Ford opted for the BDA-engined RS1600 in 1972 and sailed to victory with that elusive win and four Escorts in the top ten finishers.

Safari Rally 1972. Gunnar Palm lifts a glass of bubbly to toast their victory while Hannu Mikkola tries to find something to say for the Voice of Kenya reporter.

Safari Rally 1972. It was not going to be a hat-trick for Edgar Herrmann and Hans Schuller. This time, the best they could do with their Datsun 240Z was to finish fifth overall.

Moroccan Rally 1972, Simo Lampinen/Solve Andreasson, Lancia Fulvia Coupé 1.6. Lancia only entered one car on this rally but, at the finish, Lampinen had been quick and reliable enough to win.

From Nairobi to Dar-es-Salaam, there were more problems for Edgar Herrmann with a broken suspension while both Mäkinen and Aaltonen missed a passage control near Mkomazi and had to go back for it while Andersson was stopped for welding repairs to the 1800 SSS's rear cross-member. Even Zasada ran into trouble, losing first half his exhaust and then going off the road and breaking the windscreen. But Mikkola drove on, seemingly with no problems to collect the champagne. And the result was really good news for Ford's Escorts as Preston was third, Robin Hillyar fourth and Mäkinen eighth so they collected the team prize as well as twenty IRCM points.

The IRCM stayed in Africa for its next round, the Rallye du Maroc, held at the end of April. Citroën turned up with the largest team and the biggest hopes after winning this rally for the previous three years. They had two Group 2 SMs for Waldegård and Aaltonen, a Group 1 SM for Deschazeaux, two Group 2 DS21s for Neyret and Bochnicek, and two Group 1 DS21s for Raymond Ponnelle and Francisco Romãozinho. For Alpine there were three A110s for Thérier, Nicolas and Ove Andersson while Peugeot had four 'unofficial' works 504s from their factory in Sochaux, two Group 2 cars for Mikkola and Chasseuil and two Group 1 cars for Jean Guichet and Fall. Lancia, hoping to show that there was not strength in numbers entered just one Fulvia 1600 for Simo Lampinen and they were eventually proved to be correct. There had been some doubt as to whether Lampinen should take the start as it looked as if there were not going to be enough starters for the rally to count for points. Eventually enough taxis and private cars were found to make up the numbers to fifty-two and Cesare Fiorio gave his manager on the spot, Daniele Audetto, the green light to go ahead with the rally.

Moroccan Rally 1972, Simo Lampinen.

Moroccan Rally 1972, Bob Neyret/Jacques Terramorsi, Citroën DS21. Here the second-placed Citroën crosses the river at Rich. This was a Group 2 version of the big Citroën and not the shortened Group 6 DS21 with which Neyret had won this rally in 1969 and 1970.

Alpines dominated on the first leg to Fez with Nicolas leading from Lampinen, Andersson and Thérier. Once into the longer desert stages, the Citroëns and Peugeots fared better so, at Marrakech, it was Thérier in the lead from Andersson – after Nicolas lost time with a broken hub – followed by Waldegård, Lampinen, Neyret and Mikkola. With just two days left and only five special stages, the rest might have appeared to be easy but the stages south of the Atlas were often hundreds of kilometres long. There was plenty of action and, by way of example, Andersson set fastest time on the longest stage despite having two punctures and being stuck in a dry river bed for five or six minutes. Retirements came thick and fast with three Peugeots dropping out with broken head gaskets while various suspension and radiator problems assailed the Alpines and Citroëns. Just six cars came to the finish and the winner was the lone Lancia of Lampinen that came through practically unscathed.

A month later, it was the turn of the Acropolis Rally and here there were ninety-eight cars on the start line due in part to the involvement of Sears Roebuck with selected entries from Saab, Porsche, Datsun and BMW. Lancia and Fiat stuck with their normal Pirelli tyres as did one of the works BMW 2002 TIs driven by Warmbold. The Saab 96 V4s of Blomqvist and Eklund both retired with transmission failures while the two Ford Escort RS1600s of Mikkola and Hillyar joined them after a halfshaft breakage and an alternator failure respectively. The BMWs went well though the Sears-supplied cars of Aaltonen and Fall did have several punctures on their standard road tyres and Aaltonen finally retired in the Peloponnese with a broken differential. But Warmbold took something of a starring role and would almost certainly have won the rally had he not lost seven minutes road time with a puncture and a recalcitrant jack on the very tight section from Arnea to Stavros. The early leader was Waldegård in a loaned factory Porsche 911S but the air filters on his car proved inadequate to keep out the Greek dust that was being generated on a hot and dry rally. The dust eroded the Porsche piston rings and, after consuming large quantities of oil, it came to a halt during the last night.

Lancia lost Källström with a broken engine but Lampinen took things easy on the many rough and impossible road sections in the north so that he lost eighteen minutes at time controls compared to Lindberg's fifteen minutes. But, since the Lancia was nearly always quicker than Lindberg's Fiat 124 Spider on the special stages, coming to the night halt at Loutraki before crossing to the final sections in the Peloponnese, it appeared on unofficial calculations – the Acropolis organisers were never prompt to issue results – that Lampinen had a comfortable lead on Lindberg. There were suggestions later that Lancia might have been the victims of misinformation from their Turinese colleagues, but whatever the reason, Lampinen took it easy in the Peloponnese and lost the rally to Lindberg by just twenty-nine seconds.

With the halfway point of the year now reached, Lancia had a clear lead in the IRCM with a total of 67 points with Porsche behind them with 45 points. Third was Ford with its Safari and Monte Carlo results giving it 28 points and Datsun was next with 26 points thanks to Mehta's sixth place on the Acropolis with his Sears-shod 240Z. By comparison, the ERC at mid-season looked to be more competitive since Pinto in his Fiat 124 Spider and Zasada in his Porsche 911S had both won two events outright and thus were tying for the lead with 40 points each. Behind them, three drivers were tied for third place, namely Nicolas and Darniche both driving Alpine A110s, and Barbasio in a Lancia Fulvia. And sixth was Warmbold with a BMW 2002 TI. With thirteen more events to come, there were still plenty of possibilities.

In the original calendar, there was to have been a date clash between the traditional 1000 Lakes Rally and the weeklong, pan-German Olympus Rally, held to celebrate the Olympic Games in Munich and both of which were ERC events. The 1000 Lakes accommodatingly moved forward to the beginning of August and received its normal entry with 95 cars starting the event. The rally was also being observed by FIA representatives for possible inclusion in the first World Rally Championship that had already been announced for 1973. Because of its ERC status where Groups 5 and 6 were welcome, both Saab and Ford took the opportunity to throw weight off their cars and enter in the prototype class.

Predictably, the 1000 Lakes turned out to be a straight fight between the Group 5 Saabs of Blomqvist and Lampinen with the lightweight Escort RS1600 of Mäkinen that was running with the new aluminium block BDA engine. After a rainy first half, Mäkinen led by five seconds from Lampinen who was forty seconds ahead of Blomqvist thanks to a speeding penalty for the Swede. When the rally restarted, both those gaps started to decrease. Four stages later, Lampinen had got into the lead, albeit by just a few seconds, and soon Blomqvist had passed the Escort as well. Blomqvist then closed to within six seconds of his Finnish team-mate before his engine blew spectacularly when its crankshaft broke. Mäkinen had problems with his engine mounts and complained that the engine always seemed to be losing power. Behind the two leaders, now separated by over a minute, Alén was setting fastest times with his Group 2 Volvo 142 thus assuring himself of third place ahead of Tapio Rainio's Opel Ascona 1.9 and compensating for the early retirement with a broken propeller shaft of Mikkola's Group 5 Volvo 142.

The Olympia Rally was a real tour of Germany starting in Kiel on the northern coast and passing through most of the ten states on its way to the finish in Munich. A route of 3,270 kilometres (2,031 miles) with sixty-seven special stages all to be tackled by 300-plus competitors made this one-off event one of the biggest rallies in Europe for many years. Ford entered two Escort RSs for Mikkola and Glemser but neither was destined to go far with Mikkola breaking a half-shaft and Glemser going off the road. Ford honour was however maintained by their two Ford Germany entries of a Group 2 Capri for Röhrl and a Group 1 Capri for Jochi Kleint. Indeed Röhrl was the revelation of this rally as far as the non-Germans were concerned and he carried the fight to the works Alpines of Nicolas and Darniche plus the works BMW 2002 TIs of Warmbold and Fall. Right up to the last day, Röhrl and Fall were pressing the then leader, Nicolas, until Fall's BMW broke the rear axle and Röhrl's Capri dropped a valve in its engine.

Five days earlier on the first night of the rally when the roads were being drenched in rain, the leader was Warmbold ahead of the two Alpines and Röhrl. Darniche made a mistake of three minutes checking in at a time control and thus dropped back. The test on the Nürburgring was in fog for the early numbers and a chap called Alfred von Langen driving a Group 1 Opel Commodore with a late number did it in sunshine and was credited with fastest time. Shortly after that, Warmbold left the road and broke first the BMW's radiator and then its head gasket while Darniche was motoring to such effect that he had caught up his three minutes lost on the road and now led the rally until, during a night of difficult gravel stages, he inverted his Alpine. After the retirements of Röhrl and Fall, the only possible challengers to a victorious Nicolas were the Opel Asconas of Kulläng (Group 2) and Ragnotti (Group 1) and that was the order in which they finished.

Back with the IRCM, the Austrian Alpine proved to be a great success on its new date and attracted over seventy entries with works cars from Saab, Fiat, Lancia and BMW plus the Porsche Salzburg VW 1302 Ss. The attrition rate was high for a European rally with only eight cars finally classified as finishers. There were

1000 Lakes Rally 1972. The relative simplicity of Timo Mäkinen's Ford BDA engine.

1000 Lakes Rally 1972, Simo Lampinen/Klaus Sohlberg, Saab 96 V4.

◄ 1000 Lakes Rally 1972, Markku Alén/Juhani Toivonen, Volvo 142 S.

▼ Acropolis Rally 1972, Håkan Lindberg/Helmuth Eisendle, Fiat 124 Spider. In a very close battle with Simo Lampinen's Lancia, Lindberg managed to pull off the victory by just over twenty seconds.

Olympia Rally 1972, Hannu Mikkola/Jim Porter, Ford Escort RS1600. The best place for a half-shaft that does not want to drive its wheel is on the roof. Then passing cars like the Detlef Mühleck/Siegfried Zepfel Porsche 911S can tell the next Ford service what is wrong. Mühleck eventually finished sixth overall.

many sad tales to tell not the least of which was from Lancia who had seen all its three Fulvias retire with Lampinen going out with a split oil filter just hours from the finish while leading. This was a particularly harsh result for the championship leaders since Munari had convincingly won the ERC San Martino di Castrozza Rally ahead of the works Fiats just three days before the start in Austria.

The initial running had been made by the BMWs with Warmbold leading from Lampinen and with his team-mate, Aaltonen, third. But then Warmbold rolled out of the rally and Aaltonen broke his BMW's differential while Fall in the third BMW had his distributor break. Blomqvist in the lone works Saab was already out with his car running on three wheels after an accident caused by brake failure so that the rally almost immediately became a straight fight between Lampinen's Lancia and the leading Fiat 124 Spider of Lindberg. As for the other Lancias, Källström had gone out with a broken driveshaft while Barbasio was to break a connecting rod and Lindberg's Fiat team-mate, Paganelli, had been delayed by punctures before his engine broke. Even the normally reliable Salzburg VWs had their problems with Dr Gernot Fischer being the first to retire with broken suspension followed later by Georg Fischer who had a rocker arm break in his engine. However, Günther Janger and Herbert Grünsteidl came through in the somewhat depleted field to take second and fourth places respectively behind Lindberg. Third was Per Eklund in his own Saab and that might well have been placed higher had he been able to do a reconnaissance and thus not make so many navigational mistakes during the rally.

If Acropolis, Olympia and Austria had not been kind to Warmbold and his BMW, the TAP Rally gave him some comfort. Against a formidable entry of works or semi-works cars from Citroën, Datsun, Alpine, Fiat and Porsche, he managed to hold off all challengers and take first place with a Group 2 BMW 2002 TI ahead of Darniche in one of the new 1.8-litre Alpine A110s, Waldegård in a Citroën SM prototype, Fall in a Datsun 240Z and Paganelli in a prototype of the new Abarth 124 Rallye with a 1.8-litre engine. The two Alpines of Nicolas and Darniche were fastest on the classification test so that they would run first over the majority of the rally. This was good if there was dust on the stages but also conveyed the disadvantage that it was hard to know what stage times were being recorded behind you and on the early stages there was rain.

At the main halt in Porto, Nicolas headed Warmbold by just over a minute. In the better weather of the following day, he was setting lots of fastest stage times in anticipation of being able to take it easy on the infamous rough stages of the coming night. On the first of those, he broke the gearbox, the same failure that had sidelined Andersson and Darniche on the Monte Carlo. This made Darniche careful and with Warmbold, running behind Darniche and thus knowing his times, the German driver was able to maintain a seven-minute lead right to the end of the rally. The Austrian driver, Bochnicek, had been going very well with a Citroën DS21 but he came to a halt late in the rally with a wiring fire initiated by the steering column rubbing on the Citroën's electrical loom.

With three IRCM events to go, Fiat had narrowed the gap to their Italian rivals but thanks to Erich Haberl's fifth place in Austria with his 911S, Porsche still lay second, fourteen points behind Lancia and ten ahead of Fiat. But now came the all-Italian fiesta of rallying, the Sanremo Rally, where no less than six Lancia Fulvias, all in their new red-and-white Marlboro livery were going up against four works Fiats. One surprise in the Lancia line-up was the inclusion of Jean

Olympia Rally 1972, Anders Kulläng/Donald Carlsson, Opel Ascona 1.9 SR.

Olympia Rally 1972, Bernard Darniche/Alain Mahé, Alpine Renault A110 1.6.

Austrian Alpine Rally 1972, Håkan Lindberg/Helmut Eisendle, Fiat 124 Spider. With a high rate of attrition amongst the works cars from Lancia, Saab, BMW and Citroën, Lindberg was able to take his second major win of the season for Fiat.

▲ Austrian Alpine Rally 1972, Günther Janger/Harald Gottlieb, VW 1302S. Günther Janger driving one of Porsche Salzburg's VWs finished eight minutes behind Lindberg in second place.

▶ TAP Rally 1972. Achim Warmbold is interviewed in the Autódromo do Estoril after winning the TAP Rally in his works BMW 2002 TI accompanied by John Davenport.

Ragnotti, the young French driver who had been impressing with his drives in French Opels. The most feared opposition to the Italian legions came from Alpine who had sent two A110s to be driven by last year's winner, Ove Andersson, and by Thérier.

The Sanremo Rally had shaken off the connection with Turin and Sestriere and was 'back to normal' with everything focussed on the city of Sanremo and the action centred in the mountains behind it. In three stages, Andersson had opened out a lead over Thérier but on the fourth stage his gearbox failed, and his team-mate now led Ballestrieri and Munari in their Lancias. Lampinen's Lancia was soon sidelined with a failed oil pump and Lindberg's Fiat – the only one of the four Abarths to be running a Fiat gearbox instead of a non-synchromesh Colotti – was delayed with it jumping out of gear. At the halt in Sanremo, Thérier led from Munari who in turn was a few seconds ahead of Ballestrieri. After two stages, Thérier's gearbox failed in the same manner as Andersson's and all looked set for a Lancia 1-2-3 until Munari had his differential break, Källström his engine and Ragnotti a drive shaft all within a short distance of each other. This left Ballestrieri and Barbasio in charge with three Fiats behind them and, when Giorgio Bisulli who was the leading one of the three ran into problems with the gear-change on his Colotti box, it was Lindberg who charged through to claim third.

It was an Italian victory in more ways than one since Lancia were now virtually certain to be IRCM champions. Fiat had no plans to go to the rally in the USA and, with Lancia on 87 points to Fiat's 55 points and Porsche still on 53 points, they were practically invincible. Still, Lancia did send a car to the Press on Regardless, a lone Fulvia for Källström who flew out straight away after Sanremo. The initial leader over the soft, sandy stages of Michigan's Lower Peninsular was John Buffum in his Escort RS with Källström and Gene Henderson in a 5.3-litre Jeep Wagoneer dicing for second place. Then Buffum went off and retired while, on the firmer gravel stages of the Upper Peninsular, Källström was able to go quicker. He was soon eight minutes ahead of the formidable Jeep that had taken a wrong turning on a stage at a place called, aptly enough, 'Henderson's Stump'. But then trouble hit the Lancia as sand had built up inside the wheel against one of the rear calipers and worn through a brake pipe. With the leak impossible to fix himself, Källström had two more stages to do before Lancia service and, sadly, rolled on the second. The winner was thus Henderson ahead of a Datsun 240Z driven by Canadian, Tom Jones, and it was this car that scored IRCM points as the Jeep did not belong to any of the FIA Groups.

Therefore, this result did nothing to alter the IRCM results table though it did temporarily elevate Datsun to fourth place ahead of Ford. The British team were able to put that right on the final IRCM round, the RAC Rally, where Clark won for them and thus became the first Briton to win his home event since Gerry Burgess back in 1959. There was satisfaction too for his regular co-driver, Jim Porter, who had been co-opted onto the organising team and the result was one of the best organised RAC rallies to date with prompt results, standardised arrowing on the stages, and a big increase in spectator numbers. The rally was based on York and this too proved popular with the competitors.

The main contest was fought out between the works teams of Saab, Lancia, Ford, Fiat, Datsun and the dealer teams of Opel Sweden and Volvo Finland. Three of the Escort RS1600s went out in the first half with Mikkola's car breaking a cylinder head gasket, Mäkinen's shearing its wheel studs and Andrew Cowan's having an ECU fail in the middle of a forest. Fiat too were in the wars and lost all three of their works 124 Spiders before halfway with Lindberg and Paganelli going off the road and Pinto's engine stopping with a burnt-out valve. However Clark, the new British Rally champion-elect with Tony Mason standing in for Porter, swept through the modest quantities of rain, snow and fog to lead Blomqvist's Saab by a minute and a half at the halfway halt in York with Eklund in another Saab third ahead of Källström's Lancia and Fall's Datsun 240Z.

Press on Regardless Rally 1972, Gene Henderson/Ken Pogue, Jeep Waggoneer. Not your average rally car by any means, but Henderson was able to make this large machine – nicknamed "Moby Dick" as it was all-white – move rapidly in the Michigan forests. It was a landmark victory in several ways: first American driver to win a major FIA rally, first American car to do so, and – most importantly – the first 4WD car to do so.

Sanremo Rally 1972, Amilcare Ballestrieri/Arnaldo Bernacchini, Lancia Fulvia Coupé 1.6.

On the second leg, Fall stopped with a fuel blockage while Eklund rolled and the Swedish Opels moved up into contention behind Clark and Blomqvist. Saab had been hoping for worse weather and some snow on the northern route but it did not materialise and Clark finally won by three and a half minutes. The best of the rest was Kulläng in an Ascona 1.9 some six minutes behind Blomqvist. The Opel driver admitted that he had taken the rally too carefully as he was expecting there to be more retirements after what he had seen during the first part of the event. The Lancias of Källström and Lampinen recovered from minor problems with springs and dampers to claim fourth and fifth places respectively but, as one of the few teams still intact, Opel picked up the manufacturer team prize and, in addition to Kulläng's third place they also claimed sixth, seventh and eighth places overall.

One significant appearance on this RAC Rally was Ove Andersson in a Toyota Celica. The reason for this change was that Renault had just bought out Alpine and were committing themselves 100% to winning the new World Championship announced for 1973. But they only wanted to do it with French crews since they had realised – even if the CSI had not – that, for PR purposes, the general public are more interested in the personalities of the drivers than the provenance of the cars. So Andersson had guessed that he was going to be unemployed for 1973, had started looking for an alternative and had found one with Toyota. By taking one of their cars, preparing it himself, obtaining some sponsorship and finishing tenth on the RAC Rally, he laid the foundations for what was to become Toyota Team Europe, multiple World Champions and eventually participants at Le Mans and in Formula One.

Meanwhile, the ERC had given Fiat some consolation in that Raffaele Pinto and his co-driver, Gino Macaluso, had romped away with the title. As the second half of the year started, they had won in Poland where Zasada crashed and they had managed to keep Röhrl and his Capri 2600RS behind them. Then a second place in San Martino di Castrozza behind Munari's Lancia almost doubled their score from what it had been at the end of June. Zasada came back with a second place to Röhrl's winning Capri 2600RS on the Baltic Rally at the end of September and less than a week later, Zasada won the Munich–Vienna–Budapest. This put the two protagonists on level pegging at 75 points each but when they came together a week after the Hungarian event on the Yugoslav Rally it was Pinto who took the victory with Zasada second. Pinto and Macaluso owed that win to the Fiat mechanics as their 124 Spider hit a cow on the very first stage and it needed a roadside rebuild before they could continue and catch up with the Porsche.

Zasada's bolt was just about shot but he entered both the TAP and the Spanish rallies that were held two weeks apart in October. When he retired in Portugal and Pinto won the 1000 Minutes Rally in Austria at the same time as the TAP, it gave the Fiat driver a twenty-five point advantage that not even an outright win in Spain would be able to beat. Neither of them had any plans to go to the Tour de Corse – won by Andruet for Alpine – or to the Tour de Belgique – won by Staepelaere in a Ford Escort RS1600 – so that was how the ERC for 1972 ended with Pinto winning the title by a comfortable margin from Zasada.

For 1973, there was a whole new vista of top flight rallying awaiting the teams and rally fans. Back in July, the FIA had issued the provisional dates for the new World Rally Championship with eleven events listed, mainly the ones that had formed the IRCM plus the 1000 Lakes, but the final list had swelled to thirteen with the further addition of the Poland Rally and the TAP while the Tour de Corse had been introduced to replace the Rallye des Alpes when it was clear that it would definitely not be running in 1973. The ERC stayed very much the same but here too there was an influx of new events to replace those that had been elevated to the WRC of which examples were the Costa Brava Rally, the Welsh Rally and the Cyprus Rally. The total number of events scheduled to be held remained at twenty-four and the scoring system stayed the same. The time of experiment was over – or was it?

▲ RAC Rally 1972. Plenty to grin about for Roger Clark as he had just become the first British driver to win the RAC Rally since Gerry Burgess in 1959.

◄ RAC Rally 1972. By finishing ninth overall in this Toyota Celica, Ove Andersson started on the road that was to take him to the establishment of Toyota Team Europe and success in the World Rally Championship. Andersson (the tallest one in the photo) is pictured with his co-driver, Geraint Phillips (to his R) and the Toyota engineers.

RAC Rally 1972, Roger Clark/Tony Mason, Ford Escort RS1600. In its delicate Esso Uniflo colours and with an autumnal setting, Clark's Escort sets fastest time on the Blenheim Palace special stage. This was one of ten "spectator" stages run during the first half of the rally. The other sixty-two stages comprised more serious going in the British forests.

Champions **1972**

Raffaele "Lele" Pinto was European Driver Champion for Fiat.

The Makes Championship trophy went to the "other" side of Turin, to Lancia.

Chapter 08

The works teams,
their managers and their cars
Alfa Romeo/Alpine/British Motor Corporation
BMW/Citroën/DAF/DKW Auto Union
Fiat/Ford Germany/Ford GB/Lancia/Mercedes
Opel/Porsche/Renault/Rootes/Rover/Saab
Standard Triumph/Volvo

Chapter 08
The works teams, their managers and their cars

The use of major rally results in advertisements, especially those after the Monte Carlo Rally, had always meant that car manufacturers took an interest in their products when they were entered on events. In many cases, such interest only manifested itself in rather 'hands off' ways such as offering prizes or bonuses for private entrants that did well. Then, for the better drivers, there came the possibility of borrowing a car from the manufacturer, or of having one's own car prepared with their help. During the 1950s, it did not take long before this background enthusiasm for good rally results manifested itself in what we would recognise as works teams with cars owned, prepared and entered by the manufacturers.

It is almost impossible to say when and which manufacturer first took that major step of creating a dedicated competition department with the object of competing in rallies. During the early 1950s, works teams from DKW, Renault and Mercedes made an appearance. They were swiftly followed by similar involvements from BMC, Sunbeam-Talbot and Standard Triumph in Britain while in the 1960s, there was a positive explosion of such efforts with Citroën, Alfa Romeo, Porsche, BMW, Alpine, Lancia, Opel, DAF and Ford – with their companies in GB, Germany and USA – getting involved.

Very often, the way it happened was that there was a person employed within the company who had both access to the engineering departments and a personal enthusiasm for motor sport through his own experiences behind the wheel. His initiative, sometimes aimed merely at having a car to drive himself, was often to be the catalyst for bigger things. No two of these manufacturer involvements were identical in that there were many ways in which a 'works team' could exist. It could be housed 100% within the manufacturer's premises either with a regular workforce or by 'borrowing' resources from engineering and service departments. Or it could be established outside the company but with a manager employed by the company. Or it could even 'adopt' a preparation and tuning firm that specialised in its products.

Here are a few of those that existed in the 1950s and 1960s.

The three Group 1 Opel Rekords entered by the Swedish Opel importer on the 1967 Monte Carlo Rally line up before the start in Frankfurt am Main.

Bert Shankland (left) and Chris Rothwell pose beside the car in which they won the 1966 Safari – TDH 404 – with their trophies from the Safari and other rallies.

Volkswagens occupied the first five places in the general classification of the 1957 Safari. They also won the team prize with these three cars.

Alfa Romeo

There was no direct factory involvement with rallying during this period though it could be argued that Italian companies such as Autodelta and Conrero were for all practical purposes, factory-supported teams. Alfa Romeo private owners used first the 1,300 cc Giulietta and then the 1,600 cc Giulia and enjoyed a good measure of success. For instance, the Kalpala brothers, Osmo and Eino, used a Giulietta to win the 1958 1000 Lakes Rally. But by far the most successful Alfas were the ones with bodies produced by Zagato.

Bernard Consten and his cousin, Jean Hébert, used a Giulietta Sprint Veloce Zagato to win the Liège–Rome–Liège in 1958. This was just one of three Alfas prepared by Conrero for them to use in rallies and races: a Group 1 Giulietta, a Group 2 Giulietta and the SV Zagato. They used the Group 2 car to win the touring category of the Tour de France Automobile in 1958. Then in 1959, Jean Rolland started rallying a Giulietta SV and won the Ronde Cévenole. Over the next two years, he twice finished second on the Tour de Corse and was third in 1962 before winning the Rallye des Alpes in 1963. In 1964, he won again but this time driving a 1,600 cc Giulia Tubolare Zagato (GTZ) prepared by Virgilio Conrero and he used the same car to take second place again on the Tour de Corse. Luck was not with his GTZ in 1965 but in 1966 he won the Rallye des Alpes again, this time using an Alfa GTA and picked up a Coupe d'Argent for winning three non-consecutive Coupes. As from late 1964, the Alfa Romeo France competition activity was co-ordinated by François Landon who had an Alfa connection through his Corsican dealership that sold both Renault and Alfa Romeo cars. Under his direction, Consten also drove again for Alfa using first a GTZ winning the Rallye des Alpes in 1965 and then a GTA on rallies. In 1967 Consten won the French rally championship with a GTA but this was one of the last major successes for Alfa Romeo until they returned in the late 1970s with the GTV Turbodelta and the GTV6.

Alfa Romeo made a special homologation of the GTA that gave them results in racing but it was not a big success in rallying.

Alpine

It sounds illogical but it is almost true that Alpine was involved in rallying before the company of that name was formed and started making cars. The reason is that Jean Rédélé, the founder and prime mover of Alpine, was competing in rallies before he founded the company and the activities of both are virtually synonymous. Rédélé ran a Renault dealership in Dieppe with his father. He started driving a self-modified Renault 4CV in rallies and races of which one of the earliest was the Mille Miglia of 1952 where he won his class. In 1954, he finished sixth on the Liège–Rome–Liège and won a Coupe on the Rallye des Alpes. When in 1955 he started to build cars based on the 4CV with its 747 cc engine, he decided to call his company Alpine in memory of winning that Coupe and to call the first car, the A106, the 'Mille Miles'.

This little GT car was very popular with private owners and was driven successfully in competition by people like Jacques Féret and Henri Greder. In 1960, a new Alpine made its debut on the Tour de France Automobile. This was the A108 that was based on the Renault Dauphine and powered by a 904 cc engine. Only a year later, it was followed by the A110. This had a steel backbone chassis, fibreglass bodywork and was based on mechanical parts from the Renault R8. It was soon homologated with a 1,106 cc engine into Group 3 and started to rack up everything from class wins to outright victories on French events.

One of the men driving Alpines at the time was Jacques Cheinisse whose career kicked off with a win on the Rallye d'Automne in 1963 with an A108. He subsequently drove for Rédélé four times at Le Mans with a best result of eleventh overall in 1966 sharing an A210 prototype with Roger de Lageneste. It was also with De Lageneste that he had finished fourth on the Tour de Corse of 1965 in an A110. As Rédélé's company grew – in 1961/62 they built twenty-five A108s while in 1965/66 they sent out over 270 A110s – he extended his deal with Renault so that they sold Alpines through the Renault dealer network while at the same time buying 30% of Alpine's equity. Furthermore, at the end of 1967, Renault decided to put their rally budget into rallying Alpines from Dieppe. The man who was put in charge was Jacques Cheinisse who for some time had been Rédélé's Commercial Director.

By this time the A110 was homologated into Group 4 with a 1,296 cc engine though, if it was entered as a prototype, then it often ran with a 1,440 cc version of the R8 engine. The drivers that Cheinisse had at his disposal were Alpine stalwarts like Gérard Larrousse, Jean Vinatier, Bernard Darniche and Jean-Claude Andruet who were soon joined by refugees from the Renault R8 programme like Jean-Luc Thérier, Jean-François Piot and Jean-Pierre Nicolas. During his first three years, Cheinisse achieved a great deal on relatively small budgets where the drivers were largely unpaid but expenses generous. However, he did have a staff of some thirty-five people engaged full-time on rallying activities. André de Cortanze was in charge of technical matters while Bernard Dudot looked after the engines that were built under the direct supervision of Marc Mignotet.

For 1970, the little blue cars got an upgrade with a 1,565 cc engine pinched from the Renault R16 and more serious results started to come with both Thérier and Nicolas starting to win major events outside France. For 1971, they were joined by Ove Andersson, himself a refugee from the Ford team, and suddenly they were winning everything. Andersson won Monte Carlo, Sanremo, Austria and Acropolis so that Alpine scooped the IRCM with double the points of their nearest challenger. Perhaps their only sadness was that Nicolas only had time to do a handful of the rallies counting for the ERC for Drivers and thus finished third behind Zasada and Munari.

For 1972, the A110 lost a little of the formidable reliability that had seen it achieve those 1971 results. This was mainly due to an increase in engine capacity to 1,796 cc without the benefit of a major overhaul of the now over-stressed gearbox and transaxle. Towards the end of 1972, this was addressed by the addition of internal parts from the Renault R12 gearbox and, in quick succession, Nicolas won the Olympia Rally and Andruet the Tour de Corse and Rallye du Var. It was also in 1972 that Alpine suffered economic problems including a strike at their Dieppe factory and Renault decided to take a majority shareholding. It was a good move as the A110 1800, now a Renault Alpine rather than an Alpine Renault, swept to victory in the first year of the WRC.

◀ David Stone, Ove Andersson and Jean Rédélé (front row, from L to R) at the prize-giving of the 1971 Monte Carlo Rally.

▼ Jacques Cheinisse

◀ Sanremo-Sestriere Rally 1971, Ove Andersson/Tony Nash, Alpine-Renault A110

▼ At first, the Alpine A110s were considered to be tarmac machines. However, they soon proved otherwise and Jean-Luc Thérier and Marcel Callewaert would have finished third on the 1970 RAC Rally had they not broken a drive shaft on the very last stage.

British Motor Corporation

Before 1939, the MG company had taken part in all manner of motor sport including rallies and, in the post-war era, its Abingdon factory became the focus for BMC's involvement in motor sport. Morris Motors had acquired MG in 1935 and Morris had become part of BMC in 1952. The Managing Director of the MG factory in Abingdon, John Thornley, successfully lobbied the BMC board to start a competition department. Marcus Chambers was hired to start in 1955 as the manager of the new department on the Abingdon site under the benevolent eye of Thornley. Over the next seven years, BMC entered a wide variety of cars including Austin A90s, Morris Minors, Austin A40s, Riley 1.5s and, of course, MG TFs and Magnettes. Gradually the trophy cupboard filled up with team awards, class wins plus European Ladies titles in 1956 and 1957 won by Nancy Mitchell mainly in MGs. During this period, John Gott was 'team captain' and undertook most of the recces for long events like the Liège–Rome–Liège and Monte Carlo Rally, preparing detailed road books and advice on road conditions and severity of the sections. Pat Moss joined the team in 1958 and was soon at home in the Austin Healey 100-6 and 300 sports cars, winning the European Ladies title in 1958 and again in 1960, the year that she won the Liège–Sofia–Liège outright.

Already by 1961, the BMC team was beginning to look more professional every day. The advent of the Mini 850 and the continued success of the big Healey with drivers like Pat Moss, Don Morley, Peter Riley and David Seigle-Morris boded well for the future when Chambers stepped down and handed over the reins to Stuart Turner. By profession an accountant, Turner was a top international rally co-driver and journalist and had experience of seeing the other teams and drivers in action. Crews were now encouraged to do their own recces and also to make their own pace notes for stages and difficult sections. Turner had won the RAC Rally in 1960 sitting beside Erik Carlsson and was convinced that Scandinavian drivers had what was needed to produce major wins. He was also able to give them the machines to do it for the mild 850 Mini first became the Mini Cooper and finally the Mini Cooper S. Multiple Monte Carlo victories soon ensued and a legend was born; British car, British engineering and Finnish drivers, but with that notable exception, Paddy Hopkirk, who proved himself their equal in both Healeys and Minis.

Turner left to pursue a career with Castrol in 1967 after a Cooper S had won the Monte Carlo for the third time (or should that be fourth?). He was succeeded by Peter Browning who carried on with the programme adding wins on the Acropolis and Rallye des Alpes to the BMC trophy cupboard. But when Leyland took over BMC in 1968, its competition department was considerably shrunk and, though Austin 1800s were successfully run on the 1968 London to Sydney and Triumph 2.5 PIs on the 1970 World Cup Rally (London to Mexico), the competition activities were mainly a mixture of racing, rallying and rallycross. Finally, in September 1970 on the eve of the 84-hours of Nürburgring (the new Marathon de la Route) where the Abingdon department had a lightweight Cooper S and a V8-engined Rover 3500 entered – neither came to the finish but both distinguished themselves before that – the employees were told that the competition department was to close. Browning left and the only remaining activity was that of Special Tuning Department, run by Basil Wales, that sold competition parts for British Leyland vehicles to private owners.

It was from Special Tuning that the phoenix of a Leyland competition department rose from the ashes of the old BMC department by virtue of preparing Triumph Dolomite Sprints and Morris Marinas for rallying and getting funds to run them in events from Leyland importers and dealer principals. In 1974, through the intervention of Leyland International, a more serious competition programme was launched that saw the re-establishment of a competition department at Abingdon under Richard Seth-Smith.

"Ecurie Safety Fast" was the unofficial name for the all-conquering BMC team.

It was often said that Stuart Turner (on R) was the God of the BMC team. In which case, that must be the BMC Bible that he is showing to senior mechanic, Den Green.

▲ By 1968, the famous BMC workshop at Abingdon had started to diversify and Minis are being prepared for both rallies and races while in the background, other models are awaiting evaluation for long-distance events.

◄ Now under the British Leyland flag, Abingdon chose Triumph 2.5 PIs for their works entries on the 1970 World Cup Rally but they also prepared five Austin 1800s (seen here) and two Maxis as a second-string to the big Triumphs.

BMW

The BMW 328 was a successful competition car in the 1930s with examples winning events as diverse as the RAC Rally and the Mille Miglia. The 328 was still doing well in the 1950s when one of the men who helped to design it, Alex von Falkenhausen, won a Coupe on the Rallye des Alpes in 1952. Von Falkenhausen was also involved in running the Formula 2 AFM cars with BMW. Indeed, until the late 1960s he was the principal adviser to BMW on their sporting activities. As far as rallying was concerned, very little happened until the early 1960s with the arrival of first the 1800 TI and then the TI/SA. Some success was achieved with these cars in semi-private hands with parts and advice from the factory and on occasions even the loan of cars. But it was in 1968 when the 2002 and its even more powerful derivative, the 2002 TI arrived that there was a real chance to do well in rallies.

BMW promptly hired in Helmut 'Helle' Bein who, as a driver, had already won three German rally championships of which the last two were at the wheel of BMWs. He started work at the end of 1969 and quickly built up a team that would run drivers like Rauno Aaltonen, Tony Fall and Achim Warmbold in European rallies. The results were not astounding though Warmbold showed that he could hold his own with the best on the Olympia Rally before retiring and went on to win the TAP Rally in 1972. Bein was also responsible for loaning a works car to Sobieslaw Zasada for the 1971 season and was rewarded by the Polish driver winning the European title for that year.

Bein left BMW in 1973 to go to Opel and become their rally manager. After that, BMW's focus turned ever more to motor racing, which was understandable in the light of a comment made by a main board director at the time that 'On rallies, no one can see our cars because they are always covered in dirt!'

From BMW driver to BMW rally manager: Helmut Bein.

A year later and BMW would have won a WRC round with their 2002 TI. Achim Warmbold and John Davenport were winners on the Portugal Rally in 1972.

Citroën

Citroën cars were active in rallying throughout the 1950s and, in private hands, notched up many successes with their machines. But the idea of having a proper competition department did not come to fruition until after the success of Paul Coltelloni on the 1959 Monte Carlo Rally. But before that, just after launching the DS and ID19s at the Paris Motor Show, Citroën had decided to provide six DS19s to well-known rally drivers to enter the Monte Carlo Rally of 1956. The cars were not yet in full-scale production. Indeed the story is that just 42 had been built when the car was homologated by the FIA on the basis that there was a clear intention from Citroën to build thousands more before the year was out.

Sadly, the results were rather disappointing as the cars were highly underdeveloped plus there was little snow and ice on a rally where they could have shown Citroën's unique abilities. Coltelloni's eventual victory in 1959 driving his own ID19 was achieved with the help of a private team run by René Cotton. Cotton was an experienced driver who had notched up many class wins in rallies and races with Panhards, had been second overall on the 1955 Liège–Rome–Liège with a Salmson, and had finished sixteenth on the 1958 Monte with a Citroën. There was no immediate rush to form an official competition department but Cotton was provided with funds to prepare and run cars in rallies where they were entered under the name of his team, 'Paris Île-de-France'. There was soon more success with René Trautmann winning in French national rallies and then Coltelloni winning the Adriatic Rally to clinch the 1959 European title. It was more of the same in 1960 and then Lucien Bianchi drove an ID19 to win the 1961 Liège–Sofia–Liège with Bob Neyret third and Roger de Lageneste fifth. Pauli Toivonen got support to win the 1000 Lakes and the Finnish championship in 1962 while in 1963 Trautmann was the French and Bianchi the Belgian champion.

In 1965, the team became official with Cotton taking the title of Chef du Service Compétition Citroën and from that point onwards, the cars were entered as works cars. Accommodation was also found for the team within a Citroën factory outside Paris. Depending on which way you look at it, the high point was when, in 1966 and with both driving DS21s, Toivonen won the Monte Carlo Rally and Neyret was fourth. Cotton's organisational skill and the typically French way in which the comfort and refreshment of the rally crews was provided were legendary. But, except on long distance rallies, the DS was beginning to be outclassed by more modern machinery. However, in 1968, only an eleventh hour accident with a private car prevented Bianchi from winning the London to Sydney in a DS21. Neyret won the Rallye du Maroc twice – 1969 and 1970 – in a prototype DS21 that had been lightened by considerably shortening the chassis while Jean Deschazeaux won the 1971 event in a V6-engined Citroën SM. But success was tempered by sadness since Cotton died literally weeks after returning from the SM's winning debut in Morocco. Someone who had been helping him organise the team for years succeeded him, his wife Marlène. She continued to run the team until Guy Verrier took over during 1980.

▲ Citroën notched up a win on the Rallye du Maroc in 1971 when the local ace, Jean Deschazeaux drove this Maserati V6-engined SM to win.

◀ The 1971 Rallye du Maroc was included in the IRCM and thus did not allow Bob Neyret and Jacques Terramorsi to drive the Citroën DS prototypes. Instead, they were entered in this Group 2 version of the DS21.

DAF

The first DAF car was the 600 that sent the power from its flat-twin 590 cc engine to the rear wheels via a constant velocity transmission (CVT) involving rubber belts and called the Variomatic. This hardly sounds like a recipe for motor sport success but the fact was that, in slippery low traction conditions, the CVT acted like a super limited slip differential. The first man to see this was Rudi Hunger who drove one in Austrian events starting in 1960. The DAF factory came out with the 'Daffodil' in 1961 with an uprated engine of 746 cc and André Ransy, the DAF dealer in Spa, Belgium decided to enter one in the Liège–Sofia–Liège of 1963. Together with his co-driver, Norbert Rebetez, they got the little machine to the finish in nineteenth place, the smallest-engined car to ever finish the original Marathon de la Route.

This result fired the enthusiasm of Martien van Doorne, the son of the founder of DAF, and he decided to start a competition department in 1965 to run rally cars and F3 racing cars with Variomatic transmission. The man he chose to run it was Rob Koch who was put in charge of the team's debut at the 1965 Swedish Rally. Rob Slotemaker and Claude Laurent both finished but were defeated in their class by works Saabs. There was a much better result on the Tulip Rally two months later when all five DAFs finished and won the team prize for manufacturers.

The reliability of the DAF proved to be its best feature and, once the DAF 44 with its two-cylinder 844 cc engine arrived in 1967, the class wins and team prizes started to mount up. The rally cars were prepared in a workshop that was an offshoot of DAF's experimental area from which the mechanics were also drawn. The rally cars and service cars were driven to the start of the rallies – for example, Monte Carlo, Corsica, TAP Rally, Acropolis – where the service cars were often pressed into service as recce cars. When the rally was over, the cars were then driven home to Holland. Of the drivers, Claude Laurent was by far the most successful but he was rivalled by the young Belgian, Jean-Louis Haxhe, a protégé of André Ransy.

The team's most ambitious task was to enter two of their new DAF 55s on the 1968 London to Sydney. The DAF 55 was powered by a 1,100 cc four-cylinder in-line engine supplied by Renault and the entries on the London to Sydney were crewed by Rob Slotemaker/Rob Janssen and David van Lennep/Peter Peters. Both cars finished and Slotemaker was seventeenth overall. There were no prizes for classes but certainly the DAF was the highest placed car with a capacity of less than 1,600 cc. And in 1969, they achieved their best result when Laurent finished third overall behind Pauli Toivonen's Porsche and Roger Clark's Escort TC on the Acropolis Rally.

The 'fuel crisis' of 1972 caused the company to disband its team but both Laurent and Haxhe continued to rally the little cars with the support of DAF France and DAF Belgium. And a chap called Jan de Rooy developed a DAF rallycross car powered by a Ford BDA using a Variomatic with one belt driving the front wheels and one driving the rear. He anticipated the Audi Quattro by ten years and won the inaugural Dutch Rallycross championship in 1971.

▲ Swedish Rally 1965, Rob Slotemaker/Wim Loos, DAF 33

◀ The most tireless campaigner behind the wheel of a DAF rally car was Claude Laurent. In 1971, he and co-driver, Jacques Marché, tackled the Safari Rally in this DAF 55 powered by a 4-cylinder Renault engine.

DKW / Auto Union

One of the earliest companies to get involved in rallying was DKW. Heinz Meier was the head of Auto Union's 'Factory Repair Department' and he was something of a star on trials behind the wheel of a DKW F89 – 684 cc, two-cylinder, two-stroke with a three-speed gearbox. Thus when, during 1953, DKW opened a motor sport department in Düsseldorf with Karl-Friederich Trübsbach as manager, Meier was one of the first volunteers to drive the new three-cylinder 3=6 Sonderklasse. Joining him in the team for 1954 was Walter Schlüter who had an experience of big rallies from helping Helmut Polensky to win the European Championship of 1953. Schlüter used it to good effect to win the European Championship title that year. Drivers such as Gustav Menz and Hubert Brand joined Meier and Schlüter – these new men were both test engineers for Auto Union – during the next years and racked up an impressive list of class wins and even the occasional outright victory. However, the commercial strength of Auto Union started to fade and after 1956, the in-house team gave way to support for private owners like Wolfgang Levy who very nearly repeated Schlüter's 1954 success by narrowly failing to win the European Championship in 1959.

As a works team, DKW/Auto Union put most of their effort into European rallies but their knowledge helped Eric Cecil and Tony Vickers to win the 1956 Safari.

Monte Carlo Rally 1954, Gustav Menz/Hubert Brand, DKW 900

Fiat

Despite having cars that had participated in rallies and won them during the 1920s – Jacques Bignan (Monte Carlo 1928) and Ernest Urdăreanu (Rallye dei Fiori 1928 and 1929) – Fiat was largely absent from the sport until the late 1960s. At that time, they started to help private owners in 124s and 125s through an unofficial Squadra Clienti based first in the Corso Bramante and later in the old Fiat Export Delivery area in the Corso Giulio Cesare. They had just a few mechanics under the direction of Giovanni Maruffi who did some basic preparation and attended the rallies almost incognito. It was, however, clear that Fiat was gradually building up its competition activities in regard to rallying. The 125 Special was homologated on January 1st, 1969 into Group 1 along with the 124 Special and of course, suitably tuned, these could also run in Group 2. In January 1970, the 124 Sport Spider was homologated and Maruffi's team was rewarded with some good results. They were particularly pleased that Alcide Paganelli/Ninni Russo won the Italian rally championship of 1970 thus bringing to an end Lancia's run of five consecutive Italian titles.

Fiat acquired the Abarth company in August 1971 and promptly merged the racing activities of Abarth and their own rally programme under the direction of Giovanni Sguazzini. They also moved everything under a single roof at Corso Marche 72. The motive for all this was that Abarth's contract with Fiat was coming to an end and, rather than see it snapped up by a rival company, Fiat decided to make sure that its expertise with Fiat cars was not lost. The Abarth side of things continued with racecar builds, exhaust development and engine tuning under the direction of Lorenzo Avidano with Mario Colucchi as its technical head. Things now moved at a quicker pace and the cars were entered by Fiat and the name of the company started to appear on service vans and overalls. The first big result for Maruffi was when Raffaele Pinto and Gino Macaluso won the European Rally Championship in 1972 driving a 124 Sport Spider.

Fiat's return to rallying was mainly with the 124 and 125 saloons. But their programme started to show results when they developed the 124 Sport Spider.

Ford Germany

The first formal competition department run by Ford Germany from Cologne was opened in July 1968 under the direction of Jochen Neerpasch. His background was mainly in racing and indeed he had won the Daytona 24 Hours in February of that same year driving a Porsche 907. Much of the department's activities were focused on racing but, building on the involvement of drivers like Joachim Springer and Gilbert Staepelaere with the 20 MTS, teams of 20 MRS were entered in both the London to Sydney of 1968 and the Safari Rally of 1969. They so nearly won London–Sydney as the car driven by Simo Lampinen and Gilbert Staepelaere was leading when it went off the road just 200 miles from the finish. Earlier that year, Alfred Burkhart won the Tour d'Europe in a 20 MRS but their most significant victory came on the 1969 Safari Rally when local man Robin Hillyar clinched an outright win for them in the face of strong opposition. As well as racing Escorts, Cologne also entered rallies with them and Staepelaere took fourth place on the 1968 Geneva Rally with one of their cars.

During 1969, Neerpasch decided that the Capri 2600RS was the car to go rallying with and, though a three-car entry on the Safari Rally saw all the Capris retiring, one of his cars won the Tour d'Europe with Günther Klapproth. He lent a works Capri to Jean-François Piot for Corsica who rewarded him with a third place overall. Ford Köln also gave some help to Walter Röhrl who was rallying a Group 1 Capri and then a Group 2 version and results in German rallies started to come. During 1972, Neerpasch moved to BMW and Mike Kranefuss took over. Not much more happened on the rally side except for the Olympia Rally where Dieter Glemser drove an Escort RS while Röhrl and Jochi Kleint took part in Capri RSs. All three of them retired but Röhrl made a major impression by leading at one point and this performance was key to his later career.

◀ Team Manager: Jochen Neerpasch

▼ Safari Rally 1969, Robin Hillyar/Jock Aird, Ford Taunus 20 MRS

Ford GB

Ford Great Britain got involved in rallying and racing during the 1950s and ran a low-key operation out of the old Lincoln Cars building along the Great West Road in West London. The principal occupation of the people working in this area was to prepare and maintain Ford GB's considerable fleet of press and courtesy cars. Some of Ford's early rally successes came from cars lent from this press fleet to rally drivers such as Ken Wharton who won the Tulip Rally of 1950 with a Pilot V8 from Lincoln Cars. He then won the Tulip again in 1952 with a Ford Consul though this second victory was with his own car. This embarrassment was enough to spur Ford, during 1953, into creating its first UK-based competition department within Lincoln Cars under Edgell 'Edgy' Fabris.

Fabris was a friendly ex-colonial whose primary qualities lay in the PR area so for several years he relied on the crews competing in his cars to sort out much of the organisational arrangements. This changed for the better when he acquired the services of Bill Barnett who was able to take over much of those activities and improve upon them. It is interesting to note that Barnett was still performing that function when Ford won the Safari Rally in 1972 and that two of the mechanics assigned to the new department in 1953 – Jack Welch and Norman Masters – also served throughout the 1960s.

The instant the new arrangement was in place, Maurice Gatsonides won the Monte Carlo Rally of 1953 in a Zephyr prepared by Lincoln Cars and then two years later D.P. Marwaha won the Safari Rally in a Zephyr with similar help. But it was not until 1959 that another big victory came their way when Gerry Burgess won the RAC Rally. Victories like this gave senior management a taste for more rallying success and, when Walter Hayes joined the company in 1961 as their head of Public Affairs, he soon proposed two ideas: one was to fund a Formula One engine with Cosworth and the other was to build a motorsport centre at Boreham in Essex. In 1963, the Lincoln Cars operation moved out to the new set-up at Boreham. Before that, Fabris had moved on within the company and Sid Henson, previously Ferodo's competition manager, had been brought in to run things. But Ford Competitions at Boreham was destined to have a new manager, Alan Platt, recruited from the ranks of Ford management.

The arrival of the team from Lincoln Cars at Boreham coincided with the arrival of the Mk1 Cortina GT and the enlarged workforce under the direction of Bill Meade was soon preparing cars for events. Success was reasonably quick in coming and they won the Safari Rally in 1964 with Peter Hughes. Their early attempts with the Lotus Cortina in rallying were frustrated by its A-frame linkage and coil sprung rear axle. However, once Meade had engineered leaf springs into the car, it started to produce a string of victories at home with Roger Clark and abroad with Bengt Söderström. At the end of 1965, Henry Taylor, until then a Cortina driver on both rallies and races, took over from Alan Platt and the Lotus Cortina in both Mk1 and Mk2 form continued its winning ways despite a few legal traumas during the 1966 season.

But something better was needed and it was Taylor and Meade who during the latter part of 1967 decided to try and fit a Lotus twin-cam engine into one of the new Escorts. Persuading senior Ford management to make sufficient of these to get FIA homologation was not easy but the new car did make its debut in February 1968. Stuart Turner replaced Taylor for 1970 and he masterminded both the Escort push-rod's win on the 1970 World Cup marathon rally and the historic first win for an overseas crew at the 1972 Safari Rally with an Escort RS1600. On both of those occasions, Hannu Mikkola and Gunnar Palm drove the winning car.

Almost production-line techniques were used by the Ford GB team at their competition department at Boreham to build the Escorts required for their entry on the 1970 World Cup Rally.

Ford GB's policy of lending cars to good rally drivers paid off with Ken Wharton winning both the Tulip and Lisbon rallies in 1950 with one of their V8 Pilots.

The Ford Anglia 105E was the first of Ford's 'modern' cars to be rallied with success. This is Peter Hughes on their way to second place on the 1963 Safari.

Lancia

Looking at the success that Lancia had with versions of their Aurelia during the early 1950s, including an outright win on the Monte Carlo Rally in 1954 with Louis Chiron at the wheel, one might have imagined that they had an active competition department right from the start. In fact, like many other European factories, they had a customer service department whose employees would try to help those clients who were going to enter a car on a major rally. And frequently, they would get invited along to go in a service car. In Italy, there were also a lot of private establishments preparing cars for racing and it was not too hard for them to turn their efforts to preparing the occasional rally car.

One of the more successful co-drivers in Lancias during this period was Sandro Fiorio. By the beginning of the 1960s, he was working for Lancia and eventually rose to become their PR and Marketing Director. His son, Cesare, had ambitions to be a racing driver and in 1961 won his class in the Italian GT championship before going off to do his national service with the Italian navy. When he returned, Cesare started working for a Lancia dealer and formed a team that they called HF Squadra Corse. The 'HF' stood for 'High Fidelity' and the team was also something of a club for people who not only competed in Lancias but also were faithful to the marque when they bought a new car. Fiorio had shared a Flaminia 3B Coupé entered by the Anglo-Italian Racing Team with Piero Frescobaldi at the 1962 Brands Hatch 6-Hours where they had finished fifth overall. When the team returned there over the next two years, it was as HF Squadra Corse and Leo Cella finished fifth with a Flavia Sport Zagato in 1964.

In January 1964, the young Fiorio had organised a team of Flavia Coupés to enter the Monte Carlo Rally and had a modicum of success with Frescobaldi finishing thirteenth and Franco Patria twentieth. René Trautmann was also driving Lancia now with the aid of the French concessionaire and when he won two French national rallies, it was all Cesare needed to make a strong plea to his father for support. He got it and HF Squadra Corse became a semi-official Lancia team in 1965. The most important thing was that Lancia gave the team cars to prepare free-of-charge and also a small workshop to use as their Reparto Corse. During 1965, the team started using the Fulvia saloon and Cella won the Rallye dei Fiori for them. By 1966, the Fulvia Coupé had arrived and Cella finished fifth in Monte Carlo, won the Rallye dei Fiori and was second in the Three Cities Rally. Joining him in the team for 1966 was Ove Andersson, the first of Fiorio's Scandinavian signings and it soon brought results with Andersson finishing third in Monte Carlo with a Flavia and third on the Rallye dei Fiori with a Fulvia. In 1967 Andersson went one better and finished second in Monte Carlo and won the Spanish Rally, but it was Italian talent in the person of Sandro Munari who astoundingly won the Tour de Corse and set Fiorio and his little team en route for the big time.

In fact, it was not such a little team any more and apart from a cluster of Italian talent headed by Munari, Fiorio was soon recruiting drivers like Pauli Toivonen, Jorma Lusenius, Pat Moss, Hannu Mikkola, Harry Källström, Simo Lampinen and Timo Mäkinen. However, the first of these to deliver Squadra Corse a championship was Källström who won the European title in 1969, winning the RAC Rally that year and following it up with a second victory in Britain in 1970. All this time, the team was just getting by financially. Lancia had been 'acquired' by the Fiat group in late 1969 and, at least for the time being, Fiorio was left to carry on with his rally programmes while they were showing results at least as good as those of the nascent Fiat team.

As in 1967, it was Munari that gave Fiorio the lift that he needed to face down the internal challenge from within Fiat. At the beginning of 1972, Munari won the Monte Carlo Rally in a Fulvia Coupé. Naturally, in the corridors of power, Fiorio now received more smiles than frowns and he was able to convince both sets of Fiat and Lancia directors that it was possible to build a rally winner from scratch that owed nothing to any production car. It was so simple: all that was necessary was to build 500 of them for homologation with the FIA and there were plenty of technical and practical resources within Turin to do that. When they bought the idea, this was the beginning of the Lancia Stratos that launched the Group 4 era.

Safari Rally 1971, Lancia team

Monte Carlo Rally 1972, Sandro Munari/Mario Mannucci, Lancia Fulvia HF 1.6

▲ Lancia's competition department – its Reparto Corse – at 118 via San Paolo in Turin may have been modest in size but it was not modest in aspiration.

▶ Competition Director: Cesare Fiorio

▶▶ Acropolis Rally 1965, René Trautmann/Claudine Bouchet, Lancia Flavia 1800

Mercedes

Mercedes had a long history in motor sport dating back to 1923. In 1952 under the management of Alfred Neubauer, they started a very successful participation in sports car racing with their 300SL. It was only natural that someone would start using it on rallies and it made its first appearance as a private entry on the Tulip Rally of 1955 with Willem Tak who went home with first prize. And, with a little help from Stuttgart, Werner Engel drove a 300SL to win the European Rally Championship in 1955 with a third place on the Tulip and an outright win in Yugoslavia. 1955 was also the year of the Le Mans disaster where a works Mercedes crashed and killed seventy-seven people, one consequence of which was that Mercedes withdrew from racing at the end of the year and Neubauer retired. His replacement was Karl Kling who had been a successful driver in both sports cars and Formula One for Mercedes.

Kling's idea was to use the Mercedes facilities and knowledge – he himself had won the 1952 Carrera Panamericana road race in Mexico with a prototype 300SL – to do more in the world of rallying. With Walter Schock and Rolf Moll, they aimed for the European Championship again. With wins on the Sestriere and Acropolis rallies plus tenth in Geneva, ninth in Germany and a second place on the Monte Carlo in a 220A, Mercedes had a European Rally Champion for the second year running. Kling had developed a core of excellent mechanics who were not only adept at preparing cars for rallies, but also attended the rallies and serviced the cars where this was possible under the regulations. He also instituted a regime of recceing where crews went with proper cars and made sure that they knew where the roads were going and where time would be short.

The next sporting foray for Mercedes was when the 220SE arrived at the end of 1959 and the new car was put to work in rallies. Schock was once again European Champion in 1960 and he now had companions in the team like Eugen Böhringer, Eberhard Mahle and Dieter Glemser. Böhringer finished third in the 1961 championship and won it for Mercedes in 1962. His most famous victory was on the 1963 Liège–Sofia–Liège with the untried 230SL. That model and the big 300SE were rallied during 1964 but with diminishing success as other manufacturer teams became as efficient as that of Mercedes. Ewy Rosqvist was signed by Kling from Volvo for 1962 and rewarded Mercedes by an outright win on the Gran Premio Turismo d'Argentina with a 220SE, a victory that was repeated by Böhringer in 1964 with a 300SE.

Mercedes did send a team of 300SEs to the Safari in 1964 but failed to make an impression. From 1965 until Mercedes started the 450SLC rally programme in 1979 under Erich Waxenberger, the only Mercedes involvement was in some 280SEs for long distance events like the London to Sydney and the World Cup Rally.

Team Manager: Karl Kling

Opel

As part of General Motors, there was a high-level resistance to anything connected to motor sport within Opel during the 1960s. This would change and the man who did most to change it was Ragnar Ekelund. An active rally driver himself, he managed to persuade the Swedish Opel dealers that they had nothing to fear from supporting a bit of rallying. It all started in a small way in 1964 with Ekelund himself driving a 998 cc Kadett in a team with Håkan Lindberg with the latter winning the 851 cc–1,000 cc class on the Midnight Sun Rally. By the following year, Lindberg had moved to Renault but Dealer Opel Team Sweden soon recruited Ove Eriksson and Bertil Söderström to drive 1,900 cc Rekord Coupés and these too proved to be class winners with Ekelund himself finishing fifth in class on the Midnight Sun.

By 1966, Lillebror Nasenius had joined the team and drove a standard Rekord winning the Group 1 championship in both Sweden and Europe. He was to go on to win the Swedish title in Group 1 for another three years still using the Rekord before the team changed to the Rallye Kadett B also with a 1,900 cc engine for 1970. Their trips outside Sweden to major rallies were generally restricted to Finland's 1000 Lakes and the RAC Rally of Great Britain. The team had made the pilgrimage to Britain's forests a couple of times in the late 1960s and shown considerable promise but on the 1970 RAC Rally it all came good and Eriksson, Nasenius and Jan Hendriksson finished second, third and fourth with their Kadetts and easily claimed the team prize awarded to manufacturers.

The Opel Sweden ranks were swelled for 1971 when Anders Kulläng started driving for them and he was soon matching Eriksson as the Kadetts pursued the Group 1 Saab 96 V4s of Stig Blomqvist and Tom Trana. And they also had their fast lady when Sylvia Österberg joined them in 1968 and regularly won the Ladies prize driving from the outset in a Kadett. In 1972, the team changed to the new Ascona A and finished second and third with Kulläng and Eriksson on the Swedish Rally while Kulläng took third overall on the RAC Rally. These results did not go unobserved in Rüsselsheim and it was not long before tuners like Irmscher and Steinmetz were devising ways of making the Ascona into a truly competitive car. Of course, they needed a good driver and, at just the right moment, along came Walter Röhrl and after winning the European Championship in 1974, the way was open to that World Rally Championship title in 1982.

Rally to the Midnight Sun 1964, Ragnar Ekelund/Ake Sotterman, Opel Kadett,

Team Manager: Ragnar Ekelund

On the 1963 Monte Carlo Rally, Eugen Böhringer and Peter Lang were the best classified of the Mercedes works team at eleventh overall while Ewy Rosqvist and Ursula Wirth won the Ladies Award.

Porsche

There was never exactly a Porsche competition department as such even when the activity with the 911 reached its peak in the late 1960s. At that time, Helmuth Bott ran them out of his Research and Development department in Werk Zwei. Even a major project – for example, the Formula 1 participation with their 718 and 804 racing cars from 1957 to 1962 – was run out of the engineering area and indeed many of the entries in both racing and later rallying were made in the name of Porsche System Engineering.

Huschke von Hanstein started working for Porsche in the spring of 1951 with a brief to improve sales outside Germany. He immediately recognised motor sport as the best way to promote sales of a German car in post-war Europe. It turned out to be not such a difficult task and, for rallying at least, drivers from many countries rushed to acquire 356s and their derivatives. Von Hanstein himself took a 356 to the 1952 Midnight Sun Rally and finished third in class behind two other Porsches. In 1953, his friend Helmut Polensky won the European Championship with a 356. On occasions, Von Hanstein was able to lend a car from his promotional fleet to drivers but 'works' cars on events were fairly rare in the 1950s.

When the 911 was announced in 1964, Von Hanstein was keen to have one finish the Monte Carlo Rally of 1965 since it would be excellent publicity to have the new car photographed at the prize giving with the Monegasque royal family. Porsche already had two cars entered, 904 GTSs for Eugen Böhringer and Pauli Toivonen, so he took a press car, gave it to Peter Falk in the engineering division to fit spotlights and paired him with Herbert Linge. Their instructions were clear: get this car to the finish – undamaged! It says as much for the abilities of Linge and Falk as for the inherent ability of a 911 that, on a rally with the worst weather in living memory, they got to the finish and in sixth place. Böhringer, of course, was second overall in the 904 but other efforts with the 904 and 904/6 in rallies proved largely unsuccessful.

Porsche entered Günther Klass in the ERC during 1966 and he won the Group 3 title for them. Towards the end of 1966, Vic Elford met Von Hanstein and suggested that he would like to drive a 911 in 1967. The deal was done and Elford nearly won the Monte Carlo Rally for them, only denied victory by the unique tyre regulation. But he won other rallies and at year's end was European Champion in Group 3 and went on to win the Monte Carlo in 1968. That year Pauli Toivonen was also driving a 911 for the factory and became the European Champion. Meanwhile in Sweden, initially without direct support from Stuttgart, Björn Waldegård had been driving a 911 for the Swedish importer, Scania-Vabis. He won the Swedish Rally in 1967/1968/1969 and for 1969 became part of the works team where he promptly delivered two Monte Carlo wins on the trot and thus, with Elford's 1968 victory, enabling Porsche to claim a hat trick.

Within Porsche, the management felt that Von Hanstein was not perhaps concentrating enough on sales so that Rico Steinemann was brought in to be the team manager. During his three-year rule, competition activities in Porsche reached a peak with the 917 racing programme, but they also continued on the rally side. With Waldegård, Gérard Larrousse and Åke Andersson driving regularly and Zasada joining for the Safari, they had a very strong team and, as well as success in individual events, Porsche won the IRCM in 1970. When Steinemann left at the end of 1971, rally activities became – among many other things – the responsibility of Jürgen Barth. His title was Director of Customer Racing Services but he took every opportunity to keep Porsche involved in rallying. This extended to occasionally driving himself, for example, taking a 924 GTS on the 1982 Monte Carlo Rally with engineer Roland Kussmaul and finishing tenth overall. He was also the driving force behind several further attempts at conquering the Safari Rally with Porsche claiming second place twice, once with Zasada in 1972 and once with Waldegård in 1974.

Monte Carlo Rally 1971, Gérard Larrousse/Jean-Claude Perramond, Porsche 914/6

On the Monte Carlo of 1968, Jürgen Barth, later to be in charge of the team, puts the finishing touches to a tyre change for the winning 911S of Vic Elford.

▲▶ The hallmark of Porsche rally car preparation was simplicity combined with functionality almost as if they had taken instruction from the Bauhaus school. This is one of two Porsche 911Ss entered for the 1972 Monte Carlo Rally.

Renault

Renault was also involved in the early 1950s and started a competition department in 1951. Its first manager was François Landon who also drove a 4CV in rallies and races, winning a Coupe on the Rallye des Alpes in 1951 and also finishing twenty-third in a 4CV at Le Mans. Jean Rédélé drove for Landon, but after driving a 4CV to win a Coupe himself on the 1954 Rallye des Alpes, he started his own car manufacturing company and called it Alpine after the Rallye des Alpes. When the Dauphine arrived in 1956, almost its first major assignment was to go to the Mille Miglia. And soon Landon was able to deploy special Group 5/6 Dauphines developed by Amédée Gordini with five-speed gearboxes and improved engines with inclined valves and better manifolds.

It was under Landon that the company sent a team of five Ondine Gordinis to the Safari in 1961 (three finished) while in 1962 he sent six R4Ls and again three were at the finish. His next move was to persuade Renault to manufacture a production run of special Dauphines called the 1093 – the figure is Renault's internal code and not its cylinder capacity since that stayed at 848 cc – so that it could be homologated into Group 2. This little rocket with its standard four-speed gearbox, uprated suspension and larger Solex carburettor was ideal for tuning and it was soon notching up results. The Dauphine had always been successful in Corsica with three victories to its credit in the 1950s and now in 1962 Pierre Orsini took one to his second victory on that island.

The next Renault rally car was the R8 Gordini in which Gordini not only had a hand in the development but also lent his name to the model. This came out in 1964 with a 1,108 cc engine, four-speed gearbox and the option of five speeds in Group 2. This new car had its teething troubles and then, in February of 1965, Landon departed for Ajaccio to run the dealership that he owned there and that sold both Renault and Alfa Romeo cars.

His replacement at Renault was Jacques Féret who had been a partner with Guy Monraisse during his victories in Monte Carlo Rally 1958, Tour de Corse 1958 and in the touring category of the Liège–Rome–Liège in 1959. Gradually the R8 Gordini became reliable and accepted as a good performer in both Group 1 and Group 2. It was a great success with drivers like Jean-François Piot, Gérard Larrousse, Jean-Pierre Nicolas and Jean-Luc Thérier who used the R8 to rise up the ranks and become works drivers for first Renault and later for Alpine. Relations were a little strained between Renault competitions and its 'client' company, Alpine, since both were heavily involved in rallying and, by the end of the 1960s, it was Alpine that were delivering better results. Féret eventually concentrated on promotion formulae like the Coupe Renault Gordini while Renault bankrolled the Alpine efforts that were directed by Jacques Cheinisse and run from their factory in Dieppe. When Renault bought out Alpine just before 1973, the Alpine team became synonymous with Renault and in that form, they won the first WRC in 1973.

▲ In the late 1960s, Renault encouraged young French drivers to compete with the R8 Gordini. This is Jean-Luc Thérier on the 1968 Lyon-Charbonnières who went on to win Group 1 and finish fourth overall.

◀ Renault entered six Dauphine Gordinis for the 1961 Safari Rally and were given the first six numbers in a year when the cars with small engines started first.

Rootes

The Rootes Group had one of the longest running manufacturer teams though the company did go through some changes of ownership along the way. There were also a large number of marque names associated with the team including Sunbeam, Hillman, Humber and Talbot, all of whom had a role in competition activities under the umbrella of first Rootes ownership, then Chrysler UK and finally Peugeot.

At the beginning of the 1950s, Norman Garrard, an engineer who had been a successful rally driver before 1939, took charge of a team of Sunbeam Talbot 90 saloons. Rally success was not long in coming. With drivers like Stirling Moss, Mike Hawthorn, veteran George Murray-Frame – a man who won three Coupes on the Rallye des Alpes in five years between 1948 and 1952 – and Sheila van Damm, the Sunbeams always shone in the Alps. Moss in particular was outstanding by writing history as the second man to win a Coupe d'Or for three consecutive Coupes. So successful was the 90 and its derivatives that Rootes named its most sporty version the Alpine and it was this model that was used in the 1953 Rallye des Alpes.

Moss also netted sixth place for Garrard on the 1953 Monte Carlo though this commendable performance was eclipsed in 1955 by Per Malling and Gunnar Fadum, private entrants from Norway who only took delivery of their new Sunbeam Talbot three weeks before the rally. They were meticulous in their approach to the new timing system and went on to win outright with two works Sunbeams of Peter Harper and Sheila van Damm ninth and eleventh. Van Damm also won the Coupe des Dames and went on to win the Ladies prize in the ERC for the second time.

The 1,500 cc Sunbeam Rapier was the next car chosen for rallying and Harper notched up its first big victory on the 1958 RAC Rally having already won a Coupe on the Rallye des Alpes that year. Garrard had committed to enter a team of Hillman Huskies on the Safari Rally in 1959 and when Hawthorn was unable to go, he signed up Paddy Hopkirk who had just left Triumph. Neither Hopkirk nor Harper finished the Safari in the little estate cars but the third Rootes entry, a Humber Super Snipe driven by ex-Monte winner, Ronnie Adams finished in twenty-seventh place. That same year, Hopkirk and Peter Jopp both won Coupes on the Rallye des Alpes in Rapiers and took third and sixth places overall.

Garrard always liked to make sure that the team included a ladies crew. When Rootes started rallying the Hillman Imp and homologated a special 'Rally Imp' in 1964, he had Rosemary Smith already in the team. She had won the Coupe des Dames on the Circuit of Ireland in a Rapier and was invited to stay with the team to drive the new Imp. However, at the beginning of 1964, Garrard had stepped aside and been replaced by ex-BMC boss, Marcus Chambers, making his return to motor sport.

Chambers found that there was insufficient engineering input going into the cars and, during his reform of the competition department, in late 1964 brought in Des O'Dell, someone who had experience of racing with Aston Martin, John Wyer and GT40s. Their rally programme over the next few years involved making entries with Imps and with the Ford V8-engined version of the Series 2 Sunbeam Alpine known as the Sunbeam Tiger.

Behind the scenes, things were happening in the main company that did not bode well for its motor sport activities. Chrysler bought out Rootes in June 1967 and, when they found that there was insufficient room to replace the Ford V8 engine in the engine compartment of the Tiger with one of their own, the car was dropped from production. Things carried on for a while with the Imp while O'Dell looked at other cars in the Chrysler/Rootes range. When it came to the 1968 London to Sydney, he and Chambers chose a Hillman Hunter and crewed it with Andrew Cowan, his regular co-driver Brian Coyle and Colin Malkin who had just won the British rally championship in an Imp. They won the event and gained the company worldwide publicity but this did not stop Chambers being made redundant in early 1969 as the company was reshuffled to become Chrysler UK. The competition department in Humber Road continued now under the direction of O'Dell who continued to develop cars like the Avenger mainly for use in national rallies. By keeping the workforce intact, it meant that when the opportunity arrived at the end of the 1970s to produce a real rally winner, the Sunbeam Lotus, O'Dell was able to take the chance and go on to win the WRC.

Monte Carlo Rally 1955, Jack Fairman/L. Smith, Sunbeam-Talbot Mk III

Monte Carlo Rally 1964, Keith Ballisat/Andrew Cowan, Hillman Imp

Rover

In 1962, the Rover Company decided to take an interest in rallying. This was largely stimulated by the fact that, Richard, the son of the Managing Director, at that time, William Martin-Hurst, was an active participant in British events. Through a small department in their Solihull factory, they prepared four three-litre P5 saloons for the 1962 Safari Rally. The team manager was Ralph Nash and his chief engineer – and sometimes works driver – was Toney Cox. To many people's surprise, Ronnie Adams was lying fifth overall at the halfway point in Nairobi. He later broke the steering but two of the other P5s did finish the rally. The cars were then shipped home and re-prepared for the Liège–Sofia–Liège where one, driven by Ken James, finished sixth overall out of just eighteen finishers. The team went back to the Safari in 1963 this time with three cars. It was an appallingly wet year when only seven cars got to the finish and one of the Rovers driven by Bill Bengry was the seventh finisher of 'The Magnificent Seven'. Later that year, they entered a team of P5s on the RAC Rally all of which finished and they only failed to win their class thanks to the fact that they were running in the same class as the rally winner, the Volvo PV544 of Tom Trana and the similar car of Gunnar Andersson. Again it was Bengry who was the one to take third in class

From 1964, the team started to develop the Rover 2000 (also known as the P6) which was a much more lively and better handling proposition despite only having a two-litre engine. Nash recruited a good team of drivers including Roger Clark, Andrew Cowan and Anne Hall. They entered events like Coupe des Alpes where Cowan was third in the touring category for them in 1965. However, Rover had possibly their best result the same year on the Monte Carlo Rally with Clark when, amid all the snow and chaos, he finished sixth overall and won Group 1. It is possible, had Group 1 risen to be the dominant force in rallying as the CSI hoped it would, that the P6 might have gone on to more success but it was not to be. Clark went off to drive for Ford while Cowan went back to Rootes and Rover competition activities ground to a halt until the mid-1980s.

The Rover importer entered four of these three-litre Rover P5 saloons on the 1962 Safari Rally. This one driven by P.A. Brochner was forced to retire.

Saab

Rolf Melde was one of the fifteen original engineers who were taken from aircraft production to work on Saab's first efforts at automobile design and manufacture. As chief development engineer for the company, Melde, who had previously rallied himself with a DKW, realised that the new Saab 92 could be its own best publicity. Somehow he managed to get two pre-production 92s released for him and Greta Molander to compete on the Monte Carlo Rally of 1950 where they both finished.

Since the departments dealing with chassis and engine development were under the supervision of Melde, for most of the 1950s the competition activities of Saab were run out of his area. Melde was also one of the principal drivers and used feedback from the rallies to help improve the standard production cars. Already in 1950 when he finished fourth overall on the Rally to the Midnight Sun and won the Rikspokalen (National Trophy) – an event billed as 'the toughest motoring event in Europe' – in a 92, it was clear that this two-cylinder, 764 cc powered front-wheel drive car had competition potential. Greta Molander won the Coupe des Dames with one on the 1951 Midnight Sun – the first of many – as well as on the 1952 Monte Carlo while in 1953 she won the Ladies European title and Melde won the Swedish championship. Two years later Erik Carlsson won the Rikspokalen with a 92 supplied by Melde and made his name with that car by winning innumerable national rallies and races.

In 1956 using the new 93 with its three-cylinder 750 cc engine, Carlsson was third overall on the Midnight Sun with Melde fourth while that September, Carl-Magnus Skogh won the Viking Rally with Carlsson second. Gradually, things were becoming more professional with mechanics dedicated to rally – and race – car preparation. Melde was not slow to pick up on the idea of having proper service cars especially when they took cars to events like the 1959 Le Mans 24 Hours where a 93 Sport finished twelfth out of the twelve classified finishers and was supported by a fully equipped 95 Estate car.

Carlsson and Skogh continued their winning ways on major rallies in Sweden, Finland and Britain in the early 1960s and Carlsson took a fourth place on the 1961 Monte Carlo Rally driving a 95 Estate car. With major events requiring more complex service arrangements than in the past and non-Scandinavian events – with the exception of the RAC Rally – requiring the provision of recce cars, Saab decided that they would create their own dedicated competition department. They chose Bo Hellberg, a man with plenty of competition experience having been a co-driver in Volkswagens and Porsches and who had also been working with the Swedish automobile club, the KAK, on the organisation of events. They also took the preparation of the rally and recce cars out of the engineering area and moved it to premises that had been a workshop for the local Saab dealer in Trollhättan.

Apart from completing a hat trick of victories on the RAC Rally from 1960 to 1962, Carlsson also won the Monte Carlo Rally twice in 1962 and 1963 and finished a remarkable second on the Liège–Sofia–Liège of 1963. That same year, he married Pat Moss and not long afterwards she also joined the official Saab team though even prior to that she had been driving a 96 in some rallies, notably the Safari Rally. Hellberg acquired a number two in his organisation, Bo Swanér, who was promptly nicknamed 'Baby Bo' while the chief mechanic was Per-Olof Rudh. Between them, they established a reputation for efficiency and achieving a lot from modest resources. Eventually the old guard of Saab drivers decided to hang up their helmets and this happened around the time that the 96 became the

96 V4. Hellberg was able to find some good replacements in Stig Blomqvist, Håkan Lindberg and Per Eklund. Simo Lampinen who had been driving for the Finnish Saab team – with whom he had already won the 1000 Lakes twice – also joined them. Hellberg was always a realist and realised that the 96 V4 was no match in certain conditions for Porsches, Escorts and Alpines so he chose his events wisely and was rewarded with multiple wins on rallies like the RAC and Swedish. The Saab Competition department was to carry on in the 1970s with turbocharged cars but the same levels of success were never repeated though, especially on the Swedish Rally, the combination of Blomqvist and Saab could still astound their rivals.

Between 1960 and 1971, Saab won the RAC Rally five times. This is Stig Blomqvist and Arne Hertz driving their works Saab 96 V4 to victory in 1971.

This is a photograph of a Saab Sport engine taken before the Monte Carlo Rally of 1964. The three-cylinder, 841cc two-stroke engine was fed by three Solex carburettors with six air filters.

Standard Triumph

The person that kick-started Triumph's involvement in rallying was Ken Richardson, an engineer who had worked on the testing of aircraft engines during the war and had then worked at the British race car constructors, ERA and BRM, as both engineer and test driver before moving to Triumph at the beginning of 1952. Richardson's first job was to sort out Triumph's prototype sports car, the TR1, that he was later to recall was originally 'a death trap' and the result was the TR2 – which was not!

In 1953, he was asked to prepare a prototype TR2 to try and beat the speed records recently set up by Rootes. With his motor sport engineering credentials well established, Richardson was able to set up a competition department within the development and service departments on the western outskirts of Coventry. One of the other spurs for this was that the factory had released four of its new TR2s to well-known drivers in time for the 1954 RAC Rally where Johnny Wallwork promptly won it with two more TR2s finishing second and fifth with Peter Cooper and Bill Bleakley.

Triumph had already forged a relationship with Maurice Gatsonides, the Monte Carlo winner of 1953 with a Ford, who had agreed to drive Triumphs in 1954. Their first major effort was on the Rallye des Alpes where they came away with a Coupe and sixth overall for Gatsonides and with Richardson finishing fourth in class. With a private owner in a TR2, they won both the team and manufacturer prizes.

Richardson was good at reading the regulations both for the individual rally and the FIA's technical regulations by which the cars had to be prepared. The result was that, in the ensuing years, Triumph would compete with whatever car he thought suited the rally best. For instance, in 1955, they had all four of their Standard 10s finish the Monte Carlo. Then in August of that year, Richardson and Gatsonides driving TR2s finished fifth and seventh overall on the Liège. They also entered Standard Vanguards on the 1956 Safari Rally, Group 1 Standard 8s on the Tulip Rally of 1956 and Group 2 Standard Pennants on the RAC Rally of 1958.

Thanks to a policy of providing cars to top drivers, by the start of the 1960s the Triumph marque had a good reputation in the rally world. But dark clouds were on the horizon since the Standard Triumph Company was in the red and, at the end of 1960, it was gobbled up by the Leyland company. By the middle of 1961, the new management had a 'night of the long knives' with 800 employees and all but two of the board of management being made redundant. Despite Geoff Mabbs having just won the Tulip Rally with a Herald Coupé and all three twin-cam TR4Ss finishing at Le Mans, Richardson was amongst those 800 leaving the company.

Not all was lost, however, as within a year, Harry Webster had employed Graham Robson to be competition secretary and to run a new department. With Vic Elford, Jean-Jacques Thuner and Mike Sutcliffe on its driving strength they ran TR4s, Spitfires, Vitesses and finally the 2000 saloon in a variety of international rallies. The department continued through 1965 and 1966 under the direction of Ray Henderson and picked up a win with a Spitfire in the Rallye des Alpes prototype category driven by Lampinen. But with the arrival of the new Appendix J in 1966, the 2000 became much less competitive and activity dwindled until Leyland bought BMC and the BMC competition department was given the job of rallying Triumph 2.5 PIs.

Triumph entered three cars on the 1969 RAC Rally as a test for the 1970 World Cup Rally. Andrew Cowan and Brian Coyle brought this 2.5 PI home in eleventh place.

Volvo

The popularity of the Volvo PV444 with drivers in all branches of Scandinavian motor sport in the mid-1950s was not matched by a similar enthusiasm on behalf of Volvo management. Indeed, Assar Gabrielsson, one of the founders of the company who was now its managing director, was worried that motor sport and the accidents that it produced would have a negative effect for the general public to whom Volvo were selling their cars on an image of safety. He may have disliked rallying and racing but the introduction of the 1.6-litre engine for the PV444 in 1957 only made matters worse as did the arrival of the PV544 a year later with its four-speed gearbox. These cars handled well and adapted themselves perfectly to the demands of rallying.

One of the best exponents of the PV's abilities was Gunnar Andersson who, with his own cars, won the European Rally Championship in 1958. By this time Gabrielsson had become chairman and the new managing director was Gunnar Engellau who was much more supportive of motor sport and of rallying in particular. By 1959, Andersson – and other drivers – were getting support from the company in the form of parts and development. The company started to spread their motor sport wings by, for instance, entering cars in the Gran Premio Internacional Turismo d'Argentina in 1960 where Andersson brought them an outright win. As a result of that and their increasing success in both Scandinavian and European rallies, in early 1962, Engellau asked Andersson if he would consider doing slightly less driving and instead organise a proper rally team with on-event service and a team of professional drivers.

One suspects that Andersson was not too keen on this idea as he liked driving and competing. Even after he got support for his own efforts from the company, he entered his own PV in the Swedish racing championship and won the title in 1959. Anyway, he agreed to Engellau's suggestion and fairly quickly organised the team. He soon had drivers like Tom Trana, Carl-Magnus Skogh, Bengt Söderström and Sylvia Österberg doing events for him. Trana in particular was a big success while Sylvia Österberg proved equally adept at lifting the Coupe des Dames as had her predecessor, Ewy Rosqvist, with her semi-works PVs at the end of the 1950s. Andersson managed to combine his running of the team with a driving role and did so to such effect that he won the European Rally Championship again in 1963 with Trana taking the title in 1964. Andersson also took a team of four PV544s to the Safari in 1964 but none of them finished. However, this did eventually give Volvo one of its biggest wins of the decade when Joginder Singh took over one of the PV544s they had left behind and won the Safari with it in 1965.

But success was also tempered by accidents during the team's activities on rallies, two of which produced fatalities. The first trauma came in 1964 on the Polish Rally where no one as killed though Andersson was badly injured and partially paralysed. For some time, it was thought that he would not be able to drive again but his mobility was soon fully restored. However, on the Gulf London Rally of 1965, Trana had a road accident in Britain where his co-driver, Gunnar Thermaenius was killed. And less than a year later, two Volvo mechanics were killed in a freak road accident during the Acropolis Rally leading to Volvo withdrawing their cars from that event. None of this went down terribly well with senior management at Volvo and thus, at the end of the 1965 season, with the advent for 1966 of the new Appendix J and new homologation requirements diminishing the performance of their cars, works activity dwindled to almost nothing. The competition department continued to look after cars for private entrants and sell competition parts with all such activity all still under the direction of Andersson. Trana bought two of the 122Ss from him and rallied them during 1966 before migrating to the Saab team for 1967 while Sylvia Österberg left immediately and already drove for Renault in 1966.

▲ Acropolis Rally 1965, Carl-Magnus Skogh/Lennart Berggren, Volvo Amazon 122S

◀ In 1964, Volvo's rally car of choice was still the PV544 and at the competition department in Gothenburg prior to the 1964 Monte Carlo Rally, there was a lot of work needed to be ready for the coming season.

Chapter

Appendix
The fairer sex
Getting technical
Tour de Corse
East African Safari Rally
Long Distance Information
Odds and Ends
Epilogue

09

Chapter 09
Appendix

The fairer sex

There are many differences between international rallying in the 1950s and the sport as it is today in the 21st century. But none so marked as the number of lady drivers participating in rallies. Right through the 1950s and 1960s, the Coupe des Dames was fought over with as much passion as for the outright win. And occasionally, the ladies fought for that as well.

Right from the start of the European Touring Championship in 1953, there was always a Coupe des Dames awarded at the end of the year alongside the other championship trophies. In the beginning, points were only awarded to driver and co-driver if there were more than five ladies crews starting a rally. To a certain extent this weakened its appeal since, on some of the lesser-known events, that criterion was not achieved, while on other rallies, there were sometimes dozens of ladies crews. Also in order to score, both – or all if there were more than two persons in the crew – people in the car had to be feminine. Had that not been the case then lady co-drivers like Pat Appleyard, Mirielle Landon, Nicole Angevin and later Eva Zasada might well have scored points by accompanying their husbands to rally success.

The first Ladies Champion was Greta Molander who, co-driven by Helga Lundberg, took the 1953 title with a Saab 92. Molander was Swedish by birth and Norwegian by adoption – she married Kaare Barth in 1938 – and was a prolific travel writer. Like so many of the ladies who drove on rallies in the 1930s and 1950s, she was what the British refer to as 'a character'. Molander was as famous for her hats as she was for writing and rally driving. And many others were equally interesting. Sheila van Damm, who won the Ladies title in 1954 and 1955 for Sunbeam Talbot, only entered her first rally – the 1950 Daily Express Rally – with her sister Nona navigating as a bit of publicity for the legendary Windmill Theatre in London, home of 'Revudeville' and other delights, that she ran with her father, Vivian.

There was nothing quite that exotic in Nancy Mitchell's background though she had raced HRGs, Daimlers and Allards with success before she joined the BMC team under Marcus Chambers for 1956. She drove a wide variety of cars during her four years in the BMC team including MG Magnettes, Riley 1.5s, Austin Healey 100-6s and even a Mini Minor 850 but she was far and away most successful with the MGA 1500. She narrowly missed winning the Ladies title in 1956 when Greta Molander was crowned for the second time driving various Mercedes and Peugeots. Mitchell was unlucky in that her high placings on the Geneva, Rallye des Alpes and Liège-Rome-Liège that year did not count as there were less than five ladies crews starting on those events. However she did win the title in 1957 that included winning the Ladies Prize on the 1957 Liège–Rome–Liège.

However in Mitchell's championship year, a young lady called Pat Moss had started driving rallies for the BMC team and in 1958, rose to win the title herself. Moss's background was as a highly successful international equestrienne but the fact that her brother, Stirling, as well as her mother, Aileen, and father, Alfred, were competitive drivers all tended to ease her into the driving seat of a rally car. Once there she proved to be one of the outstanding lady drivers of all time by winning the Ladies title five times in 1958, 1960, 1962, 1964 and 1965. If further proof were needed, her outright win on the 1960 Liège–Rome–Liège with a Healey 3000 plus other outright wins and podium finishes on major internationals confirm that accolade. Her drives to fourth place on the 1964 Liège–Sofia–

Greta Molander was the first European Ladies Champion, securing the title in 1953.

Pat Moss drove for Ford in 1963 with both Cortina GT and Lotus Cortina.

Appendix - The fairer Sex

▲ Headscarves and handbags. During the 1970s, Ford ran a competition to find the next Pat Moss. Heading this line-up are Jill Robinson and Liz Crellin.

◄ Acropolis Rally 1964. Pat Moss – or Pat Moss-Carlsson as she was more correctly titled after marrying Erik Carlsson – and Valerie Domleo pick up the prize for finishing third overall in their Saab 96 Sport from the new King of Greece, Constantine II.

Pat Moss-Carlsson and Liz Nystrom with their trophies after finishing ninth overall and winning the Coupe des Dames on the RAC Rally of 1966

While Pat Moss and Erik Carlsson only have eyes for each other, Graham Hill looks to the camera.

Sometimes you think you are dreaming but wake up to discover it is real ! Gunnar Palm was persuaded – with difficulty? – to do this PR shot at the 1967 Acropolis Rally. Dear me, what hardships one had to suffer in rallying during the 1960s …

Liège and third overall on the 1963 Safari Rally in a Saab 96 were particularly notable. And it was with a Lancia Fulvia that she also won the Sestriere Rally outright in 1968. Pat Moss effectively retired in the early 1970s at which point many gentlemen drivers must have sighed with relief when they realised that a rival had gone.

It would be all too easy to pass on from this period without mentioning two non-champions. Firstly, Gilberte Thirion whose main claim to fame was that she won the Tour de Corse outright in 1956 with Nadège Ferrier driving a Renault Dauphine Spéciale. Before that, she had competed mainly in races often alongside her good friends, Olivier Gendebien and Annie Bousquet. Her father was the importer of Champion spark plugs based in Belgium and in 1952 he bought her a Porsche 356 Gmünd with which they went rallying together. It was, for instance, in this car that they met Helmut Polensky on the Rallye des Alpes of 1952 and, when his car was not ready, she lent him her Porsche to win the Liège–Rome–Liège of that year.

Accompanying Sheila van Damm on many of her successful rallying outings was Anne Hall from Huddersfield in Yorkshire who soon turned to driving as a number one. Initially she drove for Ford with Anglias, Zephyrs and Falcons and was rewarded by a string of Ladies awards on major rallies including on the Monte Carlo Rally of 1961 when she drove a Ford Anglia with Valerie Domleo. That same year, she drove a Ford Zephyr Mk2 on the Safari Rally with Lucille Cardwell and finished a very creditable third overall behind the two winning Mercedes 220SEs. When Ford America were choosing their team for the 1964 Monte Carlo, Hall was paired with the American driver, Denise McCluggage, and they brought their Falcon Futura Sprint, a V8-engined monster, home to take fourth in the Ladies prize behind Pat Moss (Saab 96), Sylvia Österberg (Volvo 122S) and Ewy Rosqvist (Mercedes 220SE). Anne Hall went on to drive Rover 2000s for a couple of years and then retired.

With the Scandinavians beginning to take over rallying in the late 1950s, it was no surprise that a second Swedish lady should win the Ladies title in 1959. This was Ewy Rosqvist whose glamorous blonde exterior concealed a very tough competitor. She had learnt her driving skills in her job as a veterinary assistant when she had to go around the country roads of Southern Sweden in both summer and winter conditions. A friend persuaded her to have a go at a rally and by 1956 she was good enough to finish sixth in the Ladies class of the Midnight Sun Rally with a Fiat 1100. On that same rally in 1957, she came fourth in the Ladies class with a Saab 93 while, in 1958, also in a Saab, she was second. She finally won it in 1959 with a Volvo PV544 and repeated that victory with Volvos in 1960 and 1961 before moving to Mercedes for 1962 when she won it again in a 220SEb. It was with Volvo that she won the European Ladies title in 1959 and 1961. But it was with Mercedes that she stunned the world by winning outright the Gran Premio Turismo d'Argentina in 1962 with Ursula Wirth.

In the 1959 European Championship Rosqvist actually tied on points with Annie Soisbault, the works Triumph TR3A driver, with the decision going to the Swedish lady on the basis of number of outright wins in the Ladies class. Curiously, these two ladies proved to have quite a lot of other things in common since they were both keen tennis players – Soisbault was a seven-times French champion and also played at Wimbledon – and eventually both married into the aristocracy. Rosqvist married Baron von Korff who had been working for the Mercedes team while Soisbault married the Marquis de Montaigu. Since de Montaigu's interest was more in racing than rallying, her subsequent rally exploits were limited though they did rally a Ferrari GTO together in 1965. But before that, Soisbault's achievements in rallying were substantial. In 1959 alone she took fourth place overall on the Liège–Rome–Liège and ninth overall on the Acropolis in a TR3A with René Wagner, won the Coupe des Dames on the Tour de France Automobile in a soft-top TR3A and, together with two other Triumphs, won the manufacturer team prize on the RAC Rally.

Ursula Wirth co-drove for both Ewy Rosqvist and, briefly, with Pat Moss.

Big car, little lady. Anne Hall was a very determined driver in all kinds of cars and never lacked for courage or skill.

Eva-Maria Falk, a German journalist, co-drove for Ewy Rosqvist in a Mercedes 220SE on the 1964 Monte Carlo Rally.

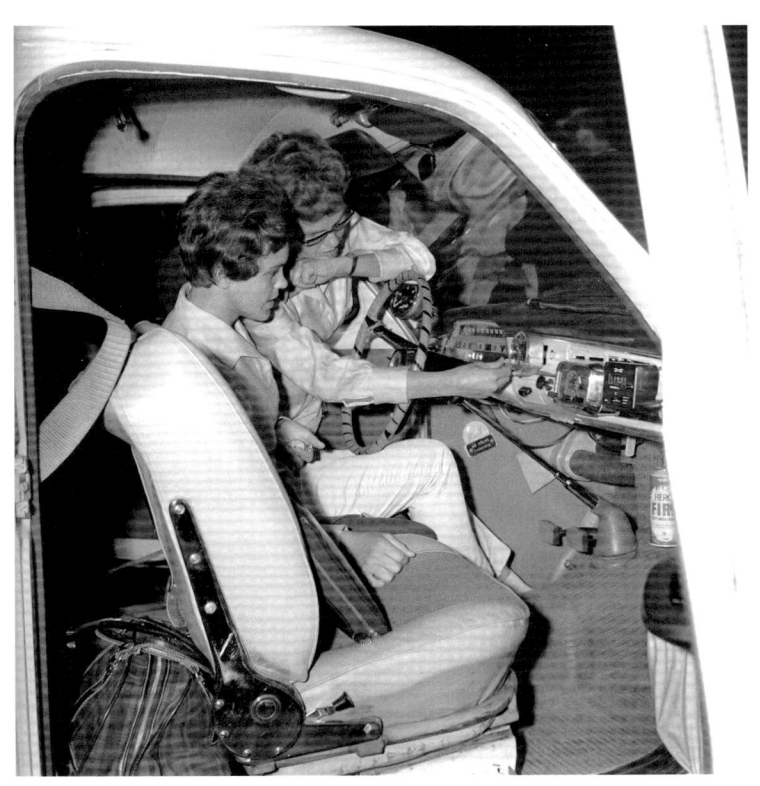

Sylvia Österberg explains all the dashboard instruments of their Volvo PV 544 to Siw Sabel before the Acropolis Rally of 1964.

When Pat Moss defected from BMC to Ford, her replacement at BMC was Pauline Mayman (on the L) who together with Valerie Domleo were European Ladies Champions in 1963. Here they are seen before the Rallye des Alpes of 1964 with their Cooper S 970.

Appendix - The fairer Sex

With the adoption in 1966 of new regulations for both the cars and the European Championship, a Ladies title became less influential, partly due to the fact that, with three male champions, life was too complicated to take in a fourth. At the same time, as the number of all-lady crews being entered on events was diminishing, the status gained by winning a Ladies Prize on individual events also shrunk. But things went on as normal for a couple of years with Sylvia Österberg winning the title in 1966. Österberg had been Rosqvist's successor at Volvo and finished second to the Mercedes driver on her debut event with the Volvo team in Finland in 1962. Then in 1963 and 1964 she won the Ladies Prize on the Midnight Sun Rally. When Volvo stopped with its works team for 1966, she started driving an R8 Gordini for Renault Sweden and during that year amassed enough points to win the title. She subsequently went to drive for Opel Sweden in a Group 1 Rallye Kadett accompanied by her husband, Ingemar. She was also one of the drivers who in January 1971 helped Opel to set two World Records with a special diesel-powered Opel GT.

The only publicity given to Sylvia Österberg's title appears to have come from Volvo and indeed during the six years that followed the introduction of the new Appendix J and European Rally Championship rules at the beginning of 1966, an annual title for lady drivers seemed to be far from the thoughts of the men in Paris.

For 1967 there was no formal announcement of a Ladies title but if one was looking for the outstanding lady in the rallies of that year, it would have to be Lucette Pointet. Initially she co-drove for Citroën but, after a few years, started taking the wheel herself. It was in that role she finished fourteenth overall and won the Ladies Prize on the 1965 Safari Rally and she was also top lady driver on the 1966 Monte Carlo Rally. However, for 1967, she went back to co-driving, sitting alongside Jean-Claude Ogier – who she later married – in a Group 1 Citroën DS21. The points scoring was such that she was listed equal with Ogier as eleventh overall in the Group 1 driver's listing for the ERC and was thus the best lady driver of the year though her performance was not recognised with a trophy. She teamed up with Rosemary Smith in 1968 to drive a Ford Cortina Lotus on the London to Sydney and they finished second in the Ladies Prize.

The FIA did announce a 'Ladies Cup' for the European Rally Championship of 1968 and 1969. However, the phrase 'lady driver of an exclusively female crew' was clear in the wording. Thus, despite the excellent performance of Eva Zasada who was ninth in the European Rally Championship for Drivers of 1969 by virtue of accompanying her husband, Sobieslaw Zasada, no such award was made. In a way, things got slightly worse for 1970 and 1971 since, in the European Championship regulations published for those years, there was not even the passing mention of a Ladies Cup or any similar trophy or title.

However, for 1972 there was a positive trumpeting of the new 'European Rally Cup for Ladies'. Scoring was only for drivers in 'exclusively female teams' and points would be awarded in the same way as for all the other drivers and not on the basis of a separate classification for lady drivers. Furthermore, there was no requirement as there had been in the past for there to be a minimum number of ladies teams starting the event.

The lady who stepped forward to claim the 1972 title was Marie-Claude Beaumont, née Marie-Claude Charmasson, whose father ran the Citroën dealership in Gap and had competed himself on rallies with a Citroën 15. Her rally career kicked off when she accompanied Claudine Bouchet (later Trautmann) in a works Lancia Flavia on the 1964 Liège–Sofia–Liège. Bouchet was already four times ladies rally champion of France (1960-63) and her young companion learnt fast. She adopted the pseudonym of 'Beaumont' so that driving in cars that were not Citroëns did not embarrass her father's business. She was soon driving NSU 1000s on rallies and then, in company with Henri Greder, American Fords. In 1969 she formally joined the Greder Racing Team that was by then firmly linked to Opel and, over the next years, drove everything from Kadetts and Commodores to Corvettes and Camaros. In 1972 with good results from half a dozen ERC rounds, including a fifth place overall on the Tour de France Automobile in a Corvette, she clinched the Ladies title with ease.

It would be fair to say that in the rallying world of the last forty years, lady drivers have not played a major part except for the one astonishingly amazing exception, Michèle Mouton. During the 1980s, this lady won no fewer than four WRC rallies outright and so very nearly became World Rally Champion in 1982. It is appropriate therefore that she now works with the FIA as President of their 'Women in Motorsport Commission' with a mandate to get more ladies participating in a sport in which they have done so well in the past.

Before the start of the 1970 World Cup Rally (London to Mexico), the ladies crew of (from L to R) Rosemary Smith, Ginette Derolland and Alice Watson are interviewed in front of their Austin Maxi 1500 with which they finished tenth overall and won the Coupe des Dames.

▲ Marie-Claude Beaumont's rally career started with the French NSU team. She quickly graduated to the French Opel team where she drove Commodores, Kadetts, Chevrolet Camaros and Asconas. In 1972, she won the re-instituted European Ladies Championship. Here she is seen on the RAC Rally of 1971 where she drove an Ascona with Martine de la Grandrive where they won the Coupe des Dames.

◀ On her way to a Coupe des Dames on the 1966 Acropolis Rally with a Hillman Imp, Rosemary Smith grabs some quick refreshment from team manager, Des O'Dell.

▼ And my other car is a Porsche … but most of Rosemary Smith's victories came with another rear-engined car – the Hillman Imp.

Getting technical

When Paul Newman, as the character Butch Cassidy, asked in the famous Western film 'Butch Cassidy and the Sundance Kid' about the rules for a knife fight, the answer he got was that there were none. In many ways, that is how it was in rallying for quite a while. What people did to their cars to 'prepare' them for rallying was not under any kind of overall control. This meant that the only thing the organisers could do was to list the recognised Groups and Classes in their regulations and add any caveats that occurred to them about not doing certain things to them or using particular equipment. There had been an attempt in 1931 to define what was meant by a series-production touring car but until the CSI issued their first regulations for series-production cars in late 1952, there was no common guidance on such matters.

Let us choose the Tulip Rally to give an example of what we are talking about here. The 1952 event was won by Ken Wharton driving his own Ford Consul with a bit of help from Ford. The Consul had been modified in that it had a twin carburetor conversion and used a Zephyr rear axle. The British were not the only ones trying to ensure that their cars were properly competitive since on the same event, a Dutch MG TD was observed to have a shortened and lowered chassis. Such things were not easily spotted and would have needed comparison with a standard car to discover them, unless one was very familiar with the particular model. However, many of the cars being driven on the rally sported plastic windows in place of the standard glass and even plywood body parts where a standard car would have steel. These were easily seen but no one did anything.

Naturally, the Tulip organisers came in for some criticism for allowing such liberties and, like officialdom everywhere when put under pressure, swung a bit too far in the opposite direction. At post-rally scrutineering in 1953 and wielding the new regulations, they came down on the competing cars like a wolf on the fold. Nine cars were thrown out for being 'over modified' and eight of these belonged to British entrants. Sadly, the departure of cars from his class meant that Bill Banks and his Bristol 401 who would otherwise have won the event could only finish second. Ian Appleyard, who was classified fourth overall and won his class, was not above suspicion and the cylinder head came off his Mk VII Jaguar to ensure that it was not of the C-type variety.

Over the next few years, rallies veered between the Liège–Rome–Liège attitude of 'modify it all you like, it won't help you' and the more restrictive approach. This was where scrutineers expected to find a car in conformity with what they understood to be a production version plus any declaration of modifications that the entrant had made on his entry form. It was not an easy situation for either officialdom or the competitors and eventually the FIA took a hand. In time for the 1957 season, they published a more detailed Appendix J to the International Sporting Code. There were to be four modified versions of the 1952 rules published in the fifteen years after 1952 of which this was the first.

The idea was very simple: define the kind of cars that one is talking about and then set out a list of modifications that may – or may not – be carried out on them for use in competition. Prior to 1957, there had been a definition of cars that tried to make the distinction between 'touring' and 'sports' cars. The 'touring' category was split into three sub-groups of 'normal series', 'GT series production' and 'special series production touring cars' while 'sports' was split into 'series production sports cars' and 'sports cars'. All of these five sub-groups had different annual production quantities. The new rules gave a much better scientific basis by using 'Touring cars' and 'Grand Touring cars' as the two major categories and within each of these two categories there were three identically named groups. These were 'normal series production' (Group 1 for Touring and Group 4 for GT), 'improved series production' (Group 2 for Touring and Group 5 for GT) and 'special' (Group 3 for Touring and Group 6 for GT). 'Touring cars' were defined as being four-seaters (unless the engine's capacity was below 1,000 cc when it was enough to have two) while GT cars had two seats. Furthermore to be recognised as a Touring car, a manufacturer had to make 1,000 of them within twelve months while for a GT – this category included sports cars – there had to be 100 constructed within twelve months or, if they were open cars, 200 per annum.

In addition, the FIA designed a Recognition Form, a document unique to each car that would later be called a Homologation Form. This had to be drawn up by the national automobile club (ASN) of the manufacturer concerned and would contain 'the principal data enabling the identification of each model'. Each model would thus have a single form to use as a basis for its entry into any particular group. If there was a weakness in all this it was that the form was stamped by the ASN and they also certified the number of cars manufactured without any reference to actual production figures. Once completed, this form was then valid anywhere in the world.

In any case, the data required was pretty basic stuff and one of these forms for an average touring car was rarely more than a couple of pages of A4. But the big step forward was the detailing, within Appendix J itself, of the 'permitted changes' that could be made to a car for competition use. For a 'normal series' car, things like brake linings, lights, tyres, suspension dampers, spark plugs, batteries were freed up and could be replaced by different brands to those fitted to the production car while keeping – in the case of the electrical system – the same voltage. This was a big step in helping to persuade component manufacturers to come in and support rallying. Appendix J also went so far as to allow re-boring of the engine and replacement of pistons and cylinder sleeves in a 'normal series' car. For 'improved series', the menu of freedoms extended further to road wheels, ignition parts, silencing systems, dual-circuit brakes, battery voltage, air and oil filters plus alternative carburettors, gearboxes and axle ratios that could be supplied by the car manufacturers while tuning was allowed by means of rectifying, lightening or balancing of standard parts. Except on those events where there was a timing handicap for Group 2 cars, the arrival of the new rules led to a much greater interest in running modified cars.

Then in 1964, the FIA appointed a sub-committee to examine how these regulations were working out in practice and to suggest any changes that might make Appendix J function better. Their recommendations were accepted during 1965 and implemented from the beginning of 1966. The biggest differences were in the number of cars that had to be manufactured within twelve months in order to be 'recognised' or homologated. For the 'normal series touring cars' – now formally identified as Group 1 – this was to be increased to a minimum production of 5,000 per annum while 'improved series touring cars' – Group 2 – would require 1,000 cars. The old 'special touring cars' group was combined with the 'special GT cars' and were popped into an assembly of effectively rallying prototypes in Group 5. For the production GT and sports cars, there would be a Group 3 of 'normal series grand touring cars' requiring a minimum production of 500 cars per annum and a Group 4 needing only 50 cars to be manufactured for the 'improved series grand touring' cars.

At the same time, the lists of permitted and non-permitted modifications were lengthened, as was the amount of data required for the homologation form. As a consequence of this latter requirement, the manufacturers were more involved in the process and had to provide all the data for the form plus a certification of car production signed by a person of authority within the company.

However, the CSI introduced one concept that they were probably to regret later and this was the procedure whereby a car could be homologated directly into any one of the four Groups that were dependant on production quantities, i.e. Groups 1 to 4. This was a fundamental change from what had gone on before. Previously it had been necessary to first get a car recognised as a normal series production in either touring cars or grand touring cars and only then could the tuning and modification freedoms allowed for 'improved' and 'special' varieties of these two categories be applied and the car then entered in a higher Group. Now, if you could only produce 500 cars – as happened with the first rallies for the Escort Twin Cam in 1968 – you could apply for homologation in Group 3 and get on with running your works rally team. It only took a few years and then it gradually dawned on manufacturer's works teams that with a production of just 500 cars per annum, it was possible to homologate any car, touring or grand touring, straight into Group 4. One of the first to do this was the Chrysler UK team who had the 998 cc version of the Hillman Imp/Singer Chamois – a small, four-seater saloon – homologated into Group 4. Soon the floodgates opened and everyone was doing it.

This open door in the regulations was one of the things that gave rallying its big leap forward during the late 1970s with cars like the Lancia Stratos, the Fiat 131 Abarth, the Ford Escort RS1800, the Opel Ascona 400 and, of course, the Audi Quattro. But its effect was probably regretted by the men of the CSI who, when they had launched their new rules for the 1966 season, had hoped that it would swing things towards everyone competing in practically standard cars with just a few choosing to go the 'improved' route. How wrong they were – and how much less interesting rallying would have been if they had been right.

Tour de Corse

There are two major rallies that were born and flourished during the period of this book that scarcely get a mention since they were not part of the European Rally Championship scene. One is the East African Safari that started in 1953, took international status in 1957 and was finally accorded championship status when it became part of the IRCM in 1970. But the other major rally is the Tour de Corse and that deserves more than just a passing mention.

If ever there was a rally that could truly be called a Rallyman's Rally, it has to be the Tour de Corse. To start with the tarmac roads that cover the island of Corsica could have been created solely with rallying in mind. Seen from above, they look like the wanderings of myriads of drunken beetles trying to find their way over steep mountains from one valley to another. The original subtitle of this rally was 'Rallye des Dix Mille Virages' – the rally of the ten thousand corners – but, as anyone will tell you who has driven the event, that is a statistical under-estimate of considerable proportions. As you drive these little roads over the hills and mountains of Corsica, the bends come at you relentlessly, one after another with hardly time to take a breath between them.

With such wonderful material available to them, the Association Sportive Automobile Club de la Corse (ASACC) devised an elegant format for their event that made it appeal even more to the rallying fraternity. A route of about 1,200 kilometres (745 miles) would start in the late afternoon and run through the night to finish some twenty-four hours later. From 1960 it would start from either Ajaccio or Bastia – alternating between the two largest towns to avoid any possible vendetta between them – and would run in November when the tourist season had finished and the weather could be, in a word, changeable.

The first event was held in 1956 and the international auspices were not promising. The previous year had seen the terrible accident at Le Mans with its negative effect on French motor sport events in general. Now in September 1956 there was the occupation of the Suez Canal by French and British forces and then at the beginning of November, the Russian invasion of Hungary. Nothing daunted, the new rally went ahead and twenty-four starters left Bastia and headed for Ajaccio. At the finish, the best of the seventeen classified finishers was the Renault Dauphine Spéciale of the ladies, Gilberte Thirion and Nadège Ferrier. Though Renaults – mainly the 4CV 1063 variety – were the most popular choice with seventeen of them at the start, there were also examples of Porsche Carrera 356, Mercedes 300SL, Alfa Romeo Giulietta, Fiat Abarth, Triumph TR3 and even a Saab 93 among the starters.

It was quickly realised that this rally was a true test of ability and did not favour just the most powerful cars. From its second edition in 1957, it was accepted as a round of the French GT Championship and as the 1950s progressed, so its entry list swelled until it regularly saw in excess of eighty cars at the start. Some measure of its ability to test both the skill of the drivers and the hardiness of their cars can be gathered from the fact that it was rare indeed for more than a third of the starters to be classified as finishers. It goes without saying that the nimble Renaults continued to do well with Jacques Féret winning in 1958 and Pierre Orsini, himself a Corsican, winning in 1959 both in Dauphine Spéciales. However, other makes did get a look in. The outright winner in 1957 was an Alfa Romeo Giulietta Sprint Veloce driven by Roger de Lageneste and in 1960 it was a Porsche Carrera 356 driven by Paul Ernst Strähle.

The weather always seemed to cooperate and provide November mist and rain but, in 1961, it exceeded all expectations. For the first time the rally was a round of the French Rally Championship for drivers and the entry list included Pat Moss in an Austin Healey 3000, Strähle with Robert Buchet in a Porsche Carrera Abarth and Jo Schlesser in a Ferrari 250 GT. The Bastia start may have been in sunshine but it shortly started to rain and then, on higher ground, to snow. The main road over the Col de Vizzavona (1,163 m) from Bastia to Ajaccio was closed to normal traffic, a fact that made life difficult for the organisers, while heavy rain elsewhere was dislodging rocks into the road and strong winds were blowing down trees. Retirements were high even before the rally reached the foot of the Col de Vergio (1,478 m) where a notice saying 'Danger sans chaînes' welcomed them. At the summit, there was in fact more than half a metre of snow and only two cars managed to reach it. They were the Citroën ID19s of René Trautmann and Lucien Bianchi and they only managed it by using the highest setting of their hydropneumatic suspension – position crick – and then turning one car round and tying them bumper to bumper so that they had an eight-wheel, four-wheel drive car.

Even then, their ordeal was not over for, going down the other side of the Col, they found their way blocked by a fallen tree. This was eventually moved and they reached the time control after taking four hours to cover fifty-two kilometres. And when they got there, there were no marshals for they had gone home when no rally cars came. There were just the gendarmes charged with making sure the road was closed. The Citroën drivers got the gendarmes to sign their time cards to show that they had been there and went on to Ajaccio where the rest of the rally cars that were still able to move joined them having travelled via Calvi and the coast road. The remainder of the rally was cancelled, Trautmann was declared the winner ahead of Bianchi, and the rest of the people who had reached Ajaccio were classified behind them on the basis of penalties before the Col de Vergio.

Heavy rain was present again during the 1962 rally but thankfully without the additional complications of snow and fallen trees. The new Renault Dauphine 1093s fared well in those conditions and occupied eight of the top ten places – indeed of the twenty-three finishers, fourteen were Dauphine 1093s – with Pierre Orsini taking his second outright victory. Orsini tried to win again in 1963, this time with an Alpine A110, and indeed led from the start only to retire when the electrical system could not keep up with running both the heated windscreen and an array of eight iodine lights. The leader then was Jo Schlesser in a magnificent soft-top AC Cobra but he fell back after a service halt near Bastia. A customs strike had meant that his special racing tyres were late arriving from the USA and, in the service point, his mechanics had to strip off the worn ones and re-fit the wheels with new tyres. The time lost dropped him behind the winning Citroën ID19 of René Trautmann. It was truly a year for bigger cars since third overall was Henri Greder with a Ford Falcon while Guy Verrier was fourth in another Citroën ahead of Bernard Consten in one of rallying's rarer cars, a Lotus Elan.

Rain and fog were on the menu again in 1964 and this time it was the turn of the new Renault 1,100 cc R8 Gordini to shine with Jean Vinatier leading everyone home. The poor conditions meant that there were only eight cars from the seventy-nine starters that managed to keep within their thirty minutes of lateness on the road sections and of those, four were R8 Gordinis. After a very short rally the previous year, Jean Rolland was happy to finish second in his Alfa Romeo GTZ while it was Günter Klass who had the brief outing this time, retiring on the first test with a Porsche 904 GTS. In 1965, Orsini added another win to his total with a 1,300 cc version of the R8 Gordini but it was clear from the second and fourth positions gained by Alpine A110s driven by Mauro Bianchi and Roger de Lageneste, that the little GT car from Dieppe was making progress and would shortly be a threat.

Not all the roads in Corsica were asphalted when the Tour de Corse started life in the 1950s. This is the winning Porsche Carrera 356 of Paul-Ernst Strahle and Herbert Linge in 1960 tackling a steep downhill section. This was Porsche's first victory in Corsica.

Appendix - Tour de Corse

The entry for the 1966 rally had a very much more international flavour about it with Lancia, Ford, Porsche and Alfa Romeo all ready to challenge the supremacy of Renault and Alpine. Even DAF sent a works team. Leo Cella led from the start but put his Fulvia Coupé off the road leaving Orsini with his Alpine A110 ahead of Jean-François Piot in a very special lightened R8 Gordini with a 1,440 cc engine. Corsica was always happy to welcome cars from Groups 5 & 6 and the ASACC seemed to have adopted the same attitude as the Liège organisers. Their view was that their event was tough enough that no matter what you did to your car, the challenge of 1,200 km of Corsican roads might well defeat it. This was not the case for Piot since, after Orsini broke a drive coupling 100 km after leaving the turning point in Ajaccio, the R8 romped home to win by more than five minutes from second-place man, Rolland, this time in an Alfa Romeo GTA. After trying his luck with a 1.6-litre Ford Anglia in 1965, Vic Elford had returned with a works-loaned Porsche 911 and finished in third place. Ford too had some success with Henri Greder taking fifth place with a Lotus Cortina and Jochen Neerpasch finishing seventeenth in a Taunus 15 M, a difficult task in a modestly powered front-wheel drive car.

The French Rally Championship proper was created in 1967 and the Tour de Corse was a natural choice for inclusion. It also attracted its biggest entry yet with ninety-eight cars taking the start and, with eight full works teams present, it was always going to be a superb event. However, the battle to be first came not from the ranks of the 1.4-litre R8 Gordinis and Alpine A110s but from the Lancia Fulvia 1.4-litre of Sandro Munari and the Porsche 911R of Elford. These two drivers fought it out over the four timed-to-the-second tests and innumerable tight road sections during a night and a day that were damp, foggy and slippery. Munari took the advantage on the opening tests and sealed certain victory by only dropping a single minute on the road sections compared with two lost by Elford. On the last of the four tests, Elford went off the road briefly trying in the daylight to reduce Munari's advantage and dropped back behind another Lancia driven by Pauli Toivonen so that just three seconds separated them at the finish. The best Renault in 1967 was an Alpine A110 driven by Orsini to fourth place, but a year later, it was an Alpine that took Renault's revenge when Jean-Claude Andruet won the 1968 rally with a 1.4-litre A110. In his third year in a Porsche 911, Elford had started as the favourite but a broken oil filter sidelined his 2.1-litre, fuel injected, four-camshaft prototype just five kilometres into the first test. Toivonen was back but in a Porsche and led until his gearbox broke. His erstwhile team-mate, Munari who had recently returned to driving after a road accident on the 1968 Monte Carlo where a Yugoslav Mercedes had killed his co-driver, Luciano Lombardini and put Munari in hospital, retired his Lancia Fulvia with a similar fault. It was Rauno Aaltonen who thus upheld Lancia honour by taking second place ahead of Lucien Bianchi's Alfa Romeo GTA.

Naturally the French hoped that Alpine would win again in 1969 since this was the bi-centenary not only of France's conquest of Corsica in 1769 but also of the birth of Napoleon in Ajaccio. However, it was not to be and the rally was 'conquered' by a fugitive from the ranks of the Alpine team who had now signed a contract with Porsche: Gérard Larrousse. To start with, he did not have it all his own way since Andruet led for the first half in an Alpine A110 1.6-litre before hitting a rock and disabling his steering. The ever-reliable Orsini was second for Alpine in a 1.4-litre A110 with a truly commendable third for the 1966 winner, Piot, in a Ford Capri 2600 loaned by Ford Germany.

By 1970, the Alpine A110 was a much more reliable rally car and this was emphasised by the result in Corsica where the diminutive GT car occupied the first three positions in general classification. This

Citroën may have won the Tour de Corse in 1961 and 1963 but life was getting more difficult by 1966. After the first few hours of this 24-hour event, this Group 1 DS 21 of Lucien Bianchi/"Vic" was proceeding with only third gear available. It was a fine tribute to the flexibility of the big Citroën that they finished at all, albeit in twentieth place overall.

On the bi-centenary of the birth of Napoleon, it was a German car that won in Corsica in 1969. The factory Porsche 911R of Gérard Larrousse and Maurice Gélin waits for its crew in *parc fermé* at Bastia with two Stuttgart mechanics standing guard.

Small GT cars always did well in Corsica so it seemed logical for BMC to try with a Sebring Sprite in 1967. This was crewed by Clive Baker and Mike Wood.

Jean Rolland never won the Tour de Corse but, between his first event in 1959 and his untimely death at Montlhéry in September 1967, he was second overall three times and fourth twice. All these results were obtained with various Alfa Romeos. Here he is driving a GTA with Gabriel Augias to second place in 1966.

was merely a foretaste of what was to come in succeeding years when the blue cars would win just about everything. In 1970 it was Bernard Darniche who dominated by leading from start to finish and winning all twelve of the secteurs chronométrés. He finished almost four minutes ahead of his team-mate Andruet who in his turn was eight minutes ahead of Jean-Pierre Manzagol in a third A110.

Sadly there was no Tour de Corse in 1971 when the required finance to run the event was not found. However, it returned in 1972 with an even bigger and better rally featuring eight secteurs chronométrés and a further eighteen secteurs de classement rather similar to the sélectifs of the Rallye des Alpes. These together totalled 756 km (470 miles) from a total rally distance of 1,320 km (820 miles), which implied that 60% of the rally route was flat-out. This was a bit of a change from the old system since now there was actually time in many sections to take proper service. As a consequence, the question of losing time at time controls was significantly decreased and thus more people were able to finish within the maximum time allowance. As in 1970, it was an Alpine A110 that dominated the event by leading from start to finish and this time it was Andruet at the wheel of a 1.8-litre car, the prototype of the cars that were to win the first World Rally Championship the following year. But nine minutes behind him in second place was a real prototype, an open Simca CG driven by Bernard Fiorentino followed by a queue of four more A110s. The Porsche effort of two 911 Carrera RSs for Björn Waldegård and Gérard Larrousse had faded, Waldegård with an accident and Larrousse retiring close to the finish with a broken drive shaft. Munari was back and this time with the Lancia Stratos on its first outing. The look and sound of the Stratos was right but it went out with a broken drive shaft. The other prototype from a major manufacturer, the Ford GT70, stopped about the same time with a seized wheel bearing.

From 1973, the Tour de Corse was accepted as a round of the WRC and consequently flourished. By 1986, it possessed a format that, though different from the original rally where the road sections were more important than the épreuves (tests), was equally tough. With twenty-six special stages totalling 1,017 km in a total distance of 1,551 km spread over three days with no night sections, it was a very different rally but still dearly loved by the rally community. With the advent of Group A in 1987 and the tendency for the FIA to shorten and emasculate WRC events in the name of the Great God TV, by the beginning of the 21st Century the Tour de Corse had shrunk to fifteen stages totalling 366 km in a total of 854 km. Eventually shunned by the WRC authorities in favour of a mainland France event, for 2009 the Tour de Corse was left to its own devices and is currently re-inventing itself for 2013 as a pillar of the new European Rally Championship. Its old glory may have gone but the challenge of its roads and the beauty of its scenery will hopefully never fade.

With the help of Claudio Maglioli, Cesare Fiorio's Reparto Corse created the F&M Special, a cut down spyder based on the 1.6 litre Fulvia rally car. One example finished ninth overall at the 1969 Targa Florio and thus Fiorio decided to enter two F&Ms for Corsica. Driven by Timo Mäkinen (seen here helping Paul Easter with his seat belt) and Sandro Munari/John Davenport, they finished eleventh and thirteenth respectively. Looking on in the background is Luca di Montezemolo who was co-driving for Cristiano Ratazzi in a Fulvia Coupé with a roof.

Released from his BMC contract when they stopped competition, Rauno Aaltonen finished seventh overall for BMW on the Tour de Corse in 1969 with Tony Ambrose. With this factory 2002 TI in 1970, this time accompanied by Mike Wood, he was not so fortunate as multiple punctures caused their retirement.

Tour de Corse 1970, Jean-Claude Andruet/Michel Vial, Alpine Renault A110. In 1970, the result in Corsica was a 1-2-3 for Alpine with their A110s powered on this occasion by 1,440cc engines.

Tour de Corse of 1972, the Port of Ajaccio. Nestling together are forty-nine starters comprising Alpine 110 1800s, Porsche 911Ss, Ligier JS2s, Opel Ascona 19 SRs, Renault R12 Gordinis, Peugeot 304 Ss, a Simca CG spyder, a Ford Capri 3.0, a Lancia Stratos, a Ford GT70, an Opel GT, DAFs, Skodas, Alfa Romeos – the old days certainly had variety!

East African Safari Rally

This event, one of the greatest and toughest challenges that has ever come from motor rallying, has had little mention in this book since it was not chosen to be part of the CSI's Grand Plan until 1970. In fact, the inaugural Coronation Safari Rally took place in 1953 just as the European Touring Championship was starting up. The Safari took its title at that time from the excuse that it was an event celebrating the coronation of Queen Elizabeth II of England. In fact, the Kenyans had long wanted to hold a major rally and now, since everyone was getting a few days off work at the time of the coronation, it seemed like as good a time as any to run one.

That first event set the model for the years that followed by using the roads and tracks of all three East African countries – Kenya, Tanganyika (Tanzania from 1964) and Uganda – though they did abandon the mass start for the second year. The Safari was always about survival and one could paraphrase a cowboy song by saying that if the roads, rivers and wild animals did not get you, then the weather certainly would. This was territory in which knowing how to drive into a mud hole and come out the other side was as important as being able to drive fast. Many of the early arrivals from Europe who came to test their skills in these conditions either drove too fast and broke their cars, or found that some of the local conditions – like the infamous 'black cotton', a mud offering no grip to tyres but which would stick and cling to almost everything else –defeated them.

The Safari took an international permit for 1957 after a very positive report to the FIA from Maurice Gatsonides who had taken part in the 1956 event with a Standard Vanguard III and finished third in Class C. At that time, the classes were based on the price of the car in Nairobi, a habit that continued until 1960 when normal cylinder capacity classes were adopted. With good weather conditions, the percentage of finishers on these early events could be quite high but with the move of the date from May to the Easter weekend in 1957, the chances of hitting the rainy season were increased and the result was often devastating. In 1963, for example, there were just seven finishers from eighty-four starters with Nick Nowicki claiming the win in a Peugeot 404 after the long-time leader, Erik Carlsson, had a close encounter of the first kind between his Saab 96 and an aardvark that forced him to retire. In 1964 – a somewhat drier year – the winner was the man who had been second to Nowicki in 1963, Peter Hughes, now driving a Ford Cortina GT rather than the Anglia he had used previously while behind him was the indefatigable Erik Carlsson, recording the best-ever Safari result for Saab.

Many teams came and saw but, unlike Caesar, failed to conquer. Volvo had a five-car team of PV544s in 1964 but failed to get one to the finish. However, after the rally they sold a couple of their cars to Joginder Singh who prepared one himself and promptly went and won the 1965 event with it. In 1965, Mercedes were there in strength but Eugen Böhringer, Lucille Cardwell and David Lead all failed to finish in their 300SEs and it was left to John Sprinzel and Jim Wilson in Wilson's own Mercedes 190 to uphold Stuttgart honour by finishing fourth overall. Nissan came for the first time with works Datsun Bluebirds in 1963 but it was not until 1966 that they got a reasonable result with John Greenly and Jock Aird finishing fifth and sixth in Bluebirds. There was even a team of Lincoln Mercury Comets that came to the 1964 Safari to pit their 4.7-litre V8 muscle against the sub-two-litre cars that were currently dominating the results. Of the ten Comets entered, five to be driven by Americans and five by East Africans, six started and just two finished with Kim Mandeville eighteenth and Joginder Singh twenty-first out of twenty-one finishers.

The end of an epic drive. On the 1968 Safari, the weather was so bad that there were only seven finishers and the seventh car was the Datsun 2000 Cedric of Gerry Davies (on L) and Lucille Cardwell. Such were the delays in mud and water that these two ladies took twenty hours longer to cover the route than the allowed time.

The ability of a Safari rally car to tackle deep water had to be matched by the courage and experience of its driver. Joginder Singh was a connoisseur of African road conditions and knew just how fast – or slow – to tackle obstacles of all kinds. Here accompanied by his brother, Jaswant, he takes his VW 1200 through deep water on the 1960 Safari where they finished ninth on Joginder's second appearance on the Safari Rally.

By now a legend was building about the inability of overseas drivers to ever win the Safari. In fact, Kenyan drivers had won every one of the thirteen events held between 1953 and 1965. This changed slightly for 1966 when Bert Shankland and Chris Rothwell won in a Peugeot 404 injection since both members of the crew were from Tanzania. They won again in 1967 and then so very nearly completed their hat trick in 1968 when they were denied by a broken connecting rod just three time controls from the finish in Nairobi. The winner on that occasion was Nick Nowicki also in a Peugeot 404 injection. It was no coincidence that this was another wet year, particularly on the second half in Tanzania, and that, as with Nowicki's previous win, just seven cars made it to the finish from ninety-three starters. To give some idea of the severity of the conditions on that Tanzanian leg, the initial leader, Peter Huth in a Ford Lotus Cortina, lost his lead at the Kiroka Pass where it took him an hour and a half to cover twenty miles of steep and muddy road.

In complete contrast, 1969 was dry throughout and, as with Joginder Singh in 1965, Robin Hillyar benefited somewhat in drawing number one in the starting order for his works Ford Taunus 20 MRS. The rally did not use Tanzania this year as their authorities wanted to see the Safari start rotate from Nairobi to the other capitals and were 'on strike'. Thus much more use was made of the twisty Ugandan roads along the Congo border and this suited rear-wheel drive cars to the extent that Bengt Söderström, also in a Taunus, was leading coming back into Kenya. However, he then broke his axle leaving Hillyar in close pursuit of Vic Preston Senior's Lotus Cortina with Joginder Singh's Volvo 122S over an hour behind them in third. Hillyar's car had an unsolvable problem in that its clutch was worn out and in Mombasa they said to Preston that this was the case and they were going to drive slowly back to Nairobi to finish second. Unfortunately, Preston took it that these were 'mind games' intended to distract him and went like hell away from the coast only to crash into a bridge and retire.

For Hillyar and his co-driver Jock Aird, the rally might have appeared won provided that they could limp back to the finish but the Safari is never that simple. An hour out from Nairobi they were in collision with a Morris Oxford taxi and severely damaged their car. In fact, Joginder Singh drove past and reported at the next control that the leaders were out. However, in fifteen minutes unaided labour at the side of the road, they had taken out the radiator, re-connected the throttle, levered the wing off the tyre and got the car running. When they got to the finish, no one was expecting them but they had clinched victory by thirty-four minutes.

These stories of survival, whether self-repair of a stricken car or taking hours to negotiate a flooded river or a sea of mud, were typical of the Safari rallies of the 1960s. With the event being inducted into the IRCM for 1970 and then being a founder member of the WRC in 1973, the organisational approach was to back off from routes that could be inundated and concentrate more on establishing a hard, fast run through all-weather roads that would make the event yet more attractive to European teams and drivers. Thus it was no great surprise when Hannu Mikkola and his Ford Escort RS1600 rudely interrupted the succession of local winners in 1972 followed by Ove Andersson (Peugeot 504, 1975), Björn Waldegård (Ford Escort RS1800, 1977) and Jean-Pierre Nicolas (Peugeot 504 V6 Coupé, 1978) as overseas winners. But the basic challenge of the Safari was to remain for many more years until it hit the twilight zone in the late 1990s and faded from sight after the farcical episode of the 'Sands of Suswa' in 2002.

[Further reading in 'Safari Rally – 50 years of the toughest rally in the world'. Bi-lingual text English/German. By Reinhard Klein / John Davenport / Helmut Deimel. Published by McKlein. ISBN 978-3-927458-08-6. 49.00 Euro]

The natives are friendly and this was certainly the case throughout the majority of the Safari route which in 1972 still took in all three countries of East Africa: Kenya, Uganda and Tanzania. This Peugeot 504 injection of Hugh Lionnet and Philip Hechle was lying ninth at half-distance in Kampala but later dropped out with mechanical problems.

A welcome at the finish in 1970 for Mike Kirkland (on L) and John Rose who, despite losing their windscreen, battled through to seventh place in their Datsun 1600SSS.

Many hands make light work when Timo Mäkinen's Escort Twin Cam is stuck in the mud on the 1971 Safari. Co-driver, Henry Liddon, is in the left foreground showing where he wants the car to go.

Long Distance Information

Memphis, Tennessee may never have featured in any long distance rallies, but it was certainly the Americans – if not actually Chuck Berry's rock-n-roll hit – who inspired marathon events to choose that continent as their first post-war home. In 1950, after the completion of the Pan-American Highway, the Mexican government organised a race from border-to-border lasting six days. They called it the Carrera Panamericana and in 1950 it was American cars that dominated with Herschel McGriff winning in an Oldsmobile 88 while in 1951, works Ferrari 212 Intervignales driven by Piero Taruffi and Alberto Ascari finished first and second.

Not to be outdone, Mercedes sent a full team of 300SLs to the 1952 race and also took a 1-2 finish with Karl Kling and Hermann Lang. It could so easily have been a 1-2-3 but their third car driven by John Fitch was excluded for having service while under *parc fermé* conditions. Also, Kling was lucky to finish since he had hit a vulture on the first day and the bird had broken the windscreen and briefly knocked his co-driver, Hans Klenk, unconscious. They carried on almost without stopping and Klenk carried on reading their 'pacenotes', an invention that was to help Mercedes succeed in many of their later rally activities not to mention Stirling Moss's Mille Miglia victory with a 300SLR in 1955.

At the end of the 1953 event, Juan-Manuel Fangio had won with a Lancia D24 Pininfarina while in 1954 it was the Italians again with Umberto Maglioli winning for Ferrari in a 375 Pininfarina. However, with every successive year, the death toll steadily mounted as did the speeds achieved by the winners. In 1950, McGriff had averaged 142 kph (88 mph) while in 1954, Maglioli had averaged 220 kph (137 mph). With the accident at Le Mans in 1955, it was wisely decided to end the Carrera Panamericana. And when two years later, there was a similarly dreadful accident on the Mille Miglia in Italy, for all practical purposes this was the end of motor racing on open roads from town to town. The end of one thing is often the birth of something else, so similar events on dirt roads in South America picked up the idea using saloon cars rather than sports-prototypes.

Mercedes team manager, Karl Kling doubtless recalled his experiences in Mexico when from 1959 onwards other German manufacturers such as NSU and Borgward started to have some success in the Gran Premio Turismo d'Argentina (GPTA). NSU had people like Paul Frère, Edgar Barth and Juan-Manuel Bordeu (a protégé of Fangio's) driving for them. Poor Barth got his knuckles rapped by the FIA for 'taking part in a competition not registered on the international calendar'. So for 1960, the Argentinean Automobile Club had the GPTA put on the FIA calendar as an 'International Regularity Test'. Which of course it was not, since it was a race. More Europeans came to try their luck on the 4,000 km (2,500 miles) event much of which was on unsurfaced roads and it was one of these visitors, Gunnar Andersson in a Volvo PV544, who won outright in 1960.

All this resulted in a team of four cars being entered by Mercedes for 1961 with Fangio now helping with team management. These were 220SEbs to be driven by Walter Schock, Eberhard Mahle, Hans Herrmann and ex-Formula One driver, Carlos Menditeguy. At the finish, Schock won easily from Herrmann after the others had had transmission problems. Mercedes were back in 1962 with two 300SEs for Eugen Böhringer and Menditeguy and two 220SEbs for Hermann Kühne and Ewy Rosqvist. There seemed to be little good luck around for the Stuttgart team as Böhringer's engine took in water at a river crossing and broke while Menditeguy was late going into *parc fermé* and was promptly excluded. Next Kühne went off the road to miss a flock of sheep, hit a tree and was killed in the impact when his seat and seat belt mounting broke. Happily, his co-driver, Manfred Schiek, was practically unharmed. At this point, Gunnar Andersson driving one of twelve Volvo 122Ss entered, mainly for South American drivers, was leading. Rosqvist wanted to retire when she heard of Kühne's accident but Fangio persuaded her to continue and, when Andersson's Volvo ran into suspension problems, the winners of the toughest 'regularity event' on the planet were Ewy Rosqvist and Ursula Wirth.

Mercedes returned in 1963 with five cars: four 300SEs for Böhringer, Bordeu, Hermann Eger and Dieter Glemser and a 220SEb for Rosqvist. With less opposition, Böhringer and Glemser rather ran away with things to finish first and second with Rosqvist third. Böhringer's win came after a problem on the very first stage where he went off the road, rolled the car and broke away half of the windscreen. Later on that stage, they hit a large bird that came in through the hole in the windscreen and expired on the back seat. Böhringer could see how this could let him avoid having to tell the truth about his accident so he explained that all the damage was due to hitting the bird. More than twenty years later at a sixtieth birthday party organised by Mercedes and, with a little prompting by his co-driver, Klaus Kaiser, to tell the full story, he confessed to the deception.

The following year, 1964, saw Mercedes back with four 300SEs – Rosqvist had been given one of the 'big' cars and this time was accompanied by Eva-Maria Falk – and the team managed to repeat exactly the same finishing order as the previous year with Hans Herrmann their only retirement. Opposition had come from works Lancia Flavias driven by Leo Cella and Claudine Bouchet while Rauno Aaltonen was denied the chance to drive in an MG Magnette when the event was delayed by a week by customs formalities and he had to return to Europe. The GPTA continued until 1975 but its importance as an international event gradually declined and the mainstream European teams turned to other things.

Among these was an event announced at the end of 1967 that somehow captured the imagination and set in motion the popularity of transcontinental rallies that persists until today. This was the 1968 Daily Express London to Sydney Marathon. The route, devised by Jack Sears and Tony Ambrose crossed the English Channel and then went via France, Italy, Yugoslavia, Bulgaria, Turkey, Iran, Afghanistan and Pakistan to Bombay in India. From there, cars and crews boarded the SS Chusan for a nine-day cruise to Perth in Australia. They then crossed the Nullabor Desert and the Flinders Ranges before reaching Sydney five days later. There were two 'special stages' on the way to Bombay, one in Turkey of 170 miles (273 km) and the other shorter and rougher just after leaving Kabul towards the Khyber Pass. The route in Australia did not need special stages as it was pretty much all tough going especially when it got onto gravel roads in the night.

At Bombay, Roger Clark/Ove Andersson led in a Mk2 Lotus Cortina from Simo Lampinen/Gilbert Staepelaere in a Ford Germany 20MRS while Lucien Bianchi/Jean-Claude Ogier lay third with a Citroën DS21. Once into Australia, this situation did not change significantly until, just north of Adelaide, the Cortina went onto two cylinders thanks to burnt-out valves. It was repaired using parts from Eric Jackson's Cortina but now lay third with the 20MRS leading. In the Flinders, the German Ford lost time and dropped to third with the DS21 still leading and the Cortina second. The British Ford got within two minutes of the DS21 before stopping with a seized differential and could only continue by 'borrowing' one from a spectator's standard Cortina, losing well over an hour in the process.

At the rally HQ in London, anyone could wander in and see the progress of the 1968 London to Sydney on a giant map of the route.

Ewy Rosqvist was the outright winner in Argentina in 1961 for Mercedes with a 220SEb.

In Bombay, halfway through the 1968 London to Sydney, the Citroën DS21 of Lucien Bianchi (on R) and Jean-Claude Ogier was lying third.

▲ Ewy Rosqvist – the perfect combination of glamour and performance.

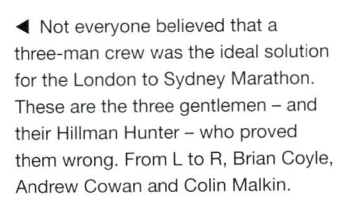

◄ Not everyone believed that a three-man crew was the ideal solution for the London to Sydney Marathon. These are the three gentlemen – and their Hillman Hunter – who proved them wrong. From L to R, Brian Coyle, Andrew Cowan and Colin Malkin.

As the rally passed Melbourne and headed for the Snowy Mountains, the 20MRS brought the gap on the DS21 down to two minutes but then it hit a post on the exit to a cattle grid and broke a steering tie rod. This dropped them down to sixteenth. Bianchi and Ogier now looked to be clear winners as they were eleven minutes ahead of their nearest challenger, the Andrew Cowan/Colin Malkin/Brian Coyle Hillman Hunter. Then, on the very last moderately difficult section, less than 100 miles before Sydney, the Citroën crashed into a private Mini that was being driven the wrong way down a road that was supposed to be closed to other traffic. Bianchi was seriously hurt in the accident but later made a full recovery. And it was the Hunter that came home with the spoils …

The London to Sydney had been sponsored by the Daily Express and, with the football World Cup of 1970 creating great interest in England (Could the national football team retain the title they won in 1966?), an Australian entrepreneur by the name of Wylton Dickson sold the idea of a marathon rally from London to Mexico to the Daily Mirror. His concept of visiting many of the countries that had qualified for the World Cup was turned into reality by two rallymen, John Sprinzel and John Brown. The route they devised would go down to Yugoslavia and thence to Lisbon via classic roads from the Liège–Sofia–Liège, the Rallye des Alpes and the TAP Rally. Once in Rio de Janeiro, the way would lie first towards Argentina in the south and then north utilizing roads in the Andes before crossing the Panama Canal and reaching Mexico City. The total distance was some 25,750 km (16,000 miles). On this event, the cars went by boat from Lisbon to Rio while the crews flew over the Atlantic – a much more popular decision than the arrangement with the SS Chusan as it gave them twelve days to relax in Rio! But one driver, Bob Neyret, used the break to go and compete in – and win – the Rallye du Maroc with a Citroën DS prototype.

In contrast to the London to Sydney, this event featured seventeen special stages called 'primes' each with its own set time. Some of them were exceptionally long and there was one example in Argentina that went on for 800 km (500 miles), started before dawn and finished after nightfall. On arrival at Lisbon after the five European primes, the leader was the Citroën DS21 of René Trautmann with just five minutes lost. Hannu Mikkola's Escort (1800 cc push-rod) was two minutes behind with Guy Verrier another two minutes further back in third with another Citroën. Indeed, the top ten was dominated by the works Citroëns and Fords with the factory Triumph 2.5 PIs of Brian Culcheth, Paddy Hopkirk and Andrew Cowan occupying sixth, eighth and eleventh places respectively.

With the pace stepping up in South America – Sprinzel was 'adjusting' downwards the times allowed for the primes once he saw just how quickly people were going – the entry started to thin out. The first to suffer, albeit after more than half the rally, were the Citroëns and Trautmann went out with an accident. Only one of their DS21s was destined to finish, that being the one driven by Patrick Vanson who finished seventh. Ford kept most of their cars running and had five Escorts at the finish with Hannu Mikkola winning, Rauno Aaltonen third, Timo Mäkinen fifth, Tony Fall (accompanied by Jimmy Greaves, the English footballer) sixth, and Sobieslaw Zasada eighth. However, the two remaining Triumphs run by the BMC/Leyland team finished strongly and Culcheth took second place, an hour and twenty minutes behind the winning Ford, while Hopkirk was fourth overall. The London to Sydney winner, Andrew Cowan, went out with an accident when trying to overtake another car in dust on that long, long prime, but was to have the last word on marathon rallies by winning the second London to Sydney with a Mercedes 280SE in 1977 and then the Vuelta a la America del Sud in 1978 with a Mercedes 450SLC.

World Cup Rally 1970, Ken Tubman/André Welinski/Rob McAuley, Austin 1800. Tubman finished eleventh overall in Mexico with this Australian-prepared "Land Crab". As to Mr McAuley's antics in this photo, perhaps he could not inhale enough dust inside the car …

World Cup Rally 1970. Police outriders for the winning Ford Escort 1850GT of Hannu Mikkola and Gunnar Palm as they approach Mexico City.

World Cup Rally 1970. The organisation for an event covering 25,750 km (16,000 miles) was impressive with travelling marshals being flown to remote controls to ensure co-ordination with the local authorities and police and consistency. Here one of the factory Ford Escorts accelerates away from a control in South America.

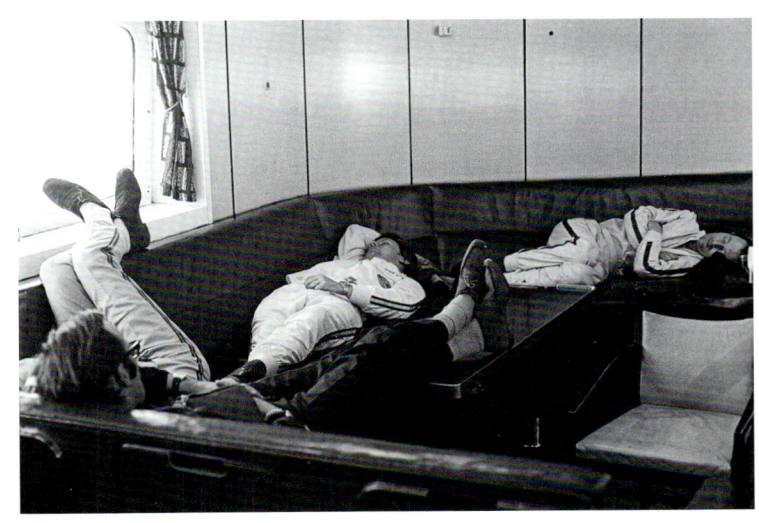

World Cup Rally 1970. Members of the Ford team take the opportunity to catch up on some sleep during the ferry crossing from Buenaventura to Panama City.

In Mexico City, Hannu Mikkola and Gunnar Palm receive the first gifts from their World Cup win – a massive sombrero for Mikkola and a necklace of flowers for Palm.

Odds and Ends

Often on rallies of the 1950s and 1960s, a control would be situated, not at the roadside, but in a restaurant or a café. This was for the comfort of the officials and the protection of the printing clocks during bad weather, but it did occasionally lead to problems. If a car was late, then the co-driver would have to descend and race inside scattering clients as they dashed to insert the time card in the clock. On the 1965 Rallye des Alpes, Pauli Toivonen – driving a German registered Porsche 904 – lost a lot of marks when at one such time control his co-driver, Anssi Järvi, could not find the clock thanks to a crowd of unhelpful locals.

In 1955, the Swedish author Astrid Lindgren wrote a book for children about a character called Karlsson who lived in a small house tucked behind a chimney on the roof of an apartment building in Stockholm. It was very popular and was serialised on Swedish radio every Saturday night. It was called 'Karlsson på taket' or 'Karlsson on the roof'. The story goes that when Erik Carlsson rolled his Saab 92 on a national rally, the marshal at the end of the stage asked the next competitor, Carl-Gunnar Hammarlund in a VW, if he had seen Saab's new test driver. Hammarlund is reported to have asked 'Which Carlsson? Do you mean Carlsson on the roof?' From that moment on, Erik was known to all as 'Carlsson på taket'.

The Acropolis Rally started out in 1952 as the ELPA Rally. ELPA is the acronym for the Automobile and Touring Club of Greece who still have the responsibility for organising the modern rally. A Chevrolet driven by an amazing character called Johnny Pesmazoglou – whose age is not known precisely but who must have been born before 1914 – won that first event. His company was the Greek importer for GM cars and, throughout his long rally career, Johnny appeared in all kinds of Chevrolets and Opels. He won the Acropolis Rally at the wheel of an Opel Kapitän in 1955 and then did not miss that event until the early 1970s though he continued to enter the Acropolis and other rallies up until 1987. He died in October 2002. 1970s.

Two stroke engines were notorious for suffering from carburettor icing on winter rallies especially when the temperature was only a few degrees below zero and the humidity was high. It happened to Rolf Melde during the 1951 Monte Carlo Rally in that first run with the Saab 92. The standard cars were subsequently fitted with a pre-heater for the air going to the carburettor. Later on rallies, the Saab team used to add about 3% of isopropyl alcohol to the fuel to reduce the risk of icing.

Erik Carlsson had the nickname of "Carlsson on the roof" and his early career was dotted with incidents like this one on the 1964 Rally to the Midnight Sun …

… however it was occasionally helpful to be able to put a Saab on its roof. He and Gunnar Palm got out of a mud hole on the 1964 Safari by rolling the car over onto its roof and then back onto the wheels again. Here they demonstrate the technique outside the prize-giving ball at the end of the rally.

How Paul Coltelloni got to drive a factory-supplied DS19 on the 1956 Monte Carlo Rally in the first place is quite amusing. He was already doing rallies in first an 11CV and then a 15CV. Shortly after the public announcement of the new Citroën ID and DS at the Paris Motor Show in October 1955, Coltelloni had just finished the Tour de Belgique when he was approached by a gentleman who introduced himself as Monsieur Labbe, PR Director of Citroën. Labbe explained that the company was looking for someone to drive one of these new cars on the 1956 Monte Carlo Rally and would he be interested? Within minutes, the deal had been struck and Labbe bade his farewell by saying 'Au revoir Monsieur Marang'. Coltelloni had to tell him that he was not Henri Marang who had finished tenth on the 1955 Monte Carlo, but the man from Citroën did not back down and Coltelloni got a drive.

It was quite common in the 1950s for some rally crews to 'make pace notes' by painting coloured spots on trees, walls, houses and road signs. The colour of the spot indicated the severity of the following bend. Perhaps the first case of these failing to work effectively was on the 1953 Carrera Panamericana when Felice Bonetto, driving alone in a single-seater Lancia D24, misread one of the spots and was killed in the resulting accident. Another disadvantage of this system was that anyone with a couple of pots of paint who came along after the first crew could very easily mess it all up if they were using a different colour code for speed.

When the first European crews arrived in Michigan in 1972 to weigh up the prospect of having an All-American rally, the Press-on-Regardless, as part of the WRC in future years, they were pleasantly surprised that it was all so much like the events that they knew – with one exception. All the timing was done using marshal's watches that read in 1/100ths of a minute rather than seconds. The local watch shops did good business.

A protest on the Liège was almost unknown. In 1962 Jacques Patte, whose Volvo 122S was classified third overall, protested the Citroën ID19 of Henri Marang and Paul Coltelloni on the basis that they had clocked in early at one of the very first controls – at Saarbrücken – and not been penalised for it. Protesting was considered infra dignitatem as far as Maurice Garot and the Royal Motor Union of Liège was concerned. They accepted the protest in silence and then published a notice saying that all penalties at the Saarbrücken control were cancelled since 'It had not been run properly'.

There was a lot of snow on the 1971 RAC Rally and, at many of the stages in northern Scotland, it had not proved possible to send any official car through the forest roads before the arrival of the rally cars. The marshals were at the start and the finish – this could be achieved by driving round on the public road – and thus the rally cars were set off into virgin snow. First car into one stage was the Alpine Renault of Jean-Luc Thérier but after half a mile it torpedoed into a snowdrift and only its rear bumper was visible. The other cars that had ventured into the stage stopped and extracted the French car and then all turned round and – very carefully – returned to the start, hoping not to meet too many rally cars coming the other way.

Time control procedures gradually evolved during the 1960s with the FIA eventually taking responsibility to design standard control signs and insisting on conformity for the checking-in process. Paddy Hopkirk and BMC's problem on the 1966 Acropolis Rally would have vanished had these been in force then. The only thing warning Hopkirk and the BMC mechanics that they were entering a control zone was an A4-size sign placed among the feet of spectators at a major crossroad in the middle of the night.

No mistaking the fact that this is a control on the 1955 Monte Carlo Rally, but there are no signs to define the control area and thus it was easy to make mistakes by checking in a minute early or late. Or even for a crew to be blocked by a car trying to check in a minute later than them.

When the RAC Rally started using forestry roads for its special stages, it was realised that some form of navigation instruction was needed since these roads were not marked on the Ordnance Survey maps that, until then, had been a reliable backup to any road book issued by the organisers. Sheets of Tulip diagrams were tried but these were made by different people in different areas of the country and thus lacked consistency. Eventually, it was decided that the forestry stages should be arrowed and companies like Dunlop and Castrol printed thousands of arrows on cardboard. One drawback here was the British weather in November when rain and wind occasionally resulted in limp cardboard and arrows that either became invisible or swung to point in the wrong direction. Plastic coated arrows finally solved the problem.

When Henri Greder did his recce for the 1964 Geneva Rally, he encountered an unusual problem that caused him to go to the organisers and request a re-route on one section of the event. The problem was that there was a bridge on the original route that was too narrow to let his Ford Falcon Futura Sprint pass through. The re-route was done and Greder went on to win the rally.

Pseudonyms often cropped up on rallies when someone did not want the folks back home to know how they spent their leisure time. One such was the Swedish co-driver to Carl-Magnus Skogh who was identified on the 1965 Acropolis entry list as 'Tandlakare'. Far from being an exotic Greek hero, this was merely the profession in Swedish of the co-driver, Lennart Berggren – he was a dentist.

No toothache problems during a rally for Carl-Magnus Skogh (on R) when he took Lennart Berggren with him. This is Acropolis 1965 when they won outright in their factory Volvo 122 S.

During 1965, Ove Andersson was getting a bit fed up with his 'second driver' status within the Saab team. He believed that he could have won the Polish Rally if his head gasket had been changed but the Saab mechanics were too busy doing something on Erik Carlsson's car. When he got home to Sweden, he wrote to Cesare Fiorio at Lancia and asked for a works drive in 1966. To his surprise he not only got a reply but he got a drive and promptly finished third for Lancia on the Monte Carlo. The Swedish press were so impressed by this that they wrote about Andersson having a special contact to Lancia's biggest shareholder – the Vatican – and nicknamed Andersson Påven (the Pope).

On the bitterly cold Swedish Rally of 1966 where temperatures dropped to below minus 40°C, the Safari Rally winner from 1965, Joginder Singh, was competing in a works Volvo 122S and, despite driving in very different conditions to those in his home country, got to the finish seventh in his class. He also drove on the Acropolis Rally of that year and won his class with a 122S.

Most of the talk before the RAC Rally of 1966 concerned the Formula One champions that were competing. Ford had an impressive Jim Clark who had been as high as sixth overall before rolling his works Lotus Cortina out of the event just after leaving his home country of Scotland. Graham Hill's rally effort finished much earlier when the gearbox failed on his works Cooper S.

Graham Hill (on L) and Jim Clark during the 1966 RAC Rally.

The CSI – and others – kept coming up with wonderful initiatives to arouse interest in rallying. By way of example, for 1967 they devised the 'Trophy of Nations National Team'. This was based on five major rallies – Sweden, Austria, Acropolis, Poland and Finland – where national teams could go head-to-head. Hardly anyone noticed when it was won by Austria with best results in Sweden and Acropolis with Sweden second and Finland third. Only two other nations elected teams: East Germany and Russia.

On many rallies where details of the special stages were not made public before the start, there was always the suspicion that drivers from the country where it was being held had some previous knowledge. But some people found an answer. Before the Swedish Midnight Sun Rally of 1962, Klaus Kaiser was taken out by Eugen Böhringer in the hills near Stuttgart and shown how to write and read pace notes. He was then dispatched to Sweden and, before the roads for the special stages were actually closed, was driven over them by a Mercedes engineer in a normal road car. The notes that he had made were then taken back for Peter Lang to read back to Böhringer in the Mercedes 220SEb. To the surprise of many Swedes, Böhringer finished fifth overall ahead of Bertil Söderström's VW and Gunnar Andersson's Volvo PV544. The points gained in Sweden for the European Championship enabled Böhringer to narrowly defeat Erik Carlsson for the 1962 title.

In the days when driver's fees were small, there was always a keen interest taken by the crews in the prize money offered on events. Every year on the Tour de Corse, Shell Berre used to offer a considerable cash prize – certainly larger than anything offered by the organisers for winning the event – to anyone who finished with no penalties at the time controls. It was a kind of 'Corsican Coupe'. Shell's money was generally considered to be pretty safe since no one normally came anywhere near achieving that target. However, they had a very close call in 1967 when Sandro Munari and Luciano Lombardini (Lancia Fulvia) so nearly pulled it off. The most difficult section of the rally started with the 50 km (31 miles) test running from Cozzano over the Col de Verde and Col de Sorba to just outside Vivario and then continued through a maze of small lanes crisscrossing the main road and containing three passage controls where cars had to stop. In the wet and slippery conditions, Munari half-spun at one point and missed getting into the arrival control at Riventosa by just eight seconds. His nearest rival, Vic Elford in a Porsche 911, was more than a minute slower on the test and two minutes late at the time control. But those eight seconds must have worried Shell since they withdrew the prize for 1968 …

When the DAF team decided to enter two of their cars on the London to Sydney in 1968, they hit upon a novel idea to provide service in Australia. They would use a small airplane, a DC3 Dakota, to carry mechanics and spare parts and put it down on one of the many bush landing strips adjacent to the route. As team manager, Rob Koch, later admitted there were two problems. The first was that more than half the load space was taken up with DC3 spares. Secondly, going across the Nullabor Plain into a head wind, the rally cars were faster than the aeroplane. However, when they got to Sydney, he was able to sell the DC3 for $AU 20,000.

Very often on a rally in the 1960s one would come across a road section with two or more special stages contained within it. It was only much later that each special stage had to have an arrival time control. Lancia turned this to good effect on the 1969 Sanremo Rally where the first competitive motoring involved going from Pigna to Rezzo, some 49 km (30 miles) over the Colle Carmo Langan – a stage uphill – down to Molini di Triora and then up the Passo di Teglia where another stage went from a few kilometres below the top all the way down to Rezzo. The surface from Pigna to Molini di Triora was smooth, damp tarmac. From the start of the second stage, it was snow over a gravel base. The whole section was going to be hard to do without losing time so what tyres to fit? Lancia solved the problem by sending its cars out from Pigna with plain road tyres on the front wheels and heavily studded snow tyres at the rear. On the tarmac, the Fulvias oversteered like anything but were still quite quick uphill and left-foot braking solved how to get down the other side. Then, just metres before the snow started, there was a Lancia pit stop where two matching studded tyres were fitted to the front of each Fulvia. The result was that that the works Fulvias did good stage times and lost nothing on the road, while their opponents – Ford and Porsche – struggled on the second stage and lost time at Rezzo. The final result was a 1-2-3 for Lancia …

Somehow the large figure of Ove Eriksson was a perfect complement to the large Opel Rekord that he drove with such vigour. His nickname in Sweden was 'Bus-Ove' and most of the non-Swedes thought that perhaps he had driven a bus before taking up rallying. In fact, 'bus' in Swedish means 'mischief' and the nickname was a comment on his sideways driving style that, as one Swedish competitor put it, 'looked as if he had stolen the car for a joy ride'.

During 1965, Ove Andersson was getting a bit fed up with his 'second driver' status within the Saab team. He believed that he could have won the Polish Rally if his head gasket had been changed but the Saab mechanics were too busy doing something on Erik Carlsson's car. When he got home to Sweden, he wrote to Cesare Fiorio at Lancia and asked for a works drive in 1966. To his surprise he not only got a reply but he got a drive and promptly finished third for Lancia on the Monte Carlo. The Swedish press were so impressed by this that they wrote about Andersson having a special contact to Lancia's biggest shareholder – the Vatican – and nicknamed Andersson Påven (the Pope).

The 1971 RAC Rally rounded off a bonanza year for Swedish co-driver, Arne Hertz. It brought his tally of major rally wins to five during the year – Sweden, 1000 Lakes and RAC with Stig Blomqvist in a Saab 96 V4 and Austria and Acropolis with Ove Andersson in an Alpine Renault A110.

Most organisers take care to arrange their rally so that it is easy to recce. This was certainly true of the 1969 Spanish Rally that comprised two loops centred on Madrid with the second loop using the identical stages but run in the opposite direction. Convenient for the organisers but very exciting for the crews during the reconnaissance!

Winning the 1965 Safari for Volvo in one of their ex-factory cars led to Joginder Singh being invited to tour the Volvo factory and to drive one of their cars in some European rallies. Here he collects his award for finishing seventh in class with a 122 S on the 1966 Swedish Rally.

Epilogue

The Longer View

With the arrival of the World Rally Championship for 1973, rallying had reached a point from which it could go on to attract worldwide interest and achieve a fan base of millions. After a great deal of experimentation, a format had been evolved by which events could be organised in any country to an agreed international standard and yet maintain their own unique character. This uniqueness frequently depended on the terrain available to the organisers allied to the weather conditions prevailing at that time of year. Thus competitors on the Monte Carlo could expect snow and ice in the mountains, while on the Swedish there would be snow and ice on undulating forest roads. Heat and dust would be common to the Safari, Morocco and the Acropolis, tarmac to Corsica and to parts of the rallies in Portugal, Poland and Sanremo. And then gravel stages completed the menu on those last three events as well as comprising almost the entirety of the Austrian Alpine, 1000 Lakes, Press-on-Regardless and RAC rallies.

To meet the challenge presented by these events that varied so much in what they had on offer to both competitors and spectators, the car manufacturers were presented with recognition and preparation rules that allowed them to develop some very exciting cars during the following decade. It was not immediately the end of Group 2 by any means just as the previous twenty-six years had not been entirely dominated by modified touring cars. But the tantalising possibility of producing a smaller run of cars and homologating them directly into Group 4 was very much in the minds of team managers.

Their interest was stimulated by Porsche's homologation of their sports racing car, the 917, into Group 4 in May 1969. Porsche was able to do this because, ever since the introduction of the new Appendix J in 1966, the annual production quantity for Group 4 had been just fifty cars. The Chevrolet Corvette, Ferrari LM, Aston Martin DB4 Zagato, Ford GT40, Lotus 47, Alfa Romeo Giulia TZ, Alpine A110, Porsche Carrera 6 and many lesser sports cars filled its ranks. Then for the 1968 season, the CSI announced that the International Sports Car Championship for Makes would be open to Group 6 (Sports Prototypes) with a maximum engine capacity of 3,000 cc, Group 4 (Sports Cars) with a maximum engine capacity of 5,000 cc, and Group 3 (Grand Touring Cars) with no maximum limit on the size of their engine. Porsche realised that they could homologate a five-litre, no-holds-barred sports racing car merely by making a fifty of them. In fact, it was even better than that. The CSI would happily accept half the production required in a Group if it was accompanied by a guarantee to build the rest within the remaining twelve months. Like this, Porsche only needed to make twenty-five in order to have the 917 recognised in Group 4.

Porsche pulled it off and showed their twenty-five cars to the CSI on April 21st, 1969. The 917 was thus homologated into Group 4 with homologation number 250 and started racing. There was a considerable backlash to this bold move that resulted in a flurry of political activity away from the racetrack. As a result of this, for 1970 the homologation rules were changed to require Group 4 (now known as Special Grand Touring Cars) to have a minimum annual production of 500 cars while Group 5 (now Sports Cars) only needed twenty-five cars whereas previously there had been no production minimum. The eligibility rules for the International Sports Car Championship for Makes were changed and it was now made open to cars of Groups 4, 5 and 6. The limits on engine size stayed for those as they had been for the three previous Groups. Group 6 was for now engines up to 3,000cc, Group 5 took over the maximum capacity of 5,000 cc while Group 4 was now free. The latter decision kept the Americans happy with the big V8s while Porsche could be relatively happy racing their 917 in Group 5 – at least until 1972 when things changed again and Group 5 was given a maximum engine limit of three litres. Sometimes motor racing is like a dodgy casino – you win too much and they change the rules.

The homologation of the 917 attracted a great deal of publicity within the motor sport world and set minds working in other competition departments despite the hike in numbers for Group 4. At Lancia's reparto corse south of the Alps in Turin, they decided that they could make 500 examples of a purpose designed rally car and call it the Stratos. This was the opening move in the Group 4 explosion of the late 1970s. The numbers required may have been bigger than those required in 1969, but the prize of a World Championship was the same.

For the competitors too, there had been a gradual development of techniques that started in the late 1950s and continued right through the 1960s. Doing a recce of a rally route was known to work as long ago as the earliest part of the Twentieth Century. On the Austrian Alpine of 1914, Mr James Radley was leading with his Rolls Royce Silver Ghost when the rally arrived at a double night halt in Innsbruck. He dined, then borrowed another Rolls and set off to recce the infamous Turracher Höhe pass. It was a loop of some 500 km to return to Innsbruck and Radley made it with little time to spare before the re-start. Tired he may have been, but he was quickest on the Katschberg and swept up the Turracher Höhe to win the rally. Thanks to teams like Mercedes and BMC, doing a recce to acquire knowledge of the route became the modus operandi for all and, by the early 1960s, making pace notes for timed sections was also an integral part of the process. Accurate measuring devices like the ubiquitous Halda became standard equipment while, as cars got noisier, electronic intercoms were devised.

For works teams and quite a lot of private owners, there was the question of servicing during the rally. To start with, it was all pretty simple stuff with a can of petrol, a couple of spare wheels and some tools crammed into an ordinary car. Then it was noticed that an estate car could carry more parts especially if it had a roof rack. There was a natural progression towards vans and eventually to small lorries. Next, two-way radios enabled a rally car to warn its service crew of what work was needed before it actually arrived in the service point. All this would be expanded as rallying swept into the 1970s.

As for the spectators, who had been appearing in steadily increasing numbers at rallies, it had already been quite an experience to go out and watch one of the bigger events. This was simply because on the Monte Carlo or the RAC for example, there was activity everywhere. This encompassed the service points – both official and impromptu ones on the side of the road – the action on the special stages and tests to which access was fairly unrestricted, and any of the main controls and rest halts where the rally crews could be found having a coffee or a meal in a café or restaurant.

If one wanted to draw an analogy of these eras of rallying with actual historical periods, you could say that the 1950s were equivalent to the Stone Age, the 1960s to the Bronze Age and the 1970s to the Iron Age. But it is perhaps preferable to choose terms taken from the Olympic Games and call them the Bronze, Silver and Gold for what was to ensue from this 'Group 2' period was indeed a Golden Age for rallying.

Keen to use their 4.5 litre, 12-cylinder 917 in sports car racing, Porsche decided to aim for homologation in Group 4. To that end, on March 29th, 1969 they lined up 25 identical 917s at their Zuffenhausen factory for the FIA to inspect.

1953–1954

Chapter 10
Statistics

1953

23ème Rallye Automobile Monte-Carlo

(20–27 January 1953)
European Touring Championship, Round 1

Pos.	No.	Driver/Codriver	Nat.	Car	Cat.	Result
1	365	Maurice Gatsonides/Peter Worledge	NL/GB	Ford Zephyr		0/ 2/ 12.10
2	228	Ian Appleyard/Pat Appleyard	GB	Jaguar MkVII		0/ 3/ 12.15
3	391	Roger Marion/Jean Charmasson	F	Citroën 15/6		0/ 3/ 12.70
4	93	Michel Grosgogeat/Pierre Biagini	F	Panhard Dyna		0/ 4/ 12.40
5	339	Cecil Vard/Arthur Jolley	IRL	Jaguar MkV		0/ 5/ 11.55
6	318	Stirling Moss/John Cooper	GB	Sunbeam Talbot 90		0/ 5/ 11.60
7	298	Emilio Cristillin/Sandro Fiorio	I	Lancia Aurelia		0/ 5/ 11.80
8	225	Don Bennett/Elsa Bennett	GB	Jaguar MkVII		0/ 5/ 11.90
9	184	Sydney Allard/Tom Allard	GB	Allard K2 Sport		0/ 6/ 10.90
10	295	Erado Matuella/Roberto Piodi	I	Lancia Aurelia		0/ 6/ 11.85

Classification in order of road penalties, then regularity, then final test. There were no categories, only capacity classes

3rd Royal Automobile Club International Rally of Great Britain

(23–28 March 1953)
European Touring Championship, Round 3

Pos.	No.	Driver/Codriver	Nat.	Car	Cat.	Result
1	166	Ian Appleyard/Pat Appleyard	GB	Jaguar XK120	S	+29.37
2	185	Ronnie Adams/John Pearman	GB	Sunbeam Talbot	T	+22.77
3	170	Goff Imhoff/Betty Frayling	GB	Allard J2X	S	+19.51
4	138	Jack Broadhead/John Lilley	GB	Jaguar XK120	S	+16.97
5	99	Don Bennett/Elsa Bennett	GB	Jaguar XK120	S	+16.31
6	164	Len Shaw/Freddie Finnemore	GB	MG YB	T	+12.45
7	71	George Turnbull/Robert Dean	GB	Vauxhall Velox	T	+8.39
8	64	Frank Grounds/Jack Hay	GB	Jaguar XK120	S	+6.05
9	51	George Hartwell/Frank Scott	GB	Sunbeam Talbot	T	-0.49
10	184	Dennis Scott/Jack Cunningham	GB	Jaguar Mk.VII	T	-2.07

3. Internationale Rallye Travemünde

(3–7 June 1953)
European Touring Championship, Round 5

Pos.	No.	Driver/Codriver	Nat.	Car	Cat.	Result
1	49	Helmut Polensky/Walter Schlüter	D	Fiat 1100	T	825,681
2	32	Gert Seibert/Alfred Bolz	SA	Citroën 15/6	T	800,618
3	43	Walter Scheube/Paul Gierke	D	Ford Taunus 12M	T	788,355
4	52	Fritz Bösmiller/Hans Wencher	D	Fiat 1100	T	765,858
5	2	Walter Deutsch/Pierre Rousselle	B	Aston Martin	S	757,353
6	54	Gustav Menz/Heinz Meier	D	DKW Sonderklasse	T	751,207
7	1	Charles Fraikin/Olivier Gendebien	B	Jaguar XK120	S	747,353
8	9	Werner Engel/Hans-Leo von Hoesch	D	Porsche 356 1300	S	746,787
9	56	Irmgard Prahl/Hans-Joachim Prahl	D	Volkswagen	T	729,045
10	62	Heinz Schwind/Wolfgang Gutbrod	D	Gutbrod Superior	T	720,673

16ème Rallye International des Alpes

(10–16 July 1953)
European Touring Championship, Round 7

Pos.	No.	Driver/Codriver	Nat.	Car	Cat.	Result
1	306	Helmut Polensky/Walter Schlüter	D	Porsche 356 1500 Super		0 / 506.779
2	302	Rudolf Sauerwein/Max Nathan	D	Porsche 356 1500 Super		0 / 490.643
3	404	Jacques Herzet/Lucien Bianchi	B	Ferrari 166MM		0 / 489.631
4	303	Kurt Zeller/Hans Wencher	D	Porsche 356 1500 Super		0 / 482.749
5	603	Ian Appleyard/Pat Appleyard	GB	Jaguar		0 / 482.190
6	407	Alex & Katharina von Falkenhausen	D	Frazer-Nash		0 / 481.782
7	304	Hans Leo von Hoesch/B. von Hoesch	D	Porsche		0 / 476.488
8	529	Ferdinando Gatta/Cottino	I	Lancia Aurelia B20		0 / 470.471
9	528	Giovanni Lurani/Vittorio di Sambuy	I	Lancia Aurelia B20		0 / 463.847
10	621	Charles Fraikin/Olivier Gendebien	B	Jaguar XK120		0 / 461.097

Note: Results decided by road penalties, then test bonus

4° Rallye Automobilistico Internazionale del Sestriere

(26 February–2 March 1953)
European Touring Championship, Round 2

Pos.	No.	Driver/Codriver	Nat.	Car	Cat.	Result
1	94	Gert Seibert/Alfred Bolz	SA	Citroën 15	T	589,0
2	204	Roberto Scala/Vittorio Mazzonis	I	Lancia Aprillia	T	586,0
3	144	Mario Damonte/Stefano Marsaglia	I	Lancia Aurelia B22	T	580,5
4	12	Piero Valenzano/Renato Sposetti	I	Lancia Aurelia B20	S	568,0
5	296	Giuseppe Maranzana/Giancarlo Carlotti	I	Panhard Dyna	T	552,0
6	136	Emilio Christillin/Sandro Fiorio	I	Lancia Aurelia B22	T	547,0
7	294	Michel Grosgogeat/Pierre Biagini	F	Panhard Dyna	T	545,0
8	130	Ferdinando Gatta/Gildo de Martino	I	Lancia Aurelia B22	T	542,5
9	50	Giovanni Pignatelli/Carlo Sonnino	I	Lancia Aurelia B20	S	531,5
10	194	Emanuelle Nasi/Michèle Ceriana	I	Fiat 1400	T	525,0

SA is Saarland

5e Internationale Tulpenrallye

(27 April–2 May 1953)
European Touring Championship, Round 4

Pos.	No.	Driver/Codriver	Nat	Car	Cat.	Result
1	53	Hugo v. Zulen v. Nijevelt/F. Eschauzier	NL	Jowett Javelin	T	90
2	178	Bill Banks/Michael Porter	GB	Bristol	T	87
3	134	Michel Grosgogeat/Pierre Biagini	F	Panhard	T	86
4	68	Petrus Jetten/Louis van Noordwijk Jr.	NL	Vauxhall Velox	T	86
5	5	Ian Appleyard/Pat Appleyard	GB	Jaguar Mk.VII	T	86
6	145	Mario Damonte/Luisa Calligaro	I	Fiat 8V	T	80
7	36	Theo Koks/Kim de Jong	NL	Volkswagen	T	72
8	102	J.Scheffer/G.J.Willing	NL	Jowett Javelin	T	72
9	196	Martin Carstedt/Gulli Carstedt	S	Simca Aronde	T	70
10	8	Goff Imhoff/Stuart Ross	GB	Allard J2	S	70

IV Svenska Rallyt till Midnattssolen

(13–16 June 1953)
European Touring Championship, Round 6

Pos.	No.	Driver/Codrivder	Nat.	Car	Cat.	Result
1	75	Sture Nottorp/Bengt Jonsson	S	Porsche 356	S	12
2	152	John Kvarnström/Sven Lundberg	S	Ford Custom	T	14
3	43	Raymond Sjöqvist/Rune Berggren	S	Citroën 15	T	14
4		Arthur Wessblad/Bo Hellberg	S	Porsche 356	S	16
5		Grus-Olle Persson/Olle Norby	S	Porsche 356	S	16
6		Owe Stålheim/Erik Frank	S	Citroën 15	T	17
7		Tage Nyström/T.Sundström	S	Vauxhall Velox	T	17
8		Karl-Evert Andersson/O.Tryggvesson	S	Fiat 1100	T	17
9		Erik Lundgren/J.Bengtsson	S	Ford Zephyr	T	18
10		Rolf Melde/Helmut Fahlén	S	Saab	T	19

Liège-Rome-Liège

(19–23 August 1953)
European Touring Championship, Round 8

Pos.	No.	Driver/Codriver	Nat.	Car	Cat.	Result
1	3	Johnny Claes/Ginet Trasenster	B	Lancia Aurelia GT		1007
2	77	Charles Fraikin/Olivier Gendebien	B	Jaguar XK120		1250
3	68	Jacques Herzet/Lucien Bianchi	B	Ferrari 166		1653
4	10	Emilio Christillin/Sandro Fiorio	I	Lancia Aurelia GT		1849
5	31	Ferdinando Gatta/Stefano Marsaglia	I	Lancia Aurelia GT		2138
6	7	Franco Caramelli/Turbiglio	I	Lancia Aurelia GT		2748
7	17	Oreste Barozzi/Siro Colombo	I	Lancia Aurelia		3422
8	48	Arthur Slater/Peter Bolton	GB	Jaguar XK120		4661
9	66	Franco Bigoni/Curie	F	Citroën		4951
10	109	René Fabre/Jean Cazon	F	Panhard		5017

3rd Viking Rally

(11–13 September 1953)
European Touring Championship, Round 9

Pos.	No.	Driver/Codriver	Nat.	Car	Cat.	Result
1	2	Carsten Johansson/Gunnar Jensen	N	Ford Zephyr Six	T	24,1
2	70	Helmuth Polensky/Walter Schlüter	D	Fiat 1100	T	27,3
3	12	Ivan Hartley/Harry Tilbjørn	S	Ford Zephyr Six	T	41,8
4	21	Per Bergan/Walter Schjølberg	N	Fiat 1100	T	42,8
5	5	Arnold Busch/Arne Lindholm	N	Fiat 1100	T	43,4
6	45	Iver Grefsen/Finn Pettersson	N	Hansa 1800	T	49,1
7	78	Erik Hellum/Knut Griff-Müller	N	Simca Aronde	T	52,7
8	39	Peder Bertelsen/Jørgen Myking	N	Ford V8	T	54,6
9	59	Aage Bye/Sverre Ekorness	N	Fiat 1100	T	55,8
10	73	Leif Toftedal/Kjell Backe	N	Plymouth	T	59,4

7° Rallye Automovel Internacional de Lisboa (Estoril)

(13–18 October 1953)
European Touring Championship, Round 10

Pos.	No.	Driver/Codriver	Nat.	Car	Cat.	Result
1	54	Joaquim Nogueira/Sousa	P	Porsche 356 1500S		21.528
2	1	Ian Appleyard/Pat Appleyard	GB	Jaguar XK120		22.021
3	15	Helmuth Polensky/Walter Schlüter	D	Porsche 356 1500S		22.870
4	31	Goff Imhoff/Raymond Baxter	GB	Sunbeam Talbot 90		23.978
5	5	Jack Reece/Peter Reece	GB	Ford Zephyr		24.305
6	6	Nancy Mitchell/Joyce Leavens	GB	Ford Zephyr		24.531
7	34	Sheila van Damm/Françoise Clark	GB/F	Sunbeam Talbot		24.867
8	4	Cuth Harrison/Reg Phillips	GB	Ford Zephyr		25.367
9	69	Fernando Stock/X	P	Porsche		25.460
10	27	Jacques Herzet/Lucien Bianchi	B	Ferrari 166 MN		25.825

There were no categories, only capacity classes

1954

24ème Rallye Automobile Monte-Carlo

(18–27 January 1954)
European Touring Championship, Round 1

Pos.	No.	Driver/Codriver	Nat.	Car	Cat.	Result
1	69	Louis Chiron/Ciro Basadonna	MC	Lancia Aurelia		204,728
2	393	Pierre David/Paul Barbier	F	Peugeot 203		206,835
3	394	André Blanchard/Marcel Lecoq	F	Panhard Dyna		207,462
4	111	Carsten Johansson/Gunnar Jensen	N	Renault 4CV		207,866
5	27	Jean Vial/Gaston Panuel	F	Renault 4CV		208,681
6	104	Ronnie Adams/Desmond Titterington	GB	Jaguar Mk.VII		210,327
7	408	Madeleine Pochon/Lise Renaud	F	Renault 4CV		211,712
8	57	Cecil Vard/Arthur Jolley	IRL	Jaguar Mk.VII		213,376
9	420	Paul Guiraud/Henri Beau	F	Peugeot 203		214,109
10	24	Georges Houel/Julio Quinlin	F	Alfa Romeo 1900		214,440

5° Rallye Automobilistico Internazionale del Sestriere

(21–25 February 1954)
European Touring Championship, Round 2

Pos.	No.	Driver/Codriver	Nat.	Car	Cat.	Result
1	4	Piero Valenzano/Renato Sposetti	I	Lancia Aurelia B20-2500	GT	7,5
2	34	Guido Brignone/Guido Meregalli	I	Lancia Aurelia B20-2000	GT	12,9
3	200	Giuseppe Maranzana/Giancarlo Carlotti	I	Panhard	T	19,1
4	162	Paul Guiraud/Henri Beau	F	Peugeot 203	T	21,9
5	124	Lucic Finucci/Gino Munaron	I	Lancia Aurelia B22	T	35,4
6	70	Heinrich Theden/Manfred Elmenhorst	D	Porsche 356 1300	GT	38,6
7	72	Werner Engel/Gilbert Armbrecht	D	Porsche 356 1300	GT	55,1
8	164	Attilio Buffa/Gian Andrea Carabelli	I	Lancia Appia	T	56
9	112	Emilio Giletti/Cinti	I	Lancia Aurelia B22	T	57,9
10	138	Luciano Crotti/Renzo Sassi	I	Lancia Appia	T	58,3

4th Royal Automobile Club British International Rally

(9–13 March 1954)
European Touring Championship, Round 3

Pos.	No.	Driver/Codriver	Nat.	Car	Cat.	Result
1	155	Johnnie Wallwork/Harold Brooks	GB	Triumph TR2	S	416,67
2	42	Peter Cooper/O.L.Leighton	GB	Triumph TR2	S	435,05
3	145	Cuth Harrison/Edward Harrison	GB	Ford Zephyr	T	440,50
4	146	Peter Harper/David Humphrey	GB	Sunbeam-Talbot	T	441,00
5	153	Bill Bleakley/Peter Glaister	GB	Triumph TR2	S	445,85
6	197	Ronnie Adams/Leslie Rawlinson	GB	Alvis	T	449,70
7	169	Jimmy Ray/Mrs K.D.Ray	GB	Morgan	S	457,35
8	7	Alec Newsham/A.Beaumont	GB	Morgan	S	458,05
9	206	George Hartwell/F.W.Scott	GB	Sunbeam-Talbot	T	462,62
10	221	John Ashworth/J.Wesley	GB	Jaguar	T	469,40

6e Internationale Tulpenrallye

(25 April–1 May 1954)
European Touring Championship, Round 4

Pos.	No.	Driver/Codriver	Nat.	Car	Cat.	Result
1	133	Pierre Stasse/Olivier Gendebien	B	Alfa Romeo 1900	T	692
2	41	Werner Engel/Gilbert Ambrecht	D	Porsche 356	GT	652
3	234	Gustav Menz/Hubert Brand	D	DKW Sonderklasse	T	640
4	90	Johnny Boardmam/Jack Duckworth	GB	Jaguar Mk.VII	T	635
5	183	Jan Martens/B.H. Eerligh	NL	Fiat 1100 TV	T	588
6	85	Bill Banks/Michael Porter	GB	Alvis	T	579
7	15	Roger Rauch/Paul Delbarre	F	Salmson 2300 Sport	S	507
8	42	Walter Ringgenberg/Wener Mader	CH	Porsche	GT	482
9	120	Reg Phillips/Denis Scott	GB	Ford Zephyr	T	459
10	104	Sheila van Damm/Anne Hall	GB	Sunbeam Talbot	T	459

16. Rallye Wiesbaden

(12–16 May 1954)
European Touring Championship, Round 5

Pos.	No.	Driver/Codriver	Nat.	Car	Cat.	Result
1	71	Gustav Menz/Walter Schlüter	D	DKW Sonderklasse		12,14
2		Ludwig Kraus/Heinz Schwind	D	BMW 501		12,85
3		Hans Wencher/Erwin Behringer	D	BMW 501		16,41
4		Heinz Meier/Heinz Schellhaus	D	DKW Sonderklasse		26,42
5		Hubert Brand/Hermann Luba	D	DKW Sonderklasse		127,54
6		Felix Vogel/Sven von Schroeter	D	DKW		134,58
7		Helmuth Glöckler/Honorée Wagner	D	BMW 501		160,79
8		Kurt Zeller/Alois Willberger	D	Fiat 1100 TV		212,56
9		Erwin von Regius/Joachim Springer	D	Ford Taunus		216,67
10		Hans Gerdum/Joachim Kühling	D	Mercedes-Benz 220		236,02

V Svenska Rallyt till Midnattssolen

(16–20 June 1954)
European Touring Championship, Round 6

Pos.	No.	Driver/Codriver	Nat.	Car	Cat.	Result
1	27	Carl-Gunnar Hammarlund/E. Pettersson	S	Porsche 1300	S	33,65
2	26	Gunnar Källström/Sune Höök	S	Porsche 1300	S	34,43
3	135	Ivar Andersson/Björn Hansson	S	Alfa Romeo	T	35,38
4	136	Joakim Bonnier/Bo Boësen	S	Alfa Romeo	T	35,39
5	25	Allan Borgefors/Åke Gustavsson	S	Porsche 1300	S	35,57
6	79	John Bengtsson/Gösta Kruse	S	Ford Anglia	T	35,89
7	159	Paul Nordström/Gunnar Själin	S	Volvo PV444	T	36,65
8	5	Heinz Meier/Bengt Friman		DKW	T	36,77
9	71	Gunnar Nilsson/Sven Nilsson	S	Fiat 1100	T	36,78
10	68	Lennart Gustavsson/Torbjörn Ström	S	Fiat 1100	T	37,58

17ème Rallye International des Alpes

(8–13 July 1954)
European Touring Championship, Round 7

Pos.	No.	Driver/Codriver	Nat.	Car	Cat.	Result
1	228	Wolfgang Denzel/Hubert Stroinigg	A	Denzel		0/3415
2	22	Jean Redélé/Louis Pons	F	Renault		0/2432
3	24	Yves Lesur/Maurice Foulgoc	F	Renault		0/2382
4	406	Hal O'Hara-Moore/John Gott	GB	Frazer Nash		0/2096
5	210	Paul Guiraud/Henri Beau	F	Peugeot		0/1838
6	434	Maurice Gatsonides/Rob Slotemaker	NL	Triumph TR2		0/1613
7	534	Bill Burton/R.Burke	GB	Aston Martin DB2		0/1587
8	116	Heinz Meier/Hermann Luba	D	DKW		0/1514
9	526	Roger Rauch/Bousson	F	Salmson 2300 Sport		0/908
10	500	Stirling Moss/John Cutts	GB	Sunbeam		0/697

Liège-Rome-Liège

(18–22 August 1954)
European Touring Championship, Round 8

Pos.	No.	Driver/Codriver	Nat.	Car	Cat.	Result
1	86	Helmut Polensky/Herbert Linge	D	Porsche 356 1500S		311
2	104	Olivier Gendebien/Charles Fraikin	B	Lancia Aurelia B20 GT		512
3	38	Claude Storez/Jack Chanal	F	Porsche 356 1500S		1.578
4	60	Georges Houel/G.Blaise	F	Alfa Romeo 1900 ti		1.617
5	75	René Cotton/Jean-Louis Lemerle	F	Salmson 2300 Sport		1.889
6	58	Jean Redélé/Louis Pons	F	Renault		1.943
7	19	Reip/Bovens	B	Fiat V8		2.088
8	37	Barre/Pellecuer	F	Porsche		2.174
9	81	Celerier/Revillon	F	Porsche		2.363
10	72	Gilbert Sabine/Leroux	F	Porsche		2.695

4th Viking Rally

(11–13 September 1954)
European Touring Championship, Round 9

Pos.	No.	Driver/Codriver	Nat.	Car	Cat.	Result
1	73	Carsten Johansson/Gunnar Jensen	N	Ford Mainline		9,0
2	24	Hans Ingier/Walther Schjølberg	N	Ford Anglia		11,2
3	39	Leiv Samsing/Elvind Hall-Torgersen	N	Fiat 1100		12,1
4	12	Lars Askersrud/Arne Ingier	NL	Volkswagen		19,2
5	68	Per Bergan/Gunnar Kjølstad	N	Fiat 1100		20,7
6	42	Carl-Axel Adolfsson/Ingmar Karlsson	S	Ford Anglia		26,4
7	69	Birger Strand/Harald Stavseth	N	Ford Zephyr		29,7
8	27	Peer Braathen/Freddy Walby	N	Volkswagen		33,0
9	32	Walter Schlüter/Leif Nyborg	D	DKW		34,4
10	87	Rune Backlund/Helmer Broberg	S	Volvo PV		35,2

24ème Rallye International de Genève

(3–6 November 1954)
European Touring Championship, Round 10

Pos.	No.	Driver/Codriver	Nat.	Car	Cat.	Result
1	15	Jean-Claude Galtier/Paul Condrillier	F	Renault 4CV	M	1,80
2	58	Walter Schlüter/Siegfried Eikelmann	D	DKW F91 3=6 Sonderklasse	T	11,32
3		Paul Guiraud/Henri Beau	F	Peugeot 203	M	12,60
4		„Deroux"/Gouteyron	F	Alfa Romeo	T	13,96
5	18	Martin/Julio Quinlin	F	Salmson 2300 Sport	GT	16,00
6		Carlo Bornand/Fleury	CH	Alfa Romeo	T	16,00
7		Heinz Meier/Hermann Luba	D	DKW F91 3=6 Sonderklasse	T	17,10
8		Gustav Menz/Frederick von Preussen	D	DKW F91 3=6 Sonderklasse	T	22,20
9		Brun/Rolf Wütherich	CH	Porsche 356 1500S	GT	23,60
10	1	Alois de Mencik Zebinsky/J. Swaters	B	Ferrari 375 America	S	24,80

M is modified touring

25ème Rallye Automobile Monte-Carlo

(17–20 January 1955)
European Touring Championship, Round 1

Pos.	No.	Driver/Codriver	Nat.	Car	Cat.	Result
1	201	Per Malling/Gunnar Fadum	N	Sunbeam Talbot MkIII	T	405,936
2	275	Georges Gillard/Roger Dugat	F	Panhard Dyna	T	430,625
3	255	Hanns Gerdum/Joachim Kuhling	D	Mercedes-Benz 220	T	442,667
4	329	Gerry Burgess/Peter Easton	GB	Ford Zephyr	T	460,924
5	225	Walter Schock/Rolf Moll	D	Mercedes-Benz 220	T	460,981
6	282	Werner Lier/Henri Ziegler	CH	Lancia Aurelia	T	478,931
7	389	Maurice Gatsonides/Marcel Becquart	NL/F	Aston Martin DB2/4	GT	484,821
8	123	Ronnie Adams/Ernest McMillen	GB	Jaguar MkVII	T	494,221
9	251	Peter Harper/David Humphrey	GB	Sunbeam Talbot MkIII	T	513,226
10	290	Henri Marang/Diran Manoukian	F	Citroën 15/6	T	555,195

6° Rallye Automobilistico Internazionale del Sestriere

(25 February–1 March 1955)
European Touring Championship, Round 2

Pos.	No.	Driver/Codriver	Nat.	Car	Cat.	Result
1	6	Ferdinando Gatta/Vittorio Mazzonis	I	Lancia Aurelia Zagato	GT	23,0
2	178	Luciano Ciolfi/Ottorino Monaco	I	Fiat 1100 TV	T	32,4
3	18	Piero Valenzano/Renato Sposetti	I	Lancia Aurelia	GT	35,0
4	98	Luigi Taramazzo/Genino Gerino	I	Alfa Romeo 1900TI	T	41,0
5	110	Giuseppe Musso/Pensa	I	Alfa Romeo 1900ti	T	43,0
6	82	Walter Schock/Rolf Moll	D	Mercedes-Benz 220A	T	51,4
7	86	Ken Wharton/Gordon Shanley	GB	Daimler Century	T	52,0
8	62	Paul Guiraud/Chevron	F	Peugeot 203	GT	56,6
9	50	Egon von Westerholt/Heinrich Theden	D	Porsche 356	GT	61,1
10	108	Guido Cestelli-Guidi/M. Cestelli-Guidi	I	Alfa Romeo	T	74,3

The 5th Royal Automobile Club British International Rally

(8–13 March 1955)
European Touring Championship, Round 3

Pos.	No.	Driver/Codriver	Nat.	Car	Cat.	Result
1	213	Jimmy Ray/Brian Harrocks	GB	Standard Ten	M	398,1
2	172	Harold Rumsey/Peter Roberts	GB	Triumph TR2	S	462,3
3	110	Goff Imhof/Ian Mackensie	GB	Allard	S	615,4
4	124	Ronnie Adams/D.A.Wilkins	GB	Alvis	T	683,4
5	215	Ken Richardson/Kit Heathcote	GB	Standard Ten	M	699,5
6	194	Denis Done/	GB	Fiat 1100	T	797,5
7	51	A.H.Greig/T.Piggott	GB	Triumph TR2	S	969,4
8	111	Ian Appleyard/J.R.J.Mansbridge	GB	MG	M	974,4
9	130	E.V.Baker/Pat Stark	GB	Ford	T	1011,7
10	86	Clive Seward/A.C.Johnson	GB	Triumph TR2	S	1025,4

7e Internationale Tulpenrallye Holland

(30 April–7 May 1955)
European Touring Championship, Round 4

Pos.	No.	Driver/Codriver	Nat.	Car	Cat.	Result
1	2	Hans Tak/W.C.Niemöller	NL	Mercedes-Benz 300SL	S	0/67m56.5
2	56	Bill Banks/A.Meredith Owens	GB	Bristol 401	GT	0/68m05.1
3	100	Werner Engel/Gilbert Armbrecht	D	Mercedes-Benz 220A	T	0/68m15.7
4	207	Maurice Gatsonides/J. St.John Foster	NL	Standard Ten	T	0/68m17.7
5	211	Rolf Mellde/H.de Montesquieu	S	SAAB 92B	T	0/68m24.1
6	131	Walter Schlüter/Siegfried Eikelmann	D	DKW F91	T	0/68m34.7
7	79	Peter Harper/John Cutts	GB	Sunbeam Talbot 90	T	0/68m53.6
8	46	John Boardman/J.W.Whitworth	GB	Jaguar Mk VII	T	0/68m55.6
9	209	Greta Molander/Monica Kjerstadius	N	Saab 92B	T	0/69m08.4
10	89	H. Stenfeldt Hansen/N.Buchsbaum	DK	Mercedes-Benz 220A	T	0/69m10.0

1. Internationale ADAC-Rallye Nürburgring

(18–22 May 1955)
European Touring Championship, Round 5

Pos.	No.	Driver/Codriver	Nat.	Car	Cat.	Result
1	12	Gustav Mentz/Sven von Schroeter	D	DKW	T	0/252.9
2	14	Heinz Meier/Hermann Luba	D	DKW	T	0/254.7
3	114	Paul-Ernst Strähle/Hans Wencher	D	Porsche	GT	0/265.4
4	86	Werner Engel/Helmuth Rathjen	D	Mercedes-Benz	T	0/274.5
5	108	Eitel Eddelbüttel/Manfred Elmenhorst	D	Porsche 1300	GT	0/278.2
6	76	Alfons Vossen/Friedrich Schorlemmer	D	BMW 502	T	0/279.2
7	82	Alex & Katharina von Falkenhausen	D	BMW 502	T	0/279.7
8	74	Hans Gerdum/Joachim Kühling	D	Mercedes-Benz 220	T	0/280.8
9	62	Gunter Kolwes/Alfred Katz	D	BMW 501	T	0/286.1
10	64	Erwin Behringer/Rolf Stahlschmidt	D	BMW 501	T	0/289.2

VI Svenska Rallyt till Midnattssolen

(13–18 June 1955)
European Touring Championship, Round 6

Pos.	No.	Driver/Codriver	Nat.	Car	Cat.	Result
1	63	Allan Borgefors/Åke Gustavsson	S	Porsche 1500S	GT	9,4
2	60	Olof Persson/Stig Pettersson	S	Porsche	GT	12,4
3	128	Stig Gruen/Sven Jonsson	S	Peugeot 403	T	12,5
4	62	Gunnar Källström/Bo Guterstam	S	Porsche	GT	13.3/36.89
5	16	Heinz Meier/Hermann Luba	D	DKW	T	13.3/38.24
6	92	Joakim Bonnier/Bo Boesen	S	Alfa Romeo TI	T	13,4
7	167	Åke Thambert/Mario Pavoni	S	Fiat 1100TV	T	13,5
8	169	Harry Bengtsson/Åke Righard	S	Volkswagen	T	14,1
9	165	Thure Jansson/Lennart Jansson	S	Fiat 1100TV	T	14,3
10	132	Martin Carstedt/Gulli Carstedt	S	Ford Taunus 15M	T	15,1

1955

IVe Rallye Adriatique

(20–24 July 1955)
European Touring Championship, Round 7

Pos.	No.	Driver/Codriver	Nat.	Car	Cat.	Result
1		Werner Engel/Heinz Straub	D	Mercedes-Benz 300SL	GT	0
2		Max Nathan/Wilhelm Glöckler	D	Porsche 356 1300S	GT	0,72
3		Georg Meier/Hans Wencher	D	BMW 502	T	
4		Edmund Gr. v. Westerholt/H. Theiden	D	Porsche 356	GT	
5		Walter Schlüter/Siegfried Eikelmann	D	DKW	T	
6		Heinz Schwind/Wolfgang Gutbrod	D	BMW 502	T	
7		Fabrizio Imbert/Michele Salvati	I	Alfa Romeo Super	T	7,32
8		Rodica/	YU	Alfa Romeo 1900		9,00
9		Holle/		Porsche 356		10,00
10		R.Sebastiani/		Fiat 1100		22,00

There is some doubt over the accuracy of these results

5th Viking Rally

(9–12 September 1955)
European Touring Championship, Round 9

Pos.	No.	Driver/Codriver	Nat.	Car	Cat.	Result
1	14	Lars Egeberg/Amund Bøhle	N	Peugeot 203		21,75
2	57	Walter Schlüter/Siegfried Eikelmann	D	DKW Sonderklasse		26,75
3	25	Leif Vold-Johansen/Carl F.Karlan	N	DKW Sonderklasse		41,90
4	9	Birger M.Strand/Harald Stavseth	N	Ford Zephyr		45,95
5	45	Ivar Andersson/Lennart Simonsson	S	Peugeot 403		46,80
6	34	Edward Gjølberg/Sten Stensrud	N	Sunbeam Mk.III		49,80
7	12	Peer Bråthen/Freddy Walby	N	Fiat 1100 TV		53,10
8	74	Ragnar Busch/Helge Mikkelsen	N	Sunbeam Mk.III		63,80
9	48	Arne Inçier/Håkon Fløysvik	N	Volkswagen		65,15
10	88	Walter Schock/Rolf Moll	D	Mercedes-Benz 220 A		66,00

Liège-Rome-Liège

(17–21 August 1955)
European Touring Championship, Round 8

Pos.	No.	Driver/Codriver	Nat.	Car	Cat.	Result
1	56	Olivier Gendebien/Pierre Stasse	B	Mercedes-Benz 300 SL		0
2	47	René Cotton/Jean-Louis Lemerle	F	Salmson 2300 Sport		0
3	110	Johnny Claes/Lucien Bianchi	B	Lancia Aurelia GT		0
4	87	Werner Engel/Heinz Straub	D	Mercedes-Benz 300 SL		60
5	41	Ken Richardson/Kit Heathcote	GB	Triumph TR2		60
6	27	Robert Leidgens/Freddy Rousselle	B	Triumph TR2		60
7	88	Maurice Gatsonides/Giuseppe Borelly	NL/F	Triumph TR2		240
8	95	Willy Mairesse/Maurice Desse	B	Peugeot		245
9	28	Guy Monraisse/Jacques Feret	F	Renault		312
10	35	Paul Condrillier/Jean Hebert	F	Renault		368

1956

26ème Rallye Automobile Monte-Carlo

(16–23 January 1956)
European Rally Championship, Round 1

Pos.	No.	Driver/Codriver	Nat.	Car	Cat.	Result
1	164	R. Adams/F. Bigger/D. Johnstone	GB	Jaguar Mk.VII	T	213
2	241	Walter Schock/Rolf Moll	D	Mercedes-Benz 220	T	219
=3	283	Peter Harper/David Humphrey	GB	Sunbeam Mk.III	T	227
=3	331	Michel Grosgogeat/Pierre Biagini	F	DKW	T	227
5	259	Wolfgang Levy/Georg Kokott	D	Volkswagen	T	229
6	350	Walter Loffler/Helmut Rathjen	D	BMW 502	T	230
7	115	Pierre Courtes/André Court-Payen	F	Citroën DS19	T	231
8	145	Maurice Gatsonides/Marcel Becquart	NL/F	Standard Vanguard	T	233
9	330	Per Maling/Einar Jensen-Lund	N	Panhard Dyna 55	T	234
10	326	Jimmy Ray/John Cutts	GB	Sunbeam Mk.III	T	236

7° Rallye Automobilistico Internazionale del Sestriere

(24–28 February 1956)
European Rally Championship, Round 2

Pos.	No.	Driver/Codriver	Nat.	Car	Cat.	Result
1	12	Walter Shock/Rolf Moll	D	Mercedes-Benz 300SL	GT&M	12,0
2	106	Wolfgang Gutbrod/Heinz Schwind	D	BMW 502	T	13,3
3	140	Luigi Taramazzo/Genino Gerino	I	Alfa Romeo 1900 TI	T	25,7
4	82	Paul-Ernst Strähle/Hans von Wencher	D	Porsche 356 1300S	GT&M	26,9
5	114	Sergio Mantovani/Morolli	I	Lancia Aurelia B12	T	46,9
6	23	Alberti/d'Errico	I	Alfa Romeo Giulietta	T	49,2
7	48	Casimiro Toselli/Lamberti Zanardi	I	Fiat 8V	GT&M	50,4
8	202	Roger Masson/Roger Laurent	F/B	Dyna-Panhard X86	T	51,1
9	154	Giorgio Superti/Fiorani	I	Fiat 1100TV	T	51,3
10	80	Paul Guiraud/Alizary de Rocquefort	F	Peugeot 203	GT&M	53,7

The Royal Automobile Club Sixth International Rally of Great Britain

(6–10 March 1956)
European Rally Championship, Round 3

Pos.	No.	Driver/Codriver	Nat.	Car	Cat.	Result
1	123	Lyndon Sims/T. Ambrose/R. Jones	GB	Aston Martin DB2/4	GT&M	29,2
2	11	Ian Appleyard/Pat Appleyard	GB	Jaguar XK140	GT&M	50,0
3	33	John Spare/M.H.Meredith	GB	Morgan Plus 4	S	54,8
4	149	Bill Bleakley/Ian Hall	GB	Jaguar 2.4	T	65,1
5	88	Peter Cooper/G.Holland	GB	Standard Ten	T	81,1
6	12	Joan Johns/Douglas Johns	GB	Austin A90 Westminster	GT&M	82,9
7	157	Arthur Senior/C.Hall	GB	Austin	T	90,0
8	143	Declan O'Leary/A.M.Canty	IRL	Volkswagen	T	91,9
9	21	Johnny Wallwork/Willy Cave	GB	Standard Ten	GT&M	112,6
10	41	Peter Harper/David Humphrey	GB	Sunbeam Mk.III	T	114,5

4th Rally Acropolis

(26–29 April 1956)
European Rally Championship, Round 4

Pos.	No	Driver/Codriver	Nat.	Car	Cat.	Result
1	9	Walter Schock/Rolf Moll	D	Mercedes-Benz 300SL	GT	6,3
2	84	N.Filines/N.Chryssikopoulos	GR	DKW	T	36,4
3	94	René Fabre/Mme M.Redon	F	Panhard X86	T	45,4
4	29	Johnny Pesmazoglou/K.Galanes	GR	Chevrolet Belair	T	48,7
5	69	Paul Guiraud/Henri Beau	F	Peugeot 203	T	51,6
6	103	G.Terementzes/Mme B.Adosidou	GR	Renault 4CV	T	61,0
7	24	P.Chenevoy/J.Deguerce	F	Porsche 356 1500S	GT	63,2
8	2	D.Stavrionos/G.Margaritis	GR	Renault 4CV	T	73,1
9	51	K.Nikolopoulos/K.Elipoulos	GR	Opel Rekord	T	79,7
10	60	K.Lykoures/A.Terzakis	GR	Opel Rekord	T	100,7

8e Internationale Tulpenrallye

(6–12 May 1956)
European Rally Championship, Round 5

Pos.	No.	Driver/Codriver	Nat.	Car	Cat.	Result
1	208	Raymond Brookes/Edward Brookes	GB	Austin A30	T	116,17
2	203	Johnny Wallwork/William Bleakley	GB	Standard Eight	T	120,49
3	201	Paddy Hopkirk/John Garvey	GB	Standard Eight	T	121,35
4	202	Dennis O'Mara-Taylor/Lew Tracey	GB	Standard Eight	T	122,02
5	210	I.M.Sutherland/T.B.Band	GB	Standard Eight	T	123,50
6	168	I.A.Langestraat/B.L.van der Wansem	NL	Rover 75	T	127,19
7	209	P.D.C.Brookes/R.E.W.Wellswest	GB	Morris Minor	T	127,43
8	219	Philippe van de Maelle/J.Langlard	F	Citroën DF	M	128,15
9	188	Gunther Issenbügel/H.Rathjen	D	Ford Taunus 12M	T	128,27
10	32	Lyndon Sims/Tony Ambrose	GB	Aston Martin DB2	GT	128,36

25ème Rallye International de Genève

(25–27 May 1956)
European Rally Championship, Round 6

Pos.	No.	Driver/Codriver	Nat.	Car	Cat.	Result
1	80	Michel Grosgogeat/Pierre Condrillier	F	DKW F91	T	
2	12	Stefan Brügger/Frederico Karrer	CH	DKW	M	0,50
3	30	Beyer/Xavier Perrot	CH	Porsche 356 Carrera	GT	1,00
4	56	Bruno Martignoni/Vittorio Vanini	I	Alfa Romeo TI	T	5,10
5	72	Ruth Lautmann/Renate Utermöhl	D	Ford Taunus	T	5,27
6	8	Georges Houel/R.Bertramier	F	Alfa Romeo Sprint Zagato	M	7,75
7	20	"Cedric"/Roger Calame	CH	Alfa Romeo 1900	GT	9,16
8	26	André Wicky/Carlo Bornand	CH	Triumph TR2	GT	10,68
9	71	Rigo Steffen/Görgen	CH	Peugeot 403	T	15,89
10	69	Robert Dubuet/Guy Dupré	F	Peugeot 403	T	17,66

1956–1958

VII Rallyt till Midnattssolen

(29 May–3 June 1956)
European Rally Championship, Round 7

Pos.	No.	Driver/Codriver	Nat.	Car	Cat.	Result
1	148	Harry Bengtsson/Åke Righard	S	Volkswagen	T	8,20
2	150	Berndt Jansson/Torsten Grenberg	S	Volkswagen	T	8,45
3	7	Carl-Magnus Skogh/Rolf Skogh	S	Saab	T	9,00
4	3	Erik Carlsson/Sten Holm	S	Saab	T	9,35
5	1	Harald Kronegård/Gustav Palmgren	S	Saab	T	10,05
6	69	Allan Borgefors/Lars Sjöberg	S	Porsche 356 1600	S	10,10
7	110	Stig Gruen/Sven Eriksson	S	Peugeot	T	11,40
8	141	Bengt Johansson/Vidar Klockare	S	Peugeot	T	11,45
9	12	Oscar Swahn/Sten Wikström	S	Saab	T	11,60
10	4	Bengt Jonsson/Gunnar Asplund	S	Saab	T	12,10

18ème Rallye International des Alpes

(6–13 July 1956)
European Rally Championship, Round 9

Pos.	No.	Driver/Codriver	Nat.	Car	Cat.	Result
1	228	Michel Collange/Robert Huguet	F	Alfa Romeo Giulietta Sprint		1913
2	320	Robert Buchet/Claude Storez	F	Porsche 356 Carrera		1630
3	332	Chuck Rickert/Dave Kriplen	USA	Porsche 356 Carrera		1517,5
4	226	André Blanchard/Guy Jouanheaux	F	Denzel 1300		1288
5	618	Jean Estager/Jean Prebel	F	Ferrari 250GT		1265,5
6	236	Paul-Ernst Strähle/Hans Wencher	D	Porsche		1242,5
7	508	Cuth Harrison/Edward Harrison	GB	Ford Zephyr		1140,5
8	412	Maurice Gatsonides/E. Pennybacker	NL/USA	Triumph TR3		1114,5
9	216	Marcel Lauga/Francia Lauga	F	Denzel 1300		1066
10	210	Pierre David/Jacques Metin	F	Peugeot 203 203C		1005

6th Viking Rally

(14–17 September 1956)
European Rally Championship, Round 11

Pos.	No.	Driver/Codriver	Nat.	Car	Cat.	Result
1	2	Carl-Magnus Skogh/Rolf Skogh	S	Saab 93	T	24,0
2	4	Erik Carlsson/Sten Helm	S	Saab 93	T	27,1
3	19	Bengt Johansson/Arne Bohm	S	Peugeot	T	34,7
4	6	Ivar Andersson/Hjalmar Ohlstrøm	S	Saab 93	T	37,7
5	53	Leif Samsing/Håkon Isdahl	N	DKW	T	44,8
6	86	Jens Jarl Jernes/Johan Solem	N	Opel Rekord	T	50,4
7	16	Olle Bromark/Stig Pettersson	S	Volkswagen	T	56,5
8	25	Lars Askersrud/Gunnar Steenslie	N	Ford Anglia	T	57,9
9	22	Ulf Strindlund/Fred Brolin	S	Peugeot 403	T	59,0
10	35	Christopher Wessel/Knut Griff-Müller	N	DKW	T	59,7

1º Rali Ibérico

(1–4 November 1956)
European Rally Championship, Round 13

Pos.	No.	Driver/Codriver	Nat.	Car	Cat.	Result
1	61	Fernando Stock/Palma	P	Mercedes-Benz 300SL	GT	42.510
2	12	Javier Sanglas Camps/	E	Alfa Romeo Giulietta Sprint Veloce	GT	43.938
3	72	José Luis Abreu Valente/	P	Porsche 356		44.837
4	5	Esteban Sala Soler/	E	Fiat 8V	GT	47.672
5	28	Gerardo de Andrés/	E	Mercedes-Benz 300SL		48.035
6	39	Paul-Ernst Strähle/Hans Wencher	D	Porsche 356	GT	49.496
7	83	Carlos Faustino/	P	Panhard	M	49.671
8	101	Francisco Silva Pereira/	P	Lancia	M	50.310
9	9	Carlos Mach Brosa/	E	Mercedes-Benz 190SL		51.437
10	88	João Vieira Azevedo/	P	Triumph TR3	S	53165

8° Rallye Automobilistico Internazionale del Sestriere

(25 February–1 March 1957)
European Rally Championship, Round 1

Pos.	No.	Driver/Codriver	Nat.	Car	Cat.	Result
1	290	Pier Carlo Borghesio/G. Bianchi	I	Dyna Panhard X86	T	11,4
2		Turri/Cocchetti	I	Alfa Romeo Giulietta	T	15,2
3	62	Carlo-Maria Abate/Mottura	I	Alfa Romeo Giulietta SV Zagato	GT	15,7
4		Stardero/"Mark"	I	Alfa Romeo Giulietta		18,0
5	60	Cabianca/Oreffice	I	Alfa Romeo Giulietta Sprint Veloce		19,3
6		Paolo Lena/Orlando Palanga	I	Ferrari 250GT	GT	22,0
7		Corcos/Janari	I	Fiat 600		24,8
8		Oscar Papais/Eros Crivellari	I	Ferrari 250GT		26,2
9		Antonio Fiorani/Gino Munaron	I	Maserati A6G	GT	26,9
10		Giorgio Superti/Fiorani	I	Alfa Romeo Giulietta	T	27,2

18. Internationale Rallye Wiesbaden

(20–24 June 1956)
European Rally Championship, Round 8

Pos.	No.	Driver/Codriver	Nat.	Car	Cat.	Result
1		Bengt Jonsson/Kjell Persson	S	Saab 93	T	
2		Max Nathan/Paul Denk	D	Porsche 356 Carrera	GT	
3		Egon Vomfell/K.H.Schöttler	D	Fiat 1100 TV	T	
4		Hubert Charton/Michael Hippau	F	Renault Dauphine	M	
5		Wilhelm Rudolf/Kurt Wüst	D	Alfa Romeo Giulietta	GT	
6		Günter Schramm/Hans Behrens	D	Borgward Isabella	T	
7		Hannes Röttger/Walther Scheube	D	Ford Taunus 15M		
8		Joachim Springer/Erwin von Regius	D	Ford Taunus 15M		
9		Walter Schock/Rolf Moll	D	Mercedes-Benz 300SL	GT	
10		Heinz Schwind/Wolfgang Gutbrod	D	BMW 502	T	

Liège-Rome-Liège

(29 August–2 September 1956)
European Rally Championship, Round 10

Pos.	No.	Driver/Codriver	Nat.	Car	Cat.	Result
1	70	Willy Mairesse/Willy Génin	B	Mercedes-Benz 300SL		540
2	36	Claude Storez/Robert Buchet	F	Porsche 356 Carrera		1.040
3	60	Olivier Gendebien/Pierre Stasse	B	Ferrari Europa		1.525
4	16	René Cotton/Jacques Leclère	F	Mercedes-Benz 300SL		1.913
5	92	Robert Leidgens/Freddy Rousselle	B	Triumph TR2		2.230
6	63	Paul-Ernst Strähle/Hans Wencher	D	Porsche		2.362
7	79	Roger de Lageneste/Michel Nicol	F	Peugeot 203		2.518
8	66	Georges Harris/Jojo Jacqmin	B	Volvo		2.690
9	90	Alain de Changy/Lucien Bianchi	B	Alfa Romeo Giulietta		2.711
10	51	Bernard Consten/Bernard Pichon	F	Triumph		2.765

Ve Rallye Adriatique

(26–29 September 1956)
European Rally Championship, Round 12

Pos.	No.	Driver/Codriver	Nat.	Car	Cat.	Result
1		Paul-Ernst Strähle/Hans Wencher	D	Porsche 356 1300S	GT,M&S	3,5
2		Siegfried Eikelman/Nedeljko Karleusa	D/YU	DKW	T	18,0
3		Milivoje Vukovic/Pavle Protic	YU	DKW	T	27,5
4		Walter Schock/Rolf Moll	D	Mercedes-Benz 300SL	GT,M&S	43,0
5		Leopold Landsmann/F. Kanles	CZ	Škoda	T	50,5
6		Vaclav Hovorka/Viktor Mraz	CZ	Škoda	T	53,0
7		H. Stenfeld Hansen/R. Rottbøl Ørum	DK	Mercedes-Benz 220A	T	59,0
8		Franjo Valencié/Milica Valencié	YU	Volkswagen		68,0
9		Max Nathan/Hans-Joachim Walter	D	Posche 356 Carrera	GT,M&S	73,5
10		Dusan Maleric/Jure Cerne	YU	Mercedes-Benz 190SL		118,5

1957

5th Rally Acropolis

(24–28 April 1957)
European Rally Championship, Round 2

Pos.	No.	Driver/Codriver	Nat.	Car	Cat.	Result
1	7	Jean-Pierre Estager/Lucille Estager	F	Ferrari 250GT		4,2
2	81	Henri Blanchoud/Berger	MC	Saab 93		6,7
3	75	Nicos Filinis/Petropoulos	GR	DKW F93		7,0
4	77	Valter Karlsson/John Kvarnström	S	DKW F93		12,2
5	14	Petros Papadopoulos/Politis	GR	MGA		14,5
6	37	M. Leto di Priolo/D. Leto di Priolo	I	Alfa Romeo 1900TI		16,9
7	39	Guido Cestelli-Guidi/Cestelli-Guidi	I	Alfa Romeo 1900TI		19,5
8	19	Alkis Michos/A.Antoniou	GR	Alfa Romeo Giulietta Sprint Veloce		22,8
9	48	Paul Guiraud/Henri Beau	F	Peugeot 403		24,9
10	66	Kostas Nicolopoulos/Kaloudis	GR	Alfa Romeo Giulietta Berline		26,8

9e Internationale Tulpenrallye

(6–11 May 1957)
European Rally Championship, Round 3

Pos.	No.	Driver/Codriver	Nat.	Car	Cat.	Result
1	163	Hans Kreisel/D.ten Hope	NL	Renault Dauphine	M	96,49%
2	1	Hans Tak/W.C.Niemoller	NL	Mercedes-Benz 300SL	GT	98,01%
3	42	T.J.Koks/R.L.G.M.Gorris	NL	Porsche 356 1600	GTM	98,74%
4	70	Martin Carstedt/Gulli Carstedt	S	Ford Fairlane 500	T	98,18%
5	226	André Jetten/Hein Korte	NL	Goggomobil	T	94,57%
6	80	Johnny Wallwork/A.Pownall	GB	Alfa Romeo 1900	T	98,78%
7	138	Jimmy Ray/Ian Hall	GB	Sunbeam Rapier	T	98,97%
8	71	C.I.de Vries/J.A.Moorman	NL	Ford Fairlane	T	99,01%
9	150	Jan Martens/B.H.Eerligh	NL	Fiat 1100	T	98,61%
10	63	Max Riess/G.R.Küfner	D	Mercedes-Benz 220S	M	99,53%

VIII Svenska Rallyt till Midnattssolen

(13–15 June 1957)
European Rally Championship, Round 5

Pos.	No.	Driver/Codriver	Nat.	Car	Cat.	Result
1	162	Thure Jansson/Lennart Jansson	S	Volvo PV444	T	10,5
2	71	Heimer Adiels/Anders Berg	S	DKW	T	11,8
3	1	Martin Carstedt/Gulli Carstedt	S	Ford Fairlane 500	T	12,0
4	157	Nisse Carlsson/Harry Happman	S	Volvo PV444	T	12,5
5	68	Valter Karlsson/Henry Karlsson	S	DKW	T	13,6
6	35	Carl-Magnus Skogh/Rolf Skogh	S	Saab 93	T	14,9
7	100	Berndt Jansson/Torsten Grennberg	S	Volkswagen	T	15,3
8	155	Stig Gruen/Sven-Erik Ericsson	S	Peugeot 403	T	16,6
9	22	Allan Borgefors/Börje Andersson	S	Porsche Speedster	GT	17,2
10	25	Arthur Wessblad/Göran Grimhall	S	Porsche 1600 S	GT	21,0

VIe Rallye Adriatique

(24–28 July 1957)
European Rally Championship, Round 7

Pos.	No.	Driver/Codriver	Nat.	Car	Cat.	Result
1	3	Ruprecht Hopfen/Kurt von Lösch	D	Saab 93		0,0
2		H.Kaufmann/K.Rappold	A	DKW		0,0
3		L.Marini/L.Tavola	I	Alfa Romeo Giulietta		0,0
4		"Pegaso"/Campidoglio	I	Alfa Romeo Giulietta Sprint Veloce		0,1
5		Arnulf Pilhatsch/Richter	A	BMW 502		5,0
6		Wolfgang Levy/Horst	D	Fiat 1100TV		7,5
7		Carlo Bornand/Michelle Vouga	CH	Alfa Romeo Giulietta Sprint Veloce		9,5
8		Paul Guiraud/Britvic	F	Peugeot 403		10,0
9		Milivoja Vukovic/Picek	YU	DKW		14,0
10		Alex & Katharina von Falkenhausen	D	BMW 507		15,0

7th Viking Rally

(20–23 September 1957)
European Rally Championship, Round 9

Pos.	No.	Driver/Codriver	Nat.	Car	Cat.	Result
1	29	Nils Fredrik Grøndal/T. Berntsen	N	Volvo PV444		7,1
2	24	Arne Ingier/Haakon Fløysvik	N	Volvo PV444		8,8
3	12	Carl Magnus Skogh/Rolf Skogh	S	Saab 93		14,0
4	81	Jens Jarl Jernes/Johan Solem	N	Mercedes-Benz 190		16,2
5	9	Leif Vold-Johansen/Carl F.Karlan	N	DKW		20,0
6	17	Harry Bengtsson/Åke Righard	S	Volkswagen		20,4
7	98	Helge Kristiansen/Even Halla	N	Simca Vedette Versailles		20,9
8	27	Rune Bäcklund/Arne Bergstrøm	S	Volvo PV444		22,4
9	5	Karl Paulsen/Finn Pettersen	N	Mercedes-Benz		22,7
10	26	Bengt Johansson/Arne Bohm	S	Peugeot 403		24,2

27ème Rallye Automobile Monte-Carlo

(21–29 January 1958)
European Rally Championship, Round 1

Pos.	No.	Driver/Codriver	Nat.	Car	Cat.	Result
1	65	Guy Monraisse/Jacques Feret	F	Renault Dauphine	GT	1520,0
2	70	Alex Gacon/Léo Borsa	F	Alfa Romeo	GT	2234,9
3	18	Leif Vold-Johansen/Finn Kopperud	N	D.K.W.	T	2559,0
4	23	Walter Loffler/Carsten Johansson	DK	Volvo	T	2907,0
5	31	Peter Harper/Peter Elbra	GB	Sunbeam Rapier	T	2928,0
6	128	Maurice Gatsonides/Marcel Becquart	NL/F	Triumph TR3	GT	3093,0
7	51	Carl Spjuth/Gino Anzil	S	Alfa Romeo	T	3152,8
8	91	Henri Ziegler/Julien Cots	CH	Sunbeam	GT	3400,0
9	80	Jean Maurin/Michel Nicol	F	Alfa Romeo	T	3609,0
10	112	Robert Nellemann/Mogens Skarring	DK	Ford	T	3800,0

5. Deutschland-Rallye (Wiesbaden)

(30 May–2 June 1957)
European Rally Championship, Round 4

Pos.	No.	Driver/Codriver	Nat.	Car	Cat.	Result
1	43	Leopold von Zedlitz/Rolf Hahn	D	BMW 502		8,10
2		E. Graf von Westerholdt/W. Scheube	D	Alfa Romeo Giulietta		9,76
3	112	Rudi Golderer/Alfred Kling	D	Mercedes-Benz 180D		21,30
4		Max Riess/Gottlieb Küfner	D	Mercedes-Benz 180D		47,79
5		Richard Weiss/Peter Falk	D	Borgward Isabella TS		52,30
6		"Max"/Dieter Lissmann	D	Porsche Carrera		54,86
7		Horst Boes/Tilo Schadrack	D	Borgward Isabella TS		57,62
8		Sven von Schroeter/S. Eickelmann	D	DKW F91		60,70
9		Fritz Hahnl/Hanshelmut Hespen	D	Borgward Isabella TS		71,35
10		Waldemar Warmbold/Kurt Henninger	D	Borgward Isabella TS		132,77

26ème Rallye International de Genève

(20–23 June 1957)
European Rally Championship, Round 6

Pos.	No.	Driver/Codriver	Nat.	Car	Cat.	Result
1	48	Massimo & Dore Leto di Priolo	I	Alfa Romeo 1900TI	T	0,00
		Stephan Brügger/W.Tiefenthaler	CH	DKW	M	0,00
3	68	F.Meyrat/R.Meyer	CH	DKW	T	0,00
4	22	Carlo Bornand/Michelle Vouga	CH	Alfa Romeo GSV	GT	0,60
5	53	Horst Boes/Ruprecht Hopfen	D	Borgward Isabella	T	9,40
6		E. Graf von Westerholdt/W. Scheube	D	Alfa Romeo Giulietta	T	11,35
7	42	P.Poncet/Simone Poncet	CH	Jaguar 3.4	T	13,75
8		G.Berger/E.Walter	CH	A.C. Ace	GT	15,00
9		Richard Weiss/Peter Falk	D	Borgward Isabella	T	16,60
10		G.Decoppet/André Wicky	CH	Alfa Romeo Giulietta	T	17,70

Liège-Rome-Liège

(28 August–1 September 1957)
European Rally Championship, Round 8

Pos.	No.	Driver/Codriver	Nat.	Car	Cat.	Result
1	4	Claude Storez/Robert Buchet	F	Porsche Carrera Speedster 1500 GS		1'20
2	101	Jo Schlesser/Annie Schlesser	F	Mercedes-Benz 300SL		11'08
3	94	Bernard Consten/Bernard Pichon	F	Triumph TR3		11'55
4	58	Roger de Lageneste/Michel Nicol	F	Peugeot 203		12'09
5	15	Maurice Gatsonides/Dries Jetten	NL	Triumph TR3		14'43
6	35	René Cotton/Jacques Leclère	F	Alfa Romeo		17'55
7	30	Paul Guiraud/Henri Beau	F	Peugeot 203		23'01
8	60	Maurice Michy/Maurice Foulgoc	F	Renault Dauphine		23'03
9	1	Alain de Changy/André Liekens	B	Triumph TR3		26'36
10	81	Paul-Ernst Strähle/Herbert Linge	D	Porsche 356 Carrera		28'05

1958

9° Rallye Automobilistico Internazionale del Sestriere

(24–28 February 1958)
European Rally Championship, Round 2

Pos.	No.	Driver/Codriver	Nat.	Car	Cat.	Result
1	74	Lanzo Cussini/Luigi Argenti	I	Fiat Abarth Zagato	GT	3
2	98	Edgar Berney/Decoppet	CH	Alfa Romeo 1900TI	T	25
3	62	Ettore Marconi/Piero Frescobaldi	I	Alfa Romeo Giulietta	GT	28
4	166	Anton Giorgio Stardero/Bonino	I	Alfa Romeo Giulietta TI	T	28
5	24	Armando Zampiero/M.Bongiasca	I	Porsche 356 Carrera	GT	37
6	164	Ferrero/Sasserno	I	Alfa Romeo Giulietta TI	T	38
7	26	Luigi Villoresi/Basadonna	I	Lancia Aurelia 2500	GT	46
8	118	G.Musso/"Pegaso"	I	Alfa Romeo 1900	T	47
9	144	Hans Bauer/Masetti Zannini	D/I	Alfa Romeo Giulietta TI	T	55
10	84	Sergio Stefani/Ferdinando Tecilla	I	Fiat Abarth Zagato	GT	61

1958–1959

The Royal Automobile Club Seventh International Rally of Great Britain

(11–15 March 1958)
European Rally Championship, Round 3

Pos.	No.	Driver/Codriver	Nat.	Car	Cat.	Result
1	173	Peter Harper/Bill Deane	GB	Sunbeam Rapier	T	652,8
2	34	Ron Gouldbourn/Stuart Turner	GB	Standard Pennant	M	1179,3
3	35	Tommy Gold/Willy Cave	GB	Standard Pennant	M	1231,4
4	201	Pat Moss/Ann Wisdom	GB	Morris Minor 1000	T	1474,5
5	200	W.H.Wadham/P.C.Wadham	GB	Morris Minor 1000	T	1789,4
6	32	Cyril Corbishley/Phil Simister	GB	Standard Pennant	M	1919,5
7	144	Eric Brinkman/Spurgeon	GB	Jaguar 3.4	T	2084,7
8	165	B.A.T.Clark/Douglas Johns	GB	Riley 1.5	T	2180,3
9	181	D.A.Smith/J.Tymon	GB	Fiat 1100	T	2244,2
10	167	K.N.Lee/A.J.Sinclair	GB	Riley 1.5	T	2407,5

10e Internationale Tulpenrallye

(26 April–2 May 1958)
European Rally Championship, Round 5

Pos.	No.	Driver/Codriver	Nat.	Car	Cat.	Result
1	103	Günther Kolwes/Ruth Lautmann	D	Volvo	T	170
2	146	Max Riess/Hans Wencher	D	Alfa Romeo Giulietta TI	T	169
3	43	W.Schorr/Willem Poll	NL	Porsche 356 1600S	GT	156
4	183	Madeleine Blanchoud/Renée Wagner	F	Auto Union 1000	T	151
5	39	Harry Bengtsson/Sune Lindstrom	S	Porsche 356 1600S	GT	150
6	113	J.A.Nielsen/V.B.Dam	DK	Volvo	T	146
7	165	S.van Schroeter/K.von Loesch	D	Auto Union 1000	T	137
8	76	Don Morley/Erle Morley	GB	Jaguar 2.4	T	137
9	102	Hans Ingier/H.Ingier	N	Volvo	T	107
10	54	Ron Gouldbourn/Stuart Turner	GB	Triumph TR3A	GT	106

IX Svenska Rallyt till Midnattssolen

(11–13 June 1958)
European Rally Championship, Round 7

Pos.	No.	Driver/Codriver	Nat.	Car	Cat.	Result
1	127	G. Andersson/N. P. Elleman-Jacobsen	S	Volvo PV444	T	3,2
2	85	Berndt Jansson/Arne Mårs	S	Volkswagen	T	4,3
3	24	Harry Bengtsson/Åke Righard	S	Porsche 1600S	T	7,7
4	32	Rolf Mellde/Bengt Carlqvist	S	Saab 93B	T	7,9
5	63	Valter Karlsson/Henry Karlsson	S	DKW	T	15,7
6	125	Nils Carlsson/Gunnar Carlsson	S	Volvo PV444	T	16,7
7	66	Heimer Adiels/Anders Berg	S	DKW	T	17,7
8	4	Rudolf Jansson/Thure Jansson	S	Alfa Romeo 1900	T	18,1
9	2	John Kvarnström/Hasse Andersson	S	Ford Edsel	T	19,0
10	44	Åke Kildén/Lennart Ström	S	Saab 93B	T	20,0

VIIe Rallye Adriatique

(23–27 July 1958)
European Rally Championship, Round 9

Pos.	No.	Driver/Codriver	Nat.	Car	Cat.	Result
1	4	Gunnar Andersson/Nils Grondal	S	Volvo		7,5
2		Wolfgang Levy/Johanna Kaszynski	D	DKW		11,1
3	26	Alex & Katharina von Falkenhausen	D	BMW Isetta 600		13,1
4		Milivoje Vuković/Ivan Picek	YU	DKW		16,0
5		Max Riess/Hans Wencher	D	Alfa Romeo		29,9
6		Kurt Otto/Hermann Henf	DDR	AWE Wartburg 353		51,9
7		Siegfried Eikelmann/Hermann Kühne	D	DKW		57,6
8		Kurt Rüdiger/Wilhelm Wöllner	DDR	AWE Wartburg 353		63,0
9		Otto Brindl/Philipp Menth	D	DKW		70,9
10		Werner Jäger/Erich Mölla	DDR	AWE Wartburg 353		86,5

8th Viking Rally

(19–21 September 1958)
European Rally Championship, Round 11

Pos.	No.	Driver/Codriver	Nat.	Car	Cat.	Result
1	76	Arne Ingier/Håkon Fløysvik	N	Volvo PV444		34,90
2	83	Arve Andersen/Edward Gjølberg	N	Volvo PV444		52,90
3	58	Harry Bengtsson/Åke Righard	S	Volkswagen		59,10
4	6	Armin Skotvedt/Thor Strandrud	N	Volvo PV444		73,20
5	24	Hans Ingier/Bjørn Gundersen	N	Volvo PV444		75,50
6	56	Lars Chrigstrøm/Görel Barckman	S	Volkswagen		77,90
7	4	Gunnar Fadum/Christopher Wessel	N	DKW		79,25
8	14	Carl Magnus Skogh/Rolf Skogh	S	Saab 93B		81,60
9	89	Rune Bäcklund/Helmer Broberg	S	Volvo PV444		90,40
10	71	Peter Harper/Jimmy Ray	GB	Sunbeam Rapier		91,15

6th Rally Acropolis

(3–8 April 1958)
European Rally Championship, Round 4

Pos.	No.	Driver/Codriver	Nat.	Car	Cat.	Result
1	2	Luigi Villoresi/Ciro Basadona	I	Lancia Aurelia GT	GT	4,003
2	25	Johnny Pesmazoglou/Costas Galanis	GR	Chevrolet	T	9,100
3	40	Gunnar Andersson/Wouter Elbers	S	Volvo PV444	T	10,400
4	1	Nicos Papamichael/S.Mourtzopoulos	GR	Jaguar XK140	GT	14,300
5	65	Heinz Meier/Sven von Schroeter	D	Auto Union 1000	T	15,921
6	19	Alkis Michos/A.Antoniou	GR	Alfa Romeo SV	GT	30,800
7	69	Nicos Filinis/S.Zannos	GR	DKW F93	T	31,021
8	23	Roger de Lageneste/P.Blanchet	F	Peugeot 203 Speciale	GT	37,000
9	56	G.Hartman/Siegfried Eikelmann	D	Auto Union 1000	T	46,521
10	77	H.Blanchoud/R.Berger	F	Saab 93	T	57,203

Deutschland-Rallye

(15–18 May 1958)
European Rally Championship, Round 6

Pos.	No.	Driver/Codriver	Nat.	Car	Cat.	Result
1	37	Bernard Consten/Jean Hebert	F	Alfa Romeo Zagato	GT	0
2	97	Max Riess/Hans Wencher	D	Alfa Romeo Berlina TI	T	0
3	72	Gunnar Andersson/Mike Widell	S	Volvo PV444L	T	0
4	27	Hans-Joachim Walter/P.-E. Strähle	D	Porsche 356 Carrera	GT	0
5	119	Hans Meier/Sven von Schroeter	D	Auto Union 1000	T	0
6	121	Siegfried Eikelmann/Hermann Kühne	D	Auto Union 1000	T	1,00
7	53	Jean-Claude Muller/J.-L. Chary	F	Jaguar 3.4 litre	T	1,46
8	12	Hubert Courtois/Raoul Martin	F	Triumph TR3	GT	2,36
9	133	Hans-Horst Hölder/Hans Klinken	D	Mercedes-Benz 180D	T	2,95
10	15	Keith Ballisat/Peter Roberts	GB	Triumph TR3	GT	3,00

XIXe Critérium International de la Montagne - "Coupe des Alpes"

(7–12 July 1958)
European Rally Championship, Round 8

Pos.	No.	Driver/Codriver	Nat.	Car	Cat.	Result
1	207	Bernard Consten/R. de Lageneste	F	Alfa Romeo Giulietta SZ		0/399
2	205	Guy Clarou/Pierre Gele	F	Alfa Romeo Giulietta Ti		0/509
3	209	Max Riess/Hans Wencher	D	Alfa Romeo Giulietta Ti		0/570
4	403	Keith Ballisat/Alain Bertaut	GB/F	Triumph TR3A		0/984
5	421	Edward Harrison/Richard Habershon	GB	Ford Zephyr		0/1044
6	306	Peter Harper/Peter Jopp	GB	Sunbeam Rapier		0/1093
7	428	Bill Shepherd/John Williamson	GB	Austin-Healey 100/6		0/1901
8	407	Desmond Titterington/B. MacCalden	GB	Triumph TR3		60
9	309	Tommy Sopwith/Bill Deane	GB	Sunbeam Rapier		120
10	423	Pat Moss/Ann Wisdom	GB	Austin-Healey 100/6		300

Liège-Rome-Liège

(28–31 August 1958)
European Rally Championship, Round 10

Pos.	No.	Driver/Codriver	Nat.	Car	Cat.	Result
1	37	Bernard Consten/Jean Hebert	F	Alfa Romeo GSV Zagato		0 pt
2	63	Paul-Ernst Strähle/Robert Buchet	D/F	Porsche 1500		0 pt
3	65	Robert Reip/Velge	B	Porsche 1500		0 pt
4	104	Pat Moss/Ann Wisdom	GB	Austin Healey 100/6		0 pt
5	95	Maurice Gatsonides/Rob Gorris	NL	Triumph TR3A		0 pt
6	98	Robert Leidgens/Claude Dubois	B	Triumph TR3A		0 pt
7	21	Roger Masson/Jean Vinatier	F	DB HBR5		0 pt
8	76	Claude Clemens/Rob Slotemaker	D/NL	Porsche 1500		0 pt
9	78	John Gott/Ray Brookes	GB	MGA		0 pt
10	105	Gerry Burgess/Sam Croft-Pearson	GB	Austin Healey 100/6		0 pt

1959

28ème Rallye Automobile Monte-Carlo

(18–25 January 1959)
European Rally Championship, Round 1

Pos.	No.	Driver/Codriver	Nat.	Car	Cat.	Result
1	176	P. Coltelloni/P. Alexandre/C. Derosiers	F	Citroën ID19	T	308
2	211	André Thomas/Jean Delliere	F	Simca Aronde	T	330
3	158	Pierre Surles/Jacques Pinier	F	DB-Panhard HBR5	GT	478
4	187	Henri Marang/Jacques Badoche	F	Citroën ID19	T	489
5	232	Ronnie Adams/Ernest McMillen	GB	Sunbeam Rapier	T	502
6	263	Gunnar Bengtsson/Carl Lohmander	S	Volvo 122	GT	537
7	132	Siegfried Eikelmann/Hans Wencher	D	DKW 1000	T	573
8	82	George Parkes/Geoffrey Howarth	GB	Jaguar 3.4	T	599
9	111	Philip Walton/Michael Martin	GB	Jaguar 3.4	T	601
10	208	Pat Moss/Ann Wisdom	GB	Austin A40 Farina	T	612

10° Rallye Automobilistico Internazionale del Sestriere

(23–26 February 1959)
European Rally Championship, Round 2

Pos.	No.	Driver/Codriver	Nat.	Car	Cat.	Result
1	402	Gianfranco Castellina/P. Frescobaldi	I	Fiat Abarth Zagato	GT	1,74
2	314	Ada Pace/Miro Toselli	I	Alfa Romeo Giulietta SV Zagato	GT	6,82
3	648	Carlo Abate/A.G.Stardero	I	Alfa Romeo Giulietta TI	T	9,72
4	208	F.Canaparo/A.Marsoglio	I	Fiat 8V	GT	10,12
5	636	Hans Bauer/Ferrero	I	Alfa Romeo Giulietta TI	T	15,82
6	308	A.Bertoglio/A.Soler Roig	I	Alfa Romeo Giulietta SV Zagato	GT	21,82
7	804	A.Capra/C.Pilone	I	Fiat 600	T	22,28
8	204	Giancarlo Sala/Ubaldi	I	Fiat 8V	GT	27,98
9	710	Wolfgang Levy/Hans Wencher	D	DKW	T	28,64
10	802	Luciano Fontana/Angela Fontana	I	Fiat 600	T	33,12

11e Internationale Tulpenrallye

(27 April–2 May 1959)
European Rally Championship, Round 3

Pos.	No.	Driver/Codriver	Nat.	Car	Cat.	Result
1	61	Don Morley/Erle Morley	GB	Jaguar 3.4	1&2	0/166
2	19	Keith Ballisat/E.Marvin	GB	Triumph TR3A	3&4	0/154
3	73	Peter Riley/Richard Bensted-Smith	GB	Ford Zephyr	1&2	0/88
4	41	Rob Gorris/R.Wiedouw	NL	Porsche 356 1600S	3&4	0/60
5	51	Erik Carlsson/Karl-Erik Svensson	S	Saab 93B	3&4	0/43
6	120	Freddy Karrer/Karl Foitek	CH	Alfa Romeo Giulietta TI	1&2	1/168
7	70	Walter Schock/Hans-Horst Hölder	D	Mercedes-Benz 220SE	1&2	1/166
8	5	Jack Sears/Peter Garnier	GB	Austin Healey 100/6	3&4	1/151
9	93	Gunnar Andersson/Valter Karlsson	S	Volvo PV544	1&2	1/149
10	78	Cuth Harrison/John Harrison	GB	Ford Zephyr	1&2	1/92

7th Rally Acropolis

(28–31 May 1959)
European Rally Championship, Round 4

Pos.	No.	Driver/Codriver	Nat.	Car	Cat.	Result
1	68	Wolfgang Levy/Hans Wencher	D	Auto Union 1000	T	171,26
2	14	Hans Walter/Max Nathan	D	Porsche 356 Carrera	GT	360,00
3	72	Nicos Filinis/S.Mourtzopoulos	GR	Auto Union 1000	T	418,96
4	19	Alkis Michos/C.Theodoracopoulos	GR	Alfa Romeo Spider Veloce	GT	452,80
5	67	Siegfried Eikelmann/H.Kuhne	D	Auto Union 1000	T	510,94
6	44	Gunnar Andersson/Valter Karlsson	S	Volvo	T	596,00
7	46	"Lailaps"/"Thor"	GR	Volvo	T	638,67
8	40	Paul Coltelloni/Henri Marang	F	Citroën ID19	T	679,08
9	6	Annie Soisbault/René Wagner	F	Triumph TR3A	GT	965,84
10	85	Kurt Rudiger/W.Wolner	DDR	Wartburg	T	1070,64

X Svenska Rallyt till Midnattssolen

(8–13 June 1959)
European Rally Championship, Round 5

Pos.	No.	Driver/Codriver	Nat.	Car	Cat.	Result
1	26	Erik Carlsson/Mario Pavoni	S	Saab 93B		110
2	35	Car-Magnus Skogh/Rolf Skogh	S	Saab 93B		135
3	17	John Kvarnström/Hans Andersson	S	Ferrari 250GT		145
4	76	Rune Larsson/Bror Hultgren	S	Volkswagen		153
5	127	Gunnar Callbo/Sigurd Höglund	S	Volvo PV544		155
6	112	Gunnar Andersson/Valter Karlsson	S	Volvo PV544		173
7	95	Carl Carlsson/Sigvard Petterson	S	Alfa Romeo Giulietta		188
8	75	Harry Bengtsson/Åke Righard	S	Volkswagen		195
9	2	Ivar Andersson/Lennart Simonsson	S	Mercedes-Benz 220SE		237
10	3	Gunnar Bengtson/Carl Lohmander	S	Mercedes-Benz 220SE		240

20ème Critérium de la Montagne - "Coupe des Alpes"

(23–30 June 1959)
European Rally Championship, Round 6

Pos.	No.	Driver/Codriver	Nat.	Car	Cat.	Result
1	94	Paul Condriller/Georges Robin	F	Renault Dauphine	T	0/3653.4
2	89	Hermann Kühne/Hans Wencher	D	DKW	T	0/3229.0
3	62	Paddy Hopkirk/Jack Scott	GB	Sunbeam Rapier	T	0/2831.0
4	81	Jacques Rey/André Guilhaudin	F	DB Panhard	GT	0/2804.0
5	41	Peter Riley/Alick Pitts	GB	Ford Zephyr	T	0/2667.4
6	64	Peter Jopp/Les Leston	GB	Sunbeam Rapier	T	0/2519.8
7	45	Cuth Harrison/John Harrison	GB	Ford Zephyr	T	0/2417.4
8	44	Edward Harrison/Fleetwood	GB	Ford Zephyr	T	0/2349.0
9	101	Tiny Lewis/Tony Nash	GB	Triumph Herald		0/2317.2
10	48	Maurice Gatsonides/Steunering	NL	Jaguar		28

VIIIe Rallye Adriatique

(22–26 July 1959)
European Rally Championship, Round 7

Pos.	No.	Driver/Codriver	Nat.	Car	Cat.	Result
1	7	Paul Coltelloni/Claude Desrosiers	F	Citroën ID19		0,0
2	79	Erik Carlsson/Karl-Erik Svensson	S	Saab 93B		12,0
3	57	Hans Wencher/Hermann Kühne	D	Auto Union		18,0
4	42	Robert Gentilini/Mme Gentilini	F	Alfa Romeo GTI		24,0
5	46	Milvoje Vukovic/Ivan Picek	YU	Auto Union		29,5
6	45	Wolfgang Levy/Otto Linzenburg	D	Auto Union		38,5
7	12	Günther Schramm/Karl-Heinz Maurer	D	Volvo		47,0
8	77	Arnulf Pilchatsch/Hans Hartinger	A	BMW 600		60,5
9	80	Horst Frischkorn/Günter Pause	D	NSU Prinz		112,5
10	14	Carl Syberg/Steffen Nielsen	DK	Volvo		124,0

IX Jyväskylän Suurajot - Rally of the Thousand Lakes

(14–16 August 1959)
European Rally Championship, Round 8

Pos.	No.	Driver/Codriver	Nat.	Car	Cat.	Result
1	59	Gunnar Callbo/Väinö Nurmimaa	S	Volvo PV544	1	5245,5
2	49	Hans Ingier/Thurbjörn Berntsen	N	Volvo	1	5287,6
3	45	Harry Bengtsson/Åke Righard	S	Volkswagen	1	5297,8
4	4	Erik Carlsson/Mario Pavoni	S	Saab GT	2,3,4&5	5326,0
5	60	Esko Keinänen/Kai Nuortila	SF	Peugeot 403	1	5361,2
6	65	Matti Salminen/Yrjö Salminen	SF	Peugeot 403	1	5361,4
7	22	Carl-Magnus Skogh/Åke Kristiansen	S	Saab 93B	1	5370,9
8	53	Gunnar Carlsson/Rune Stoltz	S	Volvo	1	5377,3
9	41	Pauli Toivonen/Heikki Ketola	SF	Simca Monthléry	1	5407,6
10	15	Arne Wernersson/Åke Gustavsson	S	Saab 93B	1	5415,8

Liège-Rome-Liège

(2–6 September 1959)
European Rally Championship, Round 9

Pos.	No.	Driver/Codriver	Nat.	Car	Cat.	Result
1	27	Robert Buchet/Paul-Ernst Strähle	F	Porsche Carrera		8m30s
2	37	Jacques Feret/Guy Monraisse	F	Renault Dauphine		9m38s
3	22	Willy Mairesse/Maurice Desse	B	Renault Dauphine		10m42s
4	36	Jean Estager/Robert Dutoit	F	Porsche		11m37s
5	24	Guy Sander/Willy Sander	B	Porsche Speedster		19m34s
6	15	Annie Soisbault/Renée Wagner	F	Triumph TR3		31m37s
7	66	Karl-Heinz Schöttler/Raker	D	Porsche		48m57s
8	9	Keith Ballisat/Alain Bertaut	GB	Triumph TR3		54m59s
9	17	Paul Coltelloni/Henri Marang	F	Citroën ID19		55m36s
10	84	Peter Riley/Rupert Jones	GB	Austin Healey		61m16s

9th Viking Rally

(18–21 September 1959)
European Rally Championship, Round 10

Pos.	No.	Driver/Codriver	Nat.	Car	Cat.	Result
1	60	Hans Ingier/Torbjørn Berntsen	N	Volvo PV544	T	70,50
2	49	Erik Carlsson/Mario Pavoni	S	Saab	T	73,90
3	39	Nils Fredrik Grøndah/lKnut Solberg	N	Volvo	T	92,00
4	52	Aatos Wassman/Köll Lycksell	SF	Škoda Octavia	T	95,15
5	47	Olle Bromark/Köll Lycksell	S	Saab 93B	T	97,15
6	53	Nils Olof Eklundh/A Ruuskanen	SF	Škoda 445	T	100,05
7	45	Edward Gjølberg/Jan Erik Martinsen	N	Škoda 445	T	101,25
8	36	Carsten A Johansson/H. Mikkelsen	N	Volkswagen	T	101,75
9	46	Arve Andersen/Walther Schjølberg	N	Volvo PV 544	T	102,80
10	#30	Gunnar Callbo/Sigurd Høglund	S	Volvo PV	T	103,30

1959–1961

Deutschland-Rallye

(1–3 October 1959)
European Rally Championship, Round 11

Pos.	No.	Driver/Codriver	Nat.	Car	Cat.	Result
1		Erik Carlsson/Karl-Erik Svensson	S	Saab 93B	T	0,00
2		Pat Moss/Ann Wisdom	GB	Austin Healey 3000	GT	0,00
3		Wolfgang Levy/Otto Linzenburg	D	Auto Union 1000	T	0,10
4		William Dodd/Donald Delling	USA	Volvo PV444	T	5,04
5		Heinz Umbach/Karl Foitek	D	Alfa Romeo TI	T	6,63
6		Roland Ott/Wolfgang Schmitz	D	Mercedes-Benz 190	T	10,26
7		Paul Coltelloni/Georges Houel	F	Citroën ID19	T	16,22
8		Egon Vomfell/Hans Wencher	D	Auto Union 1000	T	27,54
9		Peter Ruby/Franz Schüler	D	DKW F91	T	27,68
10		"Hans Falk"/Rudolf Knoll	D	Auto Union 1000		

Note: Ott may be 16.26 and thus behind Coltelloni

Rallye ACP Aveiro Estoril

(3–6 December 1959)
European Rally Championship, Round 13

Pos.	No.	Driver/Codriver	Nat.	Car	Cat.	Result
1		José Luis Abreu Valente/	P	Mercedes-Benz 300 SL		24,103
2	4	Alex Soler Roig/	E	Porsche 356		24,790
3		Henri Oreiller/Paul Coltelloni	F	Alfa Romeo Giulietta TI		24,881
4		Manuel Palma/Augusto Palma	P	Porsche 356		24,947
5		Pinca'/	P	Porsche 356		25,017
6	59	Erik Carlsson/John Sprinzell	S	Saab 93B		25,418
7		Manuel de Castro/	P			25,545
8		Manuel Fernandes/	P			25,588
9		Wolfgang Levy/	D	Auto-Union 1000		25,731
10		Carlos Faustino/	P	Volvo		25,990

29ème Rallye Automobile Monte-Carlo

(18–24 January 1960)
European Rally Championship, Round 1

Pos.	No.	Driver/Codriver	Nat.	Car	Cat.	Result
1	128	Walter Schock/Rolf Moll	D	Mercedes-Benz 220SE	T	110
2	121	Eugen Böhringer/Hermann Socher	D	Mercedes-Benz 220SE	T	298
3	135	Roland Ott/Eberhard Mahle	D	Mercedes-Benz 220SE	T	650
4	325	Peter Harper/Raymond Baxter	GB	Sunbeam Rapier	T	749
5	126	Hans Tak/Johan Swaab	NL	Mercedes-Benz 220SE	T	754
6	202	Mike Sutcliffe/George Crabtree	GB	Ford Zephyr	T	815
7	165	Werner Lier/Heinrich "Heini" Walter	CH	Sunbeam Rapier	T	844
8	269	Raymond Quilico/Raphaël Michot	F	DKW 1000	T	863
9	286	Carl-Otto Bremer/Esko Vainola	FIN	Saab 93	T	880
10	310	Henri Marang/Jacques Badoche	F	Citroën DS19	T	928

12e Internationale Tulpenrallye

(2–7 May 1960)
European Rally Championship, Round 3

Pos.	No.	Driver/Codriver	Nat.	Car	Cat.	Result
1	112	Guy Verrier/René Trautmann	F	Citroën ID19	T	0/90
2	174	Carl Orrenius/Rolf Dahlgren	S	Saab 96	T	0/90
3	82	Walter Schock/Rolf Moll	D	Mercedes-Benz 220SE	T	0/90
4	119	Hans Ingier/Nils Hagen	N	Volvo PV544	T	0/90
5	42	A.Bouwmeester/W.L.Poll	NL	Porsche 1600 S90	GT	0/75
6	162	Erik Carisson/Valter Karlsson	S	Saab 96	M	0/69
7	41	Harry Bengtsson/Sune Lindström	S	Porsche 1600 S90	GT	0/66
8	10	Pat Moss/Ann Wisdom	GB	Austin Healey 3000	GT	0/61
9	68	Gunnar Andersson/B.Martensson	S	Volvo PV544	M	1/90
10	1	Eric Haddon/Charles Vivian	GB	Jaguar XK150S	GT	1/90

Internationale Österreichische Alpenfahrt

(26–29 May 1960)
European Rally Championship, Round 5

Pos.	No.	Driver/Codriver	Nat.	Car	Cat.	Result
1	24	Ferdinand Mitterbauer/	A	NSU Prinz 600	1&2	1260
2	25	Franz Prach/	A	Steyr-Puch 500	1&2	1260
3	72	Alex Mayer/	A	Alfa Romeo	1&2	1260
4	96	Eberhard Mahle/Roland Ott	D	Mercedes-Benz 220SE	1&2	1260
5	32	Alex & Katharina von Falkenhausen	D	BMW 700	1&2	1256
6	54	O.Luschan/H.Enzinger	A	Auto Union	1&2	1248
7	43	Gert Greil/	A	DKW		1244
8	103	Arnulf Pilhatsch/Hans Hartinger	A	BMW 700	3	1242
9	36	Konrad Eckschlager/	A	DKW	1&2	1228
10	60	J.Strobl/	A	Škoda	1&2	1208

The Royal Automobile Club Eighth International Rally of Great Britain

(16–21 November 1959)
European Rally Championship, Round 12

Pos.	No.	Driver/Codriver	Nat.	Car	Cat.	Result
1	66	Gerry Burgess/Sam Croft-Pearson	GB	Ford Zephyr	1&2	33
2	51	Tommy Gold/Mike Hughes	GB	Austin Healey Sprite	3&4	42
3	103	Mike Sutcliffe/Derek Astle	GB	Riley 1.5	1&2	43
4	9	Don Morley/Erle Morley	GB	Austin Healey	3&4	44
5	98	Codger Malkin/Graham Robson	GB	Sunbeam Rapier	1&2	46
6	16	Peter Morgan/D. E. J. Thompson	GB	Morgan Plus 4	3&4	48
7	87	John Spare/J.F.Barley	GB	Singer Gazelle	1&2	49
8	139	Wolfgang Levy/Stuart Turner	D	Auto-Union DKW	1&2	50/3
9	93	Peter Jopp/Les Leston	GB	Sunbeam Rapier	1&2	50/26
10	14	E.Hodson/Allan Collinson	GB	Triumph TR3A	3&4	52

1960

29ème Rallye Internationale de Genève

(6–10 April 1960)
European Rally Championship, Round 2

Pos.	No.	Driver/Codriver	Nat.	Car	Cat.	Result
1	74	Roger de Lageneste/Henri Greder	F	Alfa Romeo Giulia SZ	M	0
2	63	René Trautmann/Jean-Claude Ogier	F	Citroën ID19	T	0
3	92	Jean-Pierre Schild/Jean Briffaud	CH	Alfa Romeo Giulietta TI	GT	0
4	69	Eberhard Mahle/Roland Ott	D	Mercedes-Benz	T	60
5	67	Walter Schock/Rolf Moll	D	Mercedes-Benz	T	60
6	94	Jacques Rey/André Guilhaudin	F	Alfa Romeo	GT	60
7	54	Siegfried Eikelmann/Hermann Kühne	D	DKW	M	120
8	112	Pat Moss/Ann Wisdom	GB	Austin Healey 3000	GT	120
9	68	Hans Tak/Rob Gorris	NL	Mercedes-Benz 220SE	T	120
10	78	Gunnar Andersson/"Jag"	S	Volvo	M	180

8th Rally Acropolis

(19–22 May 1960)
European Rally Championship, Round 4

Pos.	No.	Driver/Codriver	Nat.	Car	Cat.	Result
1	34	Walter Schock/Rolf Moll	D	Mercedes-Benz 220SE	T	0,000
2	115	Erik Carlsson/Walter Carlsson	S	Saab 95 (estate)	T	2,200
3	92	Wolfgang Levy/Walter	D	Auto Union 1000S	T	2,850
4	43	Peter Harper/Peter Procter	GB	Sunbeam Rapier	T	28,040
5	47	Nicos Filinis/S.Mourtzopoulos	GR	Sunbeam Rapier	T	44,997
6	51	Gunnar Andersson/"Jag"	S	Volvo PV544	T	83,167
7	38	Leopold von Zedlitz/	D	Mercedes-Benz 220SE	T	182,713
8	7	Helmut Busch/Zimmerman	D	Porsche 356 Super 90	GT	272,370
9	116	H.Blanchoud/R.Berger	F	Saab 93	T	274,067
10	28	Graf von Westerholt/Kühling	D	Jaguar 3.4	T	318,867

XI Svenska Rallyt till Midnattssolen

(13–18 June 1960)
European Rally Championship, Round 6

Pos.	No.	Driver/Codriver	Nat.	Car	Cat.	Result
1	81	Carl-Magnus Skogh/Rolf Skogh	S	Saab 96	1	129
2	76	Harry Bengtsson/Erik Pettersson	S	Porsche Super 90	3	156
3	52	Gunnar Andersson/Carl Lohmander	S	Volvo PV544	2	194
4	173	Rolf Carlsson/Lennart Asplund	S	Volvo PV544	1	201
5	158	Hans Ingier/Torbjørn Berntsen	N	Volvo PV544	1	232
6	127	Bengt Söderström/Bo Olsson	S	Volkswagen	1	238
7	12	Erik Berger/Billy Skoglöf	S	Fiat 2100	1	255
8	67	Berndt Jansson/Arne Mårs	S	Volkswagen	1	262
9	126	Rune Larsson/Bror Hultgren	S	Volkswagen	1	296
10	120	Henry Karlsson/Hans Lundin	S	Auto Union 1000S	1	299

21ème Critérium International de la Montagne - "Coupe des Alpes"

(27–30 June 1960)
European Rally Championship, Round 7

Pos.	No.	Driver/Codriver	Nat.	Car	Cat.	Result
1	30	Roger de Lageneste/Henri Greder	F	Alfa Romeo Giulietta SZ	GT	6748,67
2	76	Pat Moss/Ann Wisdom	GB	Austin-Healey 3000	GT	6820,95
3	63	José Behra/René Richard	F	Jaguar 3.8	T	7071,69
4	66	Eugen Böhringer/Hermann Socher	D	Mercedes-Benz 220	T	7135,02
5	65	Bobby Parkes/Geoff Howarth	GB	Jaguar 3.8	T	7158,56
6	55	René Trautman/Jean-Claude Ogier	F	Citroën ID19	T	7456,46
7	26	Henri Oreiller/Fernand Masoero	F	Alfa Romeo Giulietta SZ	GT	6678,59
8	74	John Gott/Bill Shepherd	GB	Austin-Healey 3000	GT	7085,96
9	35	Peter Harper/Peter Proctor	GB	Sunbeam Rapier	T	7476,59
10	33	Paddy Hopkirk/Jack Scott	GB	Sunbeam Rapier	T	7562,51

Liège-Rome-Liège

(31 August–4 September 1960)
European Rally Championship, Round 9

Pos.	No.	Driver/Codriver	Nat.	Car	Cat.	Result
1	76	Pat Moss/Ann Wisdom	GB	Austin Healey 3000		1h03m04s
2	36	Guy Sander/Willy Sander	B	Porsche 356 Carrera GT		1h09m11s
3	69	John Sprinzel/John Patten	GB	Austin Healey Sprite		1h10m56s
4	31	Christian Poirot/Dr.Guillemin	F	Porsche Carrera 1600 GS		1h14m49s
5	66	David Seigle-Morris/Vic Elford	GB	Austin Healey 3000		1h21m00s
6	12	Jean Demortier/Lagae	B	Auto Union		1h30m09s
7	40	Guy Verrier/Jacques Badoche	F	Citroën ID19		1h40m10s
8	43	Claudine Vanson/Renée Wagner	F	Citroën ID19		1h46m19s
9	47	Bichat/Marbaque	F	Volvo		2h11m22s
10	42	John Gott/Rev.Rupert Jones	GB	Austin Healey 3000		2h17m12s

10th Viking Rally

(16–18 September 1960)
European Rally Championship, Round 11

Pos.	No.	Driver/Codriver	Nat.	Car	Cat.	Result
1	23	Carl-Magnus Skogh/Rolf Skogh	S	Saab 96		46,3
2	27	Arne Wernersson/Tor Nilsson	S	Saab 96		58,8
3	34	Gunnar Andersson/Carl Borch	S	Volvo PV544		64,1
4	18	Arne Ingier/Ole Killingmo	N	Volvo PV544		66,8
5	31	John Unnerud/Jan Martinsen	N	Volvo PV544		67,2
6	5	Harry Bengtsson/Erik Pettersson	S	Volkswagen		71,2
7	32	Jens-Jarl Jernes/Johan Solem	N	Volvo PV544		77,1
8	38	Bo Ljungfeldt/Gunnar Häggbom	S	Ford Anglia		78,3
9	36	Lars Carlström/Carl Schlegel	S	Volvo PV544		79,2
10	14	Rune Larsson/Bror Hultgren	S	Volkswagen		81,1

The Royal Automobile Club Ninth International Rally of Great Britain

(21–26 November 1960)
European Rally Championship, Round 13

Pos.	No.	Driver/Codriver	Nat.	Car	Cat.	Result
1	178	Erik Carlsson/Stuart Turner	S	Saab	T	0/12
2	46	John Sprinzel/Richard Bensted-Smith	GB	Austin-Healey Sprite	GT	2/23
3	1	Don Morley/Erle Morley	GB	Austin-Healey 3000	GT	2/25
4	72	Peter Berry/Jack Sears/Willy Cave	GB	Jaguar 3.8	T	3/8
5	120	Johnny Wallwork/Harold Brooks	GB	Volvo PV544	T	3/8
6	183	David Seigle-Morris/Vic Elford	GB	Morris Mini Minor 850	T	3/14
7	156	Tiny Lewis/G.S.Shepherd	GB	Triumph Herald	T	3/32
8	170	Mike Sutcliffe/Derek Astle	GB	Morris Mini Minor 850	T	4/30
9	144	Phil Crabtree/Saville Woolley	GB	Ford Anglia	T	4/35
10	157	Anne Hall/Valerie Domleo	GB	Ford Anglia	T	5/29

30ème Rallye Automobile Monte-Carlo

(21–28 January 1961)
European Rally Championship, Round 1

Pos.	No.	Driver/Codriver	Nat.	Car	Cat.	Result
1	174	Maurice Martin/Roger Bateau	F	Panhard PL17	T	2701,566
2	87	Walter Loffler/Hans-Joachim Walter	D	Panhard PL17	T	2720,096
3	220	Guy Jouanneaux/Alain Coquillet	F	Panhard PL17	T	2753,907
4	53	Erik Carlsson/Karl Svensson	S	Saab 95 Break	T	2771,330
5	97	Klaus Block/Herbert Paul	D	BMW 700	T	2776,644
6	73	Esko Keinanen/Rainer Eklund	SF	Škoda Octavia	T	2790,234
7	33	Gérard Happel/Jean Guichet	F	Renault Ondine	T	2794,672
8	180	José Behra/Jean Berges	F	NSU Prinz Sport	T	2801,100
9	189	Jacques Feret/Guy Monraisse	F	Renault Ondine	T	2822,568
10	66	Paul Metternich/Hans Wencher	D	BMW 700	T	2833,254

X Jyväskylän Suurajot - Rally of the Thousand Lakes

(19–21 August 1960)
European Rally Championship, Round 8

Pos.	No.	Driver/Codriver	Nat.	Car	Cat.	Result
1	36	Carl-Otto Bremer/Juhani Lampi	SF	Saab 96	1&2	6731,4
2	39	Erik Carlsson/Lennart Simonsson	S	Saab 96	1&2	6748,7
3	26	Carl-Magnus Skogh/Rolf Skogh	S	Saab 96	1&2	6774,2
4	69	Gunnar Andersson/Bo Hellberg	S	Volvo PV544	1&2	6914,6
5	45	Harry Bengtsson/Åke Righard	S	Volkswagen	1&2	6977,2
6	32	Åke Thambert/Gunnar Häggbom	S	Ford Anglia	1&2	6977,2
7	86	Rauno Aaltonen/Pentti Siutla	SF	Mercedes-Benz	1&2	6991,5
8	48	Rune Larsson/Rolf Borg	S	Volkswagen	1&2	7005,9
9	76	René Trautmann/Jean-Claude Ogier	F	Citroen ID19	1&2	7011,7
10	19	Jorma Oksanen/Pentti Suhonen	SF	Saab 96	1&2	7050,9

XX Rajd Polski

(9–12 September 1960)
European Rally Championship, Round 10

Pos.	No.	Driver/Codriver	Nat.	Car	Cat.	Result
1	27	Walter Schock/Rolf Moll	D	Mercedes-Benz 220SE	T	155,65
2	85	Carl-Otto Bremer/Juhani Lampi	FIN	Saab 96	T	185,40
3	77	Kurt Otto/Herman Hanf	D	AWE Wartburg	T	223,25
4	72	Günther Rüttinger/Paul Thiel	D	AWE Wartburg	T	236,20
5	40	René Trautmann/Jean-Claude Ogier	F	Citroën ID19	T	241,50
6	56	Zdenek Mraz/Vojtěch Rieger	CS	Škoda Octavia	T	242,95
7	75	Kurt Rüdiger/Willy Wöllner	D	AWE Wartburg	T	250,00
8	11	Jaroslav Pavelka/Ivan Micik	CS	Tatra 603	T	263,00
9	8	Alios Mark/Lubomir Rek	CS	Tatra 603	T	264,15
10	65	Sobiesław Zasada/Ewa Zasada	PL	Simca	T	271,20

Internationale Deutschland-Rallye

(28 September–2 October 1960)
European Rally Championship, Round 12

Pos.	No.	Driver/Codriver	Nat.	Car	Cat.	Result
1	49	Gunnar Anderson/Walter Karlsson	S	Volvo PV544	T	0,0
2	32	René Trautmann/Jean-Claude Ogier	F	Citroën ID19	T	0,4
3	38	Rolf Kreder/Rolf Knoll	D	Mercedes-Benz 190B	T	6,8
4	22	Walter Schock/Rolf Moll	D	Mercedes-Benz 220SE	T	9,4
5	67	Alfred Kling/Peter Falk	D	Auto Union 1000	T	11,0
6	64	Egon Evertz/Manfred Kierdof	D	Auto Union 1000	T	15,0
7	82	Klaus Block/Herbert Paul	D	BMW 700	T	20,2
8	2	David Seigle-Morris/Stuart Turner	GB	Austin Healey 3000	GT	22,4
9	50	Ewy Rosqvist/Anita Rosqvist-Borg	S	Volvo PV544	T	23,7
10	37	Helmut Malsch/Gerhard Pfefferle	D	Mercedes-Benz 190B	T	24,0

1961

13e Internationale Tulpenrallye

(2–6 May 1961)
European Rally Championship, Round 2

Pos.	No.	Driver/Codriver	Nat.	Car	Cat.	Result
1	121	Geoff Mabbs/Leslie Griffiths	GB	Triumph Herald		94,35%
2	36	Hans Walter/Ernst Stock	D	Porsche 356 Carrera		95,37%
3	153	Carl-Magnus Skogh/Rolf Skogh	S	Saab 96		95,75%
4	53	Eugen Böhringer/Hermann Socher	D	Mercedes 220SEb		96,78%
5	113	Karl Schottler/Jürgen Sackel	D	Alfa Romeo Giulietta TI		97,03%
6	110	Odd Thrana/Leif Samsing	N	Auto Union 1000		97,96%
7	128	J.P.M.Roestenburg/M. MacKenzie	NL/GB	Auto Union 1000S		98,16%
8	97	Tom Gold/Mike Hughes	GB	Austin Healey Sprite		98,35%
9	82	Jacques Rey/Georges Burggraf	F	Alfa Romeo Giulietta TI		98,70%
10	30	H.-L. Steunebrink/K. Barendregt	NL	Jaguar 3.8		98,76%

1961–1962

9th Rally Acropolis

(18–21 May 1961)
European Rally Championship, Round 3

Pos.	No.	Driver/Codriver	Nat.	Car	Cat.	Result
1	113	Erik Carlsson/Walter Karlsson	S	Saab 96	T	468,859
2	73	Gunnar Andersson/Carl Lohmander	S	Volvo PV544	T	718,246
3	3	Peter Riley/Tony Ambrose	GB	Austin Healey 3000	GT	817,964
4	38	Eugen Böhringer/Hermann Socher	D	Mercedes-Benz 220 SEb	T	896,164
5	57	Peter Harper/Peter Procter	GB	Sunbeam Rapier	T	960,100
6	67	Keith Ballisat/Peter Jopp	GB	Sunbeam Rapier	T	1214,708
7	61	Ewy Rosqvist/Monika Walraf	S	Volvo PV544	T	1268,708
8	128	Klaus Block/Herbert Paul	D	BMW 700	T	1521,027
9	65	Jimmy Ray/Ian Hall	GB	Sunbeam Rapier	T	1558,423
10	7	Tiny Lewis/Tony Nash	GB	Triumph TR3A	GT	1722,874

Mille Miglia

(27–28 May 1961)
European Rally Championship, Round 4

Pos.	No.	Driver/Codriver	Nat.	Car	Cat.	Result
1	3	Gunnar Andersson/Carl Lohmander	S	Ferrari 250GT	GT	3h32m53.8s
2	7	Giulio Cabianca/Piergiorgio Provolo	I	Lancia Flaminia Zagato	GT	3h39m06.0s
3	1	Alberico Cacciari/Giancarlo Sala	I	Ferrari 250GT	GT	3h40m06.6s
4	27	Albino Buticchi/Nicola Camilli	I	Alfa Romeo Giulietta SZ	GT	3h48m07.0s
5	8	Hans-Joachim Walter/P.-Ernst Strähle	D	Porsche Abarth	GT	3h49m07.4s
6	22	Gianfranco Bonetto/Carlo Pelizzaro	I	Alfa Romeo Giulietta SV	GT	3h50m02.0s
7	28	Rinaldo Parmigiani/Luciano Razzuoli	I	Alfa Romeo Giulietta SZ	GT	3h52m14.4s
8	32	Armando Zampieri/Aldo Corona	I	Alfa Romeo Giulietta SV	GT	3h53m01.4s
9	47	Piero Frescobaldi/Bruno Samà	I	Lancia Appia Sport	GT	3h55m12.6s
10	21	Hans Bauer/Federico Zanotti	I	Alfa Romeo Giulietta SZ	GT	3h55m24.0s

XII Svenska Rallyt till Midnattssolen

(13–17 June 1961)
European Rally Championship, Round 5

Pos.	No.	Driver/Codriver	Nat.	Car	Cat.	Result
1	114	Carl-Magnus Skogh/Rolf Skogh	S	Saab 96	T	397
2	66	Bertil Söderström/Rune Olsson	S	Volkswagen	M	476
3	45	Arne Wernersson/Sven Jönsson	S	Saab 96	M	495
4	115	Erik Berger/Lars Andersson	S	Saab 96	T	512
5	158	Berndt Jansson/Erik Petterson	S	Volkswagen	T	516
6	6	René Trautmann/Jean-Claude Ogier	F	Citroën DS19	T	517
7	104	Harry Bengtsson/H.-Joachim Walter	S	Porsche 356 Super 90	GT	522
8	113	Olle Bromark/Kjell Lyxell	S	Saab 96	T	526
9	79	Gunnar Andersson/Hans Lundin	S	Volvo PV544	M	539
10	195	Evert Christoffersson/K.-E. Andersson	S	Volvo PV544	T	542

22ème Coupe des Alpes

(24–28 June 1961)
European Rally Championship, Round 6

Pos.	No.	Driver/Codriver	Nat.	Car	Cat.	Result
1	146	Donald Morley/Erle Morley	GB	Austin-Healey 3000	3	0
2	120	Jean Rolland/Gabriel Augias	F	Alfa Romeo Giulietta Zagato	3	60
3	33	Paddy Hopkirk/Jack Scott	GB	Sunbeam Rapier	1	120
4	107	Henri Greder/Jean Charon	F	Renault	2	189,9
5	37	Peter Harper/Peter Procter	GB	Sunbeam Rapier	1	240
6	44	René Trautmann/Jean-Claude Ogier	F	Citroën	2	240
7	41	Keith Ballisat/Tiny Lewis	GB	Sunbeam Rapier	1	420
8	137	Christian Poirot/Hughes Hazard	F	Porsche	3	540
9	51	Luçien Bianchi/Georges Harris	B	Citroën	1	540
10	134	Roger Campuzan/Martial Delalande	F	Porsche	3	624,1

XXI Rajd Polski

(3–6 August 1961)
European Rally Championship, Round 7

Pos.	No.	Driver/Codriver	Nat.	Car	Cat.	Result
1	63	Eugen Böhringer/Rauno Aaltonen	D/SF	Mercedes-Benz 220SE	T	834,6
2	25	Carl-Magnus Skogh/Karl Svensson	S	Saab 96	T	840,6
3	15	Sobiesław Zasada/Ms Ewa Zasada	PL	BMW 700	T	854,2
4	51	Gunnar Andersson/Walter Karlsson	S	Volvo PV544	T	862,4
5	33	Kurt Otto/Herman Hanf	DDR	Wartburg 311	T	920,8
6	6	Mieczysław Sochacki/C. Kozłowski	PL	NSU Prinz Sport	T	972,2
7	74	Wilhelm Heckel/Joachim Münchow	D	Porsche Super 90	GT	928,9
8	71	Günther Rüttinger/Paul Thiel	DDR	Wartburg 311	T	940,6
9		Kurt Rüdiger/Wilhelm Wöllner	DDR	Wartburg	T	951,3
10	43	Grzegorz Timoszek/K. Komornicki	PL	Simca Aronde	T	955,5

XI Jyväskylän Suurajot - Rally of the Thousand Lakes

(18–20 August 1961)
European Rally Championship, Round 8

Pos.	No.	Driver/Codriver	Nat.	Car	Cat.	Result
1	93	Rauno Aaltonen/Väinö Nurminaa	SF	Mercedes-Benz	T	1624,1
2	86	Pauli Toivonen/Jaako Kallio	SF	Citroën	T	1951,1
3	57	Esko Keinänen/Rainer Eklund	SF	Škoda TS	T	1983,6
4	25	Carl-Magnus Skogh/Fergus Sager	S	Saab 96	T	1984,7
5	75	Gunnar Andersson/Bo Hellberg	S	Volvo	T	2030,7
6	21	Carl-Otto Bremer/Juhani Lampi	SF	Saab 96	T	2041,4
7	36	Bengt Söderström/Bo Olsson	S	Saab 96	T	2062,2
8	55	Harry Bengtsson/H.-Joachim Walter	S	Volkswagen	T	2075,9
9	61	Alrik Stenström/Börje Nilsson	S	Volkswagen	T	2173,6
10	39	Sven-Erik Holm/"Ingen Vidare"	S	Austin Mini 850	T	2221,8

Liège-Sofia-Liège

(30 August–3 September 1961)
European Rally Championship, Round 9

Pos.	No.	Driver/Codriver	Nat.	Car	Cat.	Result
1	31	Lucien Bianchi/Georges Harris	B	Citroën		0h40m58s
2	46	Hans-Joachim Walter/Hans Wencher	D	Porsche Carrera		1h31m21s
3	48	Bob Neyret/Jacques Terramorsi	F	Citroën ID19		1h34m16s
4	40	Eugen Böhringer/Rauno Aaltonen	D	Mercedes-Benz		1h53m48s
5	57	Roger de Lageneste/Burglin	F	Citroën DS19		2h06m41s
6	64	David Seigle-Morris/Tony Ambrose	GB	Austin Healey 3000		2h44m20s
7	27	Francis Charlier/Jowat	B	Ford Anglia		3h10m32s
8	4	David Lead/Jim Cardwell	GB	Mercedes-Benz		3h19m19s

No other finishers

Internationale Rallye Baden-Baden - "Deutschland-Rallye"

(27 September–1 October 1961)
European Rally Championship, Round 10

Pos.	No.	Driver/Codriver	Nat.	Car	Cat.	Result
1		Hans-Joachim Walter/Hans Wencher	D	Porsche Carrera	GT	44,5
2	20	Eugen Böhringer/Rauno Aaltonen	D/SF	Mercedes-Benz 220SE	GT	117,5
3		Gunnar Andersson/Walter Karlsson	S	Volvo PV544	T	165,5
4		Hans Klinken/Hermann Socher	D	Volkswagen Spezial	GT	193,5
5		Gerhart Greil/Georg Kaufmann	D	DKW Junior	T	205,5
6		Peter Ruby/Max Moritz	D	DKW Junior	T	207,0
7		Ernst Pflugbeil/Karlheinz Panowitz	D	Porsche Carrera	GT	210,0
8	30	René Trautmann/Claudine Vanson	F	Citroën ID19	T	228,5
9		Lois John/Lothar Kohler	D	Porsche 1500 GS	GT	249,5
10		Ewald Pauli/Heinz Würfl	D	Auto Union 1000	T	252,0

The Royal Automobile Club Tenth International Rally of Great Britain

(13–18 November 1961)
European Rally Championship, Round 11

Pos.	No.	Driver/Codriver	Nat.	Car	Cat.	Result
1	1	Erik Carlsson/John Brown	S/GB	Saab 96		89
2	4	Pat Moss/Ann Wisdom	GB	Austin Healey 3000		129
3	10	Peter Harper/Ian Hall	GB	Sunbeam Rapier		150
4	9	Paddy Hopkirk/Jack Scott	GB	Sunbeam Rapier		166
5	5	David Seigle-Morris/Tony Ambrose	GB	Austin Healey 3000		170
6	7	Gunnar Anderson/Douglas Johns	S/GB	Volvo PV544		184
7	30	Jimmy Ray/John Hopwood	GB	Austin Mini		204
8	20	Anne Hall/Valerie Dolmeo	GB	Ford Anglia		204
9	17	Henry Taylor/Phil Crabtree	GB	Ford Anglia		209
10	31	Derek Astle/Peter Roberts	GB	MG Midget		217

1962

31ème Rallye Automobile Monte-Carlo

(20–27 January 1962)
European Rally Championship, Round 1

Pos.	No.	Driver/Codriver	Nat.	Car	Cat.	Result
1	303	Erik Carlsson/Gunnar Häggbom	S	Saab 96	T	2880,480
2	257	Eugen Böhringer/Peter Lang	D	Mercedes-Benz 220SEb	T	2907,035
3	155	Paddy Hopkirk/Jack Scott	GB	Sunbeam Rapier	T	2952,339
4	170	Peter Procter/Graham Robson	GB	Sunbeam Rapier	T	2997,489
5	313	Pierre Gelé/Andre Guilhaudin	F	Auto Union Junior	T	3019,587
6	281	Gunnar Andersson/Walter Karlsson	S	Volvo PV544	T	3019,970
7	149	Robert Neyret/Jacques Terramorsi	F	Citroën DS19	T	3031,074
8	11	Hermann Kühne/Hans Wencher	D	Mercedes-Benz 220SEb	T	3047,003
9	229	Pierre Frescobaldi/Marcello de Luca	I	Lancia Flavia	T	3057,253
10	130	Graham Hill/Peter Jopp	GB	Sunbeam Rapier	T	3058,255

10th Rally Acropolis

(24–27 May 1962)
European Rally Championship, Round 3

Pos.	No.	Driver/Codriver	Nat.	Car	Cat.	Result
1	31	Eugen Böhringer/Peter Lang	D	Mercedes-Benz 220SEb	T	68,000
2	97	Erik Carlsson/Karl-Eric Svensson	S	Saab 96	T	78,000
3	47	René Trautmann/Lucien Hervé	F	Citroën DS19	T	142,118
4	12	Hans-Joachim Walter/Kurt Schöttler	D	Porsche 356B	GT	329,000
5	28	Georges Harris/Pascal Ickx	B	Mercedes-Benz 220SEb	T	365,454
6	41	Gunnar Andersson/Walter Karlsson	S	Volvo PV544	T	370,117
7	33	Bob Neyret/Jacques Terramorsi	F	Citroën DS19	T	376,389
8	9	Pat Moss/Pauline Mayman	GB	Austin-Healey 3000	GT	383,678
9	83	Anne Hall/Valerie Domleo	GB	Ford Anglia	T	472,402
10	17	Henry Taylor/Brian Melia	GB	Ford Anglia	GT	496,291

XIII Svenska Rallyt till Midnattssolen

(12–16 June 1962)
European Rally Championship, Round 5

Pos.	No.	Driver/Codriver	Nat.	Car	Cat.	Result
1	138	Bengt Söderström/Bo Olsson	S	Mini Cooper	T	556
2	84	Harry Bengtsson/Rolf Dahlgren	S	Porsche Super 90	GT	571
3	44	Erik Carlsson/Gunnar Häggbom	S	Saab 96	M	615
4	81	Berndt Jansson/Eric Petterson	S	Volkswagen	GT	620
5	25	Eugen Böhringer/Peter Lang	D	Mercedes-Benz 220 SEb	T	658
6	170	Bertil Söderström/Rune Olsson	S	Volkswagen	T	667
7	3	Gunnar Andersson/Valter Karlsson	S	Volvo PV544	T	670
8	203	Evert Christofferson/K.-E. Andersson	S	Volvo PV544	T	702
9	189	Sven-Eric Holm/Tore Kyrk	S	Volkswagen	T	703
10	210	Bertram Englund/Bernt Jansson	S	Volvo PV544	T	725

XII Jyväskylän Suurajot - Rally of the Thousand Lakes

(17–19 August 1962)
European Rally Championship, Round 7

Pos.	No.	Driver/Codriver	Nat.	Car	Cat.	Result
1	37	Pauli Toivonen/Jaakko Kallio	SF	Citroën DS19	T	1618,6
2	39	Esko Keinänen/Rainer Eklund	SF	Škoda	T	1713,6
3	41	Erik Carlsson/Gunnar Häggbom	S	Saab 96	T	1742,0
4	22	Simo Lampinen/Jyrki Ahava	SF	Saab 96	T	1876,8
5	38	Bertil Söderström/Rune Olsson	S	Volkswagen	T	1890,3
6	34	Bengt Söderström/Bo Olsson	S	Mini Cooper	T	2086,5
7	36	Rune Larsson/Börje Nilsson	S	Volkswagen	T	2092,2
8	21	Nils-Olof Eklundh/Mauri Laakso	SF	Škoda	T	2194,8
9	40	John Unnerud/Einar Mortensen	N	Citroën ID19	T	2202,8
10	30	Harry Bengtson/Rolf Dahlgren	S	Porsche	GT	2210,3

Rallye Baden-Baden - "Deutschland-Rallye"

(26–30 September 1962)
European Rally Championship, Round 9

Pos.	No.	Driver/Codriver	Nat.	Car	Cat.	Result
1	65	Pat Moss/Pauline Mayman	GB	Morris Cooper	T	0/182.32
2	20	Eugen Böhringer/Peter Lang	D	Mercedes-Benz 220 SE	T	0/178.85
3	30	René Trautmann/Claudine Bouchet	F	Citroën ID19	T	0/176.9
4	3	Hans-Joachim Walter/Ewald Stock	D	Porsche 356B Carrera 2	GT	0/168.75
5	34	Rudolf Smoliner/Karl Auer	A	Citroën ID19	T	0/159.14
6	45	Arnaldo Cavallari/G. Simonetta	I	Alfa Romeo	T	0/157.27
7	80	Erik Carlsson/Gunnar Häggbom	S	Saab 96	T	0/126.06
8	12	Hans Wehner/H. von Schweinichen	D	Volkswagen Special	GT	10
9	91	Jürgen Zink/Peter Erb	D	BMW 700S	T	14,6
10	46	Walter Cordaro/Ferdinando Tecilla	I	Alfa Romeo	T	47,3

14e Internationale Tulpenrallye

(7–12 May 1962)
European Rally Championship, Round 2

Pos.	No.	Driver/Codriver	Nat.	Car	Cat.	Result
1	104	Pat Moss/Ann Riley	GB	Morris Cooper	T	0/90.78
2	71	Gunnar Andersson/Walter Karlsson	S	Volvo 122	T	0/91.08
3	135	Pierre Gelé/Claude Laurent	F	DKW Junior	T	0/91.68
4	123	Erik Carlsson/Gunnar Häggbom	S	Saab 96	T	0/91.73
5	27	Jules Meur/Freddy Rouselle	F	Porsche 356 Super 90	GT	0/91.94
6	26	D.F.Gray/Sam Actman	GB	Porsche 356 Super 90	GT	0/92.14
7	48	Eugen Böhringer/Peter Lang	D	Mercedes-Benz 220SEb	T	0/92.91
8	105	Tony Fisher/Brian Melia	GB	Austin Cooper	T	0/93.08
9	58	Peter Ruby/Gerd Raschig	D	DKW Junior	GT	0/93.58
10	94	J.Nielsen/H.Hendriksen	DK	Alfa Romeo Giulietta TI	T	0/93.80

23ème Coupe des Alpes

(7–12 June 1962)
European Rally Championship, Round 4

Pos.	No.	Driver/Codriver	Nat.	Car	Cat.	Result
1	5	Don Morley/Erle Morley	GB	Austin-Healey 3000	3	0/7718.8
2	16	Hans-Joachim Walter/Kurt Schöttler	D	Porsche 356B Carrera	3	0/7739.5
3	4	Pat Moss/Pauline Mayman	GB	Austin-Healey 3000	3	0/7869.5
4	8	Mike Sutcliffe/Roy Fidler	GB	Triumph TR4	3	0/8247.1
5	45	René Trautmann/Patrick Chopin	F	Citroën DS19	1&2	0/8479.1
6	31	Jean Vinatier/Jean Charon	F	Ford Zodiac	1&2	60/8523.2
7	50	Guy Verrier/Jacques Badoche	F	Citroën DS19	1&2	60/8970.9
8	1	David Seigle-Morris/Tony Ambrose	GB	Austin-Healey 3000	3	120/7891.5
9	10	Jean-Jacques Thuner/John Gretener	CH	Triumph TR4	3	120/8228.5
10	91	Jean Cazon/Michel Billard	F	BMW 700	1&2	240/10072.7

XXII Rajd Polski

(2–6 August 1962)
European Rally Championship, Round 6

Pos.	No.	Driver/Codriver	Nat.	Car	Cat.	Result
1	66	Eugen Böhringer/Peter Lang	D	Mercedes-Benz 220 SEb	T	412,52
2	81	Pat Moss/Pauline Mayman	GB	Austin Healey	GT	828,37
3	72	Herman Kühne/Hans Wencher	D	Mercedes-Benz 220 SEb	T	1201,39
4	35	Kurt Otto/Herman Hanf	DDR	AWE Wartburg	T	2444,47
5	62	Ever Christofferson/T.Lilienberg	S	Volvo PV544	T	2458,25
6	70	Ewy Rosqvist/Ursula Wirth	S	Mercedes-Benz 220 SEb	T	2461,41
7	7	Jerzy Dobrzański/Czesław Murawski	PL	BMW Sport	T	2640,57
8	69	Marian Repeta/Eugeniusz Stryczek	PL	FSO Warszawa	GT	2861,84
9	25	Ryszard Nowicki/Czesław Wodnicki	PL	Fiat TC SS Abarth	T	3136,76
10	45	Ludwik Postawa/Kazimierz Jaromin	PL	Simca Aronde	T	3426,89

Liège-Sofia-Liège

(29 August–2 September 1962)
European Rally Championship, Round 8

Pos.	No.	Driver/Codriver	Nat.	Car	Cat.	Result
1	82	Eugen Böhringer/Hermann Eger	D	Mercedes-Benz 220SEb		53m
2	77	Henri Marang/Paul Coltelloni	F	Citroën DS19		1h22m
3	91	Jacques Patte/Patrick Rouselle	B	Volvo 122S		1h29m
4	2	Guy Verrier/Jacques Badoche	F	Citroën DS19		1h36m
5	56	Logan Morrison/Rupert Jones	GB	Austin Healey 3000		2h11m
6	21	Ken James/Mike Hughes	GB	Rover 3-Litre		2h12m
7	28	Claudine Bouchet/Françoise Vallier	F	Citroën DS19		2h23m
8	57	David Seigle-Morris/Barry Hercock	GB	Austin Healey 3000		2h25m
9	30	Jean-Jacques Thuner/John Gretener	CH	Triumph		2h53m
10	4	Francis Charlier/Nicolas Mosbaux	B	Ford Anglia		2h57m

30ème Rallye International de Genève

(19–21 October 1962)
European Rally Championship, Round 10

Pos.	No.	Driver/Codriver	Nat.	Car	Cat.	Result
1	163	Hans-Joachim Walter/Werner Lier	D/CH	Porsche Carrera	3	152
2	110	Erik Carlsson/Gunnar Häggbom	S	Saab	2	280
3	135	Pat Moss/Pauline Mayman	GB	Mini Cooper	2	289
4	103	Jean-Pierre Hanrioud/Claude Arbez	F	Renault 1093	1	376
5	112	Pierre Gelé/Claude Laurent	F	DKW	2	495
6	115	Alfred Kling/Rolf Kreder	D	DKW	2	577
7	151	Hans Kreft/Werner Fleck	D	Jaguar	1	641
8	111	Robert Meyer/Erich Bechtel	CH	DKW	2	653
9	113	Paul Macchi/Aldo Macchi	CH	Saab	2	670
10	150	Jean Meunier/Pierre Grosrey	F	Jaguar	1	694

1962–1964

The Royal Automobile Club Eleventh International Rally of Great Britain

(12–17 November 1962)
European Rally Championship, Round 11

Pos.	No.	Driver/Codriver	Nat.	Car	Cat.	Result
1	4	Erik Carlsson/David Stone	S/GB	Saab	T	204
2	19	Paddy Hopkirk/Jack Scott	GB	Austin Healey 3000	GT	264
3	5	Pat Moss/Pauline Mayman	GB	Austin Healey 3000	GT	314
4	10	Tiny Lewis/David Mabbs	GB	Sunbeam Rapier	T	349
5	6	Rauno Aaltonen/Tony Ambrose	SF/GB	Mini Cooper	GT	352
6	30	Henry Taylor/Brian Melia	GB	Ford Anglia 1200	GT	354
7	38	Timo Mäkinen/John Steadman	SF/GB	Mini Cooper	T	394
8	2	Gunnar Andersson/Douglas Johns	S/GB	Volvo PV544	T	397
9	7	Jean-Jacques Thuner/John Gretener	CH	Triumph TR4	GT	430
10	134	Sylvia Österberg/Cecile Pattison	S/GB	Volvo PV544	T	442

1963

32ème Rallye Automobile Monte-Carlo

(19–26 January 1963)
European Rally Championship, Round 1

Pos.	No.	Driver/Codriver	Nat.	Car	Cat.	Result
1	283	Erik Carlsson/Gunnar Palm	S	Saab 96	T	2992,489
2	233	Pauli Toivonen/Anssi Jarvi	SF	Citroën DS19	T	3014,846
3	288	Rauno Aaltonen/Tony Ambrose	SF/GB	Mini Cooper	T	3055,077
4	42	Lucien Bianchi/Jean-Claude Ogier	F	Citroën DS19	T	3101,240
5	19	Bob Neyret/Jacques Terramorsi	F	Citroën DS19	T	3106,324
6	66	Paddy Hopkirk/Jack Scott	GB	Mini Cooper	T	3110,285
7	274	Roger de Lageneste/C.du Genestoux	F	Citroën DS19	T	3162,014
8	285	Olle Dahl/Lars-Erik Haag	S	Volvo 122	T	3182,000
9	237	Gunnar Andersson/Walter Karlsson	S	Volvo 122	T	3218,600
10	91	Guy Verrier/"Alec"	F	Citroën DS19	T	3228,620

15e Internationale Tulpenrallye

(22–26 April 1963)
European Rally Championship, Round 2

Pos.	No.	Driver/Codriver	Nat.	Car	Cat.	Result
1	27	Henri Greder/Martial Delalande	F	Ford Falcon Sprint	T	90,09%
2	130	Paddy Hopkirk/Henry Liddon	GB	Morris Cooper	T	91,47%
3	55	Gunnar Andersson/Lennart Bergren	S	Volvo 122S	T	91,57%
4	20	Lodewijk-Henri Bakker/H. Umbach	NL	Porsche 356 Super 90	GT	91,63%
5	148	Alfred Kling/Gerhard Kaufmann	D	DKW F11	T	91,97%
6	108	Ed Swart/Roberto Fusina	NL	Fiat 1300	T	92,66%
7	63	Tom Trana/Mario Pavoni	S	Volvo 122S	T	92,70%
8	1	Don Morley/Erle Morley	GB	Austin Healey 3000 Mk.II	GT	92,70%
9	87	Peter Harper/Ian Hall	GB	Sunbeam Rapier	T	92,77%
10	149	André Guilhaudin/Henry Balas	F	DKW F11	T	93,04%

11th Rally Acropolis

(16–19 May 1963)
European Rally Championship, Round 3

Pos.	No.	Driver/Codriver	Nat.	Car	Cat.	Result
1	41	Eugen Böhringer/Rolf Knoll	D	Mercedes-Benz 300SE	T	92,80
2	51	Gunnar Andersson/Walter Karlsson	S	Volvo 122	T	125,33
3	65	Carl-Magnus Skogh/L. Berggren	S	Volvo 122	T	125,73
4	89	Henry Taylor/Brian Melia	GB	Ford Cortina GT	T	181,75
5	37	Dieter Glemser/Klaus Kaiser	D	Mercedes-Benz 220SE	T	198,41
6	75	Pat Moss/Ann Riley	GB	Ford Cortina GT	T	213,75
7	69	Pauli Toivonen/Väinö Nurmimaa	SF	Citroën DS19	T	216,45
8	55	René Trautmann/Jean-Claude Ogier	F	Citroën DS19	T	228,13
9	59	Guy Verrier/Jacques Badoche	F	Citroën DS19	T	253,92
10	53	Sylvia Osteberg/Inga-lill Edenring	S	Volvo 122	T	261,57

24ème Coupe des Alpes

(20–25 June 1963)
European Rally Championship, Round 4

Pos.	No.	Driver/Codriver	Nat.	Car	Cat.	Result
1	19	Jean Rolland/Gabriel Augias	F	Alfa Romeo Giulietta SZ	GT	0
2	63	Rauno Aaltonen/Tony Ambrose	SF/GB	Mini Cooper S	T	0
3	50	Henry Taylor/Brian Melia	GB	Ford Cortina GT	T	0
4	49	David Seigle-Morris/Barry Hercock	GB	Ford Cortina GT	T	0
5	33	René Trautmann/Yves Cherel	F	Citroën DS19	T	0
6	73	Pauline Mayman/Valerie Domleo	GB	Mini Cooper	T	0
7	36	Guy Verrier/Jacques Jourdain	F	Citroën DS19	T	60
8	45	Tiny Lewis/David Pollard	GB	Sunbeam Rapier	T	120
9	57	John Wadsworth/Alan Cooke	GB	Mini Cooper S	T	135
10	87	Georges Nicolas/C.Cauquil	F	Renault Dauphine 1093	T	240

25. Internationale Rallye Wiesbaden

(3–7 July 1963)
European Rally Championship, Round 5 - Category GT

Pos.	No.	Driver/Codriver	Nat.	Car	Cat.	Result
1	10	Günter Wallrabenstein/K.-H. Exner	D	Porsche Carrera	GT	4,5
2	1	Hans-Joachim Walter/Otto Castell	D	Porsche Carrera GTL	GT	20,0
3	17	Wilfried Gass/Gerd Frey	D	Porsche 1600GS	GT	61,6
4	32	Rudolf-Wilhelm Moser/K. Ritterhaus	D	Alfa Romeo Giulietta SZ	GT	180,0
5	14	Hans Tenge/Hans-Georg Schuller	D	Porsche Super 90	GT	204,8
6	43	Peter Ettmüller/Xavier Perrot	CH	Fiat Abarth 1000	GT	221,8
7	6	Rudolf-Helmut Metzger/H.-J. Zander	D	Austin Healey 3000	GT	227,4
8	40	Dieter Schey/Günter Schanné	D	BMW 700S	GT	248,8
9	2	Günther Klass/Rolf Wütherich	D	Porsche Carrera 2	GT	251,4
10	11	Friedel Herborn/Ernst-Otto Müller	D	Porsche Carrera	GT	256,0

Deutschland-Rallye

(4–7 July 1963)
European Rally Championship, Round 5 - Category T

Pos.	No.	Driver/Codriver	Nat.	Car	Cat.	Result
1	100	Eugen Böhringer/Klaus Kaiser	D	Mercedes-Benz 300SE	T	0/5.43
2	111	Dieter Glemser/Martin Braungart	D	Mercedes-Benz 220SE	T	0/2.31
3	126	Gunnar Andersson/Gunnar Häggbom	S	Volvo 122S	T	0/2.08
4	112	Dieter Gerhards/Klaus Umbach	D	Mercedes-Benz 220SE	T	0/0.12
5	169	Nicolas Koob/Armand Wies	L	DKW F12	T	0/0.08
6	179	Georg Kaufmann/Alfred Kling	A	DKW Junior	T	2,0
7	189	Wolfgang Knöppel/Irmgard Knöppel	D	BMW 700S	T	6,3
8	159	Helmut Kelleners/Ferdi Bökmann	D	Fiat 1300	T	9,9
9	120	Reiner Brechler/Horst Brechler	D	Volvo 122S	T	18,6
10	127	Sylvia Österberg/Inga-Lill Edenring	S	Volvo 122S	T	22,6

VII Rallye Automobilistico della Sardegna

(4–6 May 1963)
European Rally Championship, Round 6

Pos.	No.	Driver/Codriver	Nat.	Car	Cat.	Result
1		Ernesto Prinoth/Aldo Morgantini	I	Alfa Romeo Giulia Super TI	GT	0,0
2		Arnaldo Cavallari/Enzo Martoni	I	Alfa Romeo Giulietta TI	T	0,0
3		Walter Roser/Peter Lederer	A	Steyr Puch 650	T	0,0
4		Ferdinando Frescobaldi/G. Martelli	I	Fiat Abarth 850	T	5,0
5		Mario Casula/Tonino Casula	I	Lancia Flavia	T	15,0
6		A. degl'Innocenti/F. de Benedictis	I	Fiat Abarth 850	T	24,0
7		Piero Bagnasacco/Giovanni Bonomi	I	Volvo B18	T	25,0
8		Sergio Lipizer/Ugo de Giorgio	I	Fiat Abarth 850	T	48,0
9		Gino Melis/Walter Cordaro	I	Alfa Romeo Giulietta TI	T	90,0
10		Gianluigi Sorcinelli/Enrico Bianghi	I	Mini Cooper	T	121,0

31ème Rallye International de Genève

(4–6 October 1963)
European Rally Championship, Round 7

Pos.	No.	Driver/Codriver	Nat.	Car	Cat.	Result
1		Henri Greder/Martial Delalande	F	Ford Falcon Futura Sprint	T	386,6
2		Hans-Joachim Walter/Werner Lier	D/CH	Porsche Carrera 2	GT	410,8
3		Gunnar Andersson/Gunnar Häggbom	S	Volvo 122S	T	428,1
4		Sylvia Östeberg/Ingalill Edenring	S	Volvo 122S	T	640,5
5		Paul Macchi/Aldo Macchi	CH	Saab 96 Sport	T	721,9
6		Jean-Jacques Thuner/John Gretener	CH	Triumph TR4	GT	731,0
7		Gérard Larousse/J.-Claude Perray	F	Renault Dauphine 1093	T	1071,0
8		Hervé Laurent/Michel Billiard	F	Renault Dauphine 1093	T	1533,8
9		Henri Ziegler/Malou Racle	CH	Mini Cooper	T	1622,8
10		Mauris Bernard/Guy Grasso	CH	Ford Lotus Cortina	T	1726,2

XIV Svenska Rallyt till Midnattssolen

(11–15 June 1963)
Not part of the European Rally Championship

Pos.	No.	Driver/Codriver	Nat.	Car	Cat.	Result
1	119	Berndt Jansson/Erik Petterson	S	Porsche Carrera	3	180
2		Erik Carlsson/Gunnar Palm	S	Saab Sport	2	224
3		Bo Ljungfeldt/Bo Rehnfeldt	S	Ford Cortina GT	2	228
4		Olle Bromark/Kjell Lyxell	S	Saab 96	1	245
5		Ove Andersson/Gunnar Wiman	S	Mini Cooper S	1	252
6		Carl-Magnus Skogh/Lennart Bergrren	S	Volvo Amazon	2	262
7		Carl Orrenius/Rolf Dahlgren	S	Mini Cooper S	2	265
8		Åke Andersson/Gunnar Lindén	S	Saab 96	3	272
9		Bengt Söderström/Bo Olsson	S	Volvo PV544	1	296
10		Rauno Aaltonen/Rolf Skogh	SF/S	Chrysler Valiant V200	1	333

XXIII Rajd Polski

(31 July–4 August 1963)
Not part of the European Rally Championship

Pos.	No.	Driver/Codriver	Nat.	Car	Cat.	Result
1	72	Dieter Glemser/Martin Braungart	D	Mercedes-Benz		182,99
2	64	Gunnar Andersson/Gunnar Häggbom	S	Volvo 122S		235,75
3	17	Sobiesław Zasada/Ewa Zasada	PL	Fiat 600D		715,69
4	61	Sylvia Österberg/Inga-Lill Edenring	S	Volvo 122S		774,27
5	18	Marek Varisella/Mirosław Jeżowski	PL	Syrena 102		1224,12
6	34	Kurt Otto/Hermann Hanf	DDR	Wartburg		1518,18
7	2	Eberhard Asmus/Helmuth Piehler	DDR	Trabant 600		1676,25
8	42	Jan Soczek/Ludwik Postawa	PL	Skoda Octavia		1928,04
9	20	Olle Dahl/Zdenek Treybal	S	SAAB 96		2230,00
10	60	Ksawery Frank/Zbigniew Łagutko	PL	Volvo 122S		2571,34

XIII Jyväskylän Suurajot - Rally of the Thousand Lakes

(16–18 August 1963)
Not part of the European Rally Championship

Pos.	No.	Driver/Codriver	Nat.	Car	Cat.	Result
1	32	Simo Lampinen/Jyrki Ahava	SF	Saab 96 Sport	T	9986,2
2	43	Tom Trana/Gunnar Andersson	S	Volvo PV544	T	10003,2
3	37	Rauno Aaltonen/Väinö Nurmimaa	SF	Saab 96 Sport	T	10099,4
4	38	Berndt Jansson/Erik Petterson	S	Volkswagen 1500	T	10250,3
5	36	Olle Bromark/Kjell Lyxell	S	Saab 96 Sport	T	10262,5
6	34	Bengt Söderström/Bo Olsson	S	Volvo	T	10392,5
7	46	Rune Larsson/Börje Nilsson	S	Volkswagen 1500	T	10430,6
8	42	Bertil Söderström/Rune Olsson	S	Volkswagen 1200	T	10519,4
9	41	Timo Mäkinen/Kauko Ruutsalo	SF	Mini Cooper	T	10557,9
10	55	Olli-Pekka Paroma/Veikko Villilä	SF	Mini Cooper	T	10745,1

Liège-Sofia-Liège

(27 August–1 September 1963)
Not part of the European Rally Championship

Pos.	No.	Driver/Codriver	Nat.	Car	Cat.	Result
1	39	Eugen Böhringer/Klaus Kaiser	D	Mercedes-Benz 230SL	S	0h08m
2	52	Erik Carlsson/Gunnar Palm	S	Saab 96	T	0h23m
3	85	Lucien Bianchi/Jean-Claude Ogier	B/F	Citroën DS21	S	0h28m
4	56	Henry Taylor/Brian Melia	GB	Ford Cortina	S	0h43m
5	25	Roger de Lageneste/Alain Bertaut	F	Citroën DS21	S	0h44m
6	120	Paddy Hopkirk/Henry Liddon	GB	Austin Healey 3000	GT	0h48m
7	70	Jean Guichet/Paul Coltelloni	F	Citroën DS21	GT	1h08m
8	18	Ken James/Mike Hughes	GB	Rover 3-Litre	T	1h25m
9	90	Peter Riley/Tony Nash	GB	Ford Cortina	T	1h31m
10	50	Olivier Gendebien/Jean Demortier	B	Citroën DS21	S	1h38m

The Royal Automobile Club Twelfth International Rally of Great Britain

(11–16 November 1963)
Not part of the European Rally Championship

Pos.	No.	Driver/Codriver	Nat.	Car	Cat.	Result
1	29	Tom Trana/Sven Lindström	S	Volvo PV544	T	246
2	52	Harry Källström/Gunnar Häggbom	S	Volkswagen 1500S	T	293
3	4	Erik Carlsson/Gunnar Palm	S	Saab 96	T	293
4	21	Paddy Hopkirk/Henry Liddon	GB	Mini Cooper S	T	306
5	28	Timo Mäkinen/Mike Wood	SF/GB	Austin Healey 3000	GT	311
6	27	Henry Taylor/Brian Melia	GB	Ford Lotus Cortina	T	347
7	7	Pat Moss-Carlsson/Jenny Nadin	GB	Ford Cortina GT	GT	356
8	9	Gunnar Andersson/Douglas Johns	S/GB	Volvo	T	358
9	5	Donald Morley/Erle Morley	GB	Austin Healey 3000	GT	363
10	47	Carl Orrenius/Rolf Dahlgren	S	Mini Cooper S	T	376

1964

33ème Rallye Automobile Monte-Carlo

(17–25 January 1964)
European Rally Championship, Round 1

Pos.	No.	Driver/Codriver	Nat.	Car	Cat.	Result
1	37	Paddy Hopkirk/Henry Liddon	GB	Mini Cooper		2536,2730
2	49	Bo Ljungfeldt/Fergus Sager	S	Ford Falcon		2566,7128
3	131	Erik Carlsson/Gunnar Palm	S	Saab		2573,7760
4	182	Timo Mäkinen/Patrick Vanson	SF/F	Mini Cooper S		2593,8625
5	56	Pat Moss-Carlsson/Ursula Wirth	GB/S	Saab		2596,9766
6	59	Tom Trana/Sune Lindström	S	Volvo		2609,7419
7	105	Rauno Aaltonen/Tony Ambrose	SF/GB	Mini Cooper S		2619,5565
8	110	Eugen Böhringer/Klaus Kaiser	D	Mercedes-Benz 300SE		2621,9223
9	60	Carl-Magnus Skogh/L. Berggren	S	Volvo		2646,7617
10	108	Pauli Toivonen/Anssi Jarvi	SF	Volkswagen		2685,2100

4° Rallye dei Fiori

(27 February–1 March 1964)
European Rally Championship, Round 2

Pos.	No.	Driver/Codriver	Nat.	Car	Cat.	Result
1	118	Erik Carlsson/Gunnar Palm	S	Saab 96	I	370,950
2	119	Pat Moss-Carlsson/Valerie Domleo	GB	Saab 96	I	371,269
3	159	Piero Frescobaldi/A. Degli Innocenti	I	Lancia Flavia		374,785
4	109	Velio Bartolini/Walter Bartolini	I	Alfa Romeo Giulietta TI	I	376,387
5	127	Leo Cella/Romano Ramoino	I	Lancia Flavia		376,425
6	95	Ferdinando Frescobaldi/B. Zavagli	I	Lancia Flavia		377,052
7	125	Luigi Taramazzo/Giancarlo Mamino	I	Lancia Flavia		377,679
8	8	Arnaldo Cavallari/Piero Bagnasacco	I	Alfa Romeo Giulia TI Super	I	377,767
9	48	Enrico Agostini/Leonardo Durst	i	Alfa Romeo Giulia TI Super		379,027
10	46	Luigi Cabella/Carlo Ghislandi	I	Alfa Romeo Giulia TI Super		379,153

11° Rali Internacional do Automovel Club de Portugal

(1–5 April 1964)
European Rally Championship, Round 3

Pos.	No.	Driver/Codriver	Nat.	Car	Cat.	Result
1	50	Andrea de Adamich/Aldo Morgantini	I	Alfa Romeo Giulia TI Super		96,31
2	48	Arnaldo Cavallari/Ferdinando Tecilla	I	Alfa Romeo Giulia TI Super		97,39
3	65	Dieter Glemser/Peter Lang	D	Mercedes-Benz 300SE		97,49
4	64	Eugen Böhringer/Klaus Kaiser	D	Mercedes-Benz 300SE		97,60
5	7	Jorge Passanha/Carlo Ghislandi	P	Porsche		101,23
6	52	César Torres/Paiva Rapozo	P	Mini Cooper S		104,45
7	10	Rui Martins da Silva/Carvalho	P	Alfa Romeo		105,25
8	15	Manuel Lopes Gião/L. Fernando	P	Mini Cooper S		105,77
9	16	Augusto Rodrigues Palma/P. Basto	P	Mini Cooper S		108,26
10	41	José Luis Lickfold Silva/Leal Faria	P	Mini Cooper		110,18

16e Internationale Tulpenrallye

(20–24 April 1964)
European Rally Championship, Round 4

No	Cat	Driver/Codriver	Nat.	Car	Cat.	Result
1	119	Timo Mäkinen/Tony Ambrose	SF/GB	Mini Cooper S	T	97,23
2	5	Don Morley/Erle Morley	GB	Austin Healey 3000	GT	97,41
3	21	Bernt Jansson/Erik Petterson	S	Porsche Abarth Carrera	GT	97,63
4	56	Henri Greder/Martial Delalande	F	Ford Falcon Sprint	T	98,81
5	27	Henry Taylor/Brian Melia	GB	Ford Cortina GT	GT	98,95
6	34	Julian Vernaeve/Yves Deprez	B	Mini Cooper S	GT	99,39
7	74	Carl-Magnus Skogh/L. Berggren	S	Volvo 122S	T	99,50
8	22	Wilfried Gass/Gert Frey	D	Porsche 1600 GS GT	GT	99,65
9	144	Kurt Pfnier/Wolfram Berns	D	DKW F11	T	99,91
10	147	Erik Carlsson/Gunnar Palm	S	Saab 96	T	100,54

1964–1965

12th Rally Acropolis

(14–17 May 1964)
European Rally Championship, Round 5

Pos.	No.	Driver/Codriver	Nat.	Car	Cat.	Result
1	45	Tom Trana/Gunnar Thermaenius	S	Volvo PV544		156,85
2	49	Jean-Claude Ogier/Bernhard Groll	F	Citroën DS19		298,37
3	84	Pat Moss-Carlsson/Valerie Domleo	GB	Saab 96 Sport		391,80
4	8	Erich Waxenberger/Klaus Kaiser	D	Mercedes-Benz 220SE		462,27
5	38	Ewy Rosqvist/Eva-Marie Falk	S/D	Mercedes-Benz 220SE		666,08
6	42	Patrick Vanson/Jean-Paul Joly	F	Citroën DS19		1235,01
7	3	Ken James/Mike Hughes	GB	Rover 3-litre P5		1237,31
8	62	Henny-Brit Ehringe/Annette Lindqvist	S	Volkswagen 1500S		1867,18
9	40	Richard Martin-Hurst/Roger Clark	GB	Rover 3-Litre P5		2437,15
10	30	Ove Andersson/Torsten Åman	S	Saab Sport		2651,44

Internationale Österreichische Alpenfahrt

(28–30 May 1964)
European Rally Championship, Round 6

Pos.	No.	Driver/Codriver	Nat.	Car	Cat.	Result
1	2	Paddy Hopkirk/Henry Liddon	GB	Austin-Healey 3000	GT	1930,0
2	106	Johannes Ortner/Karl-Heinz Panowitz	A/D	Steyr-Puch 650 TR	GT	1848,3
3	65	Arnaldo Cavallari/Fulvio Rubbieri	I	Alfa Romeo Giulia	T	1800,8
4	25	Wilfried Gass/Jurgen Säckl	A	Porsche	GT	1798,0
5	80	Walter Pöltinger/Ernst Merinsky	A	Mini Cooper S	T	1788,5
6	48	Otto Karger/Peter Denzel	A	Volvo 122S	T	1785,7
7	8	Carl Christian Schindler/Haber	A	MGB	GT	1769,5
8	86	Georg Kaufmann/Alfred Kling	A	Auto Union	T	1769,1
9	42	Ernst Benedikt/Herle	A	Volvo 122S	T	1754,0
10	109	König/Mauerhofer	A	Steyr-Puch 650 TR	T	1748,1

XV Svenska Rallyt till Midnattssolen

(9–14 June 1964)
European Rally Championship, Round 7

Pos.	No.	Driver/Codriver	Nat.	Car	Cat.	Result
1	89	Tom Trana/Gunnar Thermaenius	S	Volvo	II	365
2	162	Harry Källström/Ragnvald Håkansson	S	Mini Cooper S	I	403
3	193	Bengt Söderström/Bosse Olsson	S	Ford Cortina GT	I	428
4	3	Carl Magnus Skogh/L. Berggren	S	Volvo PV544	I	441
5	104	Ove Andersson/Torsten Åman	S	Saab 96S	I	444
6	48	Rauno Aaltonen/Rolf Skogh	SF/S	Saab 96S	II	460
7	32	Bo Ljungfeldt/Fergus Sager	S	Ford Falcon	I	481
8	44	Simo Lampinen/Picko Troberg	SF/S	Saab 96S	II	485
9	43	Olle Bromark/Kjell Lyxel	S	Saab 96S	II	501
10	71	Lennart Eliasson/Gunnar Trygg	S	Mini Cooper S	II	510

25ème Coupe des Alpes

(22–27 June 1964)
European Rally Championship, Round 8

Pos.	No.	Driver/Codriver	Nat.	Car	Cat.	Result
1	83	Jean Rolland/Gabriel Augias	F	Alfa Romeo Giulia TZ	III	5.303,31
2	95	Don Morley/Erle Morley	GB	Austin-Healey 3000	III	5.373,00
3	87	Jacques Rey/Jean-Pierre Hanrioud	F	Porsche 904	III	5.529,65
4	70	Rauno Aaltonen/Tony Ambrose	SF/GB	Mini Cooper S	III	5.643,06
5	29	Vic Elford/David Stone	GB	Ford Cortina GT	III	5.692,86
6	73	John Wadsworth/Allan Cooke	GB	Mini Cooper S	III	6.186,36
7	5	Erik Carlsson/Gunnar Palm	S	Saab 96	I	6.254,37
8	94	Christian Poirot/Claude Marbaque	F	Porsche 904	III	65.452,00
9	71	Terry Hunter/Patrick Lier	GB/CH	Triumph Spitfire	III	125.807,56
10	39	Jean-Claude Ogier/Lucette Pointet	F	Citroën DS19	III	185.966,06

XXIV Rajd Polski

(30 July–2 August 1964)
European Rally Championship, Round 9

Pos.	No.	Driver/Codriver	Nat.	Car	Cat.	Result
1	8	Sobiesław Zasada/Ewa Zasada	PL	Steyr Puch 650TR	I&II	376
2	20	Erik Carlsson/Gunnar Palm	S	Saab	I&II	1245
3	18	Pat Moss-Carlsson/E. Nyström	GB/S	Saab	I&II	1539
4	102	Franciszek Podstawka/Józef Zoll	PL	Volvo PV544	I&II	1877
5	23	Adam Wędrychowski/Marek Varisella	PL	Renault Dauphine	I&II	2146
6	16	Kazimierz Osiński/M. Sochacki	PL	Fiat 600D	I&II	2190
7	38	Kurt Otto/Hermann Hanf	DDR	Wartburg	I&II	2819
8	97	Giorgio Pianta/Mario Poltronieri	I	Lancia Flavia	I&II	3540
9	104	Jens Nielsen/Henning Henriksen	DK	Volvo PV544	I&II	3823
10	7	Eberhard Asmus/Helmut Piehler	DDR	Trabant 601	I&II	4339

XIV Jyväskylän Suurajot - Rally of the Thousand Lakes

(14–16 August 1964)
European Rally Championship, Round 10

Pos.	No.	Driver/Codriver	Nat.	Car	Cat.	Result
1	54	Simo Lampinen/Jyrki Ahava	SF	Saab 96 Sport		8797,8
2	48	Tom Trana/Gunnar Thermaenius	S	Volvo PV		8933,0
3	45	Rauno Aaltonen/Väinö Nurmimaa	SF	Saab		8961,6
4	50	Timo Mäkinen/Pekka Keskitalo	SF	Mini Cooper S		9105,0
5	52	Bengt Söderström/Bo Olsson	S	Ford Cortina GT		9137,0
6	34	Esko Keinänen/Anssi Järvi	SF	Ford Cortina GT		9208,2
7	35	Ove Andersson/Torsten Åman	S	Saab		9209,2
8	61	Lars Krall/Lars Andersson	S	Mini Cooper S		9243,0
9	57	Raimo Kossila/Veikko Patrikka	SF	Volvo		9268,3
10	37	Carl-Magnus Skogh/Olov Granlund	S	Volvo		9281,2

32ème Rallye International de Genève

(15–18 October 1964)
European Rally Championship, Round 11

Pos.	No.	Driver/Codriver	Nat.	Car	Cat.	Result
1	35	Henri Greder/Martial Delalande	F	Ford Falcon	I&II	85
2	23	Terry Hunter/Patrick Lier	GB/CH	Triumph Spitfire	III	189
3		Erik Carlsson/Gunnar Palm	S	Saab	I&II	210
4		Hans-Joachim Walter/Werner Lier	D/CH	BMW 1800 TI	I&II	215
5	24	Jean-Jaques Thuner/John Gretener	CH	Triumph Spitfire	III	219
6	40	Tom Trana/Gunnar Thermaenius	S	Volvo PV544	I&II	273
7		Pat Moss-Carlsson/E. Nyström	GB/S	Saab	I&II	289
8		Gérard Larousse/Jean-Claude Perray	F	Renault Dauphine	I&II	477
9		Jean-Pierre Meyer/J.-Pierre Rutsch	CH	Ford Cortina GT	I&II	481
10		Fernand Masoero/Jean Maurin	F	Alfa Romeo Giulia Super TI	I&II	486

The Royal Automobile Club's 1964 International Rally of Great Britain

(7–13 November 1964)
European Rally Championship, Round 12

Pos.	No.	Driver/Codriver	Nat.	Car	Cat.	Result
1	8	Tom Trana/Gunnar Thermaenius	S	Volvo PV544	I&II	3528
2	14	Timo Mäkinen/Don Barrow	SF/GB	Austin Healey 3000	III	3860
3	3	Vic Elford/David Stone	GB	Ford Cortina GT	III	4758
4	7	Pat Moss-Carlsson/E. Nyström	GB/S	Saab 96	III	5066
5	9	Bengt Söderström/Bo Ohlsson	S	Ford Cortina GT	I&II	5116
6	35	Roy Fidler/Don Grimshaw	GB	Triumph 2000	III	5261
7	4	Erik Carlsson/Gunnar Palm	S	Saab 96	I&II	5314
7	12	Berndt Jansson/Erik Petterson	S	Volkswagen	III	5399
9	21	David Seigle-Morris/Tony Nash	GB	Ford Cortina GT	III	5473
10	53	Sylvia Osterberg/Siw Sabel	S	Volvo PV544	I&II	5549

34ème Rallye Automobile Monte-Carlo

(16–23 January 1965)
European Rally Championship, Round 1

Pos.	No.	Driver/Codriver	Nat.	Car	Cat.	Result
1	52	Timo Mäkinen/Paul Easter	SF/GB	Mini Cooper S	III	5118,4138
2	150	Eugen Böhringer/Rolf Wutherich	D	Porsche 904	III	5613,0240
3	49	Pat Moss-Carlsson/E. Nyström	GB/S	Saab 96 Sport	III	5871,1170
4	107	Peter Harper/Ian Hall	GB	Sunbeam Tiger	III	6193,6200
5	147	Herbert Linge/Peter Falk	D	Porsche 911	III	6655,8664
6	136	Roger Clark/Jim Porter	GB	Rover 2000	II	6728,3256
7	75	Bob Neyret/Jacques Terramorsi	F	Citroën DS19	III	6883,5855
8	68	Bengt Söderström/S.-Olaf Svedberg	S	Ford Cortina	II	6911,9868
9	252	Henry Taylor/Brian Melia	GB	Ford Cortina GT	II	6983,0664
10	58	Hans-Joachim Walter/Werner Lier	D/CH	BMW 1800	II	7145,8332

1965

5° Rallye dei Fiori

(26–28 February 1965)
European Rally Championship, Round 2

Pos.	No.	Driver/Codriver	Nat.	Car	Cat.	Result
1	43	Leo Cella/Sergio Gamenara	I	Lancia Fulvia		418,939
2	44	Luigi Taramazzo/Romano Ramoino	I	Lancia Flavia Coupe		425,154
3	58	Berndt Jansson/Gunnar Liljedahl	S	Renault R8 Gordini		473,161
4	130	Giorgio Pianta/Carlo Scarambone	I	Lancia Flavia		514,116
5	116	Piero Raffa/Angelo Del Monte	I	Lancia Fulvia		622,060
6	55	Sylvia Osteberg/Siw Sabel	S	Volvo Amazon		641,325
7	50	Georges Nicolas/Latrandie	F	Renault R8 Gordini		646,936
8		Zeffirino Filippi/Panzironi	I	Lancia Flavia Sport		671,726
9	96	Enzo Martoni/Monti	I	Lancia Fulvia		675,284
10		Dino Morazzoni/Renato Mona	I	Lancia Fulvia		684,836

XVI KAK-Rallyt

(10–15 March 1965)
European Rally Championship, Round 3

Pos.	No.	Driver/Codriver	Nat.	Car	Cat.	Result
1	34	Tom Trana/Gunnar Thermaenius	S	Volvo PV544	I	672
2	26	Åke Andersson/Sven-Olaf Svedberg	S	Saab Sport	I	756
3	13	Björn Waldegård/Lars Nyström	S	Volkswagen 1500S	I	831
4	37	Carl-Magnus Skogh/L. Berggren	S	Volvo	II	922
5	88	Ove Eriksson/Stig Rosendahl	S	Opel Rekord	I	1029
6	36	Ove Andersson/Torsten Åman	S	Saab Sport	I	1103
7	29	Bengt Söderström/Bo Ohlsson	S	Ford Cortina GT	I	1129
8	95	Hans Lund/Björn Wahlgren	S	Saab Sport	II	1274
9	32	Berndt Jansson/Erik Petterson	S	Renault R8 Gordini	I	1276
10	54	Hans Lannsjö/Hans Sundin	S	Mini Cooper S	I	1284

13° Rallye Nacional del R.A.C. de España

(1–4 April 1965)
European Rally Championship, Round 4

Pos.	No.	Driver/Codriver	Nat.	Car	Cat.	Result
1	51	Juan Fernández/Jesus Sáez	E	Porsche 904	III	540,593
2	53	Estanislao Reverter/José Márquez	E	Fiat Abarth 1000 Bialbero	III	516,165
3	2	José Maria Juncadella/A. Soler Roig	E	Mini Cooper S	II	515,609
4	5	Jaime Juncosa Junior/Artemio Eche	E	Fiat Abarth 1000 TC	I	476,289
5	20	Abillio Calderón/Maria Pilar Blanco	E	Ford Lotus Cortina	I	472,711
6	7	Domingo Hergueta/Angel Sagrario	P	Renault R8 Gordini	I	469,548
7	62	Bernard Tramont/A. Ruiz-Giménez	F	Alpine Renault A108	III	468,106
8	63	Pedro Puché/Rial	E	Saab 96 Sport	III	463,745
9	17	A. García Cifuentes/J. Batista Falla	E	Ford Lotus Cortina	II	461,187
10	25	José Rubio Muños/Luiz Blasco	E	Mini Cooper S	I	460,568

17e Internationale Tulpenrallye

(26–30 April 1965)
European Rally Championship, Round 5

Pos.	No.	Driver/Codriver	Nat.	Car	Cat.	Result
1	35	Rosemary Smith/Valerie Domleo	EIR	Hillman Imp	III	85,16
2	36	Tiny Lewis/David Pollard	GB	Hillman Imp	III	85,76
3	167	Hans Lund/Björn Wahlgren	S	Saab 96 Sport	II	88,75
4	165	Olle Dahl/Lars Erik Haag	S	Saab 96 Sport	II	89,11
5	11	Jean-Jacques Thuner/John Gretener	CH	Triumph 2000	III	90,63
6	124	Timo Mäkinen/Paul Easter	SF/GB	Mini Cooper S	II	92,62
7	16	Jules Meur/Norbert Rebetez	MC	Porsche 2000 GT Carrera	III	95,30
8	4	Don Morley/Erle Morley	GB	Austin-Healey 3000 MkIII	III	95,36
9	172	Sobiesław Zasada/Kazimierz Osinski	PL	Steyr Puch 650TR	II	100,12
10	67	Giorgio Pianta/Roberto Dalla Morte	I	Lancia Flavia Coupé	II	100,29

13th Rally Acropolis

(20–23 May 1965)
European Rally Championship, Round 6

Pos.	No.	Driver/Codriver	Nat.	Car	Cat.	Result
1	32	Carl-Magnus Skogh/L. Berggren	S	Volvo Amazon	A6	453,66
2	87	Erik Carlsson/Torsetn Åman		Saab 96 Sport	A2	462,53
3	44	René Trautmann/Claudine Bouchet	F	Lancia Flavia 1800	A6	576,63
4	20	Åke Andersson/Gunnar Palm	S	Saab 96 Sport	B1	734,61
5	12	Dieter Glemser/Martin Braungart	D	Mercedes-Benz 230SL	B4	1049,40
6	8	Patrick Vanson/Jean-Paul Joly	F	Citroën DS19	B4	2329,26
7	92	Sobiesław Zasada/Kasimierz Osinski	PL	Steyr-Puch 650TR	A1	3110,47
8	46	Giorgio Pianta/Roberto Dalla Morte	I	Lancia Flavia 1800	A6	3233,51
9	34	Jan Eneqvist/Kjell Ehrman	S	Volvo PV544	A6	3422,34
10	70	Kurt Rüdiger/Günter Gries	DDR	AWE Wartburg	A3	4983,74

33ème Rallye International de Genève

(10–13 June 1965)
European Rally Championship, Round 7

Pos.	No.	Driver/Codriver	Nat.	Car	Cat.	Result
1	64	Rauno Aaltonen/Tony Ambrose	SF/GB	Mini Cooper S	II	16
2	40	René Trautmann/Claudine Bouchet	F	Lancia Flavia	II	90
3	92	Sobiesław Zasada/Kasimierz Osinski	PL	Steyr-Puch 650	II	107
4	10	Jean Rolland/Gabriel Augias	F	Alfa Romeo TZ	III	187
5	18	Jean-Jaques Thuner/John Gretener	F	Triumph Spitfire	III	193
6	65	Gérard Larousse/Jean-Claude Peray	F	Renault R8 Gordini	II	211
7	1	Don Morley/Erle Morley	GB	Austin Healey 3000	III	324
8	85	Peter Ruby/Gert Raschig	D	DKW F11	II	370
9	56	Gilbert Staepelaere/P. Christiaennes	B	Ford Cortina GT	III	469
10	3	Giorgio Pianta/Carlo Fagioli	I	Lancia Flavia	III	631

Rallye Vltava

(5–7 July 1965)
European Rally Championship, Round 8

Pos.	No.	Driver/Codriver	Nat.	Car	Cat.	Result
1	102	Rauno Aaltonen/Tony Ambrose	SF/GB	Mini Cooper S	T2	2720
2		René Trautmann/Claudine Bouchet	F	Lancia Flavia	T3	2853
3	96	Giorgio Pianta/Luciano Lombardini	I	Lancia Flavia	T3	2978
4		Alois Mark/Zdenek Cechmanek	CS	Tatra 603	T4	3270
5	60	Jaroslav Bobek/Leo Hnatevic	CS	Škoda 1000 MB	GT1	3428
6		Adolf Veřmiřovský/Stanislav Hajdusek	CS	Tatra 603	T4	3481
7		Josef Vidner/Jaroslc Wylit	CS	Škoda 1000 MB	GT1	3610
8		Oldrich Horsak/Vojtech Rieger	CS	Škoda 1000 MB	GT1	3779
9		Josef Chovanek/Jaroslv Mahyla	CS	Tatra 603	T4	4229
10		Antonin Dolejs/Milan Poldauf	CS	Škoda OTS	T2	4256

26ème Critérium International de la Montagne - "Coupe des Alpes"

(19–25 July 1965)
European Rally Championship, Round 9

Pos.	No.	Driver/Codriver	Nat.	Car	Cat.	Result
1	82	René Trautmann/Claudine Bouchet	F	Lancia Flavia Zagato	II	2h16m09.3s
2	70	Timo Mäkinen/Paul Easter	SF/GB	Mini Cooper S	II	2h16m11.0s
3	76	David Seigle-Morris/Tony Nash	GB	Ford Lotus Cortina	II	2h17m51.7s
4	60	Paddy Hopkirk/Henry Liddon	GB	Mini Cooper S	II	2h20m43.6s
5	58	Jean-François Piot/J. François Jacob	F	Renault R8 Gordini	II	2h27m12.1s
6	51	Jean Vinatier/Hubert Melot	F	Renault R8 Gordini	II	2h27m14.4s
7	93	Jean-Claude Ogier/Bernard Ogier	F	Citroën DS19	II	2h28m40.3s
8	59	Tony Fall/Mike Wood	GB	Mini Cooper S	II	2h34m33.5s
9	84	Bob Neyret/Jean-Pierre Verilhanc	F	Citroën DS19	II	2h30m40.4s
10	95	Roger Clark/Jim Porter	GB	Rover 2000 P6	II	2h34m44.0s

XXV Rajd Polski

(5–7 August 1965)
European Rally Championship, Round 7

Pos.	No.	Driver/Codriver	Nat.	Car	Cat.	Result
1	55	Rauno Aaltonen/Tony Ambrose	SF/GB	Mini Cooper S		2355,513
2	7	Sobiesław Zasada/Kazimierz Osiński	PL	Steyr-Puch 650 TR		2436,800
3	16	Erik Carlsson/Torsten Åman	S	Saab 96 Sport		2498,901
4	72	Rene Trautmann/Claudine Bouchet	I	Lancia		2517,033
5	14	Pat Moss-Carlsson/E. Nyström	GB/S	Saab 96 Sport		2606,075
6	23	Ove Anderson/Agne Nordlund	S	Saab 96 Sport		2651,403
7	73	Carl-Magnus Skogh/L. Berggren	S	Volvo		2840,894
8	9	Adam Wędrychowski/C. Wodnicki	PL	Steyr-Puch 700 TR		3356,008
9	38	Kurt Otto/Hermann Hanf	DDR	Wartburg		3601,602
10	34	Kurt Rudiger/Günter Gries	DDR	Wartburg		3672,427

XV Jyväskylän Suurajot - Rally of the Thousand Lakes

(20–22 August 1965)
European Rally Championship, Round 11

Pos.	No.	Driver/Codriver	Nat.	Car	Cat.	Result
1	28	Timo Mäkinen/Pekka Keskitalo	SF	Mini Cooper S	II	7802,8
2	26	Rauno Aaltonen/Anssi Järvi	SF	Mini Cooper S	II	7956,3
3	24	Pauli Toivonen/Kalevi Leivo	SF	Volkswagen 1500	II	8198,9
4	20	Simo Lampinen/Jyrki Ahava	SF	Saab 96 Sport	II	8220,1
5	42	Jorma Lusenius/Seppo Koskinen	SF	Mini Cooper S	II	8239,9
6	22	Paddy Hopkirk/Kauko Ruutsalo	GB/SF	Mini Cooper S	II	8241,0
7	30	Berndt Jansson/Erik Petterson	S	Renault R8 Gordini	II	8459,6
8	18	Esko Keinänen/Klaus Sohlberg	SF	Ford Cortina GT	II	8490,6
9	50	Keijo Tuominen/Jan-Ulf Ingman	SF	Volvo PV544 Sport	II	8503,5
10	9	Klaus Bremer/Raimo Hartto	SF	Mini Cooper S	II	8506,0

1965–1967

Internationale 3-Städte-Rallye - München-Wien-Budapest

(8–10 October 1965)
European Rally Championship, Round 12

Pos.	No.	Driver/Codriver	Nat.	Car	Cat.	Result
1	72	Rauno Aaltonen/Tony Ambrose	SF/GB	Mini Cooper S	II	2070,0
2	49	Herbert Tunner/Helmut Hick	A	Ford Cortina GT	II	2070,0
3	30	Arnulf Pilhatsch/Peter Lederer	A	BMW 1800TI	II	2043,3
4	102	Sobiesław Zasada/K. Osinski	PL	Steyr-Puch 650TR	II	2043,3
5	19	Bruno Martellanz/Herbert Kohlweiss	A	Alfa Romeo GSZ	III	2036,3
6	3	Wilfried Gass/Willi Bretthauer	D	Porsche 911	III	2034,3
7	32	Giorgio Pianta/Luciano Lombardini	I	Lancia Flavia Sport Zagato	II	2012,8
8	93	Kurt Otto/Wolfgang Strehlow	DDR	AWE Wartburg	II	2009,3
9	104	Günther Schörn/Hans Pail	A	Steyr-Puch 650TR	II	2005,7
10	16	Max Füss/Adolf Wendlinger	D	Porsche 1600SC	III	1991,6

Royal Automobile Club International Rally of Great Britain

(20–26 November 1965)
European Rally Championship, Round 13

Pos.	No.	Driver/Codriver	Nat.	Car	Cat	Result
1	5	Rauno Aaltonen/Tony Ambrose	SF/GB	Mini Cooper S	4	531m23s
2	5	Timo Mäkinen/Paul Easter	SF/GB	Austin Healey 3000	13	534m31s
3	77	Jerry Larsson/Lars Lundblad	S	Saab Sport	2	537m18s
4	7	Erik Carlsson/Torsten Åman	S	Saab 96 Sport	9	540m33s
5	51	Roy Fidler/Alan Taylor	GB	Triumph 2000	6	554m16s
6	44	Jorma Lusenius/Mike Wood	SF/GB	Mini Cooper S	10	560m28s
7	186	Lars-Ingvar Ytterbring/R. Håkansson	S	Mini Cooper S	4	561m04s
8	58	Sten Lundin/Nils Björk	S	Volkswagen 1600	5	576m53s
9	124	Bengt Karlsson/Lars Eriksson	S	Volkswagen 1600	5	577m06s
10	15	Pat Moss-Carlsson/E. Nyström	GB/S	Saab 96 Sport	9	577m27s

1966

35ème Rallye Automobile Monte-Carlo

(14–22 January 1966)
European Rally Championship, Round 1, Groups I & III

Pos.	No.	Driver/Codriver	Nat.	Car	Cat.	Result
1	195	Pauli Toivonen/Esko Mikander	SF	Citroën DS21	I	13.194,00
2	60	René Trautmann/J.-Pierre Hanrioud	F	Lancia Flavia	I	13.240,00
3	140	Ove Andersson/Rolf Dahlgren	S	Lancia Flavia	I	13.278,00
4	21	Bob Neyret/Jacques Terramorsi	F	Citroën DS21	I	13.560,00
5	59	Leo Cella/Luciano Lombardini	I	Lancia Fulvia Coupé	I	13.572,00
6	231	Rob Slotemaker/Rob Gorris	NL	BMW 1800	I	13.619,00
7	192	Guy Verrier/Bernard Pasquier	F	Citroën DS21	I	13.620,00
8	137	Jorma Lusenius/Anssi Järvi	SF	Lancia Fulvia Coupé	I	13.741,00
9	35	Claude Laurent/Jacques Marché	F	Citroën DS21	I	14.040,00
10	177	Geoff Mabbs/Jim Porter	GB	Rover 2000 P6	I	14.357,00

XVII KAK-Rallyt

(9–13 February 1966)
European Rally Championship, Round 2, Groups I & II

Pos.	No.	Driver/Codriver	Nat.	Car	Cat.	Result
1	19	Åke Andersson/Sven-Olof Svedberg	S	Saab 96 V4	II	44,754
2	17	Simo Lampinen/Bo Olsson	SF/S	Saab	II	45,003
3	27	Tom Trana/Solve Andreasson	S	Volvo	II	45,335
4	84	Carl Orrenius/Gustav Schröderheim	S	Saab	II	45,916
5	115	Lillebror Nasenius/Bengt Frodin	S	Opel Rekord	I	46,227
6	97	Arne Hallgren/Egon Forslund	S	Saab	II	46,734
7	6	Olof Karlberg/Sven Simonsson	S	Volvo	II	47,242
8	47	Hans Lund/Björn Wahlgren	S	Saab	II	47,541
9	66	Curt Johansson/Roland Ånöstam	S	Volkswagen 1600TL	II	47,963
10	26	Vic Elford/John Davenport	GB	Ford Lotus Cortina	I	47,997

6° Rallye dei Fiore di Sanremo

(24–26 February 1966)
European Rally Championship, Round 3, Groups II & III

Pos.	No.	Driver/Codriver	Nat.	Car	Cat.	Result
1	36	Leo Cella/Luciano Lombardini	I	Lancia Fulvia Coupé HF	III	1.030.437
2	57	Robert Buchet/Günther Klass	D	Porsche	III	1.049.402
3	22	Ove Andersson/Rolf Dahlgren	S	Lancia Fulvia Coupe HF	III	1.054.747
4	47	Sobiesław Zasada/Kazimierz Osinski	I	Steyr Puch 650TR	II	1.121.682
5	62	Wilfried Gass/Gerd Frey	D	Porsche	III	1.123.102
6	55	Sergio Bettoja/Pietro Bulla	I	Porsche 911	III	1.196.588
7	68	Giovanni Vacca/Walter Cordaro	I	Renault R8 Gordini	II	1.323.485
8	106	Sergio Barbasio/Giuseppe Giacomini	I	Renault R8 Gordini	II	1.361.643
9	88	Dieter Lambart/Heinrich Heinz	D	Opel Kadett Coupe 1100	I	1.559.915
10	135	Alberto Girardini/Gianfranco Briani	I	Lancia Fulvia Coupe HF	III	1.561.310

18e Internationale Tulpenrallye

(25–30 April 1966)
European Rally Championship, Round 4, Groups I & II

Pos.	No.	Driver/Codriver	Nat.	Car	Cat.	Result
1	89	Rauno Aaltonen/Henry Liddon	SF/GB	Mini Cooper S	II	3880,5
2	60	Vic Elford/John Davenport	GB	Ford Lotus Cortina	II	3925,4
3	1	Peter Harper/Robin Turvey	GB	Sunbeam Tiger	III	3962,5
4	42	Wilfried Gass/Willi Bretthauer	D	Porsche 911	III	3994,1
5	59	Arnaldo Cavallari/Dante Salvay	I	Alfa Romeo GTA	II	4003,0
6	43	Gijs van Lennep/David van Lennep	NL	Porsche 911	III	4027,5
7	26	Tom Trana/Lennart Berggren	S	Volvo 122S	II	4116,4
8	10	Nicolas Koob/Armand Wies	L	BMW 1800	II	4147,2
9	100	Timo Mäkinen/Paul Easter	SF/GB	Mini Cooper S	I	4171,4
10	2	John Kennerley/Digby Martland	GB	Shelby American 350GT	III	4176,8

37. Internationale Österreichische Alpenfahrt

(12–15 May 1966)
European Rally Championship, Round 5, Groups I & III

Pos.	No.	Driver/Codriver	Nat.	Car	Cat.	Result
1	58	Paddy Hopkirk/Ron Crellin	GB	Mini Cooper S	II	2500,00
2	6	Günther Wallrabenstein/Ernst Müller	D	Porsche 911	III	2443,88
3	33	Alfred Burkhardt/Franz Koch-Bodes	D	Ford Taunus 20M	II	2218,87
4	51	Jochi Kleint/Günther Klapproth	D	Ford Taunus 20M	II	2102,30
5	70	A.Buchbauer/Gerald Brandstetter	A	Renault R8 Gordini	II	2115,97
6	44	Helmut Klomfar/Ernst Marquart	A	Volvo 122S	II	2170,16
7	88	Václav Bobek/Vojtěch Rieger	CS	Škoda 1000MB	II	2114,72
8	12	Gernot Fischer/Franz Mauerhofer	A	MGB	III	2322,83
9	76	Alfred Gaberszik/G.Gaberszik	A	Saab 96	II	2155,00
10	82	Oldrich Horsak/Miroslav Fousek	CS	Škoda 1000MB	II	2101,18

14th Rally Acropolis

(26–29 May 1966)
European Rally Championship, Round 6

Pos.	No.	Driver/Codriver	Nat.	Car	Cat.	Result
1	78	Bengt Söderström/Gunnar Palm	S	Ford Lotus Cortina		106,062
2	44	Roger Clark/Brian Melia	GB	Ford Lotus Cortina		219,899
3	67	Paddy Hopkirk/Ron Crellin	GB	Mini Cooper S		641,574
4	9	Ove Andersson/Rolf Dahlgren	S	Lancia Fulvia Coupe	III	657,158
5	88	Carl Orrenius/Gustaf Schroderheim	S	Saab Monte Carlo		769,023
6	87	Sobiesław Zasada/Longin Bielak	PL	Steyr-Puch		921,800
7	95	Hans Lund/Björn Wahlgren	S	Saab Monte Carlo		954,909
8	1	Peter Harper/Ian Hall	GB	Sunbeam Tiger	III	957,300
9	20	Joginder Singh/Jan-Erik Virgin	EAK/S	Volvo 122S		2080,680
10	82	Timo Mäkinen/Paul Easter	SF/GB	Mini Cooper S		2158,386

34ème Rallye International de Genève

(9–12 June 1966)
European Rally Championship, Round 7

Pos.	No.	Driver/Codriver	Nat.	Car	Cat.	Result
1	70	Gilbert Staepelaere/André Aerts	B	Ford Lotus Cortina	I	228
2	72	Tony Fall/Henry Liddon	GB	Mini Cooper S	I	278
3		Jean-Claude Ogier/Bernard Ogier	F	Panhard 24CT	I	296
4		Guy Verrier/Jean-Claude Syda	F	Citroën DS21	I	317
5		Lucien Bianchi/"Vic"	B	Citroën DS21	I	395
6		Gerard Larousse/Simone Petit	F	NSU Prinz 1000	I	438
7		Jean-Jacques Thuner/John Gretener	CH	Triumph Spitfire	III	493
8	30	Patrick Lier/Formige	CH	Hillman Rally Imp	III	737
9	43	Charles Ramu-Caccia/B. Mauris	CH	Alfa Romeo GTA	II	755
10		Georges Theiler/Erich Bechtel	CH	Mini Cooper S	I	900

7th Rallye Vltava

(1–3 July 1966)
European Rally Championship, Round 8

Pos.	No.	Driver/Codriver	Nat.	Car	Cat.	Result
1	75	Rauno Aaltonen/Henry Liddon	SF/GB	Mini Cooper S	II	8320
2	15	Bengt Söderström/Gunnar Palm	S	Ford Lotus Cortina		8373
3	77	Timo Mäkinen/Paul Easter	SF/GB	Mini Cooper S		8377
4	16	Sobieław Zasada/Zenon Leszczuk	PL	Mini Cooper S	I	8761
5	29	Pat Moss-Carlsson/E. Nyström	GB/S	Saab	II	9098
6	18	Krzystorf Komornicki/L. Jaworowicz	PL	Mini Cooper S		9557
7	5	Jaroslav Bobek/Leo Hnatevič	CS	Škoda 1000MB	I	9670
8	101	Zdenek Cechmánek/Jiri Pelucha	CS	Tatra T2 603		9797
9	102	Alois Mark/Bohuslav Stiborek	CS	Tatra T2 603		9918
10	22	Dieter Lambart/Wolf Zink	D	Opel Kadett Coupe		10134

XXVI Rajd Polski

(3–6 August 1966)
European Rally Championship, Round 10

Pos.	No.	Driver/Codriver	Nat.	Car	Cat.	Result
1	56	Tony Fall/Attis Krauklis	GB	Mini Cooper S 970	II	5028,07
2	37	Timo Mäkinen/Paul Easter	SF/GB	Mini Cooper S 1275	II	5102,46
3	45	Sobiesław Zasada/Ewa Zasada	PL	Steyr Puch 660 TR	II	5140,95
4	38	Roger Clark/Brian Melia	GB	Ford Lotus Cortina	II	5702,00
5	49	Brian Culcheth/Johnstone Syer	GB	Mini Cooper S 1275	II	7971,54
6	66	Vladimir Krelina/Karel Stehlik	CS	Skoda 1000MB	II	7977,55
7	10	Andrzej Nytko/Jan Wojczaczek	PL	Fiat 1300	I	8454,21
8	69	Kazimierz Jaromin/Janusz Zemła	PL	Skoda 1000MB	I	9070,05
9	67	Zdenek Kec/Vaclav Per	CS	Skoda 1000MB	II	10009,12
10	20	Jan Karel/Antoni Weiner	PL	Volvo 122S	I	11484,46

27ème Coupe des Alpes

(5–10 September 1966)
European Rally Championship, Round 12

Pos.	No.	Driver/Codriver	Nat.	Car	Cat.	Result
1	61	Jean Rolland/Gabriel Augias	F	Alfa Romeo Giulia GTA	II	3h23m55.8s
2	54	Roger Clark/Brian Melia	GB	Ford Lotus Cortina	II	3h25m02.4s
3	62	Rauno Aaltonen/Henry Liddon	SF/GB	Mini Cooper S	II	3h26m29.4s
4	8	Jean-Francois Piot/J.-François Jacob	F	Renault R8 Gordini	VI	3h28m11.6s
5	53	Henri Greder/Gilbert Staepelaere	F/B	Ford Lotus Cortina	II	3h29m24.5s
6	90	Gunther Klass/Rolf Wütherlich	D	Porsche 911	III	3h38m16.6s
7	69	Noel Labaune/François Paul-Etienne	F	Alfa Romeo Giulia GTA	II	3h38m58.0s
8	26	Lucien Bianchi/Christian Delferrier	B	Citroën DS21		3h42m51.2s
9	56	Jean-Pierre Nicolas/Claude Roure	F	Renault R8 Gordini	II	3h47m15.2s
10	31	Bob Neyret/Jacques Terramorsi	F	Citroën DS21	I	3h48m23.0s

Royal Automobile Club International Rally of Great Britain

(19–23 November 1966)
European Rally Championship, Round 14

Pos.	No.	Driver/Codriver	Nat.	Car	Cat.	Result
1	11	Bengt Söderström/Gunnar Palm	S	Ford Lotus Cortina	II	475m15s
2	66	Harry Källström/Ragnvald Håkansson	S	Mini Cooper S	II	488m50s
3	19	Tom Trana/Sölve Andreasson	S	Volvo	II	489m50s
4	18	Rauno Aaltonen/Henry Liddon	SF/GB	Mini Cooper S	II	490m22s
5	21	Tony Fall/Mike Wood	GB	Mini Cooper S	II	495m17s
6	60	Jars Damberg/Rolf Riggare	S	Renault R8 Gordini	III	496m34s
7	17	Ove Andersson/John Davenport	S/GB	Lancia Fulvia Coupé 1.2	II	498m14s
8	69	Anders Gullberg/Lars Helmér	S	Opel Rekord 1900	II	502m34s
9	25	Pat Moss-Carlsson/E. Nyström	GB/S	Saab Sport	II	503m12s
10	96	Sylvia Österberg/Inga-lill Edenring	S	Renault R8 Gordini	III	504m04s

36ème Rallye Automobile Monte-Carlo

(13–16 January 1967)
European Rally Championship, Round 1

Pos.	No.	Driver/Codriver	Nat.	Car	Cat.	Result
1	177	Rauno Aaltonen/Henry Liddon	SF/GB	Mini Cooper S	II	11.491,92
2	39	Ove Andersson/John Davenport	S/GB	Lancia Fulvia Coupé	II	11.503,36
3	219	Vic Elford/David Stone	GB	Porsche 911S	III	11.556,16
4	34	Leo Cella/Luciano Lombardi	I	Lancia Fulvia Coupé	II	11.564,08
5	2	Sandro Munari/Georges Harris	I/B	Lancia Fulvia Coupé	II	11.651,20
6	205	Paddy Hopkirk/Ron Crellin	GB	Mini Cooper S	II	11.673,20
7	23	Jean-François Piot/M.Karaky	F	Renault R8 Gordini	II	11.718,24
8	79	Berndt Jansson/Miss T.Senysmann	S	Renault R8 Gordini	II	11.960,08
9	16	Jean Vinatier/Claude Roure	F	Renault R8 Gordini	II	12.006,72
10	32	Raymond Joss/Tony Fall	GB	Mini Cooper S	II	12.117,20

Internationale AvD-Rallye Nordrhein-Westfalen - "Deutschland-Rallye"

(14–17 July 1966)
European Rally Championship, Round 9

Pos.	No.	Driver/Codriver	Nat.	Car	Cat.	Result
1	4	Günther Klass/Rolf Wütherich	D	Porsche 911	III	2260,3
2	48	Arnaldo Cavallari/Dante Salvay	I	Alfa Romeo GTA	II	2525,9
3	33	Joachim Springer/Dieter Schey	D	BMW 2000TI		2700,6
4	55	Sobiesław Zasada/K. Osinski	PL	Steyr-Puch 650TR	II	2931,7
5	18	Karl-Heinz Panowitz/Rainer Strunz	D	NSU Wankel Spyder	III	3028,4
6		Theo Klinck/Hans-Christoph Mehmel	D	Glas 1300GT	III	3324,9
7		Heinz Liedl/H.Häring	D	Steyr-Puch 650TR		3564,6
8		Peter Roeder/Jan Schmitz-Gilles	D	NSU Wankel Spyder	III	3600,5
9	47	Norbert Supper/Hannelore Wirth	D	Glas 1304TS	II	3803,6
10	3	Rolf Lieb/G.Bührich	D	Porsche 911	III	3812,2

Rally of the Thousand lakes - Jyäskylän Suurajot 1966

(19–21 August 1966)
European Rally Championship, Round 11

Pos.	No.	Driver/Codriver	Nat.	Car	Cat.	Result
1	45	Timo Mäkinen/Pekka Keskitalo	SF	Mini Cooper S	II	8368
2	76	Tom Trana/Sölve Andreasson	S	Volvo 122S	II	8484
3	43	Rauno Aaltonen/Väinö Nurmimaa	SF	Mini Cooper S	II	8561
4	87	Risto Virtapuro/Alfons Strengell	SF	Volvo 122S	II	8675
5	19	Simo Lampinen/Klaus Sohlberg	SF	Saab 96 Sport	II	8726
6	27	Jorma Lusenius/Klaus Lehto	SF	Mini Cooper S	II	8823
7	39	Lars-Ingvar Ytterbring/Bo Gustafsson	S	Mini Cooper S	II	8834
8	41	Bernt Jansson/Eric Petterson	S	Renault R8 Gordini	II	8866
9	47	Atso Aho/Juha Raikamo	SF	Mini Cooper S	II	8946
10	92	Osmo Mäkelä/Timo Mäkelä	SF	Volvo PV544 Sport	II	8976

4. Internationale 3-Städte-Rallye - München-Wien-Budapest

(7–9 October 1966)
European Rally Championship, Round 13

Pos.	No.	Driver/Codriver	Nat.	Car	Cat.	Result
1	57	Timo Mäkinen/Paul Easter	SF/GB	Mini Cooper S	II	3253,2
2	114	Leo Cella/Luciano Lombardini	I	Lancia Fulvia Coupé	II	3397,0
3	111	Lilebror Nassenius/Fergus Sager	S	Opel Rekord 1900	I	3446,0
4	62	Arnaldo Cavallari/Dante Salvay	I	Alfa Romeo GTA	II	3446,9
5	6	Wilfried Gass/Gerd Frey	D	Porsche 911	III	3528,2
6	49	Arnulf Pilhatsch/Gustav Hruschka	A	BMW 1800 TI	II	3532,6
7	7	Max Füss/Adolf Wendlinger	D	Porsche 911	III	3587,9
8	119	Gilbert Staepelaere/A. Aerts	B	Ford Lotus Cortina	I	3614,2
9	82	Pat Moss-Carlsson/E. Nyström	GB/S	Saab 96 Sport	II	3663,0
10	4	Walter Pöltinger/J.-Hans Hartinger	A	Porsche 911	III	3696,4

XVIII KAK-Rallyt

(9–13 February 1967)
European Rally Championship, Round 2

Pos.	No.	Driver/Codriver	Nat.	Car	Cat.	Result
1	20	Bengt Söderström/Gunnar Palm	S	Ford Lotus Cortina	II	43726,2
2	32	Simo Lampinen/Torsten Palm	SF/S	Saab V4	II	44440,6
3	26	Rauno Aaltonen/Henry Liddon	SF/GB	Mini Cooper S	II	44720,5
4	34	Ove Eriksson/Hans Johansson	S	Opel Rekord 1900	II	45718,9
5	69	Lillebror Nasenius/Bengt Frodin	S	Opel 1900	I	46105,6
6	21	Pauli Toivonen/Jyrki Ahava	SF	Lancia Fulvia	II	46514,0
7	63	Olle Bromark/Rolf Eriksson	S	Saab V4	I	46982,7
8	60	Leif Nilsson/Kalle Riggare	S	Porsche 912		46986,3
9	68	Bertil Söderström/Rune Olsson	S	Opel 1900	I	47036,4
10	64	Anders Gullberg/Leif Wahlin	S	Opel 1900	I	47050,6

1967–1968

7° Rallye dei Fiore di Sanremo

(23–26 February 1967)
European Rally Championship, Round 3

Pos.	No.	Driver/Codriver	Nat.	Car	Cat.	Result
1	97	Jean-François Piot/Claude Roure	F	Renault R8 Gordini	II	830,418
2	67	Paddy Hopkirk/Ron Crellin	GB	Mini Cooper S	II	845,631
3	92	Ove Andersson/John Davenport	S/GB	Lancia Fulvia Coupé	II	875,243
4	82	Tony Fall/Mike Wood	GB	Mini Cooper S	II	895,377
5	84	Vic Elford/David Stone	GB	Lancia Fulvia Coupé	II	1044,223
6	40	Jean-Claude Ogier/Lucette Pointet	F	Citroën DS21	I	1044,512
7	70	Leo Cella/Luciano Lombardini	I	Lancia Fulvia Coupé	II	1045,936
8	73	Giulio Bisulli/Luigi Andreucci	I	Lancia Fulvia Coupé	II	1271,177
9	96	Zeffirino Filippi/Alberto Del Pozzo	I	Renault R8 Gordini	II	1374,405
10	51	Brian Culcheth/Johnstone Syer	GB	Mini Cooper S	II	1424,576

20ème Rallye Lyon Charbonnières - Stuttgart Solitude

(17–19 March 1967)
European Rally Championship, Round 4

Pos.	No.	Driver/Codriver	Nat.	Car	Cat.	Result
1	60	Vic Elford/David Stone	GB	Porsche 911S	III	3h 31m 30.0s
2	61	Jean-Pierre Hanrioud/Xavier Foucher	F	Porsche 911S	III	3h 47m 45.0s
3	65	Sobiesław Zasada/Eugeniusz Pach	PL	Porsche 911S	III	4h 01m 47.4s
4	59	Jean-Pierre Gaban/J.-M. Jacquemin	B	Porsche 911S	III	4h 02m 04.9s
5	39	Bob Neyret/Jacques Terramorsi	F	Citroën DS21	I	4h 10m 25.6s
6	40	Jean-Claude Ogier/Lucette Pointet	F	Citroën DS21	I	4h 12m 25.6s
7	136	René Trautmann/Philippe Leyssieux	F	Lancia Fulvia Coupé HF	V	4h 20m 03.6s
8	54	Patrick Lier/Silvio Vaglio	CH	Sunbeam Imp	III	4h 20m 55.7s
9	102	Fernand Schligler/Gérard Couzian	F	Renault R8 Gordini	II	4h 21m 44.0s
10	145	Sylvain Garant/Branco Stoikovitch	F	Porsche 911	V	4h 22m 46.0s

7. Internationale Pneumant Rallye

(6–9 April 1967)
European Rally Championship, Round 5

Pos.	No.	Driver/Codriver	Nat.	Car	Cat.	Result
1	39	Günter Rüttinger/Günter Bork	DDR	Wartburg 353	I	58,28
2		Kurt Otto/Wolfgang Strehlow	DDR	Wartburg 353	II	96,05
3		Kurt Rüdiger/Egon Culmbacher	DDR	Wartburg 353		97,83
4		Kenneth Gram Nielsen/M. Sörensen	DK	Mini Cooper		132,05
5		Hans Ullmann/Werner Lange	DDR	Trabant 501	II	154,85
6		Antoni Weiner/Jan Karel	PL	Steyr-Puch 650TR	II	167,40
7		Hans Beck/Herbert Heuser	D	Opel Kadett	I	168,55
8		Dieter Lambart/Hans Vögt	D	Opel Kadett		184,20
9		Jan Andersen/Nielsen	DK	Fiat 1500		196,64
10		Henryk Ruciński/A. Wędrychowski	PL	Volkswagen 1600		224,66

19e Internationale Tulpenrallye

(24–29 April 1967)
European Rally Championship, Round 6

Pos.	No.	Driver/Codriver	Nat.	Car	Cat.	Result
1	1	Vic Elford/David Stone	GB	Porsche 911S	III	3432,0
2	64	Timo Mäkinen/Paul Easter	SF/GB	Mini Cooper S	II	3478,3
3	65	Rauno Aaltonen/Henry Liddon	SF/GB	Mini Cooper S	II	3491,4
4	11	Björn Waldegård/Lars Helmer	S	Porsche 911	III	3495,7
5	66	Julian Vernaeve/Mike Wood	B/GB	Mini Cooper S	II	3558,5
6	14	Wilfried Gass/Gert Frey	A	Porsche 911	II	3579,8
7	93	David Friswell/Chris Nash	GB	Lotus Elan	III	3787,7
8	68	Alfred Krause/Jean Brecheisen	F	Renault R8 Gordini	II	3834,7
9	16	Rob Slotemaker/Rob Gorris	NL	BMW 2000TI	II	3862,4
10	89	Peter Harper/David Pollard	GB	Sumbeam Rally Imp	III	3916,2

38. Internationale Österreichische Alpenfahrt

(9–11 May 1967)
European Rally Championship, Round 7

Pos.	No.	Driver/Codriver	Nat.	Car	Cat.	Result
1	2	Sobiesław Zasada/Jerzy Dobrzański	PL	Porsche 911S	III	7378,4
2	35	Lasse Jönsson/Lasse Eriksson	S	Saab 96 V4	II	7550,6
3	22	Richard Bochnicek/Günther Pfisterer	A	Citroën DS21	II	7616,3
4	23	Dieter Lambart/Hans Vögt	D	Opel Rekord	II	7618,2
5	16	Klaus Reichel/Peter Pohl	D	BMW 2000 TI	II	7790,0
6	26	Rudolf Schachinger/Manfred Stepany	A	Volvo 122S	II	7902,8
7	48	Walter Roser/Jörg Andrieu	A	Renault R8 Gordini	II	7943,1
8	34	Arne Hallgren/Stig Erikson	S	Saab 96 V4	II	7954,7
9	21	Heinz Weiner/Judith Loos	A	Citroën DS21	II	7964,4
10	31	Loisl Weiner/Antonia Weiner	A	Glas 1304TS	II	7994,6

15th Rally Acropolis

(25–28 May 1967)
European Rally Championship, Round 8

Pos.	No.	Driver/Codriver	Nat.	Car	Cat.	Result
1	89	Paddy Hopkirk/Ron Crellin	GB	Mini Cooper S	II	145,989
2	39	Ove Andersson/John Davenport	S/GB	Lancia Fulvia Coupé HF	III	215,622
3	87	Bengt Söderström/Gunnar Palm	S	Ford Lotus Cortina	II	262,100
4	25	Arnulf Pilhatsch/J.-Hans Hartinger	A	BMW 2000TI	II	2336,123
5	33	Johnny Pesmazoglou/"Thor"	GR	Opel 1900	II	2383,894
6	67	Raimo Halm/A.Virtanen	SF	Datsun 1600SSS	II	2775,228
7	75	Hans Laine/Anssi Järvi	SF	Datsun 1600SSS	II	3111,299
8	18	Rune Larsson/K. Jonrup	S	Volvo 122S	II	3161,791
9	17	Jan-Eric Lundgren/Lasse Ericksson	S	Volvo 122S	II	3222,280
10	76	Eberhart Schmitthelm/W. Geltermeier	D	BMW 1600	II	3383,384

35ème Rallye International de Genève

(15–18 June 1967)
European Rally Championship, Round 9

Pos.	No.	Driver/Codriver	Nat.	Car	Cat.	Result
1	4	Vic Elford/David Stone	GB	Porsche 911S		107
2	20	Sandro Munari/Georges Harris	I/B	Lancia Fulvia Coupé HF		167
3	79	Tony Fall/Mike Wood	GB	Mini Cooper S		205
4	5	Jean-Pierre Hanrioud/J.- Claude Syda	F	Porsche 911S		358
5	80	Julien Vernaeve/Henry Liddon	B/GB	Mini Cooper S		401
6		Sobiesław Zasada/Jerry Dobrzanski	PL	Porsche 912		547
7		Claude Haldi/Guido Haberthur	CH	Porsche 912		783
8		Dieter Lambart/Hans Vögt	D	Opel Kadett		978
9		Bob Neyret/Jacques Terramorsi	F	Citroën DS21		1096
10		David Friswell/Robin Morris	GB	Mini Cooper S		1097

8th Rallye Vltava

(6–9 July 1967)
European Rally Championship, Round 10

Pos.	No.	Driver/Codriver	Nat.	Car	Cat.	Result
1		Erik Carlsson/Torsten Åman	S	Saab 96 V4		1818
2		Sobiesław Zasada/Jerry Dobrzanski	PL	Porsche 912		1860
3		Václav Bobek/Jaroslav Vylít	CS	Škoda 1000 MB		1963
4		Pat Moss-Carlsson/E. Nystrom	GB/S	Saab 96 V4		2096
5		Jaroslav Bobek/Leo Hnatevič	CS	Škoda 1000 MB		2152
6		Vladimir Hubacek/Vojtech Rieger	CS	Renault R8 Gordini		2463
7		Dieter Lambart/Hans Vögt	D	Opel Kadett		2512
8		Zdenek Trybal/Petr Štefek	CS	Saab 850S		2524
9		Franz Galle/Jochen Müller	DDR	Trabant 601		2573
10		Eberhart Schmitthelm/W. Geltermeier	D	BMW 1602		2758

4. Internationale Donau Castrol Rallye

(19–22 July 1967)
European Rally Championship, Round 11

Pos.	No.	Driver/Codriver	Nat.	Car	Cat.	Result
1	5	Tony Fall/Mike Wood	GB	Austin 1800	V	6942
2	41	Jean Vinatier/Claude Roure	F	Renault R8 Gordini	II	6962
3	22	Günter Wallrabenstein/W. Bretthauer	A	Porsche 911	II	7083
4	21	Richard Bochnicek/Sepp Kernmayer	A	Citroën DS21	II	7095
5	74	Sobiesław Zasada/Ryszard Nowicki	PL	Porsche 912	I	7130
6	40	Gerhard Tusch/Georg Hopf	A	Renault R8 Gordini		7180
7	58	Joachim Springer/Gunther Brendel	D	BMW 1600 Alpina		7357
8	38	Egon Wittig/Harald Gottlieb	D	Alfa Romeo 1300GT	III	7521
9	1	Walter Pöltinger/Ernst Merinsky	A	Volkswagen 1500	V	7554
10	4	Josef Eschey/Dieter Eymann	D	BMW 2000ti		7632

XXVII Rajd Polski

(2–5 August 1967)
European Rally Championship, Round 12

Pos.	No.	Driver/Codriver	Nat.	Car	Cat.	Result
1	47	Sobiesław Zasada/Eva Zasada	PL	Porsche 912	I	6273,962
2	57	Lille-Bror Nasenius/Matti Vigren	S	Opel Rekord	I	6798,556
3	51	Krzystorf Komornicki/M. Wachowski	PL	BMW 1600	I	7709,653

No other finishers

XVI Jyväskylän Suurajot - Rally of the Thousand Lakes

(18–20 August 1967)
European Rally Championship, Round 13

Pos.	No.	Driver/Codriver	Nat.	Car	Cat.	Result
1	29	Timo Mäkinen/Pekka Keskitalo	SF	Mini Cooper S		6891,3
2	40	Simo Lampinen/Klaus Sohlberg	SF	Saab V4		6899,6
3	32	Hannu Mikkola/Anssi Järvi	SF	Volvo 122 S		6994,6
4	36	Ove Andersson/Agne Nordlund	S	Ford Lotus Cortina		7057,9
5	35	Bengt Söderström/Gunnar Palm	S	Ford Lotus Cortina		7067,4
6	39	Ove Eriksson/Lars-Erik Carlström	S	Opel Rekord		7151,6
7	37	Pauli Toivonen/Erkki Salonen	SF	Lancia		7186,8
8	28	Carl Orrenius/Gustaf Schröderheim	S	Saab V4		7210,9
9	30	Berndt Jansson/Eric Petterson	S	Renault R8 Gordini		7222,5
10	55	Håkan Lindberg/Bo Reinecke	S	Saab V4		7263,5

28ème Coupe des Alpes

(4–9 September 1967)
European Rally Championship, Round 14

Pos.	No.	Driver/Codriver	Nat.	Car	Cat.	Result
1	107	Paddy Hopkirk/Ron Crellin	GB	Mini Cooper S	VI	18h58m14.4
2	61	Bernard Consten/Jean-Claude Peray	F	Alfa Romeo GTA	V	19h08m53.1s
3	45	Jean-Claude Gamet/Michel Gamet	F	Alfa Romeo GTA	III	19h08m58.9s
4	101	Harry Källström/Gunnar Häggbom	S	Renault R8 Gordini	VI	19h10m03.5s
5	82	Jean-Claude Andruet/Maurice Gelin	F	Alpine Renault A110	III	19h40m06.8s
6	102	Sylvia Osterberg/Ingalill Edenring	S	Renault R8 Gordini	VI	19h57m34.1s
7	26	Bob Neyret/Jacques Terramorsi	F	Citroën DS21	I	20h15m34.3s
8	114	Jacques Rey/"Fanfan"	F	Porsche 911S	VI	20h24m16.2s
9	75	Andrew Cowan/Brian Coyle	GB	Sunbeam Imp	III	20h49m40.3s
10	77	Rosemary Smith/Margaret Lowrey	IRL/GB	Sunbeam Imp	III	20h50m38.9s

15° Rallye del R.A.C. de España

(22–24 September 1967)
European Rally Championship, Round 15

Pos.	No.	Driver/Codriver	Nat.	Car	Cat.	Result
1	15	Ove Andersson/John Davenport	S/GB	Lancia Fulvia Coupé Rallye HF	VI	419,608
2	12	Sandro Munari/Luciano Lombardini	I	Lancia Fulvia Coupé Rallye HF	II	414,343
3	9	Bernard Tramont/Ricardo Muñoz	E	Alpine-Renault A110 1300 S	III	401,752
4	25	Lille-Bror Nasenius/Matti Wigren	S	Opel Commodore GS	II	398,306
5	21	José Lampreia/Jorge Nascimento	P	Renault R8 Gordini	II	396,357
6	17	José Maria Juncadella/Molins	E	Mini Cooper S	II	394,800
7	14	Jorge de Bagratión/Jorge Bárcenas	E	Lancia Fulvia Coupé Rallye HF	III	390,198
8	4	Arnaldo Cavallari/Dante Salvay	I	Alfa Romeo Giulia GTA	II	386,894
9		Dieter Lambart/Hans Vögt	D	Opel Commodore GS	II	371,366
10	10	Henri Greder/M.-Claude Beaumont	F	Opel Commodore GS	II	366,596

5. Internationale 3-Städte-Rallye - München-Wien-Budapest

(5–7 October 1967)
European Rally Championship, Round 16

Pos.	No.	Driver/Codriver	Nat.	Car	Cat.	Result
1	36	Jean-François Piot/Jacques Brenaud	F	Renault R8 Gordini	II	4408,6
2	46	Bengt Söderström/Gunnar Palm	S	Ford Lotus Cortina	II	4481,3
3	1	Klaus Reisch/Helmut Schwab	A	MGB	III	4571,3
4	33	Lasse Jönsson/Lasse Ericsson	S	Saab 96 V4	II	4626,0
5	37	Walter Roser/Peter Jakl	A	Renault R8 Gordini	II	4688,8
6	19	Klaus Reichel/Peter Pohl	D	BMW 2000 TI	II	4720,8
7	16	Detlef Mühleck/Jens Loewenhardt	D	Porsche 911	II	4739,4
8	2	Gernot Fischer/D.Queissner	A	MGB	III	4752,1
9	15	Helmut Klomfar/Georg Hopf	A	Porsche 911	II	4797,4
10	9	Egon Wittig/Gerhard Gottlieb	D	Alfa Romeo Junior	III	4818,8

XIX KAK-Rallyt

(4–7 January 1968)
European Rally Championship for Manufacturers, Round 1

Pos.	No.	Driver/Codriver	Nat.	Car	Cat.	Result
1	8	Björn Waldegård/Lars Helmér	S	Porsche 911	II	66014
2	15	Tom Trana/Sölve Andreasson	S	Saab 96 V4	II	67655
3	9	Håkan Lindberg/Bo Reinicke	S	Saab 96 V4	II	67669
4	11	Bengt Söderström/Gunnar Palm	S	Ford Lotus Cortina	II	67675
5	42	Lillebror Nasenius/Bengt Frodin	S	Opel Rekord	I	69179
6	36	Jerry Larsson/Torsten Palm	S	Saab 96 V4	II	69910
7	27	Anders Kulläng/Donald Karlsson	S	Opel Rallye Kadett	II	70061
8	21	Per Eklund/Birger Petersson	S	Saab 96 V4	II	70297
9	18	Stig Blomqvist/Lennart Blomqvist	S	Saab 96 V4	II	70397
10	1	Jan Henriksson/Lars-Eric Carlström	S	Opel Rallye Kadett	II	70932

37ème Rallye Automobile Monte-Carlo

(19–27 January 1968)
European Rally Championship for Drivers, Round 1

Pos.	No.	Driver/Codriver	Nat.	Car	Cat.	Result
1	210	Vic Elford/David Stone	GB	Porsche 911T	III	14116
2	116	Pauli Toivonen/Martti Tiukkanen	SF	Porsche 911T	III	14192
3	18	Rauno Aaltonen/Henry Liddon	SF/GB	Mini Cooper S	II	14451
4	185	Tony Fall/Mike Wood	GB	Mini Cooper S	II	14635
5	87	Paddy Hopkirk/Ron Crellin	GB	Mini Cooper S	II	14652
6	8	Ove Andersson/John Davenport	S/GB	Lancia Fulvia Coupé HF	II	14666
7	89	Jean Vinatier/Jean-François Jacob	F	Alpine-Renault A110	III	14676
8	55	Leo Cella/Alcide Paganelli	I	Lancia Fulvia Coupé HF	II	14807
9	66	Hannu Mikkola/Anssi Järvi	SF	Datsun 2000	III	14948
10	219	Björn Waldegård/Lars Helmér	S	Porsche 911T	III	15098

8° Rallye di Sanremo

(6–8 March 1968)
European Rally Championship for Manufacturers, Round 2

Pos.	No.	Driver/Codriver	Nat.	Car	Cat.	Result
1	7	Pauli Toivonen/Martti Tiukkanen	SF	Porsche 911T	III	5893,0
2	5	Pat Moss-Carlsson/E. Nyström	GB/S	Lancia Fulvia Coupé HF	II	6138,0
3	16	Ove Andersson/John Davenport	S/GB	Ford Escort TC	III	6153,5
4	42	Harry Källström/Gunnar Häggbom	S	Lancia Fulvia Coupé HF	II	6170,5
5	18	Jean Vinatier/Jean-François Jacob	F	Alpine-Renault A110	III	6183,5
6	8	Luigi Taramazzo/Luigi Pescò	I	Porsche 911S	III	6277,0
7	45	Sergio Barbasio/Alessandro Merlano	I	Lancia Fulvia Coupé HF	II	6299,0
8	55	Arnaldo Cavallari/Dante Salvay	I	Lancia Fulvia Coupé HF	II	6454,3
9	53	Jerry Larsson/Fergus Sager	S	Lancia Fulvia Coupé HF	II	6510,7
10	12	Jean-François Piot/J.-Louis Marnat	F	Alpine-Renault A110	III	6865,5

8. Pneumant Rallye - "Rallye-DDR"

(4–7 April 1968)
European Rally Championship for Drivers, Round 2

Pos.	No.	Driver/Codriver	Nat.	Car	Cat.	Result
1	38	Pauli Toivonen/Urpo Vihervaara	SF	Porsche 911T	III	10,80
2	52	Sobiesław Zasada/Zenon Leszczuk	PL	Porsche 911L	II	32,20
3	117	Antoni Weiner/Jan Karel	PL	BMW 1600ti	II	114,38
4	20	Kenneth Gram Nielsen/M. Sörensen	DK	Mini Cooper S	II	122,68
5	48	Zdenek Treybal/Petr Štefek	CS	Saab 96 V4	II	130,94
6	95	Karl Syberg/Jörn Iversen	DK	Opel Commodore	II	148,49
7	26	Kurt Otto/Wolfgang Strehlow	DDR	Wartburg 353	II	158,56
8	56	Egon Culmbacher/Paul Thiel	DDR	Wartburg 353	II	161,56
9	49	Franz Galle/Jochen Müller	DDR	Trabant 601	II	162,72
10	103	Poul Fleming Madsen/Poul Larsen	DK	Ford Taunus 20M TS	II	166,36

20e Internationale Tulpenrallye

(22–27 April 1968)
European Rally Championship for Manufacturers, Round 3

Pos.	No.	Driver/Codriver	Nat.	Car	Cat.	Result
1	18	Roger Clark/Jim Porter	GB	Ford Escort TC	III	663,5
2	19	Ove Andersson/John Davenport	S/GB	Ford Escort TC	III	668,6
3	74	Julian Vernaeve/Mike Wood	B/GB	Mini Cooper S	II	790,0
4	2	Jorma Lusenius/Klaus Lehto	SF	Datsun Fairlady	II	809,7
5	30	Rob Slotemaker/Rob Jansen	NL	BMW 2002	II	825,2
6	47	Nicolas Koob/Aly Kridel	L	Alfa Romeo GTA	II	893,3
7	63	Anders Sigurdson/Ingvar Ström	S	Saab 96 V4	II	957,5
8	15	Gérard Larousse/Marcel Callewaert	F	Alpine-Renault A110	III	1070,6
9	36	Günther Kolwes/Holger Heine	D	Volvo 122S	II	1139,7
10	83	Marie-Claude Beaumont/C. Beckers	F	NSU 1200TT	II	1178,0

1968–1969

30. Rallye Wiesbaden - "Deutschland-Rallye"

(2–5 May 1968)
European Rally Championship for Drivers, Round 3

Pos.	No.	Driver/Codriver	Nat.	Car	Cat.	Result
1	1	Pauli Toivonen/Matti Kolari	SF	Porsche 911T	III	0,0
2		Sobiesław Zasada/F. Postawka	PL	Porsche 911L	I&II	0,0
3	14	Jean-François Piot/J. Rousselot	F	Alpine Renault A110	III	15,8
4	15	Jean Vinatier/Leo Garin	F	Alpine Renault A110	III	52,0
5		Vladimir Hubacek/Vojtech Rieger	CS	Renault R8 Gordini	I&II	79,2
6		Zdenek Kec/Mojmír Klíma	CS	Renault R8 Gordini	I&II	79,4
7		Dieter Lambart/Hans Vögt	D	Opel Commodore	I&II	82,4
8		Günter Wallrabenstein/Säckl	D	Porsche 911T	III	141,8
9		Antoni Weiner/Jan Karel	PL	BMW 1600TI	I&II	253,6
10		Dieter Eymann/Rainer Strunz	D	Alfa Romeo GTA	I&II	254,8

16th Rally Acropolis

(30 May–4 June 1968)
European Rally Championship for Drivers, Round 4

Pos.	No.	Driver/Codriver	Nat.	Car	Cat.	Result
1	30	Roger Clark/Jim Porter	GB	Ford Escort TC	II	140,240
2	23	Sobiesław Zasada/Jerzy Dobrzanski	PL	Porsche 911L	II	303,500
3	7	Pauli Toivonen/Matti Kolari	SF	Porsche 911T	III	318,006
4	32	Bengt Söderström/Gunnar Palm	S	Ford Escort TC	II	325,144
5	46	Rauno Aaltonen/Henry Liddon	SF/GB	Mini Cooper S	II	370,456
6	45	Harry Källström/Gunnar Haggböm	S	Lancia Fulvia Coupé HF	II	464,309
7	43	Amilcare Ballestrieri/David Stone	I/GB	Lancia Fulvia Coupé HF	II	932,246
8	41	Pat Moss-Carlsson/E. Nyström	GB/S	Lancia Fulvia Coupé HF	II	996,830
9	28	Ove Andersson/John Davenport	S/GB	Ford Escort TC	II	1065,228
10	16	Brian Culcheth/Mike Wood	GB	Morris 1800	II	2160,963

5. Internationale Donau-Rallye für Automobile

(17–20 July 1968)
European Rally Championship for Drivers, Round 5

Pos.	No.	Driver/Codriver	Nat.	Car	Cat.	Result
1	5	Pauli Toivonen/Martti Tiukkanen	SF	Porsche 911T	III	8112,8
2	18	Walter Pöltinger/Ernst Merinsky	A	Volvo 142S	II	9660,0
3	34	David Friswell/Robert Woods	GB	Mini Cooper S	II	9815,2
4	19	Wolfgang Levy/Alfred Gomoll	D	BMW 2002	II	9866,7
5	25	Carl Christian Schindler/E. Marquart	A	Volkswagen 1500 Sport	II	10141,4
6	6	Günther Breyer/Helmut Göbel	A	Porsche 911T	III	10211,5
7	22	Günther Bohrn/Hans Gubler	A	Opel Kadett	II	10342,2
8	30	Włodzimierz Markowski/S. Delka	PL	Porsche 912	II	10362,2
9	24	Titus Majer-Kajbic/B. Köstenberger	A	BMW 2000Tilux	II	10626,4
10	52	Egon Culmbacher/G, Zimmermann	DDR	AWE Wartburg	II	10662,5

XVII Jyväskylän Suurajot - Rally of the Thousand Lakes

(16–18 August 1968)
European Rally Championship for Drivers, Round 6

Pos.	No.	Driver/Codriver	Nat.	Car	Cat.	Result
1	38	Hannu Mikkola/Anssi Järvi	SF	Ford Escort TC	II	10709,0
2	43	Simo Lampinen/Klaus Sohlberg	SF	Saab 96 V4	II	10919,4
3	44	Bengt Söderström/Gunnar Palm	S	Ford Escort TC	II	10947,4
4	37	Atso Aho/Antti Kytölä	SF	Mini Cooper S	II	11092,6
5	65	Pertti Kärhä/Heimo Poutala	SF	Isuzu Bellet	II	12289,6
6	58	Eero Soutulahti/Aimo Wirtanen	SF	Volvo Amazon	II	11440,7
7	31	Jari Vilkas/Seppo Soini	SF	Saab 96 V4	II	11445,9
8	54	Hannu Kulovesi/Timo Alanen	SF	Volkswagen	II	11462,9
9	63	Heikki Majander/Mauri Jokela	SF	Volvo 122S	II	11617,5
10	56	Seppo Utriainen/Juhani Jokonen	SF	Volvo 122S	II	11707,6

36ème Rallye International de Genève

(17–20 October 1968)
European Rally Championship for Drivers, Round 7

Pos.	No.	Driver/Codriver	Nat.	Car	Cat.	Result
1	14	Pauli Toivonen/Urpo Vihervaara	SF	Porsche 911T	III	4170
2		Lucien Bianchi/J.-Marie Jacquemin	B	Alfa Romeo GTA	II	4368
3		Guy Verrier/Francis Murac	F	Alfa Romeo GTA	II	4432
4		Gilbert Staepelaere/André Aerts	B	Ford Escort TC		4452
5		Arthur Blank/Freddy Karrer	CH	Porsche 911L		4596
6		Jean-Jacques Cochet/J.-Pierre Feuz	CH	Porsche 911T		4666
7		Bob Wollek/Jean-Pierre Delannoy	F	Renault R8 Gordini	II	4677
8		Claude Haldi/Eric Chapuis	CH	Porsche 911L		4719
9		Jean-Jacques Thuner/John Gretener	CH	Triumph TR5		4738
10		Noël Labaune/Rodet	F	Alfa Romeo GTA		4844

39. Internationale Österreichische Alpenfahrt

(15–19 May 1968)
European Rally Championship for Manufacturers, Round 4

Pos.	No.	Driver/Codriver	Nat.	Car	Cat.	Result
1	35	Bengt Söderström/Gunnar Palm	S	Ford Escort TC	II	4937,9
2	57	Hannu Mikkola/Anssi Järvi	SF	Lancia Fulvia Coupé HF	II	4952,5
3	60	Walter Roser/Roman Loibnegger	A	Renault R8 Gordini	II	5097,5
4	20	Arnulf Pilhatsch/Gustav Hruschka	A	BMW 2000	II	5140,5
5	58	Alcide Paganelli/Mario Manucci	I	Lancia Fulvia Coupé HF	II	5408,4
6	46	Hermann Bennier/Peter Urbanek	A	BMW 1600TI	II	5425,4
7	21	Klaus Reichel/Peter Pohl	A	BMW 2000TI	II	5514,7
8	24	Walter Pöltinger/Ernst Merinsky	A	Volvo 142S	II	5516,0
9	36	Tom Trana/Sölve Andreasson	S	Saab 96 V4	II	5562,1
10	10	Otto Karger/Peter Wessely	A	Matra Djet 6	III	5565,8

9th Rallye Vltava

(5–7 July 1968)
European Rally Championship for Manufacturers, Round 5

Pos.	No.	Driver/Codriver	Nat.	Car	Cat.	Result
1	8	Jean Vinatier/Marcel Callewaert	F	Alpine-Renault A110	III	6230
2	5	Simo Lampinen/Torsten Palm	SF/S	Saab 96 V4	II	6526
3	29	Gilbert Staepelaere/André Aerts	B	Ford Escort TC	II	6577
4	11	Håkan Lindberg/Bo Reinicke	S	Saab 96 V4	II	6595
5	3	Jean-François Piot/Jean Todt	F	Alpine-Renault A110	III	6638
6	32	Hermann Bennier/Berndt Bartha	A	BMW 1600TI	II	7304
7	14	Zdeněk Kec/Mojmir Klima	CS	Renault R8 Gordini	II	7542
8	17	Milan Žid/Josef Čech	CS	Škoda 1100 MB	II	8339
9	103	Franz Galle/Jochen Mülle	DDR	Trabant 601	II	8846
10	100	Eberhard Asmus/Helmut Piehler	DDR	Trabant 601	II	9210

XXVIII Rajd Polski

(31 July–4 August 1968)
European Rally Championship for Manufacturers, Round 6

Pos.	No.	Driver/Codriver	Nat.	Car	Cat.	Result
1	42	Krzysztof Komornicki/Z. Wiśniowski	PL	Renault R8 Gordini		13345,05
2	38	Zdeněk Kec/Mojmir Klima	CS	Renault R8 Gordini		14198,45
3	33	Oldrich Horsák/Jiří Motal	CS	Škoda 1100MB		14706,66
4	64	Jens Nielsen/Henning Henriksen	DK	Volvo 122S		14850,64
5	50	Haino Rüütel/Gunnar Holm	SU	Moskvitch 408		15883,40
6	60	Evgenij Andrejev/Eduard Singurindi	SU	Moskvitch 408		16170,17
7	27	Milan Žid/Josef Čech	CS	Škoda 1100MB		17277,82
8	52	Margaret Lowrey/Alice Watson	GB	Ford Escort		17764,50
9	34	Milan Břicháč/Břetislav Bil	CS	Škoda 1100		18717,51
10	1	Ryszard Żyszkowski/T. Kurmanowicz	PL	Fiat 850		19636,66

16° Rallye Internacional del R.A.C. de España

(10–13 October 1968)
European Rally Championship for Manufacturers, Round 7

Pos.	No.	Driver/Codriver	Nat.	Car	Cat.	Result
1		Pauli Toivonen/Martti Tiukkannen	SF	Porsche 911		8920,4
2		Jean-François Piot/Jean Todt	F	Alpine-Renault A110		9359,7
3		Gilbert Staepelaere/André Aerts	B	Ford Escort TC		9486,4
4		Rafaele Pinto/Mario Mannucci	I	Lancia Fulvia Coupé HF		9540,2
5		Bernard Tramont/Ricardo Muñoz	F	Alpine-Renault A110		9724,3
6	9	Estanislao Reverter/Julio Leal	E	Alfa Romeo GTA		9967,7
7		Jean-Pierre Nicolas/Claude Roure	F	Renault 8 Gordini		10014,5
8		"Pedro"/Ramón Canal	E	BMW 2002	I	10112,3
9		José Manuel Lencina/A.Caballiero	E	Mini Cooper S		10450,9
10		Christine Beckers/M. Petit "Biche"	B	Alfa Romeo Giulia GTV		10541,0

RAC International Rally of Great Britain

(16–20 November 1968)
European Rally Championship for Manufacturers, Round 8

Pos.	No.	Driver/Codriver	Nat.	Car	Cat.	Result
1	19	Simo Lampinen/John Davenport	SF/GB	Saab 96 V4	II	650m34s
2	24	Carl Orrenius/Gustaf Schröderheim	S	Saab 96 V4	II	666m04s
3	47	Jimmy Bullough/Don Barrow	GB	Ford Escort TC	II	715m08s
4	28	Phil Cooper/Mike Bennett	GB	Mini Cooper S	II	731m45s
5	67	Bruce Wilkinson/John Billet	GB	Ford Escort TC	II	747m29s
6	33	John Barnes/Tony Pettie	GB	Peugeot 204	II	759m33s
7	34	Günter Rüttinger/Günther Bork	DDR	Wartburg 353	II	761m19s
8	70	Grahame John/Ian Harwood	GB	Ford Lotus Cortina	II	764m13s
9	88	John Jago/Duncan Spence	GB	Ford Lotus Cortina	II	786m40s
10	93	John Mossop/T.Johnstone	GB	Ford Lotus Cortina	II	788m13s

1969

XX KAK-Rallyt

(12–16 February 1969)
European Rally Championship for Drivers, Round 1

Pos.	No.	Driver/Codriver	Nat.	Car	Cat.	Result
1	3	Björn Waldegård/Lars Helmér	S	Porsche 911L	II	48102
2	6	Simo Lampinen/Arne Hertz	SF/S	Saab 96 V4	II	48570
3	10	Ove Eriksson/Hans Johansson	S	Opel Rallye Kadett	II	48899
4	12	Anders Kulläng/Donald Karlsson	S	Opel Rallye Kadett	II	49086
5	8	Håkan Lindberg/Bo Reinicke	S	Saab 96 V4	II	49105
6	5	Harry Källström/Gunnar Häggbom	S	Lancia Fulvia Coupé HF	II	49331
7	7	Tom Trana/Sölve Andreasson	S	Saab 96 V4	II	49472
8	2	Stig Blomqvist/Björn Moreus	S	Saab 96 V4	II	49519
9	4	Carl Orrenius/Gustaf Schröderheim	S	Saab 96 V4	II	49619
10	39	Lillebror Nasenius/Bengt Frodin	S	Opel Rekord Sprint	I	50298

21e Internationale Tulpenrallye

(27 April–3 May 1969)
European Rally Championship for Drivers, Round 3

Pos.	No.	Driver/Codriver	Nat.	Car	Cat.	Result
1	54	Gilbert Stapelaere/André Aerts	B	Ford Escort TC	I & II	764,1
2	21	Rob Slotemaker/Ferry van der Geest	NL	BMW 2002 TI	I & II	952,0
3	39	Hans Lannsjö/Hans Sudin	S	Opel Kadett Rallye	I & II	1306,5
4	84	Jean-Louis Haxhe/Christian Delferrier	B	DAF 55	I & II	2039,3
5	83	Claude Laurent/Jacques Marché	F	DAF 55	I & II	2087,7
6	31	Manfred Gudladt/Heiko Henneking	DK	Alfa Romeo 1750 Berlina	I & II	2191,9
7	86	Theo Koks/Rob Wiedenhof	NL	DAF 55	I & II	2228,3
8	27	Theo Schoonderbeek/Hans de Jong	NL	BMW 2002 TI	I & II	2341,4
9	93	Egon Culmbacher/Wolfgang Srehlow	DDR	Wartburg 353	I & II	2579,4
10	95	Huub Vermeulen/Bob Boekhout	NL	NSU 1000TTS	I & II	2647,6

17th Rally Acropolis

(28 May–3 June 1969)
European Rally Championship for Manufacturers, Round 2

Pos.	No.	Driver/Codriver	Nat.	Car	Cat.	Result
1	1	Pauli Toivonen/Matti Kolari	SF	Porsche 911S		422,7
2	3	Roger Clark/Jim Porter	GB	Ford Escort TC		978,3
3	14	Claude Laurent/Jacques Marché	F	DAF 55		3791,1
4	39	A. Maniatopoulos/N.Zoumbroulis	GR	NSU 1200TT		4014,9
5	22	Eberhart Schmitthelm/W. Geltermeier	D	Porsche 911S		4067,4
6	44	Tassos Livieratos/M. Andriopoulos	GR	Opel Kadett		4293,4
7	17	Ioannis Psihas/George Moschous	GR	Mazda 1200		4498,7
8	79	Ioannis Hasiotis/C.Gounaras	GR	BMW 1600ti		5008,2
9	35	Constantinos Dionisopoulos/J.Vihos	GR	Toyota Corolla		5057,8
10	80	Antonis Koulendianos/E.Papakostas	GR	Datsun PL510		6152,6

XXIX Rajd Polski

(16–20 July 1969)
European Rally Championship for Drivers, Round 6

Pos.	No.	Driver/Codriver	Nat.	Car	Cat.	Result
1	100	Sobiesław Zasada/Eva Zasada	PL	Porsche 911		10.488,79
2	73	Gilbert Staepelaere/André Aerts	B	Ford Escort TC	II	10.716,46
3	58	Harry Källström/Gunnar Haggböm	S	Lancia Fulvia Coupé HF		10.726,83
4	52	Ryszard Nowicki/Marian Bien	PL	Renault R8 Gordini		11.083,81
5	105	Walter Pöltinger/Gosta Zwilling	A	Porsche 911T		11.141,55
6	88	Kurt Simonsen/Staffan Elm	S	Opel Rallye Kadett		11.721,05
7	55	Alcide Paganelli/Ninni Russo	I	Lancia Fulvia Coupé HF		11.793,22
8	56	Kenneth Gram/Morgens Boesgaard	DK	Mini Cooper S		12.156,80
9	103	Manfred Gudladt/Eberhard Kuhna	D	Porsche 911		12.207,22
10	54	Andrzej Komorowski/Longin Bielak	PL	Renault R8 Gordini		12.209,51

38ème Rallye Automobile Monte-Carlo

(18–25 January 1969)
** European Rally Championship for Manufacturers, Round 1

Pos.	No.	Driver/Codriver	Nat.	Car	Cat.	Result
1	37	Björn Waldegård/Lars Helmér	S	Porsche 911	III	21554
*	7	Harry Källström/Gunnar Häggbom	S	Lancia Fulvia Coupé 1.6	VI	21691
2	31	Gérard Larousse/J.-C. Perramond	F	Porsche 911	III	21831
3	26	Jean Vinatier/Jean-François Jacob	F	Alpine-Renault A110 1300	III	21854
*	4	Jean-Pierre Nicolas/Claude Roure	F	Alpine-Renault A110 1600	VI	22376
4	29	Jean-François Piot/Jean Todt	F	Ford Escort TC	II	22553
5	89	Jean-Luc Thérier/Marcel Callewaerts	F	Renault R8 Gordini	I	23165
6	35	Pat Moss-Carlsson/E. Nyström	GB	Lancia Fulvia Coupé 1.3	II	23513
7	115	Rob Slotemaker/Ferry van der Geest	NL	BMW 2002ti	II	23750
8	55	Jean-Louis Barailler/Philippe Fayel	F	Triumph 2.5PI	II	24351
9	36	Henri Greder/Francis Murac	F	Opel Commodore	I	24729
10	63	Giorgio Pianta/Emilio Paleari	I	Autobianchi	II	25031

* These cars were nominally competing in the Rallye Mediterranée for Group VI cars
** This event was retrospectively excluded from the ERC due to presence of non-homologated cars

9° Rallye di Sanremo

(5–9 March 1969)
European Rally Championship for Drivers, Round 2

Pos.	No.	Driver/Codriver	Nat.	Car	Cat.	Result
1	6	Harry Källström/Gunnar Häggbom	S	Lancia Fulvia Coupé HF	II	252,5
2	2	Rauno Aaltonen/Henry Liddon	SF/GB	Lancia Fulvia Coupé HF	II	278,0
3	14	Sergio Barbasio/Mario Mannucci	I	Lancia Fulvia Coupé HF	II	511,0
4	7	Luigi Taramazzo/"Gino"	I	Porsche 911	III	620,5
5	16	Jovica Palikovic/Daniele Audetto	YU/I	Porsche 911	II	1192,0
6	9	Arnaldo Cavallari/Dante Salvay	I	Lancia Fulvia Coupé HF	II	1193,5
7	24	Cristiano Rattazzi/L. di Montezemolo	I	Fiat 124 Special	II	1582,0
8	15	Alberto Smania/Giuseppe Zanchetti	I	Fiat 125S	I	1755,0
9	19	Luciano Trombotto/F. Bessola	I	Fiat 124 Spider	III	1838,5
10	3	Roger Clark/Jim Porter	GB	Ford Escort TC	II	2075,5

40. Internationale Österreichische Alpenfahrt

(15–18 May 1969)
European Rally Championship for Drivers, Round 4

Pos.	No.	Driver/Codriver	Nat.	Car	Cat.	Result
1	35	Hannu Mikkola/Mike Wood	SF/GB	Ford Escort TC	II	7483,8
2	52	Harry Källström/Gunnar Häggbom	S	Lancia Fulvia Coupé HF	II	7595,5
3	34	Carl Orrenius/Sölve Andreasson	S	Saab 96 V4	II	7626,1
4	36	Simo Lampinen/Arne Hertz	SF/S	Saab 96 V4	II	7655,1
5	39	Lasse Jönssen/Lasse Ericsson	S	Saab 96 V4	II	8015,8
6	15	Gilbert Staepelaere/André Aerts	B	Ford Taunus 20M RS	II	8138,0
7	10	Richard Bochnicek/Sepp Kernmayer	A	Citroën DS21	II	8228,8
8	2	Sobiesław Zasada/Zenon Leszczuk	PL	Porsche 911S	III	8414,3
9	1	Walter Pöltinger/Leopold Mayr	A	Porsche 911T	III	8731,1
10	45	Carl Christian Schindler/G. Hruschka	A	Volkswagen 1500	II	9738,9

10th Rallye Vltava

(4–7 July 1969)
European Rally Championship for Drivers, Round 5

Pos.	No.	Driver/Codriver	Nat.	Car	Cat.	Result
1	27	Gilbert Staepelaere/André Aerts	B	Ford Escort TC		
2	35	Harry Källström/Gunnar Häggbom	S	Lancia Fulvia Coupé HF		
3		Vladimír Hubáček/Vojtěch Rieger	CS	Renault R8 Gordini		
4		Simo Lampinen/Arne Hertz	SF	Saab 96 V4		
5		Zdeněk Kec/Bedoich Steuer	CS	Renault R8 Gordini		
6	95	Milan Žid/Jaroslav Vylít	CS	Škoda 1100MB		
7		Jaroslav Bobek/Leoš Hnatevič	CS	Škoda 1100MB		
8		Miloš Vodseďálek/Landecký	CS	Škoda 1100MB		
9		Oldřich Brunclik/Jan Gerant	CS	Škoda 1100MB		
10		Václav Chlustina/Jaroslav Řehák	CS	Wartburg 1000		

6. Internationale Donau-Rallye für Automobile

(31 July–3 August 1969)
European Rally Championship for Manufacturers, Round 3

Pos.	No.	Driver/Codriver	Nat.	Car	Cat.	Result
1	1	Walter Pöltinger/J.-Hans Hartinger	A	Porsche 911T	III	7995
2	22	Alexander Kaja/Viktor Dietmayer	A	BMW 2002	II	8102
3	46	Walter Wieltschnig/Werner Pucher	A	Renault R8 Gordini	II	8290
4	23	Titus Majer Kajbic/B. Köstenberger	A	BMW 2002ti	II	8354
5	21	Gernot Fischer/Reinhard Knoll	A	BMW 2002		8426
6	18	Wolfgang Levy/Egon Wittig	D	BMW 2002ti	II	8426
7	29	Günther Janger/Gerald Malat	A	Volkswagen 1500		8433
8	11	Richard Bochnicek/Erwin Dawid	A	Citroën DS21	II	8481
9	44	Athanas Agura/Athanas Taskow	BG	Renault R8 Gordini	II	8601
10	30	Carl Christian Schindler/G. Hruschka	A	Volkswagen 1500	II	8845

XIX Jyväskylän Suurajot - Rally of the Thousand Lakes

(15–17 August 1969)
European Rally Championship for Manufacturers, Round 4

Pos.	No.	Driver/Codriver	Nat.	Car	Cat.	Result
1	33	Hannu Mikkola/Anssi Järvi	SF	Ford Escort TC	II	10645,2
2	38	Simo Lampinen/Klaus Sohlberg	SF	Saab 96 V4	II	10949,9
3	25	Risto Virtapuro/Martti Tiukkanen	SF	Opel Rallye Kadett	II	11275,2
4	27	Timo Mäkinen/Pekka Keskitalo	SF	Saab 96 V4	II	11513,5
5	28	Risto Einto/Heikki Haaksiala	SF	Volkswagen	II	11549,8
6	36	Pertti Kärhä/Heimo Poutala	SF	Isuzu Bellet	II	11642,8
7	39	Osmo Mäkelä/Erkki Nyman	SF	Isuzu Bellet	II	11791,6
8	67	Antti Jaatinen/Antti Kivimaa	SF	Saab 96 V4	II	12006,0
9	56	Markku Alén/Juhani Toivonen	SF	Renault R8 Gordini	II	12118,4
10	68	Harras Lindroos/Teuvo Saartela	SF	Isuzu Bellet	II	12493,9

6. Internationale Rallye Baltic - "Deutschland-Rallye"

(18–21 September 1969)
European Rally Championship for Manufacturers, Round 5

Pos.	No.	Driver/codriver	Nat.	Car	Cat.	Result
1	28	Willy Jensen/Nils Thorning-Jensen	DK	BMW 2002ti	II	7780,2
2	74	Jochi Kleint/Joachim Dörfler	D	Ford Escort 1300 GT	II	7901,3
3	22	Søren Terp/Aage Olesen	DK	BMW 2002ti	II	7952,0
4	18	Gert Raschig/Wulf Biebinger	D	Opel Commodore GS	II	8038,8
5	34	Jens Nielsen/Alex Nielsen	DK	Volvo 142S	I	8123,5
6	57	Günter Schons/Rainer Zweibäumer	D	BMW 1600ti	II	8249,8
7	42	Ole Høyer/Poul Arne Christiansen	DK	Alfa Romeo GS		8318,1
8	40	Per Sendager-Holm/Poul Kristensen	DK	Fiat 124	I	8350,2
9	12	Hans Stöhr/Manfred Kröniger	D	BMW 2500	II	8427,3
10	20	Hans Lannsjö/Hans Sundin	S	Opel Rallye Kadett 1900	II	8490,4

Internationale 3-Städte-Rallye - München-Wien-Budapest

(3–5 October 1969)
European Rally Championship for Manufacturers, Round 6

Pos.	No.	Driver/Codriver	Nat.	Car	Cat.	Result
1	11	Walter Roser/Leopold Mayer	A	Alpine-Renault A110	III	4063,7
2	9	Jean Vinatier/Claude Roure	F	Alpine-Renault A110	III	4183,7
3	1	Walter Pöltinger/J.-Hans Hartinger	A	Porsche 911T	III	4195,9
4	25	Gernot Fischer/Reinhard Knoll	A	BMW 2002	II	4275,1
5	26	Hubert Neukom/Georg Hopf	A	BMW 2002ti	II	4331,1
6	32	Alexander Kaja/Victor Dietmayer	A	BMW 2002	II	4352,5
7	29	Klaus Reichel/Peter Pohl	D	BMW 2002	II	4519,6
8	34	Alfred Höber/Thomas Kieselbach	D	BMW 2002ti	II	4581,0
9	54	Günther Janger/Walter Wessiak	A	Volkswagen 1500	II	4582,5
10	53	Carl Christian Schindler/G. Hruschka	A	Volkswagen 1500	II	4616,8

17° Rallye Internacional del R.A.C. de España

(16–19 October 1969)
European Rally Championship for Drivers, Round 7

Pos.	No.	Driver/Codriver	Nat.	Car	Cat.	Result
1	2	Harry Källström/Gunnar Häggbom	S	Lancia Fulvia Coupé HF	III	3h26m11.7s
2		Gilbert Staepelaere/André Aerts	B	Ford Escort TC		3h27m08.8s
3		Rafaele Pinto/Arnaldo Bernacchini	I	Lancia Fulvia Coupé HF	III	3h34m34.1s
4	9	Alberto Ruiz-Giménez/Jaime Segovia	E	Lancia		3h45m44.6s
5		Noël van Assche/Bob De Jong	B	BMW 2002		3h47m54.9s
6		Chris Tuerlinck/Etienne Stalpaert	B	Opel Commodore GS		3h49m37.8s
7		José Manuel Lencina/A.Caballiero	E	Lancia		3h50m59.8s
8		Kurt Simonsen/A.Henrikksen	S	Opel Kadett		3h52m46.3s
9		Lucas Sáinz/Emilio Rodríguez Zapico	I	Renault R8 Gordini		3h54m41.7s
10		Claes Billstam/Synnove Billstam	S	Opel Kadett		3h57m41.9s

RAC International Rally of Great Britain

(14–21 November 1969)
European Rally Championship for Drivers, Round 8

Pos.	No.	Driver/Codriver	Nat.	Car	Cat.	Result
1	12	Harry Källström/Gunnar Häggbom	S	Lancia Fulvia Coupé HF	III	7h59m17s
2	15	Carl Orrenius/David Stone	S	Saab 96 V4	II	8h03m32s
3	7	Tony Fall/Henry Liddon	GB	Lancia Fulvia Coupé HF	III	8h14m36s
4	17	Ove Andersson/Gunnar Palm	S	Ford Escort TC	II	8h14m46s
5	19	Håkan Lindberg/Bo Reinicke	S	Saab 96 V4	II	8h15m32s
6	5	Roger Clark/Jim Porter	GB	Ford Escort TC	II	8h17m04s
7	11	Tom Trana/Sölve Andreasson	D	Saab 96 V4	II	8h17m34s
8	14	Rauno Aaltonen/Tony Ambrose	SF	Datsun 1600 SSS	III	8h18m28s
9	35	Jerry Larsson/Lars Lundblad	S	Porsche 911S	III	8h18m57s
10	26	Lasse Jonsson/Bo Eliason	S	Saab 96 V4	II	8h21m21s

1970

39ème Rallye Automobile Monte-Carlo

(16–24 January 1970)
International Rally Championship for Makes, Round 1

Pos.	No.	Driver/Codriver	Nat.	Car	Cat.	Result
1	6	Björn Waldegård/Lars Helmér	S	Porsche 911S	4	19.744
2	2	Gérard Larousse/Maurice Gelin	F	Porsche 911S	4	19.863
3	18	Jean-Pierre Nicolas/Claude Roure	F	Alpine-Renault A110	4	19.914
4	11	Åke Andersson/Bo Thorszelius	S	Porsche 911S	4	20.175
5	9	Roger Clark/Jim Porter	GB	Ford Escort TC	2	20.291
6	49	Amilcare Ballestriere/Daniele Audetto	I	Lancia Fulvia Coupé HF	4	20.417
7	130	Timo Mäkinen/Henry Liddon	SF/GB	Ford Escort TC	2	20.599
8	38	Sergio Barbasio/Mario Mannucci	I	Lancia Fulvia Coupé HF	4	20.772
9	92	Roland Charriere/Yannick Castel	F	Alpine-Renault A110	4	21.819
10	24	Giorgio Pianta/Emilio Paleari	I	Lancia Fulvia Coupé	4	22.178

XXI KAK-Rallyt

(11–15 February 1970)
International Rally Championship for Makes, Round 2

Pos.	No.	Driver/Codriver	Nat.	Car	Cat.	Result
1	2	Björn Waldegård/Lars Helmér	S	Porsche 911S	4	44.450
2	21	Stig Blomqvist/Bo Reinicke	S	Saab 96 V4	2	45.846
3	44	Lillebror Nasenius/Björn Cedeberg	S	Opel Kadett Rallye	1	46.773
4	50	Gunnar Blomqvist/Ingelöv Blomqvist	S	Opel Kadett Rallye	1	47.184
5	7	Jerry Larsson/Lars Lundblad	S	Porsche 911S	4	47.517
6	49	Anders Gullberg/Leif Wåhlin	S	BMW 2002 TI	1	47.840
7	40	Anders Kulläng/Donald Karlsson	S	Opel Kadett Rallye	1	47.933
8	75	Ingemar Frohm/Bo Ottosson	S	Ford Escort TC	2	47.978
9	28	Rolf Andersson/Claes Andersson	S	Volvo 142	2	48.670
10	54	Ove Olsson/Olof Törnkvist	S	BMW 2002 TI	1	48.791

1° Sanremo-Sestriere - "Rally d'Italia"

(3–6 March 1970)
International Rally Championship for Makes, Round 3

Pos.	No.	Driver/Codriver	Nat.	Car	Cat.	Result
1	22	Jean-Luc Therier/Marcel Callewaert	F	Alpine-Renault A110	4	810,5
2	2	Harry Källström/Gunnar Häggbom	S	Lancia Fulvia Coupé HF	4	1030,7
3	8	Jean Vinatier/Jean-François Jacob	F	Alpine-Renault A110	4	1600,0
4	10	Tom Trana/Solve Andreasson	S	Saab 96 V4	2	1796,0
5	34	Giorgio Pianta/Kuster	I	Lancia Fulvia Coupé HF	3	2146,0
6	50	Alberto Smania/Giuseppe Zanchetti	I	Fiat 125S	2	2859,7
7	38	Pino Ceccato/Helmut Eisendle	I	Fiat 125S	1	3013,5
8	20	Håkan Lindberg/Arne Hertz	S	Saab 96 V4	2	3130,0
9	26	Alcide Paganelli/Ninni Russo	I	Fiat 124 Spyder	4	3488,4
10	66	Ferdinando Tecilla/Bruno Scabini	I	Fiat 125S	1	3679,0

18th East African Safari Rally

(26–30 March 1970)
International Rally Championship for Makes, Round 4

Pos.	No.	Driver/Codriver	Nat.	Car	Cat.	Result
1	4	Edgar Hermann/Hans Schuller	EAK	Datsun 1600SSS	2	395
2	17	Joginder Singh/Ken Ranyard	EAK	Datsun 1600SSS	2	446
3	94	Bert Shankland/Chris Rothwell	TZ	Peugeot 504 Injection	2	489
4	8	Jamil Din/Mateen Mughal	EAK	Datsun 1600SSS	2	509
5	78	Chrissie Michaelides/Lyn Robinson	EAK	Volvo 122S	2	670
6	16	Kim Mandeville/Stuart Allison	EAK	Triumph 2.5 PI	2	670
7	46	Mike Kirkland/John Rose	EAK	Datsun 1600SSS	2	698
8	50	Roger Harris/Peter Austin	EAK	Peugeot 404	1	762
9	26	Chris Little/Jack Esnouf	EAK	Peugeot 304	2	810
10	20	Nick Nowicki/Paddy Cliff		Peugeot 504	1	866

41. Internationale Österreichische Alpenfahrt

(6–10 May 1970)
International Rally Championship for Makes, Round 5

Pos.	No.	Driver/Codriver	Nat.	Car	Cat.	Result
1	3	Björn Waldegård/Lars Nyström	S	Porsche 911S	4	9016,8
2	31	Håkan Lindberg/Sölve Andreasson	S	Saab 96 V4	2	9250,0
3	27	Jean-François Piot/Jean Todt	F	Ford Escort TC	2	9297,6
4	29	Adrian Boyd/Beatty Crawford	GB	Ford Escort TC	2	10038,8
5	17	Bernard Darniche/Alain Mahé	F	Alpine Renault A110	4	10067,3
6	34	Walter Lux/Hans Siebert	A	Volkswagen 1500	2	10530,1
7	36	Franz Wurz/Franz Zögl	A	Ford Escort TC	2	10563,9
8	46	Richard Zelenka/Robert Zelenka	A	Ford Escort TC	2	10727,7
9	11	Harry Källström/Gunnar Häggbom	S	Lancia Fulvia Coupé HF	4	10734,4
10	8	Klaus Russling/Gerd Eggenberger	A	Porsche 911	4	10816,0

The RAC International Rally of Great Britain

(14–18 November 1970)
International Rally Championship for Makes, Round 7

Pos.	No.	Driver/Codriver	Nat.	Car	Cat.	Result
1	14	Harry Källström/Gunnar Häggbom	S	Lancia Fulvia HF 1.6	4	541m50s
2	20	Ove Eriksson/Hans Johansson	S	Opel Kadett Rallye		544m18s
3	40	Lillebror Nasenius/Björn Cederberg	S	Opel Kadett Rallye		553m18s
4	34	Jan Henriksson/Lars-Erik Carlström	S	Opel Kadett Rallye		556m08s
5	35	Andrew Cowan/Hamish Cardno	GB	Alpine-Renault A110	4	560m20s
6	30	Gerard Larousse/Mike Wood	F/GB	Porsche 911S	4	561m04s
7	18	Rauno Aaltonen/Paul Easter	SF/GB	Datsun 240Z	4	567m19s
8	41	Brian Culcheth/Johnstone Syer	GB	Ford Escort TC	2	580m53s
9	42	Lasse Jonsson/Alf Qvist	S	Saab 96 V4		583m41s
10	95	Klaus-Joachim Kleint/Hugo Röehr	D	Ford Capri	2	590m33s

40ème Rallye Automobile Monte-Carlo

(22–30 January 1971)
International Rally Championship for Makes, Round 1

Pos.	No.	Driver/Codriver	Nat.	Car	Cat.	Result
1	28	Ove Andersson/David Stone	S/GB	Alpine-Renault A110	4	06:30:54
2	9	Jean-Luc Thérier/Marcel Callewaert	F	Alpine-Renault A110	4	06:31:34
3	7	Björn Waldegård/Hans Thorszelius	S	Porsche 914/6	4	06:32:45
3	22	Jean-Claude Andruet/Michel Vial	F	Alpine-Renault A110	4	06:32:45
5	62	Rauno Aaltonen/Paul Easter	SF/GB	Datsun 240Z	4	06:38:21
6	6	Simo Lampinen/John Davenport	SF/GB	Lancia Fulvia Coupé HF 1.6	4	06:39:47
7	24	Håkan Lindberg/Solve Andreasson	S	Fiat 124S	4	06:41:13
8	12	Bernard Darniche/Claude Robertet	F	Alpine-Renault A110	4	06:41:15
9	5	Jean Vinatier/Maurice Gelin	F	Alpine-Renault A110	4	06:45:06
10	70	Tony Fall/Mike Wood	GB	Datsun 240Z	4	06:52:27

2° Sanremo-Sestriere - "Rally d'Italia"

(14–17 March 1971)
International Rally Championship for Makes, Round 3

Pos.	No.	Driver/Codriver	Nat.	Car	Cat.	Result
1	4	Ove Andersson/Tony Nash	S/GB	Alpine-Renault A110	4	1112,0
2	5	Amilcare Ballestriere/A. Bernacchini	I	Lancia Fulvia Coupé 1.6	4	1360,0
3	12	Sergio Barbasio/Piero Sodano	I	Lancia Fulvia Coupé 1.6	4	1431,5
4	10	Bernard Darniche/Alain Mahé	F	Alpine-Renault A110	4	1439,5
5	21	Giulio Bisulli/Arturo Zanuccoli	I	Fiat 125S	1	2323,0
6	8	Jean-Pierre Nicolas/Michel Vial	F	Alpine-Renault A110	4	2380,4
7	22	Ferdinando Tecilla/Sergio Lipizer	I	Fiat 125S	1	2666,5
8	33	Orlando Dall'Ava/Silvio Maiga	I	Fiat 125S	1	3173,5
9	18	Arnaldo Cavallari/Gianti Simoni	I	Lancia Fulvia Coupé	3	3454,8
10	16	Luciano Trombotto/Maurizio Enrico	I	Fiat 124 Spyder	4	3492,6

14ème Rallye International du Maroc

(28 April–6 May 1971)
International Rally Championship for Makes, Round 5

Pos	No.	Driver/Codriver	Nat.	Car	Cat.	Result
1	16	Jean Deschaseaux/Jean Plassard	F	Citroën SM Maserati V6	4	15h56m35s
2	7	Guy Chasseuil/Christian Baron	F	Peugeot 504	1	16h22m37s
3	12	Bernard Consten/Stanislas Motte	F	Citroën DS21	2	17h26m04s
4	2	Bob Neyret/Jacques Terramorsi	F	Citroën DS21		19h09m26s
5	30	Raymond Touroul/Jean-Louis Gama	F	Porsche 911S	4	19h33m38s
6	27	Lionel Raudet/Jacques Goursolas	F	Peugeot 404	2	22h11m14s
7	24	Jacques Osstyn/Jean Kerguen	MA	Volvo 142S	2	23h44m05s
8	29	Claude Laurent/Jacques Marché	F	DAF 55	2	25h43m47s
9	59	Abdelkader Resfaoui/M. Hacem	MA	Citroën DS21	2	26h36m12s

No other finishers

18th Rally Acropolis

(27 May–2 June 1970)
International Rally Championship for Makes, Round 6

Pos.	No.	Driver/Codriver	Nat.	Car	Cat.	Result
1	2	Jean-Luc Therier/Marcel Callewaert	F	Alpine-Renault		108,1
2	5	Jean Vinatier/David Stone	F/GB	Alpine-Renault		385,4
3	9	Ove Andersson/Jim Porter	S/GB	Ford Escort TC		387,4
4	7	Jean-Francois Piot/Jean Todt	F	Ford Escort TC		943,6
5	8	Håkan Lindberg/Bo Reinicke	S	Fiat 125S		1192,9
6	12	Jean-Pierre Nicolas/Michèle Véron	F	Alpine-Renault		1406,3
7	22	Tassos Livieratos/M. Andriopoulos	GR	Opel Kadett		2765,3
8	15	Ioannis Psihas/E.Nomicos	GR	Toyota Corona		3898,4
9	27	Ali Sipahi/Dogan Zorlu	TR	BMW 2002		7476,0
10	72	"Daffy"/Minas Vourdoubakis	GR	Humber Sceptre		8027,3

1971

XXII KAK-Rallyt

(17–21 February 1971)
International Rally Championship for Makes, Round 2

Pos.	No.	Driver/Codriver	Nat.	Car	Cat.	Result
1	13	Stig Blomqvist/Arne Hertz	S	Saab 96 V4	2	30929
2	50	Lars Nyström/Gunnar Nyström	S	BMW 2002ti	2	31242
3	4	Harry Källström/Gunnar Häggbom	S	Lancia Fulvia Coupé HF 1.6	4	31296
4	3	Björn Waldegård/Lars Helmér	S	Porsche 911S	4	31395
5	17	Ove Eriksson/Börje Österberg	S	Opel Rallye Kadett	2	31512
6	1	Åke Andersson/Bo Thorszelius	S	Porsche 911S	4	31563
7	36	Anders Kulläng/Donald Karlsson	S	Opel Rallye Kadett	1	31699
8	37	Anders Gullberg/Leif Wåhlin	S	BMW 2002ti	1	31718
9	35	Lillebror Nasenius/Björn Cedeberg	S	Opel Rallye Kadett	1	31819
10	19	Tom Trana/Sölve Andreasson	S	Saab 96 V4	2	31891

19th East African Safari Rally

(8–12 April 1971)
International Rally Championship for Makes, Round 4

Pos.	No.	Driver/Codriver	Nat.	Car	Cat.	Result
1	11	Edgar Hermann/Hans Schuller	EAK	Datsun 240Z	4	217
2	31	Shekhar Mehta/Mike Doughty	EAK	Datsun 240Z	4	220
3	15	Bert Shankland/Chris Bates	TZ	Peugeot 504 Injection	2	348
4	3	Robin Hillyar/Jock Aird	EAK	Ford Escort TC	2	349
5	19	Sobiesław Zasada/Marien Bien	PL	Porsche 911S	4	368
6	17	Vic Preston Jnr./Bev Smith	EAK	Ford Escort TC	2	402
7	12	Rauno Aaltonen/Paul Easter	SF/GB	Datsun 240Z	4	437
8	21	Harry Kallström/Gunnar Häggbom	S	Lancia Fulvia Coupé HF 1.6	4	476
9	6	Robin Ulyate/Ivan Smith	EAK	BMW 2002ti	2	511
10	10	Peter Huth/John McConnell	EAK	Peugeot 404 Injection	2	559

42. Internationale Österreichische Alpenfahrt

(12–15 May 1971)
International Rally Championship for Makes, Round 6

Pos.	No.	Driver/Codriver	Nat.	Car	Cat.	Result
1	7	Ove Andersson/Arne Hertz	S	Alpine-Renault A110	4	11945
2	6	Alcide Paganelli/Ninni Russo	I	Fiat 124 Sport Spyder	4	12287
3	40	Klaus Russling/Franz Mikes	A	Volkswagen 1302S	2	12830
4	37	Gernot Fischer/Herbert Kohlweis	A	Volkswagen 1302S	2	13053
5	11	Tony Fall/Mike Wood	GB	BMW 2002ti	2	13507
6	43	Leopold Bosch/Walter Starmann	A	Volkswagen 1302S	2	14268
7	51	John Haugland/Arild Antonsen	N	Škoda 110L	2	14585
8	53	Oldřich Horsák/Jiří Motal	CS	Škoda 110L	2	15598
9	52	Milan Zid/Jaroslav Vylit	CS	Škoda 110L	2	15832
10	73	Walter Pöltinger/J.-Hans Hartinger	A	BMW 2002ti	1	15993

1971–1972

19th Rally Acropolis

(27–30 May 1971)
International Rally Championship for Makes, Round 7

Pos.	No.	Driver/Codriver	Nat.	Car	Cat.	Result
1	5	Ove Andersson/Arne Hertz	S	Alpine-Renault A110	IV	18447,00
2	2	Jean-Pierre Nicolas/Michel Vial	F	Alpine-Renault A110	IV	18619,00
3	1	Simo Lampinen/John Davenport	SF/GB	Lancia Fulvia Coupé 1.6	IV	19267,26
4	11	Pino Ceccato/Helmut Eisendle	I	Fiat 124 Abarth	IV	23992,87
5	20	Johnny Pesmazoglou/E.Mamalis	GR	Opel Kadett Rally	II	25094,95
6	16	Ali Sipahi/Erdoğan Zorlu	TR	BMW 2002ti	I	26263,33
7	24	"Lycikomos"/"Siro"	GR	Alfa Romeo 1750	II	29343,56
8	15	Antonis Koulendianos/N.Koutsavelis	GR	Datsun 510P	I	42803,80
9	43	Mario Ioannides/Patrick Langdown	CY/GB	Peugeot 404	II	88042,75

No other finishers

The RAC International Rally of Great Britain

(20–24 November 1971)
International Rally Championship for Makes, Round 9

Pos.	No.	Driver/Codriver	Nat.	Car	Cat.	Result
1	2	Stig Blomqvist/Arne Hertz	S	Saab 96 V4		07:30:47
2	3	Björn Waldegård/Lars Nyström	S	Porsche 911S		07:34:00
3	24	Carl Orrenius/Lars Persson	S	Saab 96 V4		07:40:01
4	12	Hannu Mikkola/Gunnar Palm	SF/S	Ford Escort RS1600		07:40:05
5	7	Simo Lampinen/John Davenport	SF/GB	Lancia Fulvia Coupé HF 1.6		07:45:16
6	16	Timo Mäkinen/Henry Liddon	SF/GB	Ford Escort RS1600		07:41:00
7	8	Per Eklund/Solve Andreasson	S	Saab 96 V4		07:49:12
8	1	Harry Källström/Gunnar Häggbom	S	Lancia Fulvia Coupé HF 1.6		07:52:47
9	14	Sandro Munari/Mario Manucci	I	Lancia Fulvia Coupé HF 1.6		07:53:49
10	44	Seppo Utrianen/Klaus Lehto	SF	Saab 96 V4		07:54:07

41ème Rallye Automobile Monte-Carlo

(21–28 January 1972)
International Rally Championship for Makes, Round 1

Pos.	No.	Driver/Codriver	Nat.	Car	Cat.	Result
1	14	Sandro Munari/Mario Mannucci	I	Lancia Fulvia Coupé HF 1.6	IV	05:57:55
2	4	Gérard Larousse/J.-C. Perramond	F	Porsche 911S	IV	06:08:45
3	5	Rauno Aaltonen/Jean Todt	SF/F	Datsun 240Z	IV	06:12:35
4	21	Simo Lampinen/Solve Andreasson	SF/S	Lancia Fulvia Coupé HF 1.6	IV	06:20:04
5	7	Jean-François Piot/Jim Porter	F/GB	Ford Escort RS1600	II	06:26:23
6	26	Sergio Barbasio/Piero Sodano	I	Lancia Fulvia Coupé HF 1.6	IV	06:34:17
7	33	Bob Neyret/Jacques Terramorsi	F	Alpine Renault A110	IV	06:34:53
8	27	Raffaelle Pinto/Helmut Eisendle	I	Fiat 124 Spider	IV	06:42:17
9	16	Jean Ragnotti/Pierre Thimonier	F	Opel Ascona 1900	I	06:44:10
10	60	Pat Moss-Carlsson/Liz Crellin	GB	Alpine Renault A110	IV	06:53:08

20th East African Safari Rally

(30 March–3 April 1972)
International Rally Championship for Makes, Round 3

Pos.	No.	Driver/Codriver	Nat.	Car	Cat.	Result
1	7	Hannu Mikkola/Gunnar Palm	SF/S	Ford Escort RS1600	II	553
2	12	Sobiesław Zasada/Marien Bien	PL	Porsche 911S	IV	581
3	14	Vic Preston Jnr/Bev Smith	EAK	Ford Escort RS1600	II	583
4	21	Robin Hillyar/Mark Birley	EAK/GB	Ford Escort RS1600	II	724
5	10	Edgar Herrmann/Hans Schuller	EAK	Datsun 240Z	IV	767
6	5	Rauno Aaltonen/Tony Fall	SF/GB	Datsun 240Z	IV	779
7	35	Roger Harris/Peter Austin	EAK	Peugeot 504	II	875
8	2	Timo Mäkinen/Henry Liddon	SF/GB	Ford Escort RS1600	II	879
9	4	Bert Shankland/Chris Bates	EAT/EAK	Peugeot 504	II	885
10	8	Shekhar Mehta/Mike Doughty	EAK	Datsun 240Z	IV	889

20th Rally Acropolis

(25–29 May 1972)
International Rally Championship for Makes, Round 5

Pos.	No.	Driver/Codriver	Nat.	Car	Cat.	Result
1	4	Håkan Lindberg/Helmut Eisendle	S/I	Fiat 124 Spider	IV	6h18m18.0s
2	7	Simo Lampinen/Bo Reinicke	SF/S	Lancia Fulvia HF 1.6	IV	6h18m41.4s
3	10	Achim Warmbold/Joachim Dorfler	D	BMW 2002tii	II	6h19m59.0s
4	1	Luciano Trombotto/Maurizio Ernico	I	Fiat 124 Spider	IV	6h26m12.4s
5	8	Tony Fall/Mike Wood	GB	BMW 2002tii	II	6h27m17.0s
6	2	Shekhar Mehta/Paul Easter	EAK/GB	Datsun 240Z	IV	7h03m06.0s
7	5	Alberto Smania/Arturo Zanuccoli	I	Fiat 124 Spider	IV	7h08m47.9s
8	19	Tasso Livieratos/Miltos Andriopoulos	GR	Alpine-Renault A110	IV	7h32m16.7s
9	30	Roland Fiat/Alain Beauchef	F	Opel Ascona	I	8h04m32.3s
10	32	Ali Sipahi/Oral Tan	TR	BMW 2002ti	I	8h14m36.5s

31ème Coupe des Alpes

(21–26 June 1971)
International Rally Championship for Makes, Round 8

Pos.	No.	Driver/Codriver	Nat.	Car	Cat.	Result
1	24	Bernard Darniche/Alain Mahé	F	Alpine-Renault A110	4	14h55m13.3s
2	22	Jean Vinatier/Lucette Pointet	F	Alpine-Renault A110	4	15h06m10.8s
3	14	Jean-Francois Piot/Jim Porter	F/GB	Ford Escort RS1600	2	15h39m49.6s
4	18	René Trautmann/Philippe Leyssieux	F	Lancia Fulvia Coupé 1.6	4	15h56m30.5s
5	12	Jacques Henry/Etienne Grobot	F	Alpine-Renault A110	3	16h52m01.8s
6	31	Jean-Claude Gamet/Michel Gamet	F	Opel Kadett GT	1	17h22m27.9s
7	30	Gérard Dantan-Merlin/V. Laverne	F	Porsche 911S	3	17h35m10.0s
8	33	Thierry Sabine/Bernard Surre	F	Ford Capri 2300	1	17h37m22.8s
9	16	M.-C. Beaumont/M. de la Grandrive	F	Opel Ascona SR	1	17h51m25.1s
10	21	Henri Greder/M.-Madeleine Fouquet	F	Opel Commodore	2	18h18m25.3s

Note: Due to insufficient number of starters the event did not count for points

XXIII KAK-Rallyt

(17–20 February 1972)
International Rally Championship for Makes, Round 2

Pos.	No.	Driver/Codriver	Nat.	Car	Cat.	Result
1	8	Stig Blomqvist/Arne Hertz	S	Saab V4	IV	27.808
2	4	Björn Waldegård/Lars Helmer	S	Porsche 911S	V	28.064
3	7	Harry Källström/Gunnar Häggbom	S	Lancia Fulvia Coupé HF 1.6	V	28.352
4	14	Anders Kulläng/Donald Karlsson	S	Opel Ascona	IV	28.413
5	9	Ove Eriksson/Börje Österberg	S	Opel Ascona	IV	28.882
6	40	Ingvar Carlsson/Lars-Göran Berg	S	BMW 2002tii	IV	29.025
7	28	Anders Gullberg/Leif Wåhlin	S	BMW 2002tii	IV	29.168
8	5	Per Eklund/Bo Reinicke	S	Saab V4	IV	29.381
9	29	Lillebror Nasenius/Björn Cederberg	S	Opel Ascona	IV	29.421
10	39	Bror Danielsson/Ulf Sundberg	S	BMW 2002TI1	IV	29.576

15ème Rallye International du Maroc

(27–30 April 1972)
International Rally Championship for Makes, Round 4

Pos.	No.	Driver/Codriver	Nat.	Car	Cat.	Result
1	1	Simo Lampinen/Sölve Andreasson	SF/S	Lancia Fulvia Coupe 1.6		19h42m01s
2	11	Bob Neyret/Jacques Terramorsi	F	Citroën DS21		20h14m31s
3	29	Raymonde Ponnelle/Pierre De Serros	MA	Citroën DS21		20h28m39s
4	34	J. Dupré de Boulois/G. Desgrippes	F	Renault R16 TS		24h49m50s
5	53	C.Bacchy/Richard Puigségur	MA/F	Peugeot 404		27h04m20s
6	16	Claudine Trautmann/M.-O. Desvignes	F	Renault R16 TS		28h19m39s

No other finishers

43. Internationale Österreichische Alpenfahrt

(6–9 September 1972)
International Rally Championship for Makes, Round 6

Pos.	No.	Driver/Codriver	Nat.	Car	Cat.	Result
1	1	Håkan Lindberg/Helmut Eisendle	S	Fiat 124 Spider	IV	15.425,0
2	10	Günther Janger/Harald Gottlieb	A	Volkswagen 1302S	II	15.905,5
3	12	Per Eklund/Bo Reinicke	S	Saab 96 V4	II	16.337,5
4	33	Herbert Grünsteidl/Georg Hopf	A	Volkswagen 1302S	II	16.520,7
5	18	Erich Haberl/JohannFritz	A	Porsche 911S	IV	16.914,7
6	11	Gunnar Blomqvist/Josef Kalnay	S	Opel Ascona	II	17.025,4
7	45	Vic Dietmayer/Oswald Schurek	A	BMW 2002	I	20.083,4
8	46	Wolfgang Löffelmann/Peter Wjzner	A	Alfa Romeo GS	I	22.557,9

No other finishers

10° Rallye di Sanremo

(24–26 October 1972)
International Rally Championship for Makes, Round 7

Pos.	No.	Driver/Codriver	Nat.	Car	Cat.	Result
1	2	Amilcare Ballestriere/A. Bernacchini	I	Lancia Fulvia Coupé HF 1.6	IV	45'09"
2	12	Sergio Barbasio/Piero Sodano	I	Lancia Fulvia Coupé HF 1.6	IV	48'51"
3	3	Håkan Lindberg/Lars-Erik Carlström	S	Fiat 124 Spyder	IV	58'25"
4	6	Giulio Bisulli/Arturo Zanuccoli	I	Fiat 124 Spyder	IV	1h00'13"
5	9	Luciano Trombotto/G. Zanchetti	I	Fiat 124 Spyder	IV	1h00'25"
6	20	Gianni Bossetti/P.ierpaolo Hischiatti	I	Lancia Fulvia Coupé HF	IV	1h30'27"
7	18	Giacomo Pelganta/Mauro Mannini	I	Lancia Fulvia Coupé HF	IV	1h48'25"
8	30	Alfredo Fagnola/Andrea Ulivi	I	Fiat 125S	I	1h49'03"
9	41	Luciano Corino/Pierangelo Rigo	I	Fiat 125S	I	1h54'45"
10	24	Salvatore Brai/Roberto Dalpozzo	I	Opel Kadett	I	1h55'28"

Press On Regardless International Rally

(2–5 November 1972)
International Rally Championship for Makes, Round 8

Pos.	No.	Driver/Codriver	Nat.	Car	Cat.	Result
1	124	Gene Henderson/Ken Pogue	USA	Jeep Wagoneer		122,61
2	109	Thomas Jones/Ralph Beckman	CDN	Datsun 240Z		130,19
3	117	Erhard Dahm/Jim Callon	USA	Jeep Wagoneer		134,18
4	114	Dick Zwitzer/Gail McGuire	USA	Volvo 164E		151,02
5	129	Jim Doidge/Harry Ward	USA	Dodge Colt		155,39
6	112	Walter Boyce/Doug Woods	CDN	Toyota Tezik		156,11
7	110	John Smiskol/Bernie Rekus	USA	Datsun Bluebird 1600 SSS		160,10
8	123	Jim Walker/Terry Palmer	USA	Volvo 142S		162,27
9	105	Maurice Blondin/Robert Tibault	CDN	Datsun 510		179,89
10	125	Jean Legault/Roland Poitras	CDN	Datsun PL 510		185,43

21st Daily Mirror RAC Rally

(2–5 December 1972)
International Rally Championship for Makes, Round 9

Pos.	No.	Driver/Codriver	Nat.	Car	Cat.	Result
1	4	Roger Clark/Tony Mason	GB	Ford Escort RS1600	II	410m07s
2	1	Stig Blomqvist/Arne Hertz	S	Saab V4	II	413m32s
3	14	Anders Kulllang/Donald Karlsson	S	Opel Ascona Rallye	II	419m57s
4	2	Harry Källström/Gunnar Haggböm	S	Lancia Fulvia Coupé HF 1.6	III	421m38s
5	8	Simo Lampinen/Solve Andreasson	SF/S	Lancia Fulvia Coupé HF 1.6	III	422m30s
6	19	Ove Eriksson/Lars-Eric Carlstrom	S	Opel Ascona Rallye	II	424m53s
7	23	Lillebror Nasenius/Björn Cedeberg	S	Opel Ascona Rallye	II	426m18s
8	7	Gunnar Blomqvist/Ingelov Blomqvist	S	Opel Ascona	II	430m34s
9	11	Ove Andersson/Geraint Phillips	S/GB	Toyota Celica	II	431m06s
10	30	Per-Inge Walfridsson/Kjell Nilsson	S	Volvo 142	II	431m35s

Final Standings from 1953 to 1972

European Touring Championship / European Rally Championship

1953

Pos.	Driver	Nat.	Codriver	Car	Points
1	Helmuth Polensky	D	Walter Schlüter	Porsche 1500	74
2	Ian Appleyard	GB	Pat Appleyard	Jaguar XK120 / Jaguar Mk VII	68
3	Gert Siebert	SA	Alfred Bolz	Citroën 11	42
Ladies	Greta Molander	S	Helga Lundberg	Saab 92	

1954

Pos.	Driver	Nat.	Codriver	Car	Points
1	Walter Schlüter	D		Auto Union	37
2	Heinz Meier	D		Auto Union	31
	Gustav Menz	D		Auto Union	31
4	Hans Wencher	D		Auto Union	18
Ladies	Sheila van Damm	GB	Anne Hall	Sunbeam 90	

1955

Pos.	Driver	Nat.	Codriver	Car	Points
1	Werner Engel	D		Mercedes 300SL	32
2	Walter Schlüter	D	Siegfried Eikelmann	DKW	22
3		D		DKW	22
Ladies	Sheila van Damm	GB	Anne Hall	Sunbeam 90	

1956

Pos.	Driver	Nat.	Codriver	Car	Points
1	Walter Schock	D	Rolf Moll	Mercedes	39
2	Paul Ernst Strähle	D	Hans von Wencher	Porsche 1300	34
3	Claude Storez	F	Robert Buchet	Porsche Carrera	19
Ladies	Nancy Mitchell	GB	Doreen Reece	MGA	28 **

1957

Pos.	Driver	Nat.	Codriver	Car	Points
1	Ruprecht Hopfen	D		Saab, Borgward	16
2	Martin Carstedt	S	Gulli Carstedt	Ford Fairlane	13
3	Claude Storez	F	Robert Buchet	Porsche Carrera	12
	Thure Jansson	S	Lennart Jansson	Volvo PV444	12
	Massimo Leto di Priolo	I	Salvatore Leto di Priolo	Alfa Romeo TI	12
Ladies	Nancy Mitchell	GB		MGA, Standard	8 **

1958

Pos.	Driver	Nat.	Codriver	Car	Points
1	Gunnar Andersson	S		Volvo PV444	32
2	Bernard Consten	F		Alfa Romeo Giulietta	23
	Max Reiss	D	Hans Wencher	Alfa Romeo, Porsche	23
Ladies	Pat Moss	GB	Ann Wisdom	Morris Minor, Austin Healey	23 **

1959

Pos.	Driver	Nat.	Codriver	Car	Points
1	Paul Coltelloni	F		Citroën, Alfa Romeo	40
2	Erik Carlsson	S		Saab 96	39
3	Wolfgang Levy	D		Auto Union.DKW	38
4	Hans Wencher	D		Auto Union	35
Ladies	Ewy Rosqvist	S		Volvo PV544	28 **

1960

Pos.	Driver	Nat.	Codriver	Car	Points
1	Walter Schock	D	Rolf Moll	Mercedes	
Ladies	Pat Moss	GB	Ann Wisdom	Austin A40, Austin Healey	

Note that where a driver has had more than one second driver during the year, there is no name listed alongside the winning driver's name.
Also note ** that the Ladies scoring was on an entirely different scale to that of the overall championship until 1962

1961
Pos.	Driver	Nat.	Codriver	Car	Points
1	Hans-Joachim Walter	D		Panhard, Porsche, Abarth	132
2	Gunnar Andersson	S		Volvo PV544, Ferrari	121
3	Eugen Böhringer	D		Mercedes 220SE	115
Ladies	Ewy Rosqvist	S		Volvo PV544	?

1962
Pos.	Driver	Nat.	Codriver	Car	Points
1	Eugen Böhringer	D		Mercedes	158
2	Erik Carlsson	S		Saab 96	153
3	Peter Lang	D		Mercedes	142
Ladies	Pat Moss	GB		Mini Cooper, Austin Healey	122

1963
European Rally Championship suspended for 12 months, unofficial European Cup awarded by AvD in Frankfurt

Pos.	Driver	Nat.	Codriver	Car	Points
1 – Touring	Gunnar Andersson	S		Volvo PV544	35.478
2 – Touring	Eugen Böhringer	D		Mercedes	30.458
3 – Touring	Henry Taylor	GB	Brian Melia	Ford Cortina	30.033
4 – GT	Hans-Joachim Walter	D		Porsche 356	29,182
Ladies	Pauline Mayman	GB	Valerie Domleo	Mini Cooper	17.712

1964
Pos.	Driver	Nat.	Codriver	Car	Points
1	Tom Trana	S	Gunnar Thermaenius	Volvo PV544	?
2	Erik Carlsson	S	Gunnar Palm	Saab 96	
3	Pat Moss	GB		Ford Cortina, Saab	
Ladies	Pat Moss	GB		Ford Cortina, Saab	?

1965
Pos.	Driver	Nat.	Codriver	Car	Points
1	Rauno Aaltonen	SF	Tony Ambrose	Mini Cooper S	97
2	Timo Mäkinen	SF		Mini Cooper S/Austin Healey	67
3	René Trautmann	F	Claudine Bouchet	Citroën DS 21	61
Ladies	Pat Moss	GB	Elizabeth Nyström	Saab	?

1966
Pos.	Driver	Nat.	Codriver	Car	Points
Group 1	Lillebror Nasenius	S		Opel Rekord	31
Group 2	Sobieslaw Zasada	PL		Steyr Puch	50
Group 3	Günther Klass	D	Rolf Wütherich	Porsche 911	54
Ladies	Sylvia Österberg	S		Renault R8 Gordini	

1967
Pos.	Driver	Nat.	Codriver	Car	Points
Group 1	Sobieslaw Zasada	PL		Porsche 912	64
Group 2	Bengt Söderström	S	Gunnar Palm	Ford Cortina Lotus	42
Group 3	Vic Elford	GB	David Stone	Porsche 911S	57
Ladies	Not awarded				

European Rally Championship

1968 for Manufacturers
Pos.	Manufacturer	Points
1	Ford GB	45
2	Saab	36
3	Renault	29
4	Porsche	28
5	Lancia	27
6	Alpine Renault	20

1968 for Drivers
Pos.	Driver	Nat.	Codriver	Car	Points
1	Pauli Toivonen	SF		Porsche 911	56
2	Sobieslaw Zasada	PL		Porsche 911	27
3	Rauno Aaltonen	SF	Henry Liddon	Mini Cooper S	14
Ladies	Not awarded				

1969 for Manufacturers
Pos.	Manufacturer	Points
1	Ford Europe	33
2	Porsche	31
3	BMW	30
4	Opel	20
5	Alpine Renault	13
	NSU	13

1969 for Drivers
Pos.	Driver	Nat.	Codriver	Car	Points
1	Harry Källström	S	Gunnar Haggbom	Lancia Fulvia Coupé	59
2	Gilbert Staepelaere	B	André Aerts	Ford Escort	51
3	Simo Lampinen	SF	Arne Hertz	Saab 96V4	19
Ladies	Not awarded				

International Rally Championship for Makes

1970
Pos.	Make	Points
1	Porsche	28
2	Alpine Renault	26
3	Lancia	16
4	Saab	15
5	Ford	10
6	Nissan	9

1970 European Rally Championship for Drivers
Pos.	Name	Nat.	Lyon	DDR	Irl.	Tulp.	Wies.	Semp.	Lorr.	Scott.	CH	Vltava	Rajd	Donau	SF	Castr.	TdF	3-St.	TAP	Elba	Min.	Esp.	TdC	TdB	Total
1	Jean-Claude Andruet	F	13						13	13			10					13				8			70
2	Gilbert Staepelaere	B										13	10					10				9		13	55
	Andre Aerts	B										13	10					10				9		13	55
4	Achim Warmbold	D	9				13	9						9				6							46
5	Jean Ragnotti	F	9			11			9	9												6			44
	Pierre Thimonier	F	9			11			9	9												6			44
7	Wulf Biebinger	D	9				13	9																	31
8	D Paganelli	I														3				13	4		5		25
	D Russo	I														3				13	4		5		25
10	D Stone	GB	13																			10			23

1971

Pos.	Make	Points
1	Alpine Renault	36
2	Saab	18
3	Porsche	16½
4	Lancia	15
5	Nissan	11
	Fiat	11

1971 European Rally Championship for Drivers

Pos.	Name	Nat.	Nord	Lyon	DDR	Elba	Irl.	Wies.	Semp.	Scott.	CH	Vltava	Rajd	Donau	SF	Castr.	TdF	TAP	Min.	Esp.	TdB	Total
1	Sobiesław Zasada	PL	3		13				6				13	8					6	9	10	59
2	Sandro Munari	I							10						13				13	9		45
	Mario Mannucci	I							10						13				13	9		45
4	Jean-Pierre Nicolas	F		8							6							13		13		40
5	Jean Todt	F									6							13		13		32
6	Jacques Henry	F		9							8						2			6	3	28
	Bernard-Etienne Grobot	F		9							8						2			6	3	28
8	Vic Dietmayer	A								9					9				9			27
	Hans Britth	S	1		6			6				6	4	4								27
	Hans Reppling	S	1		6			6				6	4	4								27

1972

Pos.	Make	Points
1	Lancia	97
2	Fiat	55
3	Porsche	53
4	Ford	48
5	Saab	47
6	Nissan	46

1972 European Rally Championship for Drivers

Pos.	Name	Nat.	Arctic	Brava	N.&G.	Lyon	DDR	Fir.	Elba	Scott.	Semp.	Zlatni	Vltava	Rajd	Olymp.	SF	Castr.	TdF	Baltic	3-St.	YU	TAP	Min.	Esp.	TdC	TdB	Total
1	Raffaele Pinto	I		20							20		20				15				20	20					115
	Luigi Macaluso	I		20							20		20				15				20	20					115
3	Sobiesław Zasada	PL				20						20							15	20	15						90
4	Jean-Pierre Nicolas	F			15		20								20										6		61
5	Jean-Claude Andruet	F			20													20								20		60
6	Bernard Darniche	F		20	15																		15			10		60
7	Achim Warmbold	D	15							15											20							50
8	Walter Röhrl	D												15				20										35
9	Sergio Barbasio	I						12	15		8																	35
10	Luciano Trombotto	I							20									12										32

3-St. = 3-Städte-Rallye München-Wien-Budapest, Arctic = Arctic Rally, Baltic = Baltic Rallye, Brava = Rallye Costa Brava, Castr. = Rally San Martino di Castrozza, CH = Rallye de Genève, DDR = Rallye DDR, Donau = Donau-Rallye, Elba = Rally dell'Isola d'Elba, Esp. = Rallye del R.A.C. de España, Fir. = Firestone Rally, Irl. = Circuit of Ireland, Lorr. = Rallye de Lorraine, Lyon = Rallye Lyon Charbonnières-Stuttgart-Solitude, Min. = Rallye der 1000 Minuten, N.&G. = Critérium Neige et Glace, Nord = Routes du Nord, Olymp. = Olympia Rallye, Rajd = Rajd Polski, Scott. = Scottish Rally, Semp. = Semperit Rally, SF = Jyväskylän Suurajot – The Rally of the Thousand Lakes, TAP = TAP Rally, TdB = Tour de Belgique, TdC = Tour de Corse, TdF = Tour de France Automobile, Tulp. = Tulpenrallye, Vltava = Rallye Vltava – Moldau, Wies. = Rallye Wiesbaden, YU = YU Rally, Zlatni = Rally Zlatni Piassatzi

RallyWebShop.com

McKLEIN PUBLISHING

Speed up your life ...

Group 4 – From Stratos to Quattro

Most fans still have fond memories of rallying in the 1970s. The authors describe the history of the legendary rally cars they review the first WRC years from 1973 to 1982 and tell some of the stories from that wild and tough era.

By John Davenport and Reinhard Klein
Size: 24.5 x 30 cm, 256 pages
Texts in English
ISBN: 978-3-927458-54-3
Price: 49.90 euro*

Group B – The rise and fall of rallying's wildest cars

This book tells the story of all the cars developed within Group B, from the Quattros to the outstanding Lancias and Peugeots and to the exotic sports cars from Porsche and Mazda. But all the technical development came to a head in the year 1986, when the euphoria somehow turned into an ungovernable risk.

By John Davenport and Reinhard Klein
Size: 24.5 x 30 cm, 256 pages
Texts in English
ISBN: 978-3-927458-56-7
Price: 49.90 euro*

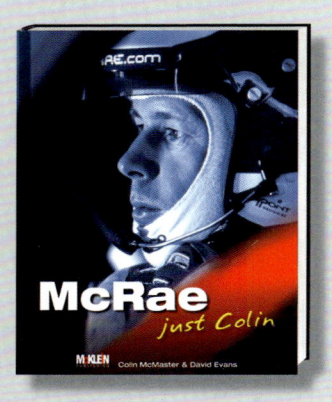

McRae, just Colin

Colin McRae, the 1995 World Rally Champion, was the most spectacular rally driver. His natural speed and win-or-bust approach made him the favourite of rally fans worldwide. The word McRae became superfluous in the end, Colin was... just Colin. This book uncovers every aspect of McRaes's character, with a collection of personal stories, told by family and friends who knew him best.

By Colin McMaster and David Evans
Size: 24.5 x 30 cm, 256 pages
Texts in English
ISBN: 978-3-927458-64-2
Price: 49.90 euro*

ALSO AVAILABLE

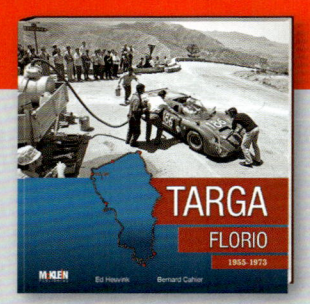

Targa Florio 1955-1973
Languages: English, German, Italian
Price: 99.90 euro*

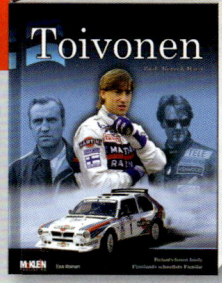

Toivonen Finland's fastest family
Languages: English, German
Price: 49.90 euro*

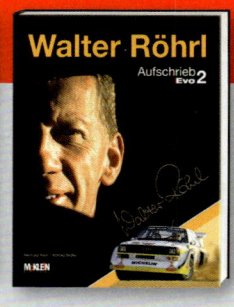

Walter Röhrl Aufschrieb Evo 2
Language: German
Price: 49.90 euro*

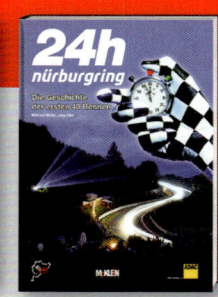

24h Nürburgring Die Geschichte der ersten 40 Rennen
Language: German
Price: 49.90 euro*

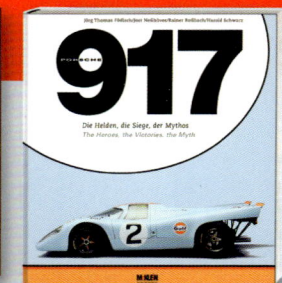

Porsche 917 The Heroes, the Victories, the Myth
Languages: English, German
Price: 59.90 euro*

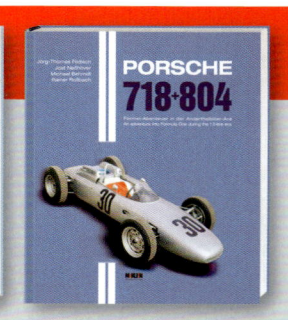

Porsche 718+804 Adventure into Formula 1 during the 1.5l era
Languages: English, German
Price: 59.90 euro*

*incl. VAT, plus shipping

RallyWebShop - Hauptstraße 172 - 51143 Köln - Germany - Tel: +49-2203-9242570 - www.rallywebshop.com